V O

BRINGING BACK *the* Black Robed Regiment

VOLUME TWO

BRINGING BACK *the* Black Robed Regiment

A Call for Preachers Who Will Fight

DAN FISHER

Published by Tate Publishing & Enterprises, LLC

127 E. Trade Center Terrace | Mustang, Oklahoma 73064 USA
1.888.361.9473 | www.tatepublishing.com

Tate Publishing is committed to excellence in the publishing industry. The company reflects the philosophy established by the founders, based on Psalm 68:11,

"The Lord gave the word and great was the company of those who published it."

Cover and interior design by Lynly D. Grider

Published in the United States of America

ISBN: 978-1-62746-233-4

1. RELIGION: Religion, Politics & State
13.07.24

Bringing Back the Black Robed Regiment

Contents

Introduction To Volume 2

There is a time for all things, a time to preach and a time to pray. But there is also a time to fight, and that time has now come!"

Rev. Peter Muhlenberg, 1776

Although many have never heard of them, they were the most outspoken proponents of truth and liberty in 18th century America. Although many have never read of their acts of valor, they bravely led their men onto the battlefield to face the cold steel of the dreaded British Redcoats. Even though their role in the birth of America has been largely forgotten, they were key leaders in the cause for American liberty and independence. Hated by the British who called them the "Black Robed Regiment," these courageous men "laid it all on the altar" for freedom.

Who were these men? They were America's "patriot preachers" and their commitment to truth and liberty and their willingness to die, if need be, defending them against tyranny is one of the most inspiring stories in American history. Convinced that the Bible impacted every area of life, including politics, these brave pastors stood in their pulpits each Sunday wearing their black robes, preaching from God's Word about spiritual ***and*** civil liberty. Because of their willingness to preach the "whole counsel" of God, their congregations were well prepared when the inevitable clash with the British came. Without their bold stand and brave deeds, the United States of America may never have come to be.

In twenty-first century America, our liberties are once again threatened by a tyranny very much like the one our Founders faced in 1776. One by one, our civil and religious liberties are being systematically stripped away. As each year passes, the assault on our liberties gains momentum. The effect of this "de-Christianizing" of America has been disastrous and our nation is becoming increasingly "amoral" – a grave departure from what our Founders originally envisioned. Consequently, Americans are "adrift" in a sea of civil and religious confusion and even worse, the silence of the American pulpit in the face of this threat to our liberties is deafening. In 1798, John Adams warned:

"[W]e have no government armed with power capable of contending with human passions unbridled by morality and religion.... Our constitution was made only for a moral and religious people. It is wholly inadequate to the government of any other."

In Volume 1 of *Bringing Back The Black Robed Regiment*, the patriotism of these preachers who rallied the men of their congregations to fight for truth and liberty is fully discussed and documented. Their personal biographies are so inspiring that before reading Volume 2 of this work, the reader would greatly benefit from learning, from Volume 1, of the daring and sacrificial stand these patriots in black robes took for liberty. May God awaken today's preachers/pastors and "Bring Back the Black Robed Regiment."

Section II:

The Preachers & Their Principles

Chapter 9

"AMERICA HAS AMNESIA"

- Christopher Columbus came to North America for the primary purpose of finding gold and natives to enslave.
- The Pilgrims came to North America mainly because they were fleeing religious persecution.
- Most of our Founders were atheists and deists.
- Thomas Jefferson and most of the other Founders believed in a "strict separation" of church and state.
- James Madison and company penned a "godless" constitution with the expressed intent of establishing a "secular" government and country.

These are the misstatements and blatant lies that are repeated over and over in America today and worse yet, they are taught as fact to our children. Was Columbus nothing more than a gold digging slave trader? Were the Pilgrims primarily religious fugitives? Did mostly atheists and deists found America? Were "strict separation of church and state" and a "godless/secular government" the goals of the people we have called "patriots" for almost two and one half centuries? The answer to all of these questions is a resounding NO! But why then, do so many Americans believe these lies?

Americans believe these lies because they have forgotten, or never knew, the message preached by those who first stepped onto the North American continent as missionaries. America has forgotten the message preached by the Pilgrims. America has forgotten the message preached by the colonial preachers. America has forgotten the message preached by the Black Robed Regiment. America has forgotten the principles that our Forefathers and Founders believed were foundational and essential to a nation that feared God and followed the law. At best, we have forgotten, and at worst, we have rejected the truths our ancestors used as the underpinning for America. As he was closing out his presidency, George Washington declared that morality and religion are the "two indispensible pillars" that support our republic. Unfortunately, for many decades it seems we have been doing our very best as a nation to take out those supports, greatly jeopardizing the strength of our country. In the process, we have forgotten who we are. It's as if we are suffering from a strange form of "national amnesia."

AMNESIA

Merriam/Webster's Dictionary defines amnesia as, a "loss of memory due usually to brain injury, shock, fatigue, repression, or illness." Of special interest is this part of the definition: "the selective overlooking or ignoring of events or acts that are not favorable or useful to one's purpose or position; a condition in which memory is disturbed or lost." Webster's Dictionary adds this: "an usually progressive condition (as Alzheimer's disease) marked by deteriorated cognitive functioning often with emotional apathy."[1]

Of all the ailments accompanying old age, Alzheimer's disease is one of the most dreaded and pitiful. Most of us have helplessly stood by as we watched this memory thief steal away the mind and personality of those we love, reducing them to nothing more than an empty shell of their former selves. People who were once loving, witty, brilliant, and productive individuals, become confused, disoriented, and completely unfamiliar with those who once meant the world to them. Callings, careers, and causes that had previously filled their lives with such purpose and meaning are no longer even a distant memory. Sad indeed.

Memory – what a phenomenal gift from God. Seldom do we think about it or stop to thank God for the mind's amazing capacity to store and recall information in an instant, but the second we cannot remember someone's name or instantaneously recall some fact we need at the moment, that is when we remember what a blessing a functioning memory is. Imagine going through life without any recollection of who you are, of what you are about, or of what has passed. Imagine starting over everyday with no recollection of what brought you to this moment or of where you are going – what a frustrating and confusing existence that would be. But for our memory, we would be like a ship without a rudder, driven by the wind and waves with no specific course, aimlessly drifting in a chaotic sea.

NATIONAL AMNESIA

Like an individual, a nation also has a memory. The collection of pertinent facts concerning its founding, its purpose for existing, its form of government, its faith, its heritage; all of these serve as the collective "memory" of a people. This "national memory" serves the same role for a nation as an individual's memory does. Without this "collective national memory," a society, like an individual, is hopelessly adrift in a sea of "historical amnesia/dementia."

It has been correctly observed that if we are not good students of history then we are destined to repeat the mistakes of the past. Even the progressive Woodrow Wilson, with whom I rarely agree, actually got it right when he said, "A nation which does not remember what it was yesterday, doesn't know what it is today or what it is trying to do–we're trying to do a futile thing if we don't know where we've come from or what we're about." Social/

political commentator and author, Mark Steyn, said, "When a society loses its memory, it descends inevitably into dementia. As I always try to tell my American neighbors, national decline is at least partly psychological …."[2]

The potential impact of this "national dementia" on a society is devastating. Communist Karl Marx clearly understood how vulnerable a nation becomes when it jettisons its heritage. Marx is credited for having said, "A people without a heritage are easily persuaded." Without a national memory, the citizens of a nation are targets for deceivers who seek to "fundamentally transform" their society. Seeing well beyond his time, George Orwell wrote in his famous book, *1984*, "He who controls the past controls the future."

Unfortunately, all indicators seem to point to the fact that we Americans have forgotten who we are as a nation. Worse than forgetting, it appears we have chosen to forget. Since we have forgotten who we were yesterday, we consequently do not seem to know who we are today, or where we are headed tomorrow. As a result, those who reject our founding principles and who seem bent on "fundamentally transforming America" are having a heyday.

Thanks, in part, to revisionist historians who have been hard at work over the past one hundred years or so, the story of America has largely been rewritten. In particular, these "historians" have focused on erasing the dominant role Christianity played in birthing and establishing our nation. Sadly, they have succeeded in painting a picture of an America that is quite different from the one our founders envisioned and created. In this way our rich Christian heritage and sacred liberties, given by God and passed down by our faithful ancestors through sacrifice and blood, have been replaced with a fabricated history that is godless, man-centered, and one few can celebrate or defend. After all, who would want to die for a nation founded by atheists/agnostics/deists who pillaged and enslaved the native peoples and exploited the land for selfish gain? In this sense, our "true" national memory has been erased and replaced, plunging Americans into Mark Steyn's version of "national amnesia."

Make no mistake – this "new American history" was not cooked up in dark backrooms out of the view of the public, but was, instead, developed and delivered out in the open where all could see. This new "American story" was not forced on us or slipped in while we were not looking; it was fed to us bite by poisonous bite – and we seemed all too willing to take it. We Americans were, in most cases, willing accomplices to the crime and now that the dirty deed has been done, we look with astonishment at the horrible carnage of a culture in decline and wonder how this could have happened in America – the once proud and powerful "land of the free and home of the brave."

How could we have willingly stood by and done little or nothing while our national heritage was systematically dismantled piece by piece? Regardless of the reason, whether due to our apathy, lack of watchfulness, and/or cowardice, the old America has essentially been replaced with a "new and improved" America. This would not be so bad if the new America was consistent with the founding principles that made the old America such a great and godly nation. But tragically, this is not the case. This new America is a radical departure from our founding principles and is a distorted monstrosity – the exact opposite of what our Founders intended. And worse yet, it is becoming more so with every passing day as historical revisionists continue rewriting the truth about our once great republic.

A good example is found in a 1997 book, *The Godless Constitution: The Case Against Religious Correctness*, written by two professors from Cornell University, Isaac Kramnick & R. Laurence Moore, and used as a textbook in colleges and universities across America. In it the authors argue that the "principal architects of our national government envisioned a godless Constitution and a godless politics." According to them, the authors of the Constitution did not include strong statements about God because they intended to "create an utterly secular state" in which religion would be kept strictly private and completely separate from the secular government. This excerpt from their book perfectly illustrates their basic premise:

"The framers erected a godless federal constitutional structure, which was then undermined as God entered first the U.S. currency in 1863, then the federal mail service in 1912, and finally the Pledge of Allegiance in 1954. … [T]he founders of this nation would regard the mixing of religion and politics in the ways now being engineered by the religious right as part of the problem of failing public morality, rather than as an answer."[3]

To one unfamiliar with America's "true" history, this argument may seem strong, but a closer look at the facts changes the picture dramatically. Like most revisionists who are dedicated to erasing our "national memory," Kramnick and Moore neglect to mention certain critical facts. For example, they fail to mention that the Declaration of Independence, our "founding" document and national purpose statement, contains strong references to God. They also fail to mention that most state constitutions of the Revolution era reflected a strong Christian influence in government, with many actually requiring a person's allegiance to Christ before taking office. Consider the following examples:

DELAWARE CONSTITUTION, 1776:

"Every person who shall be chosen a member of either house, or appointed to any office or place of trust, before taking his seat or entering upon the execution of his office, shall…make and subscribe the following declaration, to wit: 'I, __________, do profess faith in God the Father, and in Jesus Christ His only Son, and in the Holy Ghost, one God, Blessed forevermore; and I do acknowledge the Holy Scriptures of the Old and New Testament to be given by Divine inspiration.'"[4]

PENNSYLVANIA CONSTITUTION, 1776:

"And each member, before he takes his seat shall make and subscribe the following declaration: "I do believe in one God, the Creator and Governor of the Universe, the Rewarder of the good and Punisher of the wicked. And I do acknowledge the Scriptures of the Old and New Testament to be given by Divine Inspiration."[5]

MASSACHUSETTS CONSTITUTION, 1780:

"Any person chosen Governor, or Lieutenant-governor, Councilor, Senator, or Representative, and accepting the trust, shall before he proceed to execute the duties of his place or office, take, make and subscribe the following declaration, viz. 'I, ____________, do declare, that I believe the Christian religion, and have a firm persuasion of its truth;'"[6]

And these are only a few examples; many other colonies/states included similar requirements in their constitutions. These provide strong proof of Christianity's heavy influence in early America and the kind of government the citizens wanted. Granted, as the colonies became states and parts of a larger union, the "religious tests" were set aside – but the fact still remains that these constitutions reflect the religious attitude of the citizens in early America.

In responding to Kramnick and Moore's contention, Dr. Daniel L. Dreisback, Professor of Justice, Law, and Society at the American University in Washington, D.C., wrote,

"The U. S. Constitution's lack of a Christian designation had little to do with a radical secular agenda. Indeed, it had little to do with religion at all. The Constitution was silent on the subject of God and religion because there was a consensus that, despite the framer's personal beliefs, religion was a matter best left to the individual citizens and their respective state governments. ... The Constitution, in short, can be fairly characterized as 'godless' or secular only inso-far as it deferred to the states on all matters regarding religion and devotion to God."[7]

Interestingly, Kramnick and Moore who, as tenured professors, live and work in a world of footnotes and documented resources, offer no sources or footnotes to substantiate their claims. On page 179 of their book they state:

> "Because we have intended the book to reach a general audience, and because the material we have cited is for the most part familiar to historians and political scientists, we have dispensed with the usual scholarly apparatus of footnotes."[8]

This is a rather strange statement coming from two men who claim to be "correcting" more than two centuries of errors in American history. One would think that a premise so "obvious" would have volumes of sources substantiating its validity, and yet none are offered. How convenient that they simply "dismiss with the usual apparatus of footnotes" thus relieving themselves of any obligation to provide any proof for their bold claims. This is particularly ironic when we consider the fact that they and their colleagues insist that those who teach that America was founded upon Christian principles provide mountains of sources to prove their position.

The Godless Constitution simply serves to prove an important point: there is no statement too ridiculous that, if repeated often and loudly enough, people will not eventually assume is true – especially if no informed response is offered in defense. Unfortunately for Kramnick and Moore, the facts get in the way. Fortunately for us, the truth is on our side and there is a plethora of evidence that proves America was indeed founded on biblical principles – a fact that has been proven time and time again.

Because the purpose of this book is to present a compelling discussion of the Black Robed Regiment and to show how their message and leadership galvanized the Americans to fight for liberty and truth, only a brief discussion of America's Christian roots and the religious beliefs of those who founded it will be provided here. But, unlike Kramnick and Moore, in the following two chapters I will provide footnoted sources from the "mountain of evidence" that proves beyond any reasonable doubt that our Founders did indeed intend to establish a Christian America. The material in these chapters will make a useful backdrop for the discussion of the incredible contribution the "Black Robed Regiment" made to the birth and establishment of our great nation.

Chapter 10

DID THEY INTEND TO FOUND A UNION ON CHRISTIAN PRINCIPLES?

"[I have] an anxious desire that our country should be preserved from the dreadful evil of becoming enemies to the religion of the Gospel, which I have no doubt, but would be introductive of the dissolution of government and the bonds of civil society;"[9]

Elias Boudinot, Continental Army Colonel, President of the Continental Congress, 2nd president under the Articles of Confederation, U.S. Congressman, Founder of the American Bible Society

On October 25, 1780, Samuel Cooper, pastor of the Brattle Street Church in Boston, preached the following to the Massachusetts Legislature and Governor John Hancock:

"Conquest is not indeed the aim of these rising states; sound policy must ever forbid it: We have before us an object more truly great and honorable. We seem called by heaven to make a large portion of this globe a seat of knowledge and liberty ... and what is more important than all, of Christian piety and virtue. May our conduct correspond to the face of our country! ... It remains with us and our posterity, ... to invite the injured and oppressed, the worthy and the good to these shores ... by wise political institutions, by cultivating the confidence and friendship of other nations, and by a sacred attention to that gospel that breathes 'peace on earth, and good will towards men.'"[10]

Historian Carl Bridenbaugh observed, "We live in an increasingly secular society. Religiosity in our day (if not actual church-going) declines apace; whereas our fore fathers of the eighteenth century considered piety, religious observance, even theology, as part of their daily existence."[11]

In 1831, the French historian and political scientist, Alexis de Tocqueville, visited America. For almost two years he toured and studied the country. Upon returning to France he compiled his notes into his famous work, *Democracy In America.* Intrigued with the particularly strong influence Christianity had in the lives of the Americans, De Tocqueville wrote,

> "Upon my arrival in the United States, the religious aspect of the country was the first thing that struck my attention; and the longer I stayed there, the more did I perceive the great political consequences resulting from this state of things, to which I was unaccustomed. In France I had almost always seen the spirit of religion and the spirit of freedom pursuing courses diametrically opposed to each other; but in America I found that they were intimately united, and that they reigned in common over the same country.
>
> "It must never be forgotten that religion gave birth to Anglo-American society. In the United States, religion is therefore mingled with all the habits of the nation and all the feelings of patriotism, whence it derives a peculiar force. ... The greatest part of British America was peopled by men who ... brought with them into the New World a form of Christianity which I cannot better describe than by styling it a democratic and republican religion. This contributed powerfully to the establishment of a republic and a democracy in public affairs; and from the beginning, politics and religion contracted an alliance which has never been dissolved.
>
> "In the United States the influence of religion is not confined to the manners, but it extends to the intelligence of the people. ... There are certain populations in Europe whose unbelief is only equaled by their ignorance and their debasement, while in America one of the freest and most enlightened nations in the world fulfills all the outward duties of religion with fervor.
>
> "In the United States the sovereign authority is religious, and ... there is no country in the world where the Christian religion retains a greater influence over the souls of men than in America; and there can be no greater proof of its utility and of its conformity to human nature than that its influence is powerfully felt over the most enlightened and free nation of the earth.
>
> "In the United States on the seventh day of every week the trading and working life of the nation seems suspended; all noises cease; a deep tranquility, say rather the solemn calm of meditation, succeeds the turmoil of the week, and the

soul resumes possession and contemplation of itself. On this day the marts of traffic are deserted; every member of the community, accompanied by his children, goes to church, where he listens to strange language which would seem unsuited to his ear. He is told of the countless evils caused by pride and covetousness; he is reminded of the necessity of checking his desires, of the finer pleasures that belong to virtue alone, and of the true happiness that attends it. On his return home he does not turn to the ledgers of his business, but he opens the book of Holy Scripture; there he meets with sublime and affecting descriptions of the greatness and goodness of the Creator, of the infinite magnificence of the handiwork of God, and of the lofty destinies of man, his duties, and his immortal privileges. … The Americans show by their practice that they feel the high necessity of imparting morality to democratic communities by means of religion. What they think of themselves in this respect is a truth of which every democratic nation ought to be thoroughly persuaded. …

"Despotism may govern without faith, but liberty cannot. Religion is much more necessary in the republic which they set forth in glowing colors than in the monarchy which they attack; it is more needed in democratic republics than in any others. How is it possible that society should escape destruction if the moral tie is not strengthened in proportion as the political tie is relaxed? And what can be done with a people who are their own masters if they are not submissive to the Deity? …

"I have known of societies formed by Americans to send out ministers of the Gospel into the new Western states, to found schools and churches there, lest religion should be allowed to die away in those remote settlements, and the rising states be less fitted to enjoy free institutions than the people from whom they came. I met with wealthy New Englanders who abandoned the country in which they were born in order to lay the foundations of Christianity and of freedom on the banks of the Missouri or in the prairies of Illinois. Thus religious zeal is perpetually warmed in the United States by the fires of patriotism. These men do not act exclusively from a consideration of a future life; eternity is only one motive of their devotion to the cause. If you converse with these missionaries of Christian civilization, you will be surprised to hear them speak so often of the goods of this world, and to meet a politician where you expected to find a priest. … 'It is therefore our interest that the new states should be religious, in order that they may permit us to remain free.' Such are the opinions of the Americans; …"[12]

Obviously, modern Christians and conservatives are not alone in their claim that America was predominantly a Christian union in its early days. Only fifty-five years after the Declaration of Independence was signed, Alexis de Tocqueville unquestionably defined America as a Christian union. In those days, this fact was common knowledge. For instance, after visiting rural Connecticut, a British official had this to say about the Americans: "They are all politicians and they are all Scripture learnt."[13]

So why is it that today we constantly hear that America was not founded by Christians, was never intended to be a Christian union, and was never dominated by the Christian faith? It is because political progressives, statists, and atheists/agnostics, who cannot bear the thought of a Christian America, dominate the popular media and in their effort to "fundamentally change America" ignore, erase, and lie about the "true" history of our country.

So did our Founders actually intend for America to be a Christian union? Is there any evidence that can definitively answer this question for us? The answer is a resounding yes – that is if you believe what the Founders actually wrote and said instead of what today's liberal intelligentsia and media elites claim.

So what really did motivate people like Columbus and the Pilgrims to come to North America? Were they driven by nothing more than a selfish desire for wealth, power, and conquest or did higher principles inspire them to brave the dangerous waters of the Atlantic? The answer is quite easy to find if we allow these people to speak for themselves.

CHRISTOPHER COLUMBUS

Let us begin with a brief discussion of the popular claim that, while searching for a shorter trading route to the West Indies, Columbus was primarily in a search for gold and native peoples he could enslave and trade. How can we know what truly motivated Columbus more than five hundred years ago? Thankfully, we do not have to speculate – Columbus kept a diary. In his, *The Book of Prophecies*, we read in his own words what motivated him to embark upon his great journey:

> "It was the Lord who put into my mind, I could feel His hand upon me, the fact that it would be possible to sail from here to the Indies. All who heard of my project rejected it with laughter, ridiculing me. There is no question that the inspiration was from the Holy Spirit, because He comforted me with rays of marvelous illumination from the Holy Scriptures, a strong and clear testimony from the 44 books of the Old Testament [he used the Catholic Bible which includes the Apocrypha], from the four Gospels, and from the 23 Epistles of the blessed Apostles, encouraging me continually to press forward, and without ceasing for a moment they now encourage me to make haste. ... Our Lord Jesus desired to perform a very obvious miracle in the voyage to the Indies, to comfort me and the whole people of God. For the execution of the journey to the Indies I did not make use of intelligence, mathematics or maps. It is simply the fulfillment of what Isaiah had prophesied. All this is what I desire to write down for you in this book. ... No one should fear to undertake any task in the name of our Savior, if it is just and if the intention is purely for His holy service. ... Oh what a gracious Lord, who desires that people should perform for Him those things for which He holds Himself responsible!"[14]

In addition, Columbus's spiritual motivations are evident when we consider the names he and his men gave to many of the places where they landed. Names like San Salvador, Spanish for "Holy Savior," and Trinidad, Spanish for the "Trinity," indicate the deep religious beliefs of these men and are hardly the names that godless, money hungry slave traders would have used – especially if their plans included pillaging and enslaving the native peoples. Were Columbus and his men perfect, sinless individuals? No. But many of them were men of faith who were, by their own admission, motivated by something more than personal gain.

THE PILGRIMS

Today, many Americans believe that the main reason the Pilgrims came to America was to escape religious persecution in

England. It often comes as a major surprise when they learn that the Pilgrims had been enjoying religious freedom in Holland for almost twelve years before they sailed to America.

Because they were separatists, the Pilgrims believed that the Anglican Church was too worldly to be saved (contrasted with the Puritans who believed the church could be purified and remained in England attempting to do so). Believing this, in 1607 the Pilgrims "separated" themselves from the Church of England and moved to Leyden, Holland where they enjoyed the freedom to worship God as they saw fit. But in that non-Christian culture, they became concerned as they saw their children beginning to embrace the godless ways of the Dutch. After much prayer and deliberation, they determined that it was once again time to pull up stakes and renew their search for a place where they could live and worship God unencumbered by the negative influence of a decadent culture. In the process of seeking God's direction, they felt impressed by the Lord to plant a Christian community in the New World. Because of the enormity of this undertaking, not everyone in the church in Leyden was willing to go. Approximately half of the church volunteered to sail to America while the others would remain in Holland. John Robinson, the church's pastor, chose to remain behind while William Brewster, one of the church's elders, chose to go and serve as the group's pastor in the New World. Again, fortunately for us, the Pilgrims did not abandon us to speculation but left us an official document stating the very reason they were willing to spend some sixty days crossing the treacherous Atlantic Ocean to begin a new life in the wilderness of North America.

Once the Mayflower had anchored in the harbor of what would become Provincetown, Massachusetts, before disembarking for the shore, the Pilgrims drew up and signed the Mayflower Compact on November 11, 1620. This document not only detailed how they would govern themselves once they left the ship, it also stated the reason for which they had come to America in the first place. The Compact said, in part,

"[H]aving undertaken, for the glory of God, and the advancement of the Christian faith, and honor of our king and country, a voyage to plant the first colony in the Northern parts of Virginia."[15]

So in their own words, the Pilgrims came to America for the primary purpose of advancing the Christian faith. Further confirmation of the Pilgrims' missionary spirit can be found in the *History of Plymouth Plantation* written by William Bradford, the second governor of Plymouth Plantation:

"Lastly, (and which was not least,) a great hope & inward zeal they had of laying some good foundation, or at least to make some way thereunto, for the propagating & advancing the gospel of the kingdom of Christ in those remote parts of the world; yea, though they should be but even as stepping-stones unto others for the performing of so great a work."[16]

Certainly, there is no doubt that the Pilgrims were seeking a home in which to live and worship apart from the persecution of the King and his Church of England, but in their own words, "advancing the Christian faith" was their main purpose for sailing to America. Interestingly, there is a name we give to those who travel great distances to spread the Gospel – we call them missionaries. Rather than being religious refugees, the Pilgrims were actually Christian missionaries.

The preachers of the late seventeenth and eighteenth centuries knew this. In the introduction to his famous book, *The Pulpit of the American Revolution*, John Wingate Thornton wrote,

"Such was the origin of New England; such the men who founded it. Religion, the church, was the great thought, and civil interests were only incidental. This is not only evident in our history, … but it is distinctly avowed and reiterated in the writings of the fathers of New England from the very beginning. Thus Roger Conant, the first Governor of Massachusetts Colony, suggested to the Rev. John White, of Dorchester, that it might be a refuge from the coming storm 'on account of religion.' …

"In exact accordance with these teachings, the king and colonists declared 'the principal end of this plantation' of Massachusetts to be, 'to win and incite the natives of the country to the knowledge and obedience of the only true God and Savior of mankind, and the Christian faith; ... It will be a service to the church, of great consequence, to carry the Gospel into those parts of the world, and to raise a bulwark against the kingdom of antichrist,'

"When the 'governor and company,' that branch of the Massachusetts government which, under the charter, had its legal residence in England, were about emigrating to the colony, they issued a manifesto, April 7, 1630, declaring themselves to be a Church, 'a weak colony from their brethren in and of the Church of England,' as 'the Church of Philippi was a colony of the church at Rome.' The Rev. John Norton, in the Election Sermon of 1661, said that they came 'into this wilderness to live under the order of the gospel; ... that our polity may be a gospel polity, and may be complete according to the Scriptures, answering fully the Word of God: this is the work of our generation, and the very work we engaged for into this wilderness; this is the scope and end of it, that which is written upon the forehead of New England, viz., the complete walking in the faith of the gospel, according to the order of the gospel.'

"The venerable Higginson, of Salem, in his Election Sermon of 1663, stated the point with great fullness, as follows: 'It concerneth New England always to remember that they are originally a plantation religious, not a plantation of trade. The profession of the purity of doctrine, worship, and discipline, is written upon her forehead. Let merchants, and such as are increasing cent per cent, remember this: that worldly gain was not the end and design of the people of New England, but religion.'

"In the Election Sermon of 1677, the Rev. Dr. Increase Mather uttered these words: 'It was love to God and to Jesus Christ which brought our fathers into this wilderness.... They did not, in their coming hither, propound any great matters to themselves respecting this world; only that they should have liberty to serve God, and to walk with him in all the ways of His worship. ... There never was a generation that did so perfectly shake off the dust of Babylon, both as to ecclesiastical and civil constitution, as the first generation of Christians that came into this land for the gospel's sake.'

"The Rev. William Hubbard, the historian, in a Fast-day sermon, preached June 24, 1682, declared that the fathers 'came not hither for the world, or for land, or for traffic; but for religion, and for liberty of conscience in the worship of God, which was their only design.'

"The historical fact was stated by President Stiles, of Yale College [and preacher of the gospel], in 1783: 'It is certain that civil dominion was but the second motive, religion the primary one, with our ancestors, in coming hither and settling this land. It was not so much their design to establish religion for the benefit of the state, as civil government for the benefit of religion, and as subservient, and even necessary, towards the peaceable enjoyment and unmolested exercise of religion — of that religion for which they fled to these ends of the earth.'"[17]

Seventeenth century preacher William Stoughton (who saw no problem with mixing politics and religion, because, in addition to serving as a pastor, he also served as deputy-president of Massachusetts, chief justice of the Massachusetts Superior Court, and Massachusetts Lieutenant Governor[18]) understood that faith was the driving force for those who first came to America. He emphasized this point in his 1668 Massachusetts election sermon, considered one of the best election sermons delivered in early America:

"God sifted a whole nation that he might send choice grain, into this wilderness. They were men of great renown, in the nation from which the Laudian persecution exiled them; their learning, their holiness, their gravity, struck all men who knew them, with admiration. They were Timothies in their houses, Chrysostoms, in their pulpits, Augustines, in their disputations."[19]

In 1775, Moses Mather, in his sermon, *America's Appeal To The Impartial World,* also emphasized the reason the Pilgrims came to America:

"In A. D. 1620, England, torn with religious dissentions, the friends of the reformation, persecuted with unrelenting cruelty, by the intolerant spirit that influenced government, were forced to renounce their religion and liberties, or assert them with their lives. The protestants, to the number of one hundred and fifty, who before had fled to Holland for safety, having made a purchase under the Plymouth Company, and obtained the royal license, quitted their native country, preferring the enjoyment of their religion and liberty, in a howling desert, to the pomp and pleasures of luxury and sin in England; crossed the Atlantic and arrived at Plymouth in America in A.D. 1620, and by their own valor, industry, risk and expense (under the smiles of heaven) acquired plantations, subdued savage enemies, built cities, turned the wilderness into fruitful fields, and rendered it vocal with the praises of their Savior, and from small beginnings, in process of time, became great in number, and in extent of territory; great numbers, not long after, from religious considerations, emigrating from England, came and settled the other colonies in America; for, says an English historian, 'it seems that all the provinces of North America were planted from motives of religion.'"[20]

On January 17, 1776 in New York City, Samuel Sherwood declared that it was for "religion and liberty" that the Pilgrims braved the "wide Atlantic." In his sermon, *The Church's Flight Into The Wilderness: An Address On The Times,* Sherwood said,

"And what period or event is there in all the history of her [the Church] trials and persecutions, which these expressions more exactly describe, and to which they can be applied with more truth and propriety, than to the flight of our forefathers into this then howling wilderness, which was a land not sown nor occupied by any ruling power on earth, except by savages and wild beasts? It is an indisputable fact, that the cruel hand of oppression, tyranny and persecution drove them out from their pleasant seats and habitations, in the land of their nativity; and that the purest principles of religion and liberty, led them to make the bold adventure across the wide Atlantic ocean; for which they surely needed the two wings of the great eagle, to speed their flight, and to shelter and cover them from danger, while seeking a safe retreat from the relentless fury and shocking cruelty of the persecuting dragon; and a secure abode for unadulterated Christianity, liberty and peace. … This American quarter of the globe seemed to be reserved in providence, as a fixed and settled habitation for God's church, where she might have property of her own, and the right of rule and government, so as not to be controlled and oppressed in her civil and religious liberties, by the tyrannical and persecuting powers of the earth, … In all countries and kingdoms wherever Christianity had been planted, before its introduction into this American wilderness, the ruling powers in possession of the property, and right of jurisdiction and dominion, were in opposition to this benevolent institution; and the church had to make her way through the greatest possible difficulties and dangers. When God, to whom the earth belongs and the fullness thereof, brought His church into this wilderness, as on eagles wings, by His kind, protecting providence, He gave this good land to her, to be her own lot and inheritance for ever. He planted her as a pleasant and choice vine; and drove out the heathen before her. He has tenderly nourished and cherished her in her infant state and protected and preserved her amidst innumerable dangers. He has done wonders in His providence for our fathers and for us their sinful posterity: 'They, and we have many a time, stood still, and seen the salvation of the Lord.'"[21]

William Gordon made the same point about the Pilgrims in his sermon on December 15, 1774:

"Now, the ancestors of this people were eminently godly; it was the strength of their zeal for true, unadulterated religion, and the ardor of their love to God and Christ, that prevailed upon them to venture over the great deep, and to seek an abode in this then inhospitable and dangerous country, and that reconciled them to the numberless difficulties that they had long to encounter without ever attaining to the various comforts that we enjoy. They were concerned to perpetuate the same spirit of piety which they were actuated by; paid great attention to the rising generation, and wisely provided for the good instruction of succeeding ones."[22]

Episcopal Bishop James Madison, cousin to Founder James Madison, was a member of the Black Robed Regiment, served as captain of a company of militia that saw significant action in the War of Independence, was the president of the College of William and Mary, and served as the rector of James City Parish, Virginia. In his *Manifestations Of The Beneficence Of Divine Providence Towards America* preached in Richmond, Virginia on February 19, 1795, Bishop Madison declared that it was the "attachment to the inherent rights of man" that drove our forefathers to North America:

"These considerations present to our minds the first traces of the beneficent designs of providence in the history of this new world. Nor ought it ... to be here forgotten, that the ... general tendency of providence is also to be traced back to the source, whence the present free and enlightened race of America sprung. For surely, our forefathers, amidst the wreck of human rights, and the convulsive tempests with which ambition had so often overwhelmed the nations of the east, still evinced, at times, no small portion of that ethereal spirit, that ardent love of liberty, which glows in the American breast. It was this indomitable spirit, this attachment to the inherent rights of man, stronger infinitely than the fear of those storms, which agitate the immense Atlantic, or of the fierce and cruel tenants of the howling wilderness, or the ravages of disease, and famine and death itself, which urged our forefathers to these distant shores. Yes, brethren, it was this noble principle, this love of liberty, which defying all dangers, conducted our forefathers to America; … Who doth not see, that thus to have transported it to America, thus to have incorporated it with the primary social institutions of this country, may be justly deemed an event most fortunate for mankind, nay, most worthy of providence itself?"[23]

As far as the preachers of early America were concerned, a missionary spirit, not a fear of religious persecution, drew the Pilgrims to the New World.

- The settling of America and the establishment of the colonies:

With the success of the Plymouth Colony and the increasing religious persecution directed toward those in England who dared to disagree with the King and his Anglican Church, the Puritans, who had originally chosen to work toward purifying the Church of England, came to believe their only hope was to move to the new world just as the Pilgrims had done a few years before. So, around 1630, the Great Puritan Migration began as ships filled with Puritan Christians sailed to America to settle in Massachusetts. As religious intolerance spread across Europe, many other Christian denominations found themselves at odds with their state-sponsored churches and in response, also made their way to America's shores to establish their own colonies. According to historian Bill Federer, all thirteen original colonies were founded by Christian denominations:

1. Virginia was founded in 1607 by the Anglicans
2. New York was founded in 1626 by the Dutch Reformed
3. Massachusetts was founded in 1630 by the Puritans
4. Maryland was founded in 1633 by the Catholics
5. Rhode Island was founded in 1636 by the Baptists
6. Connecticut was founded in 1636 by the Congregationalists

7. New Hampshire was founded in 1638 by the Congregationalists
8. Delaware was founded in 1638 by the Lutherans and Dutch Reformed
9. North Carolina was founded in 1653 by the Anglicans
10. South Carolina was founded in 1663 by the Anglicans
11. New Jersey was founded in 1664 by the Lutherans and Dutch Reformed
12. Pennsylvania was founded in 1682 by the Quakers and Lutherans
13. Georgia was founded in 1732 by the Protestants[24]

Clearly, the original thirteen colonies were undeniably Christian and the faith of those who settled them became the dominant force in the society and government of early America.

- Faith in 1776 America:

Although many today concede that there were a good number of Christians in seventeenth and eighteenth century America, they are shocked to discover just how many Christians there actually were. These same people are also surprised to learn how much these Christians' strongly held biblical beliefs influenced the framing of the political structures of early America. Amazingly, the facts reveal the overwhelming majority of Americans in 1776 claimed to be Christians. Based upon the research of Patricia Bonomi, Professor Emeritus of New York University, and Dr. James Kennedy, President and Founder of Coral Ridge Ministries, in 1776, 99.8% of Americans professed to be religious.[25] Of those:

- 98% identified themselves as Protestant Christians
- 1.6% identified themselves as Catholic Christians

- .2% identified themselves as Jewish

This means that 99.6% of Americans claimed to be Christians in 1776. Although it is reasonable to concede that not all of these were "born again" in the biblical sense, it is equally undeniable that America was overwhelmingly a Christian nation when the Declaration of Independence was signed.

(A "bit" of good news: almost two and one half centuries later, even with the rise of religious skepticism and anti-Christian sentiment, a Pew Forum Research Center study revealed that the religious beliefs of Americans today remain strongly Christian. The study indicates that Americans are – .5% Hindu, 1% Muslim, 1% Buddhist, 2% Jewish, and a whopping 78.5% Christian[26] – so much for the claim that today's America is not a Christian nation.)

GEORGE WASHINGTON, "THE FATHER OF OUR COUNTRY"

The official statements and writings of George Washington are so filled with evidence of his Christian faith that it is practically impossible to read anything he wrote or said without finding references to Christ or the Christian religion. For example:

On May 12, 1779 General Washington said to the Delaware Indian Chiefs who were bringing three youths to be trained in American schools:

> "You do well to wish to learn our arts and ways of life and, above all, the religion of Jesus Christ. These will make you a greater and happier people than you are. Congress will do everything they can to assist you in this wise intention."[27]

On June 14, 1783 in Newburgh, New York at the close of the war, George Washington wrote "A Circular Letter Addressed to the Governors of all the States on the Disbanding of the Army." In it, he offered the following prayer for the nation:

> "I now make it my earnest prayer that God would have you, and the State over which you preside, in his holy protection; that he would incline the hearts of

the citizens to cultivate a spirit of subordination and obedience to government, to entertain a brotherly affection and love for one another, for their fellow-citizens of the United States at large, and particularly for brethren who have served in the field; and finally that he would most graciously be pleased to dispose us all to do justice, to love mercy, and to demean ourselves with that charity, humility, and pacific temper of mind, which were the characteristics of the Divine Author of our blessed Religion, and without an humble imitation of whose example in these things, we can never hope to be a happy nation."[28]

PRESIDENT WASHINGTON'S FAREWELL ADDRESS

After serving two terms as President of the United States completing some forty-five years of combined public service, Washington declined to run for a third presidential term for which he would have certainly been elected. His farewell address was published in the *American Daily Advertiser* on September 19, 1796. In it he wrote of his belief that Religion (Christianity) was essential to America:

"Of all the dispositions and habits, which lead to political prosperity, Religion and Morality are indispensable supports. In vain would that man claim the tribute of Patriotism, who should labor to subvert these great pillars of human happiness, these firmest props of the duties of Men and Citizens. The mere Politician, equally with the pious man, ought to respect and to cherish them. … Let it simply be asked, 'Where is the security for property, for reputation, for life, if the sense of religious obligation desert the oaths, which are the instruments of investigation in Courts of Justice?' And let us with caution indulge the supposition, that morality can be maintained without religion. Whatever may be conceded to the influence of refined education on minds of peculiar structure, reason and experience both forbid us to expect, that national morality can prevail in exclusion of religious principle. It is substantially true, that virtue or morality is a necessary spring of popular government. The rule, indeed, extends with more or less force to every species of free government. Who, that is a sincere friend to it, can look with indifference upon attempts to shake the foundation of the fabric?"[29]

Significantly, Washington believed that religion and morality were the primary and indispensable supports to America's political prosperity and that anyone who attacked those pillars was no patriot. He emphasized that morality, essential to a republic, could not be maintained without religion. It is also important to note that throughout Washington's life, when he referred to "Religion" he was normally referring to Christianity – not Buddhism, Hinduism, etc. So the "Father of our country" believed Christianity was the primary support for America.

DR. BENJAMIN RUSH

(signer of the Declaration of Independence, Surgeon General for the Continental Army, physician and pioneer of medical science, & founder of Dickinson College, Carlisle, PA)

Writing to Elias Boudinot on July 9, 1788, Benjamin Rush said,

"I do not believe that the Constitution was the offspring of inspiration, but I am as perfectly satisfied that the Union of the United States in its form and adoption is as much the work of a Divine Providence as any of the miracles recorded in the Old and New Testament."[30]

In 1798, after the adoption of the Constitution, he declared,

"The only foundation for...a republic is to be laid in Religion. Without this there can be no virtue, and without virtue there can be no liberty, and liberty is the object and life of all republican governments."[31]

In 1806, Dr. Rush wrote,

"Let the following sentence be inscribed in letters of gold over the doors of every State and Court house in the United States: 'The Son of Man came into the world, not to destroy men's lives, but to save them.'"[32]

SAMUEL CHASE

(signer of the Declaration of Independence, Chief Justice of Maryland, and U.S. Supreme Court Justice)

For those of us living in the twenty-first century, it is hard to believe that a Supreme Court Justice could talk like this, but in 1799, Supreme Court Justice Samuel Chase said,

"By our form of government, the Christian religion is the established religion;"[33]

This statement flies in the face of those who believe the Founders intended for the Constitution to demand a "strict separation of church and state."

JOHN JAY

(delegate to the first and second Continental Congresses, President of the Continental Congress 1778-79, co-author of the *Federalist Papers*, and first Chief Justice of the U.S. Supreme Court)

On October 12, 1816, commenting to John Murray, Jr., Jay wrote,

"Providence has given to our people the choice of their rulers, and it is the duty, as well as the privilege and interest of our Christian nation, to select and prefer Christians for their rulers."[34]

In a letter Jay wrote to the Rev. Uzal Ogden on February 14, 1796, he said,

"[T]he evidence of the truth of Christianity requires only to be carefully examined to produce conviction in candid minds... they who undertake that task will derive advantages."[35]

In a prayer written by his own hand, Jay prayed,

"Condescend, merciful Father! To grant as far as proper these imperfect petitions, to accept these inadequate thanksgivings, and to pardon whatever of sin hath mingled in them for the sake of Jesus Christ, our blessed Lord and Savior; unto Whom, with Thee, and the blessed Spirit, ever one God, be rendered all honor and glory, now and forever."[36]

In his speech at the Annual Meeting of the American Bible Society on May 13, 1824, Jay said,

"By conveying the Bible to people ... we certainly do them a most interesting act of kindness. We thereby enable them to learn that man was originally created and placed in a state of happiness, but, becoming disobedient, was subjected to the degradation and evils which he and his posterity have since experienced. The Bible will also inform them that our gracious Creator has provided for us a Redeemer in whom all the nations of the earth should be blessed – that this Redeemer has made atonement "for the sins of the whole world," and thereby reconciling the Divine justice with the Divine mercy, has opened a way for our redemption and salvation; and that these inestimable benefits are of the free gift and grace of God, not of our deserving, nor in our power to deserve. The Bible will also [encourage] them with many explicit and consoling assurances of the Divine mercy to our fallen race, and with repeated invitations to accept the offers of pardon and reconciliation.... They, therefore, who enlist in His service, have the highest encouragement to fulfill the duties assigned to their respective stations; for most certain it is, that those of His followers who [participate in] His conquests will also participate in the transcendent glories and blessings of His Triumph."[37]

On June 29, 1826, as his health was beginning to fail, just three years before his death, Jay responded to the Committee of the Corporation of the City of New York on their invitation for him to participate in their approaching celebration of Independence Day:

"I cannot forbear to embrace the opportunity afforded by the present occasion, to express my earnest hope that the peace, happiness, and prosperity enjoyed by our beloved country, may induce those who direct her national councils to recommend a general and public return of praise and thanksgiving to Him from whose goodness these blessings descend. The most effectual means of securing the continuance of our civil and religious liberties is always to remember with reverence and gratitude the source from which they flow."[38]

SAMUEL ADAMS

(called "the voice of American independence," leader in establishing the Committees of Correspondence, delegate to the Continental Congress, instrumental in the adoption of the Declaration of Independence, assisted in drafting the Articles of Confederation, and worked to see that the Bill of Rights was added to the U.S. Constitution)

Adams said,

"[Divine] Revelation assures us that 'Righteousness exalteth a nation.' Communities are dealt with in this world by the wise and just Ruler of the Universe. He rewards or punishes them according to their general character."[39]

In 1772, Adams wrote in his *The Rights of the Colonists as Christians*,

"The right to freedom being the gift of God Almighty, the rights of the Colonists as Christians may best be understood by reading and carefully studying the institutions of The Great Law Giver and the Head of the Christian Church, which are to be found clearly written and promulgated in the New Testament."[40]

In a letter to James Warren, February 11, 1789, Adams wrote about the importance of virtue in America:

"A general Dissolution of Principles & Manners will more surely overthrow the Liberties of America than the whole Force of the common Enemy. While the People are virtuous they cannot be subdued; but when once they lose their Virtue, they will be ready to surrender their Liberties to the first external or internal Invader. How necessary then is it for those who are determined to transmit the Blessings of Liberty as a fair Inheritance to Posterity, to associate on public Principles in Support of public Virtue. ... I hope our Countrymen will never depart from the Principles and Maxims which have been handed down to us from our wise forefathers. This greatly depends upon the Example of Men of Character & Influence of the present Time. This is a Subject my Heart is much set upon."[41]

While Lieutenant Governor of Massachusetts, Adams wrote the following in his *Proclamation for a Day of Fasting and Prayer* on March 10, 1793:

"[That] we may with one heart and voice humbly implore His gracious and free pardon through Jesus Christ, supplicating His Divine aid ... [and] above all to cause the religion of Jesus Christ, in its true spirit, to spread far and wide till the whole earth shall be filled with His glory."[42]

While governor of Massachusetts, Adams stated in a Fast Day Proclamation on March 20, 1797:

"I conceive we cannot better express ourselves than by humbly supplicating the Supreme Ruler of the world ... that the confusions that are and have been among the nations may be overruled by the promoting and speedily bringing in the holy and happy period when the kingdoms of our Lord and Savior Jesus Christ may be everywhere established, and the people willingly bow to the scepter of Him who is the Prince of Peace."[43]

In his *Last Will and Testament*, Adams wrote, "I … [rely] upon the merits of Jesus Christ for a pardon of all my sins.[44]

PATRICK HENRY

(Governor of Virginia, leader of Virginia in the fight for liberty, Colonel of the 1st Virginia Regiment, member of the Continental Congress, delivered the famous "give me liberty or give me death" speech to the Virginia House of Burgesses on March 23, 1775, and helped lead the struggle for the addition of the Bill of Rights to the U.S. Constitution)

Concerning his personal faith, Henry said, "Being a Christian… is a character which I prize far above all this world has or can boast."[45]

Writing to Archibald Blair on January 8, 1799, Patrick Henry wrote that America's morality and religion were its armor:

"And, whilst I see the dangers that threaten ours [America's government] from her [France] intrigues and her arms, I am not so much alarmed as at the apprehension of her destroying the great pillars of all government and of social life; I mean virtue, morality, and religion. This is the armor, my friend, and this alone, that renders us invincible. These are the tactics we should study. If we lose these, we are conquered, fallen indeed."[46]

Henry wrote in his *Last Will & Testament*:

"This is all the inheritance I can give to my dear family. The religion of Christ will give them one which will make them rich indeed."[47]

And as he was dying, Henry said to his attending physician:

"Doctor, I wish you to observe how real and beneficial the religion of Christ is to a man about to die …"[48]

JOHN ADAMS

(a key promoter of independence, member of the Committee of Five that drafted the Declaration, served as foreign ambassador of the U.S. for the Continental Congress, served as the first Vice President of the U.S. and second President of the U.S.)

Adams wrote in his diary on July 26, 1796:

"The Christian religion is, above all the religions that ever prevailed or existed in ancient or modern times, the religion of wisdom, virtue, equity and humanity."[49]

Adams pronounced the following to the Militia of Massachusetts on October 11, 1798:

"We have no government armed with power capable of contending with human passions unbridled by morality and religion. Avarice, ambition, revenge, or gallantry, would break the strongest cords of our Constitution as a whale goes through a net. Our Constitution was made only for a moral and religious people. It is wholly inadequate to the government of any other."[50]

Writing to Dr. Benjamin Rush on August 28, 1811, Adams said,

"I agree with you in sentiment, that religion and virtue are the only foundations, not only of republicanism and of all free government, but of social felicity under all governments and in all the combinations of human society."[51]

On June 28, 1813, in a letter to Thomas Jefferson, Adams discussed the principles that had united the American army during the Revolution:

"The general principles on which the fathers achieved independence, were the only principles in which that beautiful assembly of young men [Continental army] could unite, and these principles only could be intended by them in their address, or by me in my answer. And what were these general principles? I answer, the general principles of Christianity, in which all those sects were united, and the general principles of English and American liberty, in which all those young men united, and which had united all parties in America, in majorities sufficient to assert and maintain her independence. Now I will avow, that I then believed and now believe that those general principles of Christianity are as eternal and immutable as the existence and attributes of God; and that those principles of liberty are as unalterable as human nature and our terrestrial, mundane system."[52]

In another letter to Thomas Jefferson written on December 25, 1813, Adams said, "I have examined all religions, and the result is that the Bible is the best book in the world."[53]

NOAH WEBSTER

(best known as the author of the *An American Dictionary of the English Language*, called the "Father of American Education," strong supporter of America's separation from Great Britain, soldier in the War of Independence, strong proponent for a national constitution, and extremely influential in the political scene of early America)

In the introduction to his 1832 book, *History of the United States*, Noah Webster wrote,

"It is the sincere desire of the writer that our citizens should early understand that the genuine source of correct republican principles is the Bible, particularly the New Testament or the Christian Religion."[54]

Writing to James Madison on October 16, 1829, Webster said,

"The Christian religion, in its purity, is the basis, or rather the source of all genuine freedom in government...and I am persuaded that no civil government of a republican form can exist and be durable in which the principles of that religion have not a controlling influence."[55]

On October 25, 1836, Webster wrote,

"In my view, the Christian religion is the most important and one of the first things in which all children, under a free government, ought to be instructed...No truth is more evident to my mind than that the Christian religion must be the basis of any government intended to secure the rights and privileges of a free people."[56]

Although these are only a few examples from the hundreds of statements made by the Founding Fathers, they are a good representation of the positions and beliefs of the vast majority of them. Again, even though it is impossible to prove that most of the Founders were "born again" Christians, it is undeniable that all of them, even the least religious, possessed a deep respect for the Bible, its teachings, Christ, and the Christian faith.

CONGRESS AND THE SUPREME COURT IN THE 19TH CENTURY

In the 1850s, a lawsuit was filed claiming that America was never founded as a Christian union. In response, Congress assigned the Judiciary Committees of both the House and the Senate with the task of researching our founding documents to determine whether or not America was truly founded as a Christian union. On March 27, 1854, the House committee submitted its report which was practically identical to the one submitted by the Senate committee. It said in part,

> "Had the (founding fathers), during the revolution, a suspicion of any attempt to war against Christianity, that Revolution would have been strangled in its cradle. ... At the time of the adoption of the constitution and its amendments, the universal sentiment was that Christianity should be encouraged ... In this age, there is no substitute for Christianity...That was the religion of the founders of the republic and they expected it to remain the religion of their descendants."[57]

In 1856, the House added these comments to its official records:

> "The great, vital and conservative element in our system is the belief of our people in the pure doctrines and the divine truths of the Gospel of Jesus Christ."[58]

Thirty-eight years later on February 29, 1892, U.S. Supreme Court Justice, David Brewer, writing in the decision *Holy Trinity vs. The United States*, said,

> "These and many other matters which might be noticed, add a volume of unofficial declarations to the mass of organic utterances that this is a Christian nation."[59]

Of course, John Adams had already confirmed this fact when he said in 1813 that America was founded on the "general principles of Christianity."[60] On July 4, 1837, his son and the sixth President of the United States, John Quincy Adams, echoed this truth in a speech he delivered during a Fourth of July celebration in Newburyport, Massachusetts:

"Why is it that, next to the birthday of the Saviour of the World, your most joyous and most venerated festival returns on this day? ... Is it not that, in the chain of human events, the birthday of the nation is indissolubly linked with the birthday of the Saviour? ... Is it not that the Declaration of Independence first organized the social compact on the foundation of the Redeemer's mission upon earth? That it laid the corner stone of human government upon the first precepts of Christianity ..."[61]

Adams's comments are amazingly similar to those of the Black Regiment preacher William Smith spoken sixty-two years earlier on June 23, 1775 in his sermon, *The Crisis of American Affairs*:

"[W]e know that our civil and religious rights are linked together in one indissoluble bond, we neither have, nor seek to have, any interest separate from that of our country; nor can we advise a desertion of its cause. Religion and liberty must flourish or fall together in America. We pray that both may be perpetual."[62]

A casual study of the writings of the Founding Fathers makes it clear that the Founders drank deeply from the sermons and writings of the Black Regiment. In these sermons they not only found the principles that influenced their own personal beliefs but they also found the ones they used to design our republican form of government.

In 1860, the great historian John Wingate Thornton noted,

"The Fathers of the Republic ... invoked God in their civil assemblies, called upon their chosen teachers of religion for counsel from the Bible, and recognized its precepts as the law of their public conduct. ... Indeed, the clergy were generally consulted by the civil authorities; and not infrequently the suggestions from the pulpit, on election days and other special occasions, were enacted into laws. The state was developed out of the church."[63]

It is not uncommon to find key phrases from the sermons of the popular preachers of that time in the correspondence and political writings of many of the Founders. Amazingly, parts of those sermons even made their way into the Declaration of Independence and the Constitution.

One such example is the sermons of Massachusetts pastor John Wise. In the early 1700s, Wise was preaching the biblical principles of government as he spoke about such concepts as taxation without representation, governmental power originating from the consent of the governed, and the equality of all men. In 1772, to help re-educate the colonists about the biblical principles of government, the Sons of Liberty reprinted two of his pamphlets, *The Churches' Quarrel Espoused* (1710) and *A Vindication of the Government of New-England Churches* (1717). In 1864, Benjamin Morris pointed out the incredible impact Wise's sermons had on the Founders:

> "[S]ome of the most glittering sentences in the immortal Declaration of Independence are almost literal quotations from this essay of John Wise.... It was used as a political text book in the great struggle for freedom."[64]

In 1926 President Calvin Coolidge confirmed this fact in a speech he delivered in Philadelphia during the 150th anniversary of the signing of the Declaration of Independence. In it he said, "The thoughts [in the Declaration] can very largely be traced back to what John Wise was writing in 1710."[65] Alice Baldwin confirmed the same truth when she wrote in 1918, "The Constitutional Convention and the written Constitution were the children of the pulpit."[66]

Regardless of one's religious faith or lack thereof, one fact is abundantly clear and undeniable: America was founded on Christian principles by people with deeply held Christian beliefs who believed that, even though liberty allowed for the practice of all faiths in America, Christianity should be the dominant faith.

Chapter 11

THE FOUNDERS WERE NOT ATHEISTS AND DEISTS!

God be thanked! Deists are very thinly sown [in America]; although, like another set of men among us of illaudable and invidious description, they magnify themselves into legions."[67]

Ezra Stiles' sermon to the General Assembly of Connecticut, May 8, 1783

With the Founding Fathers so heavily influenced by the preaching of the Black Robed Regiment, how is it that we've become convinced that the majority of them were Atheists and Deists? We have been told AD *infinitum,* AD *nauseum* by the liberal intelligentsia and media elites that this is exactly what the Founders were. But just a cursory study of the lives of these great patriots should convince the most skeptical that the facts prove otherwise. If just the quotes cited thus far are considered, the legitimate claim can be made that the Founders were anything but atheists and deists.

But before we determine whether or not the Founders were practicing atheists and deists, it is imperative to first define what atheists and deists believe. Most people understand that atheists deny the existence of God so that one is easy, but few today are familiar with what deists believe. *Webster's New World Dictionary* defines deism as:

"the 17th and 18th century doctrine that God created the world and its natural laws, but takes no further part in its functioning"[68]

A deist, then, believes that after God created the universe and the natural laws that govern it, He went "on vacation" and not only does not interface or interfere with men's activities and destinies, but also is not there to hear men's prayers.

As far as we know, none of the Founders claimed to be atheists, at least none did publicly, and although no matter how remote, there is the possibility that a few may have even been deists to some degree. But if we examine the writings, statements, and actions of most of the Founders, it becomes obvious that the beliefs of the vast majority, if not all, were exactly opposite to those of the deists.

THE YOUNG COLONEL GEORGE WASHINGTON

In the mid eighteenth century, Great Britain and the American colonies were at war with France who was allied with many of the Indian tribes of northeastern America. On July 9, 1755, the British and American forces, led by Major General Edward Braddock, marched through the wilderness of Pennsylvania to capture Fort Duquesne located in western Pennsylvania in the area of present day Pittsburgh. A relatively unknown and untried twenty-three year old Colonel from Virginia, by the name of George Washington, served as Gen. Braddock's aid-de-camp.

When the British and American troops, numbering around 1300, were some ten miles from their objective, a force of some 900 French regulars, Canadians, Potawatomi, and Ottawa Indians ambushed them from the cover of the rocks and trees near the banks of the Monongahela River. Taken completely by surprise, the British/American troops were overwhelmed. With musket balls filling the air, the British/American troops were thrown into confusion – even finding it difficult to know exactly in which direction to return fire. It was a blood bath as some 456 British soldiers were killed and 422 were wounded. In a matter of moments, almost seventy-five percent of the British/American soldiers had fallen. Of the eighty-six officers, twenty-six were killed and thirty-seven were wounded including General Braddock who received a mortal wound to the chest.

With guns firing in every direction, visibility at zero from the smoke, the maddening shouts and groans of men locked in mortal combat, the shrieks of terrified and wounded horses, and with the majority of their commanders down, the British/American troops began to panic. Battle formations began to melt away as the soldiers started to run.

At the critical moment, in the midst of this confusion, realizing the situation was quickly transforming from a battle to a complete massacre, one man took control. Riding from place to place, shouting out orders, and pulling the troops together – that man was Col. George Washington. As the ranking commander still standing, Washington succeeded in organizing the troops into an orderly retreat, saving his soldiers from total annihilation. Although the rout effectively ended the British/American offensive in Pennsylvania, it helped launch the illustrious military career of George Washington.

With sixty-three of the eighty-six British officers killed or wounded, it is easy to understand how Col. Washington was erroneously listed among the dead. Although it had been a close call, Washington had escaped unscathed. As the news of the battle began to spread, Washington discovered that people believed he had been killed in the action. To correct this rumor, Washington wrote to his brother, John, assuring him of his health and describing how he had been Providentially protected throughout the entire ordeal. A portion of that letter says,

"As I have heard, since my arrival at this place, a circumstantial account of my death and dying speech, I take this early opportunity of contradicting the first, and of assuring you that I have not composed the latter. By the all-powerful dispensations of Providence, I have been protected beyond all human probability or expectation; for I had four bullets through my coat, and two horses shot under me, yet escaped unhurt, although death was leveling my companions on every side of me!"[69]

As Washington's letter attests, he was a man of deep faith and understood that his miraculous escape from harm at the Battle of Monongahela River was the work of Providence – God having preserved him for some task that lay ahead. Certainly a deist would not believe or admit this, but a Christian would.

As intriguing as this story is, one more amazing story emerges from the drama of the Battle of Monongahela River. Fifteen years later, Washington and a friend were surveying the old battlefield when an aged Indian chief approached them. Speaking through an interpreter, the Chief said,

> "I am a chief and ruler over my tribes. My influence extends to the waters of the great lakes and to the far blue mountains. I have traveled a long and weary path that I might see the young warrior of the great battle. It was on the day when the white man's blood mixed with the streams of our forests that I first beheld this chief [Washington]. I called to my young men and said, mark yon tall and daring warrior? He is not of the red-coat tribe – he hath an Indian's wisdom, and his warriors fight as we do – himself alone exposed. Quick, let your aim be certain, and he dies. Our rifles were leveled, rifles which, but for you, knew not how to miss – 'twas all in vain, a power mightier far than we, shielded you. Seeing you were under the special guardianship of the Great Spirit, we immediately ceased to fire at you. I am old and soon shall be gathered to the great council fire of my fathers in the land of shades, but ere I go, there is something bids me speak in the voice of prophecy: 'Listen! The Great Spirit protects that man [pointing at Washington], and guides his destines – he will become the chief of nations, and a people yet unborn will hail him as the founder of a mighty empire. I am come to pay homage to the man who is the particular favorite of Heaven, and who can never die in battle.' … Washington was never born to be killed by a bullet! I had seventeen fair fires at him with my rifle, and after all could not bring him to the ground!"[70]

GEN. WASHINGTON'S COMMAND TO HIS TROOPS

The importance George Washington placed on the Christian faith is clearly illustrated by one of the earliest orders he issued to his troops after taking command of the Continental Army. On July 4, 1775, General Washington issued this command from Cambridge, Massachusetts:

"The General most earnestly requires and expects a due observance of those articles of war established for the government of the army which forbid profane cursing, swearing and drunkenness; and in the like manner requires and expects of all officers and soldiers not engaged on actual duty, a punctual attendance on Divine Service to implore the blessings of Heaven upon the means used for our safety and defense."[71]

On October 21, 1778, he issued a similar order from Fredericksburg, Virginia:

"Purity of morals being the only sure foundation of public happiness in any country, and highly conducive to order, subordination, and success in an army, it will be well worthy the emulation of officers of every rank and class to encourage it both by the influence of example and the penalties of authority. It is painful to see many shameful instances of riot and licentiousness among us; the wanton practice of swearing has risen to a most disgusting height. A regard to decency should conspire with a sense of morality to banish a vice productive of neither advantage or pleasure."[72]

In another order issued on July 9, 1776, Gen. Washington encouraged the soldiers of the Continental Army to "live and act" like Christians:

"… the blessing and protection of Heaven are at all times necessary but especially so in times of public distress and danger. The General hopes and trusts that every officer and man will endeavour to live and act as becomes a Christian soldier, defending the dearest rights and liberties of his country."[73]

In his General Orders issued on May 2, 1778, Washington made a similar declaration:

"While we are zealously performing the duties of good citizens and soldiers, we certainly ought not to be inattentive to the higher duties of religion. To the distinguished character of Patriot, it should be our highest glory to add the more distinguished character of Christian."[74]

In his inaugural speech on April 30, 1789, Washington said,

"... it would be peculiarly improper to omit in this first official Act, my fervent supplications to that Almighty Being who rules over the Universe, who presides in the Councils of Nations, and whose providential aids can supply every human defect, that his benediction may consecrate to the liberties and happiness of the People of the United States, a Government instituted by themselves for these essential purposes: and may enable every instrument employed in its administration to execute with success, the functions allotted to his charge. In tendering this homage to the Great Author of every public and private good I assure myself that it expresses your sentiments not less than my own; nor those of my fellow-citizens at large, less than either. No People can be bound to acknowledge and adore the invisible hand, which conducts the Affairs of men more than the People of the United States. Every step, by which they have advanced to the character of an independent nation, seems to have been distinguished by some token of providential agency. And in the important revolution just accomplished in the system of their United Government, the tranquil deliberations and voluntary consent of so many distinct communities, from which the event has resulted, cannot be compared with the means by which most Governments have been established, without some return of pious gratitude along with an humble anticipation of the future blessings which the past seem to presage. These reflections, arising out of the present crisis, have forced themselves too strongly on my mind to be suppressed. You will join with me I trust in thinking, that there are none under the influence of which, the proceedings of a new and free Government can more auspiciously commence."[75]

George Washington, a Christian? Yes. An atheist/deist? No.

THE FIRST OFFICIAL ACT OF THE CONTINENTAL CONGRESS

On September 5, 1774, the delegates from the thirteen colonies to the Continental Congress gathered in Philadelphia to determine the course the colonies would take concerning their relationship with England. The next day, September 6, they met for the first time in Carpenters' Hall. As the meeting began, Mr. Thomas Cushing promptly suggested that the meeting should begin with prayer. Some objected claiming that the number of Christian denominations and the diversity of theological opinions represented would make it impossible for the delegates to join together in one, unified prayer.

Samuel Adams rose and said, "I am no bigot. I can hear a prayer from a man of piety and virtue, who, at the same time, is a friend to his country."[76] His statement having found agreement with the delegates, a motion was made to secure the services of a local Episcopal minister by the name of Jacob Duche and that he be invited to lead in a time of prayer the following day. The motion was approved and on September 7, 1774, Rev. Jacob Duche stood before the assembly and read from his daily devotions in the Anglican Common Prayer Book that, providentially, focused that day on Psalm 35 which begins:

> "Plead my cause, O Lord, with them that strive with me: fight against them that fight against me. 2Take hold of shield and buckler, and stand up for mine help. 3Draw out also the spear, and stop the way against them that persecute me: say unto my soul, I am thy salvation. 4Let them be confounded and put to shame that seek after my soul: let them be turned back and brought to confusion that devise my hurt."

No more perfect passage could have been read to that particular group on that particular day. Oh, for the overseeing eye of God! After reading this passage, Duche then broke into this extemporaneous prayer:

> "Our Lord, our Heavenly Father, high and mighty King of Kings, Lord of Lords, who dost from thy throne behold all the dwellers upon the earth, and reignest with power supreme and, uncontrolled over all kingdoms, empires, and governments, look, down in mercy, we beseech thee, upon these American States who have fled to Thee from the rod of the Oppressor, and thrown themselves upon Thy gracious protection, desiring to be henceforth dependent only upon Thee. To Thee have they appealed for the righteousness of their cause. To Thee do they now look up for that countenance and support which Thou alone canst give. Take them, therefore, Heavenly Father, under Thy nurturing care. Give them wisdom in council and valor in the field. Defeat the malicious design of our cruel adversaries. Convince them of the unrighteousness of their cause, and if they still persist in their sanguinary purpose, O let the voice of Thine own unerring justice, sounding in their hearts, constrain them to drop their weapons of war from their unnerved

hands in the day of battle. Be Thou present, O Lord of Wisdom, and direct the Council of the honorable Assembly. Enable them to settle things upon the best and surest foundation, that the scene of blood may speedily be closed; that order, harmony, and peace may effectually be restored, and truth and justice, religion and piety, prevail and flourish amongst Thy people. Preserve the health of their bodies, the vigor of their minds. Shower down upon them, and the millions they here represent, such temporal blessings as Thou seest expedient for them in this world and crown them with everlasting glory in the world to come. All this we ask in the name and through the merits of Jesus Christ, Thy Son, our Savior. Amen."[77]

As the prayer swept across the room like a thunderstorm, it had an incredible effect on the delegates. Writing about his experience to his wife, Abigail, John Adams said,

"... Accordingly, next morning he appeared with his clerk and in his pontificals, and read several prayers in the established form; and then read the Collect for the seventh day of September, which was the thirty-fifth Psalm. You must remember this was the next morning after we heard the horrible rumor of the cannonade of Boston. I never saw a greater effect upon an audience. It seemed as if Heaven had ordained that Psalm to be read on the morning ... I must beg you to read that Psalm. ... [R]ead this letter and the thirty-fifth Psalm to them [your friends]. Read it to your father. ... After this Mr. Duche, unexpected to everybody, struck out in an extemporary prayer which filled the bosom of every man present. I must confess I never heard a better prayer or one so well pronounced. ... with such fervor, such ardor, such earnestness and pathos and in language to elegant and sublime – for America, for the Congress, for the Province of Massachusetts Bay, and especially the town of Boston. It has had an excellent effect upon everybody here."[78]

The prayer moved other delegates as well. Silas Deane wrote,

"The Congress met and opened with a prayer made by the Revd. Mr. Duche which it was worth riding one hundred mile to hear. He read the lessons of the day [Scriptures] which were accidentally extremely applicable, and then prayed without book about ten minutes so pertinently, with such fervency, purity, and sublimity of style and sentiment, and with such an apparent sensibility of the scenes and business before us, that even Quakers shed tears."[79]

The insistence of the Founders to open the first session of the Continental Congress with prayer was hardly the act of a group of atheists and deists. Atheists/deists would not have even believed there was a God to hear their prayer.

DR. BENJAMIN RUSH

(First signer of the Declaration of Independence, physician, Surgeon General for the Continental Army, pioneer of medical science, and founder of Dickinson College in Carlisle, Pennsylvania)

Dr. Benjamin Rush possessed a strong Christian faith evidenced by his life and many writings and statements. The following examples are representative of his authentic faith:

- "If moral precepts alone could have reformed mankind, the mission of the Son of God into all the world would have been unnecessary. The perfect morality of the Gospel rests upon the doctrine which, though often controverted, has never been refuted: I mean the vicarious life and death of the Son of God. … I have alternately been called an Aristocrat and a Democrat. I am neither. I am a 'Christocrat'."[80]

- "The Gospel of Jesus Christ prescribes the wisest rules for just conduct in every situation of life. Happy they who are enabled to obey them in all situations! … My only hope of salvation is in the infinite transcendent love of God manifested to the world by the death of His Son upon the Cross. Nothing but His blood will wash away my sins [Acts 22:16]. I rely exclusively upon it. Come, Lord Jesus! Come quickly! [Revelation 22:20]"[81]

- "The great enemy of the salvation of man, in my opinion, never invented a more effective means of limiting Christianity from the world than by persuading mankind that it was improper to read the Bible at schools."[82] (Letter to Jeremy Belknap, July 13, 1789)

- "[C]hristianity is the only true and perfect religion; and… in proportion as mankind adopt its principles and obey its precepts, they will be wise and happy."[83] (Letter to Jeremy Belknap, March 2, 1791)

- "The Bible, when not read in schools, is seldom read in any subsequent period of life… [T]he Bible… should be read in our schools in preference to all other books because it contains the greatest portion of that kind of knowledge which is calculated to produce private and public happiness."[84] (Rush's "A Defense of the Use of the Bible as a School Book")

ROGER SHERMAN

(the only person to sign all four of our founding documents – the Continental Association, the Articles of Confederation, the Declaration of Independence, and the U.S. Constitution and a member of the Committee of Five that drafted the Declaration)

In what could be called his "Declaration of Dependence on Christ," Roger Sherman wrote,

"I believe that there is one only living and true God, existing in three persons, the Father, the Son, and the Holy Ghost, the same in substance equal in power and glory. That the Scriptures of the old and new testaments are a revelation from God, and a complete rule to direct us how we may glorify and enjoy Him. … I believe that the souls of believers are at their death made perfectly holy and immediately taken to glory: that at the end of this world there will be a resurrection of the dead and a final judgment of all mankind when the righteous shall be publicly acquitted by Christ the Judge and admitted to everlasting life and glory, and the wicked be sentenced to everlasting punishment."[85]

On June 28, 1790, Sherman wrote to Samuel Hopkins,

"God commands all men everywhere to repent. He also commands them to believe on the Lord Jesus Christ, and has assured us that all who do repent and believe shall be saved… [G]od… has absolutely promised to bestow them on all these who are willing to accept them on the terms of the Gospel – that is, in a way of free grace through the atonement. "Ask and ye shall receive [John 16:24].

Whosoever will, let him come and take of the waters of life freely [Revelation 22:17]. Him that cometh unto me I will in no wise cast out" [John 6:37]."[86]

The August 15, 1837 issue of Washington D.C. newspaper the, *Globe*, said of Sherman:

"The volume which he consulted more than any other was the Bible. It was his custom, at the commencement of every session of Congress, to purchase a copy of the Scriptures, to peruse it daily, and to present it to one of his children on his return."[87]

Roger Sherman certainly did not sound like an atheist or deist.

JAMES MADISON

(considered by many to be the "Chief Architect of the Constitution," Secretary of State under President Thomas Jefferson, and the fourth President of the United States)

James Madison attended Princeton University, founded by the Presbyterians in 1746. Princeton's first president, Rev. Jonathan Dickinson, declared, "Cursed be all that learning that is contrary to the cross of Christ."[88] Princeton's motto from the beginning was "Under God's Power She Flourishes." While at Princeton, Madison studied under the tutelage of Dr. John Witherspoon, president of Princeton. It was in this "faith-rich" atmosphere that Madison was educated, such was the education of many of our Founders.

In emphasizing the importance of "active Christianity," Madison wrote, "It is not the talking but the walking and working person that is the true Christian."[89]

In a November 9, 1772 letter to his friend, William Bradford, Madison encouraged Bradford to make certain of his salvation:

"[A] watchful eye must be kept on ourselves lest, while we are building ideal monuments of renown and bliss here, we neglect to have our names enrolled in the Annals of Heaven."[90]

Desiring all who served the public in government to openly declare their Christian beliefs and testimonies, Madison writing again to William Bradford, said on September 25, 1773,

"I have sometimes thought there could not be a stronger testimony in favor of religion or against temporal enjoyments, even the most rational and manly, than for men who occupy the most honorable and gainful departments and [who] are rising in reputation and wealth, publicly to declare their [temporal enjoyments] unsatisfactoriness by becoming fervent advocates in the cause of Christ; and I wish you may give in your evidence in this way."[91]

WILLIAM SAMUEL JOHNSON

(delegate to the Constitutional Convention, Signer of the U.S. Constitution, Senator, and first president of Columbia University)

In 1772, Johnson wrote to his friend Robert Temple,

"For my part, I have seen so much of the follies of the world, particularly the political part of it, ... that I am heartily sick of politics, and am endeavoring to forget all I have observed upon that subject; to erase from my mind every political idea as relative to the present conduct of affairs, and to attend to my own duty only as a Christian, a man, and a member of society. When iniquity abounds, the love of many will wax cold. Iniquity does now abound: let us take care that our Christianity, though put to the test, as I doubt not yours has sufficiently been, be not shaken, and that our love for things really good wax not cold."[92]

As president of Columbia University, William Johnson delivered the following commencement speech to a graduating class of Columbia University not long after the War of Independence in the mid 1790's. He said in part:

"You have, by the favor of Providence and the attention of friends, received a public education, the purpose whereof hath been to qualify you the better to serve your Creator and your country. ... Fulfill the expectations your friends have a right to form of you, and the demands which your country hath upon you. Your first great duties, you are sensible, are those you owe to Heaven, to your Creator and Redeemer. Let these be ever present in your minds, and exemplified in your lives and your conduct. Imprint deep upon your minds the principles of piety towards God, and a reverence and fear of His holy name. The fear of God is the beginning of wisdom and its consummation is everlasting felicity. Possess yourselves of just and elevated notions of the Divine character, attributes, and administration, and of the end and dignity of your own immortal nature as it stands related to Him. Reflect deeply and often upon those relations. Remember that it is in God you live and move and have your being … and that He will one day call you to a strict account for all your conduct in this mortal life. Remember, too, that you are the redeemed of the Lord, that you are bought with a price, even the inestimable price of the precious blood of the Son of God. Adore Jehovah, therefore, as your God and your Judge. Love, fear, and serve Him as your Creator, Redeemer, and Sanctifier. Acquaint yourselves with Him in His word and holy ordinances. Make Him your friend and your protector and your felicity is secured both here and hereafter. And with respect to particular duties to Him, it is your happiness that you are well assured that he best serves his Maker, who does most good to his country and to mankind."[93]

JOHN JAY

(delegate to the first and second Continental Congress, President first Chief Justice of the U.S. Supreme Court)

On April 8, 1784, John Jay wrote to his eldest son, Peter Augustus:

"The Bible is the best of all books, for it is the word of God and teaches us the way to be happy in this world and in the next. Continue therefore to read it and to regulate your life by its precepts."[94]

Writing to Pastor Uzal Ogden on February 14, 1796, Jay commented on how he believed Christianity would survive the attack of Thomas Paine's book, *The Age of Reason*:

"I have long been of the opinion that the evidence of the truth of Christianity requires only to be carefully examined to produce conviction in candid minds …"[95]

PATRICK HENRY

(Governor of Virginia, leader of Virginia in the fight for liberty, Colonel of the 1st Virginia Regiment, member of the Continental Congress, delivered the famous "give me liberty or give me death" speech to the Virginia House of Burgesses on March 23, 1775, and helped lead the struggle for the addition of the Bill of Rights to the U.S. Constitution)

In a letter to his daughter, Betsy, on August 20, 1796, Patrick Henry wrote,

"The view which the rising greatness of our country presents to my eyes, is greatly tarnished by the general prevalence of deism, which, with me, is but another name for vice and depravity. I am, however, much consoled by reflecting that the religion of Christ has, from its first appearance in the world been attacked in vain by all the wits, philosophers and wise ones, aided by every power of man, and its triumph has been complete. What is there in the wit or wisdom of the present deistical writers or professors that can compare them with Hume, Shaftsbury, Bolingbroke and others; and yet these have been confuted, and their fame is decaying, insomuch that the puny efforts of Paine are thrown in to prop their tottering fabric, whose foundations cannot stand the test of time. Among other strange things said of me, I hear it is said by the deists that I am one of their number; and, indeed, that some good people think I am no Christian. This thought gives me much more pain than the appellation of tory, because I think religion of infinitely higher importance than politics, and I find much cause to reproach myself that I have lived so long and have given no decided and public proofs of my being a Christian. But, indeed, my dear child, this is a character which I prize far above all this world has, or can boast."[96]

A friend who visited Henry not long before his death, found him engaged in reading the Bible. Holding it up, Henry said, "[H]ere, is a book worth more than all the other books that were ever printed."[97]

BENJAMIN FRANKLIN

(member of the second Continental Congress, member of the Committee of Five that drafted the Declaration of Independence, first U.S. Postmaster General, Ambassador to France, member of the Constitutional Convention, and signer of the Declaration of Independence and the U.S. Constitution)

Although quite possibly the least religious of all the Founders, today Franklin is commonly labeled a deist. The note Benjamin Franklin wrote to George Washington, president of the Constitutional Convention, on June 28, 1787 certainly does not sound like one written by someone who believed that God was disconnected and uninterested in the affairs of mankind. With the Constitutional Convention deadlocked in disagreement and the members preparing to adjourn and return home in frustration, Franklin made the following motion:

"In this situation of this Assembly, groping as it were in the dark to find political truth, and scarce able to distinguish it when presented to us, how has it happened, Sir, that we have not hitherto once thought of humbly applying to the Father of lights to illuminate our understandings ? In the beginning of the Contest with G. Britain when we were sensible of danger we had daily prayer in this room for the divine protection. Our prayers, Sir, were heard, and they were graciously answered. All of us who were engaged in the struggle must have observed frequent instances of Superintending providence in our favor. To that kind of providence we owe this happy opportunity of consulting in peace on the means of establishing our future national felicity. And have we now forgotten that powerful friend ? Or do we imagine that we no longer need his assistance ? I have lived, Sir, a long time, and the longer I live, the more convincing proofs I see of this truth – that God governs in the affairs of men. And if a sparrow cannot fall to the ground without his notice, is it probable that an empire can rise without his aid? We have been assured, Sir, in the sacred writings, that 'except the Lord build the House they labor in vain that build it.' I firmly believe this; and I also believe that without his concurring aid we shall succeed in this political building no better than the Builders of Babel: We shall be divided by our little partial local interests; our projects will be confounded, and we ourselves shall become a reproach and bye word down to future ages. And what is worse, mankind may hereafter from this unfortunate instance, despair of establishing Governments by Human Wisdom and leave it to chance, war and conquest. … I therefore beg leave to move – that henceforth prayers imploring the assistance of Heaven, and its blessings on our deliberations, be held in this Assembly every morning before we proceed to business, and that one or more of the Clergy of this City be requested to officiate in that service."[98]

Benjamin Franklin an atheist or deist? Hardly.

NOAH WEBSTER

(author of *An American Dictionary of the English Language*, called the "Father of American Education," strong supporter of America's separation from Great Britain, soldier in the War of Independence, strong proponent for a national constitution, and extremely influential in the political scene of early America)

In his 1832 book, *History of the United States*, Webster wrote,

"Almost all the civil liberty now enjoyed in the world owes its origin to the principles of the Christian religion. … civil liberty has been gradually advancing and improving, as genuine Christianity has prevailed. … the religion which has introduced civil liberty, is the religion of Christ and his apostles, which enjoins humility, piety, and benevolence; which acknowledges in every person a brother, or a sister, and a citizen with equal rights. This is genuine Christianity, and to this we owe our free constitutions of government.

Let your first care through life, be directed to support and extend the influence of the Christian religion, and the observance of the Sabbath. This is the only system of religion which has ever been offered to the consideration and acceptance of men, which has even probable evidence of a divine original; it is the only religion that honors the character and moral government of the Supreme Being; it is the only religion which gives even a probable account of the origin of the world, and of the dispensations of God towards mankind; it is the only religion which teaches the character and laws of God, with our relations and our duties to him; it is the only religion which assures us of an immortal existence; which offers the means of everlasting salvation, and consoles mankind under the inevitable calamities of the present life.

But were we assured that there is to be no future life, and that men are to perish at death like the beasts of the field; the moral principles and precepts contained in the scriptures ought to form the basis of all our civil constitutions and laws. These principles and precepts have truth, immutable truth, for their foundation; and they are adapted to the wants of men in every condition of life. They are the best principles and precepts, because they are exactly adapted to secure the practice of universal justice and kindness among men; and of course to prevent crimes, war, and disorders in society. No human laws dictated by different principles from those in the gospel, can ever secure these objects. All the miseries and evils which men suffer from vice, crime, ambition, injustice, oppression, slavery, and war, proceed from their despising or neglecting the precepts contained in the Bible.

As the means of temporal happiness then the Christian religion ought to be received, and maintained with firm and cordial support. It is the real source of all genuine republican principles. It teaches the equality of men as to rights and duties; and while it forbids all oppression, it commands due subordination to law and rulers. It requires the young to yield obedience to their parents, and enjoins upon men the duty of selecting their rulers from their fellow citizens of mature age, sound wisdom, and real religion—'men who fear God and hate covetousness.' The ecclesiastical establishments of Europe, which serve to support tyrannical governments, are not the Christian religion, but abuses and corruptions of it. The religion of Christ and his apostles, in its primitive simplicity and purity, unencumbered with the trappings of power and the pomp of ceremonies, is the surest basis of a republican government.

Never cease then to give to religion, to its institutions, and to its ministers, your strenuous support. … those who destroy the influence and authority of the Christian religion, sap the foundations of public order, of liberty, and of republican government.

For instruction then in social, religious, and civil duties, resort to the scriptures for the best precepts and most excellent examples for imitation. … Christ and his apostles presented, in their lives, the most perfect example of disinterested benevolence, unaffected kindness, humility, patience in adversity, forgiveness of injuries, love to God; and to all mankind. If men would universally cultivate these religious affections and virtuous dispositions, with as much diligence as they cultivate human science and refinement of manners, the world would soon become a terrestrial paradise."[99]

This certainly does not sound like something written by an atheist or deist.

ROBERT AITKEN AND THE AITKEN BIBLE

Assuming America was founded mostly by atheists and deists who intended to create a completely secular government, one in which religion and the state would be kept strictly separate as Cornell professors Isaac Kramnick and Lawrence Moore contend, it is incredibly odd that Congress would officially "authorize" the printing of the first English Bible printed in America.

On January 21, 1781 Robert Aitken, a printer from Philadelphia, petitioned Congress, then assembled in that same city, to officially sanction a publication of the Old and New Testaments that he was preparing at his own expense. The following entry is from the official *Journals of the Continental Congress*:

"September 12, 1782

"The committee, consisting of Mr. [James] Duane, Mr. [Thomas] McKean and Mr. [John] Witherspoon, to whom was referred a petition memorial of Robert Aitken, printer, dated 21 January, 1781, respecting an edition of the holy scriptures, report,

"That Mr. Aitken has at a great expense now finished an American edition of the holy scriptures in English; that the committee have, from time to time, ~~conferred with him~~ attended to his progress in the work: that they also recommended it to the two chaplains of Congress to examine and give their opinion of the execution, who have accordingly reported thereon: The recommendation and report being as follows:

"Philadelphia, 1 September 1782.

"Rev. Gentlemen, Our knowledge of your piety and public spirit leads us without apology to recommend to your particular attention the edition of the Holy Scriptures publishing by Mr. Aitken. He undertook this expensive work at a time, when from the circumstances of the war, an English edition of the Bible could not be imported, nor any opinion formed how long the obstruction might continue. On this account particularly he deserves applause and encouragement. We therefore wish you, reverend gentlemen, to examine the execution of the work, and if approved, to give it the sanction of your judgment and the weight of your recommendation. We are with very great respect, your most obedient humble servants,

"(Signed) James Duane, Chairman, In behalf of a committee of Congress on Mr. Aitken's memorial. Rev. Dr. White and Rev. Mr. Duffield, chaplains of the United States in Congress assembled.

"REPORT.

"Gentlemen, Agreeably to your desire, we have paid attention to Mr. Robert Aitken's impression of the holy scriptures, of the old and new testament. Having selected and examined a variety of passages throughout the work, we are of opinion, that it is executed with great accuracy as to the sense, and with as few grammatical and typographical errors as could be expected in an undertaking of such magnitude. Being ourselves witnesses of the demand for this invaluable book, we rejoice in the present prospect of a supply, hoping that it will prove as advantageous as it is honorable to the gentleman, who has exerted himself to furnish it at the evident risk of private fortune. We are, gentlemen, your very respectful and humble servants,

"(Signed) William White, George Duffield.

"Philadelphia, September 10, 1782. Hon. James Duane, Esq. chairman, and the other hon. gentlemen of the committee of Congress on Mr. Aitken's memorial.

"Whereupon, Resolved, That the United States in Congress assembled, highly approve the pious and laudable undertaking of Mr. Aitken, as subservient to the interest of religion as well as an instance of the progress of arts in this country, and being satisfied from the above report, of his care and accuracy in the execution of the work, they recommend this edition of the Bible to the inhabitants of the United States, and hereby authorize him to publish this recommendation in the manner he shall think proper."[100]

How strange that atheists and deists would take the time and effort to officially authorize the printing of the first English Bible in America – a book about a God they believed either did not exist or was unreachable.

RULES FOR THE REGULATION OF THE NAVY OF THE UNITED COLONIES OF NORTH AMERICA, NOV. 28, 1775

If the Founders truly intended for America's government and its agencies to be a "religion-free zone," then how can we explain the following regulations imposed by the Navy of the United Colonies in 1775? The official regulations stated,

"The Commanders of the ships of the Thirteen United Colonies are to take care that divine service be performed twice a day on board, and a sermon preached on Sundays, unless bad weather or other extraordinary accidents prevent it. ... If any shall be heard to swear, curse or blaspheme the name of God, the Captain is strictly enjoined to punish them for every offence, by causing them to wear a wooden collar or some other shameful badge of distinction, for so long a time as he shall judge proper:–If he be a commissioned officer he shall forfeit one shilling for each offence, and a warrant or inferior officer, six-pence: He who is guilty of drunkenness (if a seaman) shall be put in irons until he is sober, but if an officer, he shall forfeit two days pay."[101]

THOMAS JEFFERSON, CHRISTIANITY, AND CHURCH ATTENDANCE

Of all the Founders, Thomas Jefferson is the one most quoted by modern historians and media personalities. In their attempt to paint the Founders as non-Christians, those on the political left make a habit of grossly misquoting and mischaracterizing Jefferson – especially when it comes to the concept of "separation of church and state." They would have us believe that, because of his famous "separation" phrase in his letter written to a group of Baptists in Danbury, Connecticut on January 1, 1802, Jefferson was a godless, irreligious man who believed that church and state should never mix. This relatively recent interpretation of Jefferson's comments in his 1802 letter completely turns the meaning of what he actually wrote on its head.

Before we make Thomas Jefferson "the authority" on the First Amendment, it is interesting to note that Jefferson was not even in America when Congress adopted the First Amendment – he was in France. In addition, Jefferson did not write the First Amendment – it was written by James Madison.

In the famous "separation" letter, Jefferson was responding to a group of Baptists in Danbury, Connecticut who had heard that Congress was planning to "establish" a state denomination. The phrase "wall of separation between church and state" is found in this incredibly long sentence in Jefferson's letter:

> "Believing with you that religion is a matter which lies solely between a man and his God, that he owes account to none other for his faith or his worship, that the legislative powers of government reach actions only, and not opinion, I contemplate with solemn reverence that act of the whole American People which declared that their legislature should 'make no law respecting an establishment of religion, or prohibiting the free exercise thereof,' thus building a wall of separation between church and state."[102]

It is understandable why the Baptists in Danbury were so concerned. Had the rumor that the U.S. government was about to designate an "official" denomination for the country been true, the Baptists had a legitimate fear. A "government established religion/church" was one of the very things Americans had fought and died in the War of Independence to prevent. Although America had been founded squarely on biblical principles by a mostly Christian population, Americans certainly did not want the federal government, or anyone else for that matter, telling them how or where they could/should worship. Jefferson correctly reminded the Baptists in Danbury that the Constitution erected a "wall of separation" between religion and government that restricted the government from establishing any "official" church in America.

Jefferson actually said that this "wall" existed mainly to protect religion from government – not government from religion. The very purpose for which the Constitution and the Bill of Rights were written was to limit government – not the people. The thought that Jefferson believed the country needed protection from religion is ludicrous in the highest degree, is the exact opposite of what he was saying, and is contrary to what the Founders had intended. The Constitution and subsequent Bill of Rights established freedom "of" religion – not freedom "from" religion. As James L. Adams correctly observed,

> "With those words Jefferson was not formulating a secular principle to banish religion from the public arena. Rather he was trying to keep government from darkening the door of the church. … We dare not muzzle morality in the marketplace or permit the wall of separation to turn into an Iron Curtain of religious repression."[103]

Today, the political left has crafted a "myth of separation" by twisting and distorting Jefferson's letter. Consequently, our courts have been using this "myth" as the basis of bad constitutional law for almost fifty years. This was the opinion of William Rehnquist, former Supreme Court justice. In 1985, Rehnquist wrote:

> "But the greatest injury of the "wall" notion is its mischievous diversion of judges from the actual intentions of the drafters of the Bill of Rights. … The 'wall

of separation between church and State' is a metaphor based on bad history, a metaphor which has proved useless as a guide to judging. It should be frankly and explicitly abandoned."[104]

As we assess Jefferson's faith, it must be conceded that he may never have become a born again Christian. Even so, it is obvious that he possessed a great respect for Scripture and the Christian faith and was no atheist or deist. It is also important to remember that most people go through a number of different phases throughout a lifetime. What they believe during one period of their lives may not necessarily reflect what they believe in a later period. Multiple examples can be found of people who at one time rejected Christianity only to become fervent believers later on – the Apostle Paul comes immediately to mind. Even though some of these people were even hostile towards the Christian faith, in time they came to embrace the very faith they had once worked to destroy.

When assessing someone's beliefs and convictions, especially when it comes to religious beliefs, great care must be taken to consider the entirety of his life rather than "selectively picking" the parts that support particular presuppositions. Unfortunately, if someone is committed to casting a person in a particular light, it is easy enough to emphasize what he said or did during one period of his life while ignoring later statements and positions to the contrary. In doing so, they can create a caricature that does not accurately reflect what that person actually believed in the end. This is absolutely what many in our era have done with Thomas Jefferson and his position on Christianity and the relationship between church and state.

A number of historians have studied the life and writings of Jefferson extensively and believe that his life can be divided into a number of phases. During each of these phases, based upon his intellectual/spiritual development and his life experiences – especially the difficult times, his religious beliefs appear to move from one position to another.

For example, with the death of his oldest sister, Jane, who was only twenty-five years of age at the time of her death, Thomas, only twenty-two, was so overwhelmed that he fell into a period of deep mourning and depression. The effect of her death on him was magnified even more by the fact that his two other older sisters had moved away from home after getting married, leaving him with only younger siblings who offered little of the intellectual exchange he so craved.

Then in 1772, at the age of twenty-eight, he married Martha Skelton. But married life proved to be short and difficult for Thomas. Even though he and Martha had six children born to them, only two survived to adulthood. A daughter died at the age of one year in 1775, a son was still born in 1777, another one-year-old daughter died in 1781, and in 1785 another daughter died at the age of three. Only a few months after the birth of this daughter, Martha, his wife of only ten years, died. Her death devastated Thomas, and he greatly mourned her; often taking long rides on secluded roads grieving her loss. Keeping the promise he made to her, he never remarried.

Experiences like these cut deep marks into a person's soul – greatly affecting his psyche, beliefs, and actions. So when quoting someone as complicated and as brilliant as Thomas Jefferson, we must carefully consider the life context within which particular statements or actions were made in order to correctly figure them into a much larger whole-life equation.

If one considers the whole of Thomas Jefferson's life rather than its parts, it is relatively easy to prove that many of the modern, commonly held opinions that present him as an irreligious man who believed in a strict separation of church and state are in direct contradiction with his official statements and deeds. In many ways, this "modern portrait" is more a fabrication created from misquotes and bad interpretations than it is a truthful reflection of the facts. Again, admittedly, Jefferson was a complicated person who is difficult to completely understand, and whose spiritual condition is highly debatable. But by considering the following examples, it becomes obvious that he was quite different from the "anti-Christian" picture modern leftists have painted of him.

HIS CHURCH ATTENDANCE

Genuine Christian or not, Thomas Jefferson made it a practice to attend church regularly. Writing about this, the Reverend Ethan Allen said that, while president, Thomas Jefferson sometimes attended church in a Tobacco House located at or near an old market, which stood on the NW corner of the Virginia and Jersey Avenues in Washington D.C. There he listened to sermons by a preacher named McCormick. Allen wrote of Jefferson,

> "Here it was that Mr. Jefferson was coming one Sunday morning across the fields leading to it with his large red Prayer Book under his arm when a friend riding [beside] him, after their mutual good morning, said 'Which way are you walking Mr. Jefferson?' To which he [Jefferson] replied, 'To Church Sir.' 'You going to church Mr. Jefferson? You do not believe a word in it.' 'Sir,' said Mr. Jefferson, 'no nation has yet existed or been governed without religion, nor can be. The Christian religion is the best religion that has been given to man & I, as the chief magistrate of this nation, am bound to give it the sanction of my example. Good morning Sir.'"
>
> (Note: Although the Monticello website questions Rev. Allen's story, Dr. James H. Hutson, who has served in the History Departments at Yale and William and Mary and as the Chief of the Library of Congress's Manuscript Division since 1982, offers proof to the validity of Allen's account.)[105]

According to a Maryland Episcopal Bishop by the name of Mr. Claggett, while vice president, Jefferson regularly attended church services held in the chamber of the House of Representatives.[106] He continued this practice after becoming President, attending his first church service in the Capitol as President on January 3, 1802 (just two days after writing his infamous "separation of church and state" letter) where he listened to the preaching of his friend, the Rev. John Leland.[107]

Mrs. Samuel Harrison Smith (Margaret Bayard Smith), a frequent attendee of the services at the Capitol, also confirmed Jefferson's faithful attendance:

> "Mr. Jefferson, during his whole administration, was a most regular attendant. … The seat he chose the first Sabbath, and the adjoining one (which his private secretary occupied), were ever afterwards by the courtesy of the congregation, left for him and his secretary."[108]

Manasseh Cutler, himself a preacher, a U.S. Representative, Revolutionary War chaplain, and fellow church attendee at the Capitol, recorded in his diary: "He [Jefferson] and his family have constantly attended public worship in the Hall."[109] Cutler noted that Jefferson was so committed to attendance that he would not even allow inclement weather to deter him: "It was very rainy, but his [Jefferson's] ardent zeal brought him through the rain and on horseback to the Hall."[110]

It is quite an irony of history that Jefferson attended a worship service held in the nation's Capitol Building just days after writing his now famous letter containing the "wall of separation" metaphor. If he were the "strict separationist" that many claim, why did he not protest the apparent unconstitutional use of a government building, especially the Capitol Building, for a church service? In addition, according to Margaret Smith, the marine band was used for a time to provide the music for the worship services (presumably while they were on the government payroll). Amazingly, Mr. "Separation of Church and State" Jefferson, never, to anyone's knowledge, protested this "unconstitutional" use of government personnel and property.[111]

During Jefferson's presidency, church services were also held in the Treasury Building and the old Supreme Court Chamber[112] all of this without the slightest whimper of protest from the man modern historians claim was the most ardent "separation of church and state" warrior this nation has ever known.

(Note: the church that met in the capitol building was so popular that by the years just prior to the Civil War, it was the largest evangelical church in America.)

HIS ACTIONS AS PATRIOT AND PRESIDENT

Of all Jefferson's actions that bring into question his ardent "separation of church and state" sentiments, the following is possibly the most compelling. In July 1776, the Continental Congress assigned to Thomas Jefferson, Benjamin Franklin, and John Adams the task "to bring in a device for a seal for the United States of America."[113] Jefferson suggested that the seal depict the "Children of Israel in the Wilderness, led by a Cloud by Day, and a Pillar of Fire by night."[114] Franklin proposed that the seal incorporate the story of the parting of the Red Sea. The committee of three came to an agreement by merging the two designs into one. Their design consisted of a circle with the words, "Rebellion To Tyrants Is Obedience To God" written around the perimeter. The center of the seal contained a drawing depicting the Egyptian army drowning in the Red Sea as Moses and the Israelites looked on with the Pillar of fire/cloud between them and the Egyptians.[115]

Jefferson, Adams, and Franklin presented their proposal to Congress on August 20, 1776. Interestingly, the Library of Congress website cites the following:

> "Although not accepted, these drafts reveal the religious temper of the Revolutionary period. Franklin and Jefferson were among the most theologically liberal of the Founders, yet they used biblical imagery for this important task."[116]

In addition to approving of and regularly attending church services in the Capitol Building and proposing a biblically based national seal, Jefferson also reflected his deep and abiding respect for, if not acceptance of (at some level), the Christian faith by signing numerous pieces of legislation that clearly "mixed" government and religion.

For example, on March 4, 1787, responding to a plea from Bishop John Ettwein, Congress set aside 10,000 acres of public land on the Muskingum River, in the present state of Ohio. The legislation directed the land "be set apart and the property thereof be vested in the Moravian Brethren … or a society of the said Brethren for civilizing the Indians and promoting Christianity." Congress extended this act three times during Jefferson's presidency and each time he signed the extensions into law without any apparent concern for violating the principle of "separation of church and state."[117]

In 1803, Jefferson signed a treaty that provided $300 to assist the Kaskaskia Indians in "erecting a church" and "$300 to support a Catholic priest" for seven years. Article III of that treaty states:

> "And whereas, The greater part of the said tribe have been baptized and received into the Catholic church to which they are much attached, the United States will give annually for seven years one hundred dollars towards the support of a priest of that religion, who will engage to perform for the said tribe the duties of his office and also to instruct as many of their children as possible in the rudiments of literature. And the United States will further give the sum of three hundred dollars to assist the said tribe in the erection of a church."[118]

In a letter dated May 15, 1804, Jefferson assured the Nuns of the Order of Saint Ursula in New Orleans that they would receive the support of the Federal government:

> "I have received, holy sisters, the letter you have written me wherein you express anxiety for the property vested in your institution by the former governments of Louisiana. The principles of the constitution and government of the United States are a sure guarantee to you that it will be preserved sacred and inviolate, and that your institution will be permitted to govern itself according to its own voluntary rules, without interference from the civil authority. Whatever diversity of shade may appear in the religious opinions of our fellow citizens, the charitable objects of your institution cannot be indifferent to any; and its furtherance of the wholesome purposes of society, by training up its younger members in the way they should go, cannot fail to ensure it the patronage of the government it is under. Be assured it will meet all the protection which my office can give it. I salute you, holy sisters, with friendship and respect."[119]

In addition to this, Jefferson was instrumental in providing for the inclusion of religion in the educational system of Virginia. Peter J. Ferrara wrote,

> "Jefferson's own conception of the wall of separation between church and state did not prevent him from advocating and implementing government for religious education in the state of Virginia."[120]

Jefferson was so proud of his efforts for religious freedom in Virginia, he had that accomplishment written into his epitaph. Before he died, he left explicit instructions about the design of his tombstone and the inscription to be written thereon. His instructions included,

> "...on the faces of the Obelisk the following inscription, and not a word more: 'Here was buried Thomas Jefferson, Author of the Declaration of American Independence, of the Statute of Virginia for religious freedom, Father of the University of Virginia,' because by these as testimonials that I have lived, I wish most to be remembered."[121]

Thomas Jefferson an atheist or deist? Not a prayer!

EDUCATION IN EARLY AMERICA

The philosophy of the schools and universities in early America was decidedly Christian. One hundred and six of the first one hundred and eight schools in America, such as Princeton, Yale, and Harvard, were founded as Christian institutions and taught the principles of Christianity.[122] Fifty-percent of seventeenth century graduates were ministers and ten out of twelve of Harvard's presidents prior to the War of Independence were ministers.[123]

As already mentioned, Jonathan Dickinson, Princeton's first president, said, "Cursed be all that learning that is contrary to the cross of Christ."[124] John Witherspoon, the only vocational preacher to sign the Declaration of Independence, became Princeton's sixth president.

The original motto of Princeton was: "Under God's Power She Flourishes." The original motto of Yale was: "Lux et Verias," which is Latin for "Light and Truth." The original motto of Harvard was: "Veritas Christos et Ecclesiate," Latin for "Truth for Christ and the Church." (Significantly, though the original motto remains on Harvard's main gate, their motto today is only "Veritas" or "Truth," Christ and the Church have been omitted.)

Founded in 1636, Harvard University is distinguished as the oldest university in America. In its 1642 student handbook, *Rules and Precepts*, the students were thus instructed:

> "Let every student be plainly instructed, and earnestly pressed to consider well, the main end of his life and studies is, to know God and Jesus Christ which is eternal life, John 17:3 and therefore to lay Christ in the bottom, as the only foundation of all sound knowledge and learning. And seeing the Lord only giveth wisdom, let every one seriously set himself by prayer in secret to seek it of him Prov. 2:3."[125]

Although the main reason education in early America was so "Christian" is because Christians founded almost all of the institutions, there is another reason and historian Steve McDowell gives the explanation:

> "The important thing that has to be considered is that America's educational institutions were not merely Christian because clergymen started them; they were Christian because the memory of the atrocities in Europe such as the inquisition, the Crusades, burnings at the stake, etc., was still fresh in their minds. They knew that the reason these things occurred was that the people did not have private access to God's Word until the 16th century. Until then, everything they knew about God was subject to interpretation by those who had access to His Word. This led to abuses by those who would "censor" God's Word to fit the designs of their respective religious organizations."[126]

THE NEW ENGLAND PRIMER

The New England Primer was the first reading primer printed in the American Colonies and was first published by Benjamin Harris between 1687-1690. Of all the textbooks printed in early America, it was the most successful. It was the primary reading primer in use in early America until Noah Webster's Blue Back Speller began to replace it in the 1790s.

The following are examples of how *The New England Primer* taught the alphabet, vocabulary, and reading to young students:

The letter "A" – "In Adam's fall we sinned all"

The letter "B" – "Heaven to find the Bible mind"

The letter "C" – "Christ crucified for sinners died"

The letter "D" – "The Deluge drowned the earth around"

The letter "E" – "Elijah hid by ravens fed"

The following is another exercise used to teach students the alphabet:

"A" – "A wise son maketh a glad father, but a foolish son is the heaviness of his mother."

"B" – "Better is a little with the fear of the Lord, than great treasure and trouble therewith."

"C" – "Come unto Christ all ye that labor and are heavy laden and He will give you rest."

"D" – "Do not the abominable thing which I hate saith the Lord."

"E" – "Except a man be born again, he cannot see the kingdom of God."

(Note: It is important to note that the *New England Primer* was not a Sunday School book; it was a public school textbook used to teach spelling and grammar to elementary students.)

If the Founders were such atheists and deists, how is it that they allowed a book such as *The New England Primer*, which used the Scriptures to teach young students, to be used as a textbook in America's schools? Can you imagine the outcry that would be heard in America if a teacher attempted to use *The New England Primer* in an elementary school today?

THE NORTHWEST ORDINANCE

The Northwest Ordinance was passed by the Congress of Confederation of the United States on July 13, 1787 and was later ratified under the Constitution by the newly created Congress on August 7, 1789. It created the first organized territory of the U.S. that encompassed the area south of the Great Lakes, to north and west of the Ohio River, to east of the Mississippi River.

With the exception of the Declaration of Independence and the U.S. Constitution, the Northwest Ordinance is considered by many to be one of the most important pieces of legislation ever written in the United States. It established the process by which America would expand westward and incorporate new territory into the nation as official states.

The Ordinance serves as a critical key in unlocking the thinking and intent of the Founders. Significantly, the men who wrote the Northwest Ordinance also wrote the First Amendment to the Constitution during the same session. If they truly wanted a "strict separation" of church and state in America, how strange that the Founders would write the following in the N.W. Ordinance:

> "Religion, morality, and knowledge, being necessary to good government and the happiness of mankind, schools and the means of education shall forever be encouraged."

Given that the Founders insisted that morality and religion be taught in the schools located in the Northwest Territory, how can the First Amendment, written by the same men, be understood to insist in the "strict separation of church and state?" Obviously, it cannot. The N.W. Ordinance proves that the Founders were not atheists and deists who intended to create a "godless government," but were, instead, men who recognized the critical role Christianity played in the development of America.

YOUNG JOHN ADAMS'S DIARY ENTRY

On Sunday, February 22, 1756, a twenty-year-old John Adams made this entry in his diary:

> "Suppose a nation in some distant region should take the Bible for their only law Book, and every member should regulate his conduct by the precepts there exhibited! Every member would be obliged in conscience, to temperance, frugality, and industry; to justice, kindness, and charity towards his fellow men; and to piety, love, and reverence toward Almighty God. In this commonwealth, no man would impair his health by gluttony, drunkenness, or lust; no man would sacrifice his most precious time to cards or any other trifling and mean amusement; no man would steal, or lie, or in any way defraud his neighbor, but would live in peace and good will with all men; no man would blaspheme his Maker or profane His worship; but a rational and manly, a sincere and unaffected piety and devotion would reign in all hearts. What a Utopia, what a Paradise would this region be. Heard [Rev.] Thayer all day. He preached well."[127]

Those certainly do not sound like the words of an atheist or deist.

THEY WERE NOT DEISTS

It has been said, "there is none so blind as one who will not see." From the examples above, it would seem that the only ones who cannot see that the Founders were not atheists and deists are those who simply do not want to see it. Clearly, those who founded America did not intend to create a "godless government."

The Founders, for the most part, personally embraced Christianity, or as has already been stated, at the very least, possessed a deep respect for Scripture and the Christian faith. Their voluminous official actions, writings, and public statements make this fact so obvious that the reasonable person is compelled to concur with the Supreme Court's assessment: "These and many other matters which might be noticed, add a volume of unofficial declarations to the mass of organic utterances that this is a Christian nation." (*Trinity v. U.S.*, 1892)

Chapter 12

THEY WERE NOT REBELS & ANARCHISTS

Exactly one year after John Hancock affixed his impressive signature to the Declaration of Independence so that, as he said, "his Majesty can now read my name without glasses,"[128] William Gordon preached these words before the General Court of Massachusetts on July 4, 1777:

> "And such is the impiety of the courtiers … such the irreligion of lords and commons, that, was a messenger sent with the word of God to forbid the bloody purpose, he would be rejected without examining his credentials, and would probably be ordered into confinement as a madman. An angel from heaven would have less attention paid him than a threatening express from a neighboring power. Has not the God of nature declared again and again his disapprobation of their [British] bloody proceedings, by scattering their fleets, staying their voyages, disconcerting their plans, delivering many of their stores into our hands, and plunging them continually into greater difficulties."[129]

Gordon's words clearly reveal his and the rest of the Americans' frustrations over Britain's obstinacy toward the America. But having been taught by their pastors and instructors to honor and submit to those who ruled over them, the colonists were hesitant to enter into conflict. They simply would not take up arms hastily, but labored over the issue for more than ten years – doing all within their power to avoid bloodshed. But, they had also been taught that a tyrannical government either had to be righted or replaced.

Elizur Goodrich articulated this very message before the governor of Connecticut and the Connecticut General Assembly in his May 10, 1787 sermon, *The Principles Of Civil Union And Happiness Considered And Recommended.* Goodrich was the pastor of the Congregational Church in Durham, Connecticut, a graduate of Yale, and a close friend of Rev. Ezra Stiles, president of Yale. Because of his intellect, strength of character, and courage, Pastor Goodrich was widely accepted as a spiritual and intellectual leader throughout Connecticut. Although he believed in honoring and obeying those in power, when that government became a tyranny, he also believed those citizens had a right to resist:

> "Honor and respect are due to rulers: The order and good of society require external marks of distinction, and titles of eminence to be given them. This is due to their office; an honor paid to the institution of government; but there is a further honor due to them, when they are faithful in executing the trust committed to them, and direct all their actions to advance the true interest of the state. In this view, good rulers alone can be honored, because they alone deserve esteem and respect. We owe obedience and subjection to all rulers in the execution of their office, according to the laws of the land; but, as to cordial affection, veneration, esteem and gratitude, these are due only to the worthy magistrate; and the debt will be paid by all virtuous citizens, although he should be blasphemed, arraigned, and condemned by the factious and discontented; who wish that there should be no righteous government in the world. … When a constitutional government is converted into tyranny, and the laws, rights and properties of a free people are openly invaded, there ought not to be the least doubt but that a remedy consistent with this doctrine of the apostle, is provided in the laws of God and reason, for their preservation; nor ought resistance in such case to be called rebellion. But who will imagine, that God, whose first law, in the world of nature and reason, is order and love, has commissioned men of a private character, with a lawful power, on every pretense of some public mismanagement, to inflame and raise the multitude, embroil the state, and overturn the foundations of public peace."[130]

These are hardly the words of a wild-eyed rebel bent on anarchy. Instead, they are the thoughts and words of a logical, well-reasoned, law-abiding individual. The intention of the Americans was to execute an honorable and lawful separation from Great Britain. John Adams, who was greatly influenced by the sermons

In 1821, long after the war, John Quincy Adams debunked the theory that the Founders were anarchists:

> "[T]here was no anarchy.... [T]he people of the North American union and of its constituent states were associated bodies of civilized men and Christians in a state of nature but not of anarchy. They were bound by the laws of God (which they all) and by the laws of the Gospel (which they nearly all) acknowledged as the rules of their conduct."[135]

These men were separating from a tyrannical government – not rebelling against a good and lawful one. Our Founders did not board ships and sail to England to usurp the throne, they simply sought the freedom to live and govern the way they thought best while allowing the British to do the same. Deeply intellectual and spiritual and having thought it through completely, the Founders were well aware of the gravity of their actions and fully anticipated and embraced the potentially disastrous consequences of declaring their independence from England. As we saw earlier, Benjamin Franklin had warned the others that they could very well hang for treason for what they were doing.

Franklin's statement reflects the intense solemnity with which these men took their stand for liberty – an attitude foreign to reckless bomb throwers and mobs like those who participated in the "Occupy Wall Street" demonstrations of 2011-12. In fact, the ideology of the overwhelming majority of those who called themselves "Occupy Wall Street" was not even close to that of our Founders. Historian John Thornton commented: "His Majesty called them 'rebels,' and they soon declared and proved themselves to be neither subjects nor rebels, but a free people."[136]

In Boston on July 5, 1802 with the war nineteen years in the past and America enjoying an awkward peace with England, William Emerson, pastor of the First Church in Boston, preached the sermon, *An Oration In Commemoration Of The Anniversary Of American Independence*. In it he reminded his audience that the Founders were law-abiding men who possessed great respect for those in authority:

"Here, then, you find the principles, which produced the event, we this day commemorate. They were the principles of common law and of eternal justice. They were the principles of men, who sought not to subvert the government, under which they lived, but to save it from degeneracy; not to create new rights, but to preserve inviolate such, as they had ever possessed, rights of the same sort, by which George III then sat, and still sits, on the throne of England, the rights of prescription. Such was the American Revolution. It arose not on a sudden, but from the successless petitions and remonstrance of ten long years. It was a revolution, not of choice, but of necessity. It grew out of the sorrows and unacknowledged importance of the country; and having to obtain a definite object by definite means, that object being obtained, was gloriously terminated."[137]

In reality the Americans had shown an amazing amount of restraint in the face of repeated insults and abuses by the British government. As has already been shown, the Americans had certainly gone the second mile attempting to work out a compromise with Great Britain. So to accuse them of reckless rebellion stretches credulity beyond the breaking point. This fact was bluntly, but articulately expressed in an article in the *Boston Gazette* on November 9, 1772 written by a "Mr. Humanity" whom most believed to be a preacher:

"[It is] my firm opinion that the Americans would be justified in the sight of Heaven and before all nations of mankind, in forming an independent government of their own, and cutting off every son of Adam that dared to oppose them by force – Great Britain has robbed them, sent her armies to enslave them, and totally cancelled all obligations to continue their connection with her another day – I am however for making the King of Great Britain the offer once more, and but one, to renew the compact."[138]

In his September 8, 1774 sermon, *To The Respectable Freemen, Of The English Colony Of Connecticut*, Samuel Sherwood, pastor in Weston, Connecticut, spoke for the entire Black Regiment when he emphasized that the government should be supported as long as it promoted society's good:

"I do not mean to encourage evil jealousies and groundless suspicions of our civil rulers, the guardians of our liberties; nor to countenance seditious tumults in the state, so destructive to our civil happiness and peace. I am a firm friend to good order and regularity; that all ranks of men move in strait lines, and within their own proper spheres: That authority and government be supported and maintained so as to promote the good of society, the end for which it was instituted; perfectly consistent with which, a people may keep a watchful eye over their liberties, and cautiously guard against oppression and tyranny, which I detest and abhor, and solemnly abjure."[139]

Samuel Langdon, president of Harvard, delivered the 1775 Massachusetts election sermon in Watertown, Massachusetts. In that sermon, he emphasized that the patriot pastors were no friends to anarchy and confusion:

"On your wisdom, religion, and public spirit, honored gentlemen, we depend, to determine what may be done as to the important matter of reviving the form of government, and settling all the necessary affairs relating to it in the present critical state of things, that we may again have law and justice, and avoid the danger of anarchy and confusion."[140]

Responding to the accusation that Americans were nothing more than rebels, Pastor John Cleaveland wrote articles that were published in the April 18, 25, 1775 issues of the Massachusetts *Essex Gazette.* The articles said in part:

"To the Inhabitants of New England, Greeting. Men, Brethren and Fathers: Is the time come, the fatal era commenced, for you to be deemed rebels, by the Parliament of Great Britain? Rebels! Wherein? Why, for asserting that the rights of men, the rights of Englishmen belong to us.... But subdue us to a subjection unto the supreme legislation and taxation authority of the British Parliament over the Colonies without their consent, they will not, they shall not!... Great Britain, adieu! No longer shall we honor you as our mother; you are become cruel; you have not so much bowels as the sea monsters towards their young ones ... by this stroke you have broken us off from you, and effectually alienated us from you.... O Britain! See you to your own house. King George the Third, adieu! No more shall we cry to you for protection.... Your breach of covenant; your violation of faith;... have dissolved our allegiance to your Crown and Government.... O George! See thou to thine own house.... O my dear New England, hear thou the alarm of war! The call of Heaven is to arms! To arms!... Behold what all New England must expect to feel, if we don't cut off and make a final end of those British sons of violence, and of every base Tory among us, or confine the latter to

Simsbury mines.... We are, my brethren, in a good cause; and if God be for us, we need not fear what man can do.... O thou righteous Judge of all the earth, awake for our help. Amen and Amen."[141]

That same year, Moses Mather preached an almost identical message in a sermon delivered in Hartford, Connecticut:

"Thus, these liberties and privileges are not only granted and confirmed, but a power is expressly given to the colonies to defend them to the utmost, against those who should invade or attempt to destroy them. And are the Americans chargeable with treason and rebellion, for yielding to the irresistible impulses of self-preservation and acting under and in pursuance of the royal license and authority of their king?"[142]

Emphatically stating that submission to tyranny was "no tenet of the church," William Smith pointed out that before declaring themselves independent from England, Americans had warned King George that he must govern lawfully if he intended to retain the cooperation of the colonies. Having not only ignored their warning, King George had doubled down on his oppressive rule, forcing the Americans to pull back. Smith applauded this pull back in his sermon, *The Crisis of American Affairs,* preached at Christ Church in Philadelphia on June 23, 1775:

"A continued submission to violence is no tenet of our church. When her brightest luminaries, near a century past, were called to propagate the court doctrine of a *dispensing power above law,* did they treacherously cry, 'Peace, peace, when there was no peace?' Did they not magnanimously set their foot upon the line of the constitution, and tell majesty to its face, that 'they could not betray the public liberty,' and that the monarch's only safety consisted in 'governing according to the laws?'"[143]

Further contrasting the difference between a people in rebellion and a people fighting for their God-given rights, Samuel West, pastor in Dartmouth, Massachusetts, made this impassioned statement in his 1776 Massachusetts election sermon:

"... the British Parliament has virtually declared us an independent state by authorizing their ships of war to seize all American property, wherever they can find it, without making any distinction between the friends of administration and those that have appeared in opposition to the acts of Parliament. This is making us a distinct nation from themselves. They can have no right any longer to style us rebels; for rebellion implies a particular faction risen up in opposition to lawful authority, and, as such, the factious party ought to be punished, while those that remain loyal are to be protected. But when war is declared against a whole community without distinction, and the property of each party is declared to be seizable, this, if anything can be, is treating us as an independent state. Now, if they are pleased to consider us as in a state of independency, who can object against our considering ourselves so too?"[144]

Clearly, only those willing to ignore the facts could possibly claim that the Founders and the preachers who urged them on were reckless rebels or crazed anarchists. The Black Regiment preachers were intelligent, law-abiding, and godly men who believed they were fighting for a righteous cause, their God-given, unalienable rights. But many still wonder, how could preachers in good faith, urge their congregations to overthrow one government to establish another?

DEFENDING THEIR UNALIENABLE RIGHTS

Jonathan Mayhew was one of the men who understood long before the war began that the God-given, unalienable rights of Americans were in jeopardy. He knew that the taxes levied without the colonists' consent and intolerable acts like the Stamp Act were only symptoms of a greater, deeper problem – a tyrannical government bent on enlarging its power at the expense of the colonists' rights.

Even when Great Britain repealed the Stamp Act on March 18, 1766, only one year after it had been enacted, they had done it only because they had to, not because it was the right thing to do. Mayhew understood that Parliament had not "seen the light" but had "felt the heat" from the lost income of diminished trade caused by colonial boycotts of British goods. Mayhew's suspicions were confirmed when Parliament, while in the process of repealing the Stamp Act, passed the Declaratory Act. This act declared that Parliament had the same authority in the American colonies as it did in England and could pass any laws it chose – laws as equally binding on the colonists as they were on the British. Actions like these made the Americans realize that the time for reasonable discourse was running out.

On May 23, 1766, just weeks after the repeal of the Stamp Act, Mayhew made it clear that the real point of contention between the Americans and the British was the abuse of the colonists' natural rights by the British. In his *The Snare Broken* preached at the West Church in Boston, he declared:

"The colonists are men, and need not be afraid to assert the natural rights of men; they are British subjects, and may justly claim the common rights, and all the privileges of such, with plainness and freedom. … it shall now be taken for granted, that as we were free-born, never made slaves by the right of conquest in war, if there be indeed any such right, nor sold as slaves in any open lawful market, for money, so we have a natural right to our own, till we have freely consented to part with it, either in person, or by those whom we have appointed to represent, and to act for us. It shall be taken for granted that this natural right is declared, affirmed, and secured to us, as we are British subjects, by Magna Carta; all acts contrary to Which are said to be *ipso facto,* null and void: and, that this natural constitutional right has been further confirmed to most of the plantations by particular subsequent royal charters, taken in their obvious sense; the legality and authority of which charters were never once denied by either house of Parliament; but implicitly, at least, acknowledged, ever since they were respectively granted, till very lately. It is taken for granted also, that the right of trial by juries, is a constitutional one with respect to all British subjects in general, particularly to the colonists; and that the plantations in which civil government has been established, have all along, till of late, been in the uninterrupted enjoyment of both the rights aforesaid, which are of the utmost importance, being essential to liberty. …

"It shall, therefore, be taken for granted, that the colonies had great reason to petition and remonstrate against a late act of Parliament, as being an infraction of these rights, and tending directly to reduce us to a state of slavery. It is, moreover, taken for granted, whatever becomes of this question about rights, that an act of that sort was very hard, and justly grievous, not to say oppressive; … yet they had great reason to remonstrate against the act aforesaid on the footing of inexpedience, the great hardship, and destructive tendency of it, as a measure big with mischief to Britain as well as to themselves; and promoted at first, perhaps, only by persons who were real friends to neither. … History, one may presume to say, affords no example of any nation, country or people, long free, who did not take some care of themselves; and endeavor to guard and secure their own liberties. Power is of a grasping, encroaching nature, in all beings, except in Him to whom it emphatically 'belongeth;' and who is the only king that, in a religious or moral sense, "can do no wrong." Power aims at extending itself, and operating according to mere will, wherever it meets with no balance, check, control or opposition of any kind. For which reason it will always be necessary, as was said before, for those who would preserve and perpetuate their liberties, to guard them with a wakeful attention; and in all righteousness, just and prudent ways, to oppose the first encroachments on them. … After a while it will be too late."[145]

In 1777, with the war in full swing, Abraham Keteltas was preaching the same message that Mayhew had preached eleven years earlier. He too, was convinced that the war was about men's unalienable rights. In his sermon, *God Arising And Pleading His People's Cause*, Keteltas argued that fighting to defend men's God-given rights was "God's own cause":

"From the preceding discourse, I think we have reason to conclude, that the cause of this American continent, against the measures of a cruel, bloody, and vindictive ministry, is the cause of God. We are contending for the rights of mankind, for the welfare of millions now living, and for the happiness of millions yet unborn. If it is the undisputed duty of mankind, to do good to all as they have opportunity, especially to those who are of the household of faith, if they are bound by the commandment of the supreme law-giver, to love their neighbor as themselves, and do to others as they would that others should do unto them; then the war carried on against us, is unjust and unwarrantable, and our cause is not only righteous, but most important: It is God's own cause: It is the grand cause of the whole human race, and what can be more interesting and glorious. If the principles on which the present civil war is carried on by the American colonies, against the British arms, were universally adopted and practiced upon by mankind, they would turn a vale of tears, into a paradise of God: … cannot therefore doubt, that the cause of liberty, united with that of truth & righteousness, is the cause of God."[146]

SO, WHEN IT IS RIGHT TO OVERTHROW A GOVERNMENT?

"There is no reason they should be fools because their rulers are so."[147]

So said Elisha Williams, Congregational minister in Connecticut, Colonel in the French and Indian War, member of the Connecticut legislature, and Judge of the Connecticut Superior Court. His remarks referred to the unreasonable, deplorable way in which the British were ruling over the colonies. Williams's words perfectly summed up the sentiments of the Black Regiment. Convinced that unscriptural government was "illegitimate," they taught and preached that it was the duty of Christians to rise up and replace such a government.

In 1918, Alice Baldwin explained just how the patriot preachers defined "proper" law and the kind of government that deserved the submission of the people:

> "Probably the most fundamental principle of the American constitutional system is the principle that no one is bound to obey an unconstitutional act. … No single idea was more fully stressed, no principle more often repeated, through the first sixty years of the eighteenth century, than that governments must obey law and that he who resisted one in authority who was violating that law was not himself a rebel but a protector of law."[148]

As the Founders saw it, God first gave rights to the people, and the people, by consent, could enter into a covenant and form a government to protect and administer those rights. In this covenant, the same laws that bound the people bound the government as well. They believed that the primary function of government was to protect and foster those rights and as long as government did not violate God's laws in the process, both written and natural, then it could rightfully require the respect and submission of the people. But the Founders also believed that if government ever violated God's laws or man's written constitutions, it forfeited its right to govern and therefore invalidated itself. They believed this principle so strongly that they were willing to stand up to the awesome might of the Redcoats to defend it.

This is exactly the message Samuel Cooke preached on May 30, 1770 to the Massachusetts House of Representatives in Cambridge, Massachusetts while delivering that year's election sermon:

"Justice also requires of rulers, in their legislative capacity, that they attend to the operation of their own acts, and repeal whatever laws, upon an impartial review, they find to be inconsistent with the laws of God, the rights of men, and the general benefit of society. This the community hath a right to expect. … The just ruler will not fear to have his public conduct critically inspected, but will choose to recommend himself to the approbation of every man. As he expects to be obeyed for conscience' sake, he will require nothing inconsistent with its dictates, and be desirous that the most scrupulous mind may acquiesce in the justice of his rule."[149]

Moses Mather articulated this dilemma in simple terms in his sermon to his Hartford, Connecticut audience in 1775:

"The question is not whether the king is to be obeyed or not; for the Americans, have ever recognized his authority as their rightful sovereign, and liege lord; have ever been ready, with their lives and fortunes, to support his crown and government, according to the constitutions of the nation, and now call upon him as their liege lord (whom he is bound to protect) for protection, on pain of their allegiance, against the army, levied by the British parliament, against his loyal and dutiful subjects in America. … But the question is, whether the parliament of Great Britain hath power over the persons and properties of the Americans, to bind the one, and dispose of the other at their pleasure?

"If the parliament have no such power as is claimed, their invading our rights, and in them the rights of the constitution, under pretense of authority; besieging and desolating our sea ports, employing dirty tools, whose sordid souls, like vermin, delight to riot on filth; to practice every artifice to seduce, that they may the easier destroy; with money tempting, with arms terrifying the inhabitants, to induce and compel a servile submission; is treason against the kingdom, of the deepest dye, and blackest complexion: whereby the constitution, that firm foundation of the nation's peace, and pillar of government that supports the throne, is shaken to its very basis; the kingdom rent, and divided against itself; and those sons of thunder that should be the protectors of its rights, are become its destroyers."[150]

Twenty-seven years later as he looked back to the time of the war, William Emerson made the same argument that Mather had made before the war. In his July 5, 1802 sermon, *An Oration In Commemoration Of The Anniversary Of American Independence*, Emerson asked,

"Was it, then, right in the colonies to resist the parliament, and wrong to resist the king? No. For the king had joined the latter to oppress the former, and thus became, instead of the righteous ruler, the tyrant, of this country, to whom allegiance was no longer due.

"Americans called themselves free, because they were governed by laws originating in fixed principles, and not in the caprice of arbitrary will. They held, that the ruler was equally obliged to construct his laws in consonance with the spirit of the constitution, as were the people to obey them when enacted; and that a departure from duty on his part virtually absolved them from allegiance.

"Let not this be deemed a licentious doctrine. Who is the rebel against law and order, the legislator ordaining, or the citizen resisting, unconstitutional measures? It is the unprincipled minister, who artfully innovates on the custom of governing; the ambitious senator, whose self is his god; the faithless magistrate, who tramples on rights, which he has sworn to protect; these are the men, who, by perverting the purposes of government, destroy its foundations, bring back society into a state of war, and are answerable for its mischievous effects. Not those who defend, but those who attack, the liberties of mankind, are disturbers of the public peace; and not on you, my countrymen, but on thee, O Britain, who killedst thy people with the rod of oppression, be the guilt of all that blood, which was spilt in the revolutionary war!"[151]

"There is a time when it is acceptable to resist government." So declared Joseph Lathrop, pastor of the Congregational Church in West Springfield, Massachusetts, on December 14, 1787:

"Perhaps it will be asked, 'Is there no case in which a people may resist government?' Yes, there is one such case; and that is, when rulers usurp a power oppressive to the people, and continue to support it by military force in contempt of every respectful remonstrance. In this case the body of the people have a natural right to unite their strength for the restoration of their own constitutional government. And, for the same reason, if a part of the people attempt by arms to control or subvert the government, the rulers, who are the guardians of the constitution, have a right to call in the aid of the people to protect it. If the people may use force to suppress an armed usurpation of unconstitutional authority, rulers may, on the same principle, use force to suppress an armed insurrection against constitutional authority."[152]

IT WAS POSSIBLE FOR A KING TO "UN-KING" HIMSELF

The Black Regiment and their followers believed that it was possible for a king to "un-king" himself and for a seated government to "unseat" itself by violating God's laws. Emphasizing this principle in his sermon, *Discourse Concerning Unlimited Submission and Non-Resistance To The Higher Powers*, which was delivered in the Boston West Meeting House in multiple parts starting on January 31, 1749 and completed in the early days of 1750, Jonathan Mayhew declared,

> "... the Parliament which first opposed King Charles's measures, and at length took up arms against him, were not guilty of rebellion, ... for he had, in fact, un-kinged himself long before, and had forfeited his title to the allegiance of the people. ... Cromwell and his adherents were not, properly speaking, guilty of rebellion, because he whom they be headed [King Charles] was not, properly speaking, their king, but a lawless tyrant; ... Common tyrants and public oppressors are not entitled to obedience from their subjects by virtue of anything here laid down by the inspired apostle [Apostle Paul]. ... For a nation thus abused to arise unanimously and resist their prince, even to the dethroning him, is not criminal, but a reasonable way of vindicating their liberties and just rights: it is making use of the means, and the only means, which God has put into their power for mutual and self defense. And it would be highly criminal in them not to make use of this means. It would be stupid tameness and unaccountable folly for whole nations to suffer one unreasonable, ambitious, and cruel man to wanton and riot in their misery."[153]

In the event that the government "unseated" itself or the king "un-kinged" himself, the patriot preachers believed that if this government continued to rule, it was practicing tyranny. And since they believed God hated tyranny, they preached that the people not only had the right, but they had the responsibility to resist that government at all costs. Samuel Langdon preached this concept in his May 31, 1775 Massachusetts election sermon:

"If the great servants of the public forget their duty, betray their trust, and sell their country, or make war against the most valuable rights and privileges of the people, reason and justice require that they should be discarded, and others appointed in their room, without any regard to formal resignations of their forfeited power."[154]

Having concluded that King George and the British government had indeed "un-kinged" and "unseated" themselves, the pastors unashamedly declared that it was time to throw off British tyranny and follow the course Jefferson and the others outlined in the Declaration of Independence when they wrote,

"... when a long train of abuses and usurpations, pursuing invariably the same object evinces a design to reduce them under absolute despotism, it is their right, it is their duty, to throw off such government, and to provide new guards for their future security."

On December 3, 1772, four years before the Declaration had specified the citizens' "right and duty" to throw off a tyrannical government, John Allen had preached that message in his sermon, *An Oration Upon The Beauties Of Liberty*, delivered to the congregation of the Second Baptist Church, Boston. The sermon, partially inspired by the *Gaspee Affair*,* was so powerful and made such an impact on the colonists that it was reprinted seven times, making it the sixth most popular sermon pamphlet published in pre-revolution America. In it, Allen proclaimed,

"That it is not rebellion, I declare it before God, the congregation, and all the world, and I would be glad if it reached the ears of every Briton, and every American; That it is no rebellion to oppose any king, ministry, or governor, that destroys by any violence or authority whatever, the rights of the people. Shall a man be deemed a rebel that supports his own rights? It is the first law of nature, and he must be a rebel to God, to the laws of nature, and his own conscience, who will not do it. A right to the blessing of freedom we do not receive from kings, but from heaven, as the breath of life, and essence of our existence; and shall we not preserve it, as the beauty of our being? Do not the birds of the air expand their wings? The fish of the sea their fins? And the worm of the earth turn again when it is trod upon? And shall it be deemed rebellion? Heaven forbid it! … It is no more rebellion, than it is to breathe.

"If this be the case, the king of England may immediately see the reason of all his people's hard speeches, and unkindness to him: It is because he has departed, either by inclination, or persuasion, from this royal standard. … So that if the king of England is not happy let him thank himself for it: It is not his people's fault—it is his own. For that king is not worthy to reign, that does not make the *rights* of his people the rule of his actions: Knowing this, that he receives all his power, and majesty, from them; and how can he think that he has any right to rule over them, unless he rules in their hearts by inviolable maintaining their *rights*? For as the ministers of the gospel (when in their proper place) are no otherwise than the people's servants; so the king is no more than the servant of the people: And when at any time, he is unfaithful, as the people's servant, they have a right to say to him, "give an account of thy stewardship, that thou mayest be no longer steward." For what can he judge, when a free and affectionate people, lay their grievances, with tears, at his feet, praying, for years past, for redress? and yet he will not hear them!!!

"That when the king, judges, and senates, unite to destroy the rights of the people by a despotic power, or as the text expresses it, *that they may do evil with both hands*, then the prosperity of the nation totters; the crown shakes; and the destruction of the people's rights is near at hand. For the rights of the people … is the *Magna Charta* of the king as well as of the people; it is as much his privilege, as it is his glory, to maintain their rights; and he is as much under a law (I mean the law of the rights of the people), as the people are under the oath of allegiance to him. And therefore whatever power destroys their rights, destroys at the same time, his right to reign, or any right to his kingdom, crown, or glory; nay, his right to the name of a king among the people.

"This shows, that an arbitrary despotic power in a prince, is the ruin of a nation, of the king, of the crown, and of the subjects; therefore it is to be feared, abhorred, detested and destroyed, because the happiness of the king, and the prosperity of the people are hereby, not only in danger, but upon the brink of destruction. Every age and every history furnishes us with proofs, as clear as the light of the morning, of the truth of this."[155]

*(The "Gaspee Affair" occurred on June 9, 1772 when members of the Sons of Liberty boarded, took control, and burned the British ship, the HMS *Gaspée*,

after it had run aground in the Narragansett Bay off the coast of Rhode Island while chasing an American ship, the *Hannah*. Great Britain's overreaction to the "affair" helped to galvanize the Americans for the war that came a few years later.)

Samuel West was another patriot pastor who argued that it was biblical and lawful to resist a tyrannical government. On May 29, 1776, he perfectly articulated the prevailing thought of the clergy of his day:

"As our duty of obedience to the magistrate is founded upon our obligation to promote the general good, our readiness to obey lawful authority will always arise in proportion to the love and regard that we have for the welfare of the public; and the same love and regard for the public will inspire us with as strong a zeal to oppose tyranny as we have to obey magistracy. Our obligation to promote the public good extends as much to the opposing every exertion of arbitrary power that is injurious to the state as it does to the submitting to good and wholesome laws.

"No man, therefore, can be a good member of the community that is not as zealous to oppose tyranny, as he is ready to obey magistracy. A slavish submission to tyranny is a proof of a very sordid and base mind. Such a person cannot be under the influence of any generous human sentiments, nor have a tender regard for mankind. …

"Having thus shown the nature, end, and design of civil government, and pointed out the reasons why subjects are bound to obey magistrates, — viz., because in so doing they both consult their own happiness as individuals, and also promote the public good and the safety of the state, — I proceed, in the next place, to show that the same principles that oblige us to submit to civil government do also equally oblige us, where we have power and ability, to resist and oppose tyranny; and that where tyranny begins government ends. For, if magistrates have no authority but what they derive from the people; if they are properly of human creation; if the whole end and design of their institution is to promote the general good, and to secure to men their just rights, — it will follow, that when they act contrary to the end and design of their creation they cease being magistrates, and the people which gave them their authority have the right to take it from them again. This is a very plain dictate of common sense, which universally obtains in all similar cases; for who is there that, having employed a number of men to do a particular piece of work for him, but what would judge that he had a right to dismiss them from his service when he found that they went directly contrary to his orders, and that, instead of accomplishing the business he had set them about, they would infallibly ruin and destroy it? If, then, men, in the common affairs of life, always judge that they have a right to dismiss from their service such persons as counteract their plans and designs, though the damage will affect only a few individuals, much more must the body politic have a right to depose any persons, though appointed to the highest place of power and authority, when they find that they are unfaithful to the trust reposed in them, and that, instead of consulting the general good, they are disturbing the peace of society by making laws cruel and oppressive, and by depriving the subjects of their just rights and privileges. Whoever pretends to deny this proposition must give up all pretense of being master of that common sense and reason by which the Deity has distinguished us from the brutal herd. …

"In the next place, when a people find themselves cruelly oppressed by the parent state, they have an undoubted right to throw off the yoke, and to assert their liberty, if they find good reason to judge that they have sufficient power and strength to maintain their ground in defending their just rights against their oppressors; for, in this case, by the law of self-preservation, which is the first law of nature, they have not only an undoubted right, but it is their indispensable duty, if they cannot be redressed any other way, to renounce all submission to the government that has oppressed them, and set up an independent state of their own, even though they may be vastly inferior in numbers to the state that has oppressed them. When either of the aforesaid cases takes place, and more especially when both concur, no rational man, I imagine, can have any doubt in his own mind whether such a people have a right to form themselves into a body politic, and assume to themselves all the powers of a free state. For, can it be rational to suppose that a people should be subjected to the tyranny of a set of men who are perfect strangers to them, and cannot be supposed to have that fellow-feeling for them that we generally have for those with whom we are connected and acquainted; and, besides, through their unacquaintedness with the circumstances of the people over whom they claim the right of jurisdiction, are utterly unable to judge, in a multitude of cases, which is best for them? …

"Having thus endeavored to show the lawfulness and necessity of defending ourselves against the tyranny of Great Britain, I would observe that Providence seems plainly to point to us the expediency, and even necessity, of our considering ourselves as an independent state. … If representation and legislation are inseparably connected, it follows, that when great numbers have emigrated into a foreign land, and are so far removed from the parent state that they neither are or can be properly represented by the government from which they have emigrated, that then nature itself points out the necessity of their assuming to themselves the powers of legislation; and they have a right to consider themselves as a separate state from the other, and, as such, to form themselves into a body politic."[156]

HOW THE BLACK REGIMENT JUSTIFIED "RIGHTEOUS RESISTANCE"

Two sermons can be used to illustrate how the patriot preachers found biblical justification for their civil disobedience:

- Jonathan Mayhew's three-part discourse, *Discourse Concerning Unlimited Submission And Non-Resistance To The Higher Powers* preached in late 1749 and early 1750
- Samuel West's May 29, 1776 Massachusetts election sermon.

Considered two of the best Black Regiment preachers of that era, Mayhew and West captured the thinking, biblical insight, and spirit of "resistance" of the Americans better than any of their fellow preachers:

The following excerpts from those two messages show how the thinking of the spiritual leaders of the eighteenth century clearly helped mold the thinking of the Founders themselves. They could also prove quite instructional and helpful to our leaders in the twenty-first century.

Discourse Concerning Unlimited Submission and Non-Resistance To The Higher Powers by Jonathan Mayhew, 1749-1750:

(Rom 13:1-8) "It is evident that the affairs of civil government may properly fall under a moral and religious consideration, at least so far forth as it relates to the general nature and end of magistracy, and to the grounds and extent of that submission which persons of a private character ought to yield to those who are vested with authority. This must be allowed by all who acknowledge the divine original of Christianity. For, although there be a sense, and a very plain and important sense, in which Christ's kingdom is not of this world, His inspired apostles have, nevertheless, laid down some general principles concerning the office of civil ruler, and the duty of subjects, together with the reason and obligation of that duty. And from hence it follows, that it is proper for all who acknowledge the authority of Jesus Christ, and the inspiration of his apostles, to endeavor to understand what is in fact the doctrine which they have delivered concerning this matter. It is the duty of Christian magistrates to inform themselves what it is which their religion teaches concerning the nature and design of their office. And it is equally the duty of all Christian people to inform themselves what it is which their religion teaches concerning that subjection which they owe to the higher powers. It is for these reasons that I have attempted to examine into the Scripture account of this matter, in order to lay it before you with the same freedom which I constantly use with relation to other doctrines and precepts of Christianity; not doubting but you will judge upon everything offered to your consideration with the same spirit of freedom and liberty with which it is spoken. …

"[I]t has often been asserted that the Scripture in general, and the passage under consideration in particular, makes all resistance to princes a crime, in any case whatever. If they turn tyrants, and become the common oppressors of those whose welfare they ought to regard with a paternal affection, we must not pretend to right ourselves, unless it be by prayers, and tears, and humble entreaties. And if these methods fail of procuring redress, we must not have recourse to any other, but all suffer ourselves to be robbed and butchered at the pleasure of the 'Lord s anointed,' lest we should incur the sin of rebellion and the punishment of damnation! …

"But who supposes that the apostle ever intended to teach that children, servants, and wives, should, in all cases whatever, obey their parents, masters, and husbands respectively, never making any opposition to their will, even although they should require them to break the commandments of God, or should causelessly make an attempt upon their lives? No one puts such a sense upon these expressions, however absolute and unlimited. Why, then, should it be supposed that the apostle designed to teach universal obedience, whether active or passive, to the higher powers, merely because his precepts are delivered in absolute and unlimited terms? …

"'Submit yourselves to every ordinance of man for the Lord s sake.' To every ordinance of man. However, this expression is no stronger than that before taken notice of with relation to the duty of wives: 'So let the wives be subject to their own husbands in everything.' … By 'every ordinance of man' is not meant every command of the civil magistrate without exception, but every order of magistrates appointed by man, whether superior or inferior; for so the apostle explains himself in the very next words: 'Whether it be to the king as supreme, or to governors, as unto them that are sent,' etc. But although the apostle had not subjoined any such explanation, the reason of the thing itself would have obliged us to limit the expression 'every ordinance of man' to such human ordinances and commands as are not inconsistent with the ordinances and commands of God, the Supreme Lawgiver, or with any other higher and antecedent obligations. …

"As was observed above, there were some professed Christians in the apostolic age who disclaimed all magistracy and civil authority in general, despising government, and speaking evil of dignities; some, under a notion that Jews ought not to be under the jurisdiction of Gentile rulers, and others that they were set free from the temporal powers

by Christ. Now, it is with persons of this licentious opinion and character that the apostle is concerned; and all that was directly to his point was to show that they were bound to submit to magistracy in general. … So that the duty of unlimited obedience, whether active or passive, can be argued neither from the manner of expression here used, nor from the general scope and design of the passage.

"It is obvious, then, in general, that the civil rulers whom the apostle here speaks of, and obedience to whom he presses upon Christians as a duty, are good rulers, a such as are, in the exercise of their office and power, benefactors to society. Such they are described to be throughout this passage. Thus, it is said that they are not a terror to good works, but to the evil; that they are God's ministers for good; revengers to execute wrath upon him that doeth evil; and that they attend continually upon this very thing. St. Peter gives the same account of rulers: They are 'for a praise to them that do well, and the punishment of evil doers.' … If rulers are a terror to good works, and not to the evil; if they are not ministers for good to society, but for evil and distress, by violence and oppression; if they execute wrath upon sober, peaceable persons, who do their duty as members of society, and suffer rich and honorable knaves to escape with impunity; if, instead of attending continually upon the good work of advancing the public welfare, they attend continually upon the gratification of their own lust and pride and ambition, to the destruction of the public welfare; if this be the case, it is plain that the apostle's argument for submission does not reach them; …

"It is blasphemy to call tyrants and oppressors God's ministers. They are more properly 'the messengers of Satan to buffet us.' No rulers are properly God's ministers but such as are 'just, ruling in the fear of God.' When once magistrates act contrary to their office, and the end of their institution,–when they rob and ruin the public, instead of being guardians of its peace and welfare,–they immediately cease to be the ordinance and ministers of God, and no more deserve that glorious character than common pirates, and highwaymen. So that, whenever that argument for submission fails which is grounded upon the usefulness of magistracy to civil society,–as it always does when magistrates do hurt to society instead of good,–the other argument, which is taken from their being the ordinance of God, must necessarily fail also; no person of a civil character being God's minister, in the sense of the apostle, any further than he performs God's will be exercising a just and reasonable authority, and ruling for the good of the subject. …

"'Since magistrates who execute their office well are common benefactors to society, and may in that respect properly be called the ministers and ordinance of God, and since they are constantly employed in the service of the public, it becomes you to pay them tribute and custom, and to reverence, honor, and submit to them in the execution of their respective offices.' … Common tyrants and public oppressors are not entitled to obedience from their subjects by virtue of anything here laid down by the inspired apostle.

"If it be our duty, for example, to obey our king merely for this reason, that he rules for the public welfare (which is the only argument the apostle makes use of), it follows, by a parity of reason, that when he turns tyrant, and makes his subjects his prey to devour and destroy, instead of his charge to defend and cherish, we are bound to throw off our allegiance to him, and to resist; and that according to the tenor of the apostle's argument in this passage. Not to discontinue our allegiance in this case would be to join with the sovereign in promoting the slavery and misery of that society, the welfare of which we ourselves, as well as our sovereign, are indispensably obliged to secure and promote, as far as in us lies. … Suppose God requires a family of children to obey their father and not to resist him, and enforces his command with this argument, that the superintendence and care and authority of a just and kind parent will contribute to the happiness of the whole family, so that they ought to obey him for their own sakes more than for his; suppose this parent at length runs distracted, and attempts in his mad fit to cut all his children's throats. Now, in this case, is not the reason before assigned why these children should obey their parent while he continued of a sound mind namely, their common good a reason equally conclusive for disobeying and resisting him, since he is become delirious and attempts their ruin?

"What unprejudiced man can think that God made all to be thus subservient to the lawless pleasure and frenzy of one, so that it shall always be a sin to resist him? … At present there is not the least syllable in Scripture which gives any countenance to it. … These notions are fetched neither from divine revelation nor human reason; and , if they are derived from neither of those sources, it is not much matter from whence they come or whither they go. Only it is a pity that such doctrines should be propagated in society, to raise factions and rebellions, as we see they have, in fact, both in the last and in the present reign. …

"For a nation thus abused to arise unanimously and resist their prince, even to the dethroning him, is not criminal, but a reasonable way of vindicating their liberties and just rights: it is making use of the means, and the only means, which God has put into their power for mutual and self defense. And it would be highly criminal in them not to make use of this means. It would be stupid tameness and unaccountable folly for whole nations to suffer one unreasonable, ambitious, and cruel man to wanton and riot in their misery. And in such a case, it would, of the two, be more rational to suppose that they that did not resist, than that they who did, would receive to themselves damnation."[157]

Massachusetts Election Sermon by Samuel West, May 29, 1776:

(Titus 3:1) "In order, therefore, that we may form a right judgment of the duty enjoined in our text, I shall consider the nature and design of civil government, and shall show that the same principles which oblige us to submit to government do equally oblige us to resist tyranny; or that tyranny and magistracy are so opposed to each other that where the one begins the other ends. I shall then apply the present discourse to the grand controversy that at this day subsists between Great Britain and the American colonies.

"That we may understand the nature and design of civil government, and discover the foundation of the magistrate's authority to command, and the duty of subjects to obey, it is necessary to derive civil government from its original, in order to which we must consider what "state all men are naturally in, and that is (as Mr. Locke observes) a state of perfect freedom to order all their actions, and dispose of their possessions and persons as they think fit, within the bounds of the law of nature, without asking leave or depending upon the will of any man." It is a state wherein all are equal, — no one having a right to control another, or oppose him in what he does, unless it be in his own defense, or in the defense of those that, being injured, stand in need of his assistance.

"Had men persevered in a state of moral rectitude, every one would have been disposed to follow the law of nature, and pursue the general good. In such a state, the wisest and most experienced would undoubtedly be chosen to guide and direct those of less wisdom and experience than themselves, — there being nothing else that could afford the least show or appearance of any one's having the superiority or precedency over another; for the dictates of conscience and the precepts of natural law being uniformly and regularly obeyed, men would only need to be informed what things were most fit and prudent to be done in those cases where their inexperience or want of acquaintance left their minds in doubt what was the wisest and most regular method for them to pursue. In such cases it would be necessary for them to advise with those who were wiser and more experienced than themselves. But these advisers could claim no authority to compel or to use any forcible measures to oblige any one to comply with their direction or advice. There could be no occasion for the exertion of such a power; for every man, being under the government of right reason, would immediately feel himself constrained to comply with everything that appeared reasonable or fit to be done, or that would any way tend to promote the general good. This would have been the happy state of mankind had they closely adhered to the law of nature, and persevered in their primitive state. …

"Further: if magistrates are no farther ministers of God than they promote the good of the community, then obedience to them neither is nor can be unlimited; for it would imply a gross absurdity to assert that, when magistrates are ordained by the people solely for the purpose of being beneficial to the state, they must be obeyed when they are seeking to ruin and destroy it. This would imply that men were bound to act against the great law of self-preservation, and to contribute their assistance to their own ruin and destruction, in order that they may please and gratify the greatest monsters in nature, who are violating the laws of God and destroying the rights of mankind. Unlimited submission and obedience is due to none but God alone. …

"If magistrates are ministers of God only because the law of God and reason points out the necessity of such an institution for the good of mankind, it follows, that whenever they pursue measures directly destructive of the public good they cease being God's ministers, they forfeit their right to obedience from the subject, they become the pests of society, and the community is under the strongest obligation of duty, both to God and to its own members, to resist and oppose them, which will be so far from resisting the ordinance of God that it will be strictly obeying his commands. … As the public safety is the first and grand law of society, so no community can have a right to invest the magistrate with any power or authority that will enable him to act against the welfare of the state and the good of the whole. If men have at any time wickedly and foolishly given up their just rights into the hands of the magistrate, such acts are null and void, of course; to suppose otherwise will imply that we have a right to invest the magistrate with a power to act contrary to the law of God, — which is as much as to say that we are not the subjects of divine law and government. What has been said is, I apprehend, abundantly sufficient to show that tyrants are no magistrates, or that whenever magistrates abuse their power and authority to the subverting the public happiness, their authority immediately ceases, and that it not only becomes lawful, but an indispensable duty to oppose them; that the principle of self-preservation, the affection and duty that we owe to our country, and the obedience we owe the Deity, do all require us to oppose tyranny.

"If it be asked, Who are the proper judges to determine when rulers are guilty of tyranny and oppression? I answer, the public. Not a few disaffected individuals, but the collective body of the state, must decide this question; for, as it is the collective body that invests rulers with their power and authority, so it is the collective body that has the sole right of judging whether rulers act up to the end of their institution or not. Great regard ought always to be paid to the judgment of the public. It is true the public may be imposed upon by a misrepresentation of facts; but this may be said of the public, which cannot always be said of individuals, viz., that the public is always willing to be rightly informed, and when it has proper matter of conviction laid before it its judgment is always right."

West proceeded to deal with the Apostle Peter's teaching on government:

"This account of the nature and design of civil government, which is so clearly suggested to us by the plain principles of common sense and reason, is abundantly confirmed by the sacred Scriptures, even by those very texts which have been brought by men of slavish principles to establish the absurd doctrine of unlimited passive obedience and non-resistance, as will abundantly appear by examining the two most noted texts that are commonly brought to support the strange doctrine of passive obedience. The first that I shall cite is in 1 Peter 2:13-14: "Submit yourselves to every ordinance of man," — or, rather, as the words ought to be rendered from the Greek, submit yourselves to every human creation, or human constitution, — " for the Lord's sake, whether it be to the king as supreme, or unto governors, as unto them that are sent by him for the punishment of evil-doers, and for the praise of them that do well." Here we see that the apostle asserts that magistracy is of human creation or appointment; that is, that magistrates have no power or authority but what they derive from the people; that this power they are to exert for the punishment of evil-doers, and for the praise of them that do well;

i. e., the end and design of the appointment of magistrates is to restrain wicked men, by proper penalties, from injuring society, and to encourage and honor the virtuous and obedient. Upon this account Christians are to submit to them for the Lord's sake; which is as if he had said, Though magistrates are of mere human appointment, and can claim no power or authority but what they derive from the people, yet, as they are ordained by men to promote the general good by punishing evil-doers and by rewarding and encouraging the virtuous and obedient, you ought to submit to them out of a sacred regard to the divine authority; for as they, in the faithful discharge of their office, do fulfill the will of God, so ye, by submitting to them, do fulfill the divine command. If the only reason assigned by the apostle why magistrates should be obeyed out of a regard to the divine authority is because they punish the wicked and encourage the good, it follows, that when they punish the virtuous and encourage the vicious we have a right to refuse yielding any submission or obedience to them; *i. e.*, whenever they act contrary to the end and design of their institution, they forfeit their authority to govern the people, and the reason for submitting to them, out of regard to the divine authority, immediately ceases; and, they being only of human appointment, the authority which the people gave them the public have a right to take from them, and to confer it upon those who are more worthy. So far is this text from favoring arbitrary principles, that there is nothing in it but what is consistent with and favorable to the highest liberty that any man can wish to enjoy; for this text requires us to submit to the magistrate no further than he is the encourager and protector of virtue and the punisher of vice; and this is consistent with all that liberty which the Deity has bestowed upon us."

Next he dealt with the Apostle Paul's teaching on government:

"A very little attention, I apprehend, will be sufficient to show that this text is so far from favoring arbitrary government, that, on the contrary, it strongly holds forth the principles of true liberty. Subjection to the higher powers is enjoined by the apostle because there is no power but of God; the powers that be are ordained of God; consequently, to resist the power is to resist the ordinance of God: and he repeatedly declares that the ruler is the minister of God. Now, before we can say whether this text makes for or against the doctrine of unlimited passive obedience, we must find out in what sense the apostle affirms that magistracy is the ordinance of God, and what he intends when he calls the ruler the minister of God.

"I can think but of three possible senses in which magistracy can with any propriety be called God's ordinance, or in which rulers can be said to be ordained of God as his ministers. The first is a plain declaration from the word of God that such a one and his descendants are, and shall be, the only true and lawful magistrates: thus we find in Scripture the kingdom of Judah to be settled by divine appointment in the family of David. Or,

"Secondly, By an immediate commission from God, ordering and appointing such a one by name to be the ruler over the people: thus Saul and David were immediately appointed by God to be kings over Israel.

"Thirdly, Magistracy may be called the ordinance of God, and rulers may be called the ministers of God, because the nature and reason of things, which is the law of God, requires such an institution for the preservation and safety of civil society. In the two first senses the apostle cannot be supposed to affirm that magistracy is God's ordinance, for neither he nor any of the sacred writers have entailed the magistracy to any one particular family under the gospel dispensation. Neither does he nor any of the inspired writers give us the least hint that any person should ever be immediately commissioned from God to bear rule over the people; The third sense, then, is the only sense in which the apostle can be supposed to affirm that the magistrate is the minister of God, and that magistracy is the ordinance of God; viz., that the nature and reason of things require such an institution for the preservation and safety of mankind. Now, if this be the only sense in which the apostle affirms that magistrates are ordained of God as his ministers, resistance must be criminal only so far forth as they are the ministers of God, while they act up to the end of their institution, and ceases being criminal when they cease being the ministers of God, *i.e.*, when they act contrary to the general good, and seek to destroy the liberties of the people.

"That we have gotten the apostle's sense of magistracy being the ordinance of God, will plainly appear from the text itself; for, after having asserted that to resist the power is to resist the ordinance of God, and they that resist shall receive to themselves damnation, he immediately adds, as the reason of this assertion, "For rulers are not a terror to good works, but to the evil. Wilt thou then not be afraid of the power? Do that which is good, and thou shalt have praise of the same: for he is the minister of God to thee for good. But if thou do that "which is evil, be afraid; for he beareth not the sword in vain: for he is the minister of God, a revenger to execute 'wrath upon him that doth evil." Here is a plain declaration of the sense in which he asserts that the authority of the magistrate is ordained of God, viz., because rulers are not a terror to good works, but to the evil; therefore we ought to dread offending them, for we cannot offend them but by doing evil; and if we do evil we have just reason to fear their power; for they bear not the sword in vain, but in this case the magistrate is a revenger to execute wrath upon him that doeth evil: but if we are found doers of that which is good, we have no reason to fear the authority of the magistrate; for in this case, instead of being punished, we shall be protected and encouraged. The reason why the magistrate is called the minister of God is because he is to protect, encourage, and honor them that do well, and to punish them that do evil; therefore it is our duty to submit to them, not merely for fear of being punished by them, but out of regard to the divine authority, under which they are deputed to execute judgment and to do justice. For this reason, according to the apostle, tribute is to be paid them, because, as the ministers of God, their whole business is to protect every man in the enjoyment of his just rights and privileges, and to punish every evil-doer.

"If the apostle, then, asserts that rulers are ordained of God only because they are a terror to evil works and a praise to them that do well; if they are ministers of God only because they encourage virtue and punish vice; if for this reason only they are to be obeyed for conscience' sake; if the sole reason why they have a right to tribute is because they devote themselves wholly to the business of securing to men their just rights, and to the punishing of evil-doers, — it follows, by undeniable consequence, that when they become the pests of human society, when they promote and encourage evil-doers, and become a terror to good works, they then cease being the ordinance of God; they are no longer rulers nor ministers of God; they are so far from being the powers that are ordained of God that they become the ministers of the powers of darkness,1 and it is so far from being a crime to resist them, that in many cases it may be highly criminal in the sight of Heaven to refuse resisting and opposing them to the utmost of our power; or, in other words, that the same reasons that require us to obey the ordinance of God, do equally oblige us, when we have power and opportunity, to oppose and resist the ordinance of Satan.

"Hence we see that the apostle Paul, instead of being a friend to tyranny and arbitrary government, turns out to be a strong advocate for the just rights of mankind, and is for our enjoying all that liberty with which God has invested us; for no power (according to the apostle) is ordained of God but what is an encourager of every good and virtuous action, — " Do that which is good, and thou shalt have praise of the same." No man need to be afraid of this power which is ordained of God who does nothing but what is agreeable to the law of God; for this power will not restrain us from exercising any liberty which the Deity has granted us; for the minister of God is to restrain us from nothing but the doing of that which is evil, and to this we have no right. To practice evil is not liberty, but licentiousness.

Can we conceive of a more perfect, equitable, and generous plan of government than this which the apostle has laid down, viz., to have rulers appointed over us to encourage us to every good and virtuous action, to defend and protect us in our just rights and privileges, and to grant us everything that can tend to promote our true interest and happiness; to restrain every licentious action, and to punish every one that would injure or harm us; to become a terror of evil-doers; to make and execute such just and righteous laws as shall effectually deter and hinder men from the commission of evil, and to attend continually upon this very thing; to make it their constant care and study, day and night, to promote the good and welfare of the community, and to oppose all evil practices? Deservedly may such rulers be called the ministers of God for good. They carry on the same benevolent design towards the community which the great Governor of the universe does towards his whole creation. 'Tis the pensable duty of a people to pay tribute, and to afford an easy and comfortable subsistence to such rulers, because they are the ministers of God, who are continually laboring and employing their time for the good of the community. He that resists such magistrates does, in a very emphatic sense, resist the ordinance of God; he is an enemy to mankind, odious to God, and justly incurs the sentence of condemnation from the great Judge of quick and dead. Obedience to such magistrates is yielding obedience to the "will of God, and, therefore, ought to be performed from a sacred regard to the divine authority.

"For any one from hence to infer that the apostle enjoins in this text unlimited obedience to the worst of tyrants, and that he pronounces damnation upon those that resist the arbitrary measures of such pests of society, is just as good sense as if one should affirm, that because the Scripture enjoins us obedience to the laws of God, therefore we may not oppose the power of darkness; or because we are commanded to submit to the ordinance of God, therefore we may not resist the ministers of Satan. Such wild work must be made with the apostle before he can be brought to speak the language of oppression! It is as plain, I think, as words can make it, that, according to this text, no tyrant can be a ruler; for the apostle's definition of a ruler is, that he is not a terror to good works, but to the evil; and that he is one who is to praise and encourage those that do well. Whenever, then, the ruler encourages them that do evil, and is a terror to those that do well, — *i.e.* as soon as he becomes a tyrant, — he forfeits his authority to govern, and becomes the minister of Satan, and, as such, ought to be opposed."

West then asked if Paul taught that Christians should submit to the government no matter how tyrannical it became:

"I know it is said that the magistrates were, at the time when the apostle wrote, heathens, and that Nero, that monster of tyranny, was then Emperor of Rome; that therefore the apostle, by enjoining submission to the powers that then were, does require unlimited obedience to be yielded to the worst of tyrants. Now, not to insist upon what has been often observed, viz., that this epistle was written most probably about the beginning of Nero's reign, at which time he was a very humane and merciful prince, did everything that was generous and benevolent to the public, and showed every act of mercy and tenderness to particulars, and therefore might at that time justly deserve the character of the minister of God for good to the people, — I say, waiving this, we will suppose that this epistle was written after that Nero was become a monster of tyranny and wickedness; it will by no means follow from thence that the apostle meant to enjoin unlimited subjection to such an authority, or that he intended to affirm that such a cruel, despotic authority was the ordinance of God. The plain, obvious sense of his words, as we have already seen, forbids such a construction to be put upon them, for they plainly imply a strong abhorrence and disapprobation of such a character, and clearly prove that Nero, so far forth as he was a tyrant, could not be the minister of God, nor have a right to claim submission from the people; so that this ought, perhaps, rather to be viewed as a severe satire upon Nero, than as enjoining any submission to him.

"It is also worthy to be observed that the apostle prudently waived mentioning any particular persons that were then in power, as it might have been construed in an invidious light, and exposed the primitive Christians to the severe resentments of the men that were then in power. He only in general requires submission to the higher powers, because the powers that be are ordained of God. Now, though the emperor might at that time be such a tyrant that he could with no propriety be said to be ordained of God, yet it would be somewhat strange if there were no men in power among the Romans that acted up to the character of good magistrates, and that deserved to be esteemed as the ministers of God for good unto the people. If there were any such, notwithstanding the tyranny of Nero, the apostle might with great propriety enjoin submission to those powers that were ordained of God, and by so particularly pointing out the end and design of magistrates, and giving his definition of a ruler, he might design to show that neither Nero, nor any other tyrant, ought to be esteemed as the minister of God. Or, rather, —which appears to me to be the true sense, — the apostle meant to speak of magistracy in general, without any reference to the emperor, or any other person in power, that was then at Rome; and the meaning of this passage is as if he had said, It is the duty of every

Christian to be a good subject of civil government, for the power and authority of the civil magistrate are from God; for the powers that be are ordained of God; *i.e.*, the authority of the magistrates that are now either at Home or elsewhere is ordained of the Deity. Wherever you find any lawful magistrates, remember, they are of divine ordination. But that you may understand what I mean when I say that magistrates are of divine ordination, I will show you how you may discern who are lawful magistrates, and ordained of God, from those who are not."

West then designated who was worthy of submission:

"Those only are to be esteemed lawful magistrates, and ordained of God, who pursue the public good by honoring and encouraging those that do well and punishing all that do evil. Such, and such only, wherever they are to be found, are the ministers of God for good: to resist such is resisting the ordinance of God, and exposing yourselves to the divine wrath and condemnation.

"In either of these senses the text cannot make anything in favor of arbitrary government. Nor could he with any propriety tell them that they need not be afraid of the power so long as they did that which was good, if he meant to recommend an unlimited submission to a tyrannical Nero; for the best characters were the likeliest to fall a sacrifice to his malice. And, besides, such an injunction would be directly contrary to his own practice, and the practice of the primitive Christians, who refused to comply with the sinful commands of men in power; their answer in such cases being this, We ought to obey God rather than men. Hence the apostle Paul himself suffered many cruel persecutions because he would not renounce Christianity, but persisted in opposing the idolatrous worship of the pagan world.

"This text, being rescued from the absurd interpretations which the favorers of arbitrary government have put upon it, turns out to be a noble confirmation of that free and generous plan of government which the law of nature and reason points out to us. Nor can we desire a more equitable plan of government than what the apostle has here laid down; for, if we consult our happiness and real good, we can never wish for an unreasonable liberty, viz., a freedom to do evil, which, according to the apostle, is the only thing that the magistrate is to refrain us from. To have a liberty to do whatever is fit, reasonable, or good, is the highest degree of freedom that rational beings can possess. And how honorable a station are those men placed in, by the providence of God, whose business it is to secure to men this rational liberty, and to promote the happiness and welfare of society, by suppressing vice and immorality, and by honoring and encouraging everything that is honorable, virtuous, and praiseworthy! Such magistrates ought to be honored and obeyed as the ministers of God and the servants of the King of Heaven. Can we conceive of a larger and more generous plan of government than this of the apostle? Or can we find words more plainly expressive of a disapprobation of an arbitrary and tyrannical government? I never read this text without admiring the beauty and nervousness of it; and I can hardly conceive how he could express more ideas in so few words than he has done. We see here, in one view, the honor that belongs to the magistrate, because he is ordained of God for the public good. We have his duty pointed out, viz., to honor and encourage the virtuous, to promote the real good of the community, and to punish all wicked and injurious persons. We are taught the duty of the subject, viz., to obey the magistrate for conscience' sake, because he is ordained of God; and that rulers, being continually employed under God for our good, are to be generously maintained by the paying them tribute; and that disobedience to rulers is highly criminal, and will expose us to the divine wrath. The liberty of the subject is also clearly asserted, viz., that subjects are to be allowed to do everything that is in itself just and right, and are only to be restrained from being guilty of wrong actions. It is also strongly implied, that when rulers become oppressive to the subject and injurious to the state, their authority, their respect, their maintenance, and the duty of submitting to them, must immediately cease; they are then to be considered as the ministers of Satan, and, as such, it becomes our indispensable duty to resist and oppose them.

"Thus we see that both reason and revelation perfectly 'agree in pointing out the nature, end, and design of government, viz., that it is to promote the welfare and happiness of the community; and that subjects have a right to do everything that is good, praiseworthy, and consistent with the good of the community, and are only to be restrained when they do evil' and are injurious either to individuals or the whole community; and that they ought to submit to every law that is beneficial to the community for conscience' sake, although it may in some measure interfere with their private interest; for every good man will be ready to forego his private interest for the sake of being beneficial to the public. Reason and revelation, we see, do both teach us that our obedience to rulers is not unlimited, but that resistance is not only allowable, but an indispensable duty in the case of intolerable tyranny and oppression."[158]

Before concluding this chapter, it is important once again to emphasize that the Black Robed Regiment, and most Americans, did not want war – they wanted peace and a friendly relationship with Great Britain, their Mother Country. The following excerpt from William Gordon's July 4, 1777 Massachusetts election sermon reveals how the patriot preachers wanted a quick remedy to their problems with the British and a renewed friendship with them:

"May the spirit of wisdom return speedily to the British councils, that so Britain may soon recover our friendship and secure our connection by commercial treaties, ere it is too late, and her ruin is sealed! But of this I have little hope, unless some important event should take place in Europe, and oblige Britons to bethink themselves. I rather expect that they will strain every nerve to subdue us. ... I might enumerate the several interpositions of Providence whereby we have been carried safely through the first year of our independency; but your time will not permit it, and you can scarce have forgot or be ignorant of them. Notwithstanding all, the British ministry will still persist. 0! When – when – will the vengeance of Heaven overtake them, by awakening an injured, betrayed nation to avenge itself on such treasonous rulers?"[159]

Section III:

The Preachers & Their Preaching

Chapter 13

PREACHING POLITICS & RELIGION

"It is sometimes said that ministers must not preach politics. ... They would have to toe hop, and skip, and jump through two-thirds of the Bible if they did not, for there is not another book on the face of God's earth that is so full of commerce and business and government, and the relations between the governing and the governed, as this same Bible. ... And yet, in these later days, we have these ineffable men who tell us that we must not preach in the pulpit about public affairs, and who would scourge out of the sanctuary a full half of the Bible. Infidels!"[160]

This is how Henry Beecher Ward, the Presbyterian preacher and pastor of the Congregational Church in Brooklyn, New York, railed away on March 19, 1863 at those who were insisting that preachers should not address political issues from their pulpits.

"Brethren, our preaching will bear its legitimate fruits. If immorality prevails in the land, the fault is ours in a great degree. If there is a decay of conscience, the pulpit is responsible for it. If the public press lacks moral discrimination, the pulpit is responsible for it. If the church is degenerate and worldly, the pulpit is responsible for it. If the world loses its interest in religion, the pulpit is responsible for it. If Satan rules in our halls of legislation, the pulpit is responsible for it. If our politics become so corrupt that the very foundations of our government are ready to fall away, the pulpit is responsible for it.[161] ... Politics are part of a religion in such a country as this and Christians must do their duty to the country as a part of their duty to God. ... Christians seem to act as if they think God does not see what they do in politics. But I tell you He does see it, and He will bless or curse this nation, according to the course Christians take."[162]

This is how Charles Finney, the nineteenth century evangelist blamed the pulpit, specifically, and Christians, generally, for the state of America and its government.

In 1800, some sixty to seventy-five years before either Henry Ward or Charles Finney had hammered home their messages about "mixing" politics and religion, New York pastor, John M. Mason, had preached his sermon, *The Voice Of Warning To Christians*. In it Mason expressed his astonishment that there were actually people who believed it was wrong to mix the two:

"Yet religion has nothing to do with politics! Where did you learn this maxim? The bible is full of directions for your behavior as citizens. It is plain, pointed, awful in its injunctions on rulers and ruled as such: yet religion has nothing to do with politics. You are commanded 'in all your ways to acknowledge him, In every thing, by prayer and supplication, with thanksgiving, to let your requests be made known unto God, And whatsoever ye do, in word or deed, to do all in the name of the Lord Jesus." Yet religion has nothing to do with politics! Most astonishing! And is there any part of your conduct in which you are, or wish to be, without law to God, and not under the law of Christ? Can you persuade yourselves that political men and measures are to undergo no review in the judgment to come? That all the passion and violence, the fraud and falsehood, and corruption which pervade the systems of party, and burst out like a flood at the public elections, are to be blotted from the catalogue of unchristian deeds, because they are politics? Or that a minister of the gospel may see his people, in their political career, bid defiance to their God in breaking through every moral restraint, and keep a guiltless silence because religion has nothing to do with politics? I forbear to press the argument farther; observing only, that many of our difficulties and sins may be traced to this pernicious notion. Yes, if our religion had had more to do with our politics; if, in the pride of our citizenship, we had not forgotten our Christianity: if we had prayed more and wrangled less about the affairs of our country, it would have been infinitely better for us at this day. ...

"That religion has, in fact, nothing to do with the politics of many who profess it, is a melancholy truth. But that it has, of right, no concern with political transactions, is quite a new discovery. If such opinions, however, prevail, there is no longer any mystery in the character of those whose conduct, in political matters, violates every precept, and slanders every principle, of the religion of Christ. But what is politics? Is it not the science and the exercise of civil rights and civil duties? And what is religion? Is it not an obligation to the service of God, founded on his authority, and extending to all our relations personal and social?"[163]

John Mitchell Mason came by his convictions honestly. He was only six years old when the Declaration of Independence was signed and by the time the war had ended, he had entered his teen years having grown up in the midst of America's great struggle for independence. He was intimately acquainted with the price of liberty and when he preached about the Founders and their intentions, he knew well that of which he spoke. John Mitchell Mason was imminently familiar with the ministry of the Black Robed Regiment because his father, Dr. John Mason, was among its ranks. The senior Mason was a pastor in New York City when the war broke out and as such, was an outspoken critic of the British. Pastor Mason was a chaplain in the New York militia and later enlisted as a chaplain in the Continental Army. With young John Mitchell coming of age under his father's courageous example, a deep and abiding love of liberty was impressed upon him. John Mitchell went on to become a Presbyterian minister and spent his life ministering in New York. Like his father, he believed preachers should be engaged in the political, as well as the spiritual, life of the nation. Even though he was not "technically" a member of the original Black Robed Regiment, John Mitchell was certainly a bona fide member of the second generation of the "Regiment" and exerted tremendous spiritual/political influence in the early years of America. In addition to serving as a Presbyterian pastor in New York, he went on to found the Union Theological Seminary in 1804, served as trustee of Columbia College for twenty-six years, was elected as first provost of that institution in 1811, and later went on to serve as president of Dickinson College in Carlisle, Pennsylvania from 1821-1824.

The preachers of the Black Robed Regiment not only believed in mixing politics and religion; they believed that it was wrong not to do so. Unlike today, in eighteenth century America, delivering sermons with strong political content was a regular part of the preaching responsibilities of pastors and the people expected it. Because of the wide acceptance of the myth of separation of church and state, this fact comes as quite a shock to the average person living in the twenty-first century. Nonetheless, the truth is pastors of the revolution era regularly preached politics from their pulpits.

In the preface to his 1860 book, *The Pulpit of the American Revolution*, John Wingate Thornton wrote,

> "The true alliance between Politics and Religion is the lesson inculcated in this volume of Sermons ... It is the voice of the Fathers of the Republic ... They invoked God in their civil assemblies, called upon their chosen teachers of religion [pastors] for counsel from the Bible, and recognized its precepts as the law of their public conduct. The Fathers did not divorce politics and religion, but they denounced the separation as ungodly. Indeed, the clergy were generally consulted by the civil authorities; and not infrequently the suggestions from the pulpit, on election days and other special occasions, were enacted into laws. The state was developed out of the church. The annual election sermon bears witness that our Fathers ever began their civil year and its responsibilities with an appeal to heaven, and recognized Christian morality as the only basis of good laws."[164]

The accuracy of Thornton's claim is confirmed by the request the Massachusetts Provincial Congress made to the clergy of New England on November 23, 1775. The Massachusetts legislators encouraged their preachers to follow the suggestion of the Continental Congress and "make the question of the rights of the colonies and the oppressive conduct of the mother country a topic of the pulpit on weekdays."[165] The Black Regiment enthusiastically complied, but not on weekdays only; they pounded out the message in their Sunday sermons as well. Historian Alice Baldwin categorized these messages as "politico-religious sermons" and noted that the Continental Congress recognized just how valuable they were in motivating the colonists to engage in the fight for liberty and independence.[166] Believing that the church and the state were "attached at the hip," the Continental Congress and the provincial congresses of the individual colonies encouraged the setting aside of special days throughout the year for the colonists to fast, pray, and give thanks to God for His blessings and to request His aid.

Emphasizing the inseparability of church and state, Urian Oakes, pastor in Cambridge, Massachusetts and president of Harvard, wrote,

> "According to the design of our founders and the frame of things laid by them, the interest of righteousness in the commonwealth and holiness in the Churches are inseparable ... To divide what God hath conjoined ... is folly in its exaltation. I look upon this as a little model of the glorious kingdom of Christ on earth. Christ reigns among us in the commonwealth as well as in the church and hath his glorious interest involved and wrapped up in the good of both societies respectfully."[167]

In the introduction to his three-part discourse, *Unlimited Submission And Non-Resistance To The Higher Powers*, Jonathan Mayhew wrote,

> "It is hoped that but few will think the subject of it [politics] an improper one to be discoursed on in the pulpit, under a notion that this is preaching politics, instead of Christ. However, to remove all prejudices of this sort, I beg it may be remembered that 'all Scripture is profitable for doctrine, for reproof, for correction, for instruction in righteousness.' Why, then, should not those parts of Scripture which relate to civil government be examined and explained from the desk [pulpit], as well as others? Obedience to the civil magistrate is a Christian duty; and if so, why should not the nature, grounds, and extent of it be considered in a Christian assembly? Besides, if it be said that it is out of character for a Christian minister to meddle with such a subject [politics], this censure will at last fall upon the holy apostles. They write upon it in their epistles to Christian churches; and surely it cannot be deemed either criminal or impertinent to attempt an explanation of their doctrine."[168]

Then as Mayhew began the main body of his sermon, he said,

"It is evident that the affairs of civil government may properly fall under a moral and religious consideration, at least so far forth as it relates to the general nature and end of magistracy, and to the grounds and extent of that submission which persons of a private character ought to yield to those who are vested with authority. This must be allowed by all who acknowledge the divine original of Christianity. For, although there be a sense, and a very plain and important sense, in which Christ's kingdom is not of this world, his inspired apostles have, nevertheless, laid down some general principles concerning the office of civil rulers, and the duty of subjects, together with the reason and obligation of that duty. And from hence it follows, that it is proper for all who acknowledge the authority of Jesus Christ, and the inspiration of his apostles, to endeavor to understand what is in fact the doctrine which they have delivered concerning this matter. It is the duty of Christian magistrates to inform themselves what it is which their religion teaches concerning the nature and design of their office. And it is equally the duty of all Christian people to inform themselves what it is which their religion teaches concerning that subjection which they owe to the higher powers."[169]

Even though it is undeniable that the preachers of the Black Robed Regiment saw no problem with mixing politics and religion, and freely and boldly preached both from their pulpits, as preachers of the gospel, they certainly understood that the salvation of men and women's souls was of first priority. Consider the words of William Gordon in his message preached on December 15, 1774:

"The pulpit is devoted, in general, to more important purposes than the fate of kingdoms, or the civil rights of human nature, being intended to recover men from the slavery of sin and Satan, to point out their escape from future misery through faith in a crucified Jesus, and to assist them in their preparations for an eternal blessedness. But still there are special times and seasons when it may treat of politics."[170]

For that generation of preachers, preaching the Gospel meant more than just telling someone how to find Christ and receive eternal life. They believed it also meant taking the Scriptures and instructing their congregations about growing in grace and moving forward in their salvation. They found this admonition in passages such as Hebrews 6:1:

"Therefore leaving the principles of the doctrine of Christ, let us go on unto perfection; not laying again the foundation of repentance from dead works, and of faith toward God."

To them, salvation not only produced a saved soul, it also produced a saved lifestyle as well. They believed this saved lifestyle included full engagement in the civil as well as the spiritual life of the nation. But they also knew that this could never be accomplished if believers did not have the religious liberty to worship and serve God according to the dictates of their consciences. They believed external liberty allowed men to experience and express internal liberty.

So, motivated by the belief that God's word spoke to every area of life, the Black Regiment considered it their duty to instruct their people about the nature and proper function of government. As far as they were concerned, no area was "off limits" to the pulpit. They did not hesitate to give their opinions about who they thought deserved to be elected and those who did not. As was stated earlier, unlike preachers of the modern era, pastors in the eighteenth century saw no problem with preaching "politics" from their pulpits and they considered it their responsibility under God to do so.

For example, consider again Samuel West's 1776 Massachusetts election sermon. In this excerpt, West spoke directly to his fellow preachers, challenging them to preach about government to their congregations:

"My reverend fathers and brethren in the ministry will remember that, according to our text, it is part of the work and business of a gospel minister to teach his hearers the duty they owe to magistrates. Let us, then, endeavor to explain the nature of their duty faithfully, and show them the difference between liberty and licentiousness; and, while we are animating them to oppose tyranny and arbitrary power, let us inculcate upon them the duty of yielding due obedience to lawful authority. In order to the right and faithful discharge of this part of our ministry, it is necessary that we should thoroughly study the law of nature, the rights of mankind, and the reciprocal duties of governors and governed. By this means we shall be able to guard them against the extremes of slavish submission to tyrants on one hand, and of sedition and licentiousness on the other. We may, I apprehend, attain a thorough acquaintance with the law of nature and the rights of mankind, while we remain ignorant of many technical terms of law …"[171]

When Jonathan Edwards, Jr., son of the famous Great Awakening preacher, Jonathan Edwards, and pastor of the White Haven Church in New Haven, Connecticut, preached his Connecticut election sermon, *The Necessity Of The Belief Of Christianity*, on May 8, 1794, he had this to say to the preachers of his state:

"We who are employed in the work of the ministry are deeply interested in this subject [government]. We are interested in the prosperity of the state, and are peculiarly interested in this means of prosperity on which I have been insisting. It is our business to study and teach Christianity, and thus to promote the political good of the state, as well as the spiritual good of the souls of our hearers. This is a noble employment, to fidelity and zeal in which, not only the motives of religion call us, but even those of patriotism. Therefore if we have any love to religion and the souls of men; nay if we have any public spirit and love to our country, let us diligently study the evidences, the nature, the doctrines and duties of Christianity, and inculcate them with all plainness, assiduity and perseverance, giving line upon line and precept upon precept."[172]

On May 8, 1800, John Smalley, student of Rev. Ezra Stiles and pastor in Farmington (New Britain), Connecticut, preached that year's Connecticut election sermon entitled, *On The Evils Of A Weak Government*. Though lukewarm early on about America seeking its independence, later Smalley became an outspoken proponent of the struggle and encouraged his fellow preachers and Christians to stand against British tyranny. In this sermon, he encouraged preachers to "declare all the counsel of God," and rebuked those who were fearful to do so:

"The ministers of the gospel, are thought to have no concern with the temporal happiness of mankind: doubtless, the good way for them, whether the old way or not, is to confine themselves very much to their spiritual vocation. Doubtless their principal business is, to save the souls of those who hear them. But in order to [do] this, they must warn all, of that "wrath of God which is revealed from heaven, against all ungodliness and unrighteousness of men." They must 'convert sinners from the error of their ways,' or they cannot 'save their souls from death.' They must teach their converts to 'observe all things whatsoever Christ hath commanded,' by Himself or His apostles; or they cannot make them 'meet to be partakers of the inheritance of the saints in light.' And among these instructions, teaching them to 'obey those who have the rule over them, and to be cautious how they speak evil of dignities,' must not be omitted. Ministers must not 'shun to declare all the counsel of God,' both to rulers and subjects, if they would be 'pure from the blood of all men.' In a word, they must do what in them lies to make all their hearers good Christians; for without this they can never get them to heaven; and they need do no more, to make them peaceable and orderly members of society on earth. Thus far, and in this manner, Aaron may still support the hand of Moses, in ministering to the temporal good of men, even in a consistency with the modern line of separation drawn between them.

"There will always be some, and some that ought to be leaders and teachers, whose policy it is, to turn with the times; to swim with the tide, and swing with the vibrating pendulum of popular opinion. Who will trim their way to seek love; and 'become all things to all men, if by all means they may save' themselves. But a steadfast adherence to truth and duty, however great the apparent danger, is the only way of real safety. He who thus 'loses his life, shall save it'; and he shall lose his life who would save it, by deserting his post, or hiding himself under refuges of falsehood, when evil is foreseen. 'The fearful and unbelieving, shall have their part' at last, in the same lake with bolder transgressors. 'The fear of man bringeth a snare; but whoso putteth his trust in the Lord shall be safe.'"[173]

PREACHING "BOTH" KINDS OF LIBERTY

In his 1773 Massachusetts election sermon, Charles Turner of Duxbury, Massachusetts, preaching from Romans 13:4, declared,

"[W]hen the civil rights of a country receive a shock, it may justly render the ministers of God deeply thoughtful for the safety of sacred privileges – for religious liberty is so blended with civil, that if one falls it is not to be expected that the other will continue."[174]

Echoing the same theme in his June 23, 1775 sermon, *The Crisis of American Affairs*, William Smith, the Episcopalian pastor of Christ Church in Philadelphia, vocalized the Black Regiment's belief that civil and religious liberty were linked:

> "[W]e know that our civil and religious rights are linked together in one indissoluble bond, we neither have, nor seek to have, any interest separate from that of our country; nor can we advise a desertion of its cause. Religion and liberty must flourish or fall together in America. We pray that both may be perpetual."[175]

This bond was considered so indissoluble that historian Carl Bridenbaugh wrote that, in America, "Religion and politics could never again be distinguished one from another after the uproar created in the colonies by the Stamp Act."[176]

On May 17, 1776, John Witherspoon, who just weeks after would help "push" the delegates of the Continental Congress to sign the Declaration, delivered a sermon at Princeton in which he contended that civil and religious liberty were inseparable and an attack upon one was necessarily an attack upon the other:

> "You are all my witnesses, that this is the first time of my introducing any political subject into the pulpit. At this season however, it is not only lawful but necessary, and I willingly embrace the opportunity of declaring my opinion without any hesitation, that the cause in which America is now in arms, is the cause of justice, of liberty, and of human nature. So far as we have hitherto proceeded, I am satisfied that the confederacy of the colonies, has not been the effect of pride, resentment, or sedition, but of a deep and general conviction, that our civil and religious liberties, and consequently in a great measure the temporal and eternal happiness of us and our posterity, depended on the issue. The knowledge of God and his truths have from the beginning of the world been chiefly, if not entirely, confined to those parts of the earth, where some degree of liberty and political justice were to be seen, and great were the difficulties with which they had to struggle from the imperfection of human society, and the unjust decisions of usurped authority. There is not a single instance in history in which civil liberty was lost, and religious liberty preserved entire. If therefore we yield up our temporal property, we at the same time deliver the conscience into bondage. … God grant that in America true religion and civil liberty may be inseparable, and that the unjust attempts to destroy the one, may in the issue tend to the support and establishment of both."[177]

Even British preachers like Anglican Bishop, Thomas Newton, D.D., Bishop of Bristol, England, understood the strong link between civil and religious liberty. In 1754 he said,

> "Not only in this particular, but in the general, the Scriptures, though often perverted to the purposes of tyranny, are yet, in their own nature, calculated to promote the civil as well as the religious liberties of mankind. True religion and virtue, and liberty, are more nearly related and more intimately connected with each other than people commonly consider. It is very true, as St. Paul saith, that where the spirit of the Lord is there is liberty; or as our Savior himself expresseth it, 'If ye continue in my word, then are ye my disciples indeed; and the truth shall make ye free.'"[178]

Jacob Duche, the pastor who led the prayer service in Carpenter's Hall in Philadelphia when the Continental Congress met for the very first time in September 1774 (discussed in chapter 11), made such an indelible mark on the minds of the delegates of the Continental Congress that on May 17, 1776 they chose him to serve as their first chaplain. Just one year earlier on July 7, 1775 and almost one year after praying that powerful prayer in Carpenter's Hall, Duche preached the sermon, *The Duty of Standing Fast In Our Liberties*, at Christ Church in Philadelphia. In the sermon, Duche recognized and emphasized the "two-fold" responsibility of the minister to preach about religious and civil liberty:

> "The occasion is of the first importance; the subject in a great measure new to me—throwing myself, therefore, upon your candor and indulgence, considering myself under the twofold character of a minister of Jesus Christ, and a fellow-citizen of the same slate, and involved in the same public calamity with yourselves, and looking up for counsel and direction to the source of all wisdom, 'who giveth liberally to those that ask it,' I have made choice of a passage of Scripture, which will give me an opportunity of addressing myself to you as freemen, both in the spiritual and temporal sense of the word, and of suggesting to you such a mode of conduct, as will be most likely, under the blessing of Heaven, to insure to you the enjoyment of these two kinds of liberty. "Stand fast, therefore, in the liberty wherewith Christ hath made us free."[179]

(Note: Although Duche was a hardy supporter of the war in the beginning, as the fighting began to take its toll, as casualty lists began to grow, and as the Continental troops were suffering in the bitter cold with Washington at Valley Forge, Duche became increasingly disillusioned with the "cause." After the British occupied Philadelphia in 1777 and held him as their prisoner for a time, Duche reversed himself and began to speak out against the war – even going as far as to write a letter to General Washington asking him to surrender to the British. This, as you can imagine, earned him the criticism and disdain of the friends of liberty. Consequently, in 1777 Duche, having been indicted for treason by the state of Pennsylvania, fled to Great Britain where he lived for fifteen years. He eventually returned to America in 1792 after having suffered a stroke, but was never able to live down his reputation as a traitor. He died in 1798 and was buried in the church-yard of St. Peter's Church in Philadelphia, Pennsylvania.)

Again, it is extremely important to emphasize that the members of the Black Robed Regiment were first, and foremost, preachers of the gospel and believed the salvation of men and women to be their primary objective. When it came to the "two kinds" of liberty (spiritual and civil), spiritual liberty was always their first priority. But they also were keenly aware that if civil liberty was ever lost, religious liberty would be close behind. For example, consider what Henry Cumings, Congregational pastor in Billerica, Massachusetts, said in his sermon on April 19, 1781:

> "While therefore, you are engaged with a laudable zeal in the cause of civil liberty, you will permit me to remind you, that there is another kind of liberty of an higher and nobler nature, which it is of infinite importance to every one to be possessed of; I mean that glorious internal liberty, which consists in a freedom from the dominion of sin, and in the habit and practice of all the virtues of a good life. This is that noble and exalted liberty of the *sons of God*, of which our Savior speaks, when he says, *If the Son of God shall make you free, then shall ye be free indeed.* And this, once gained, will inspire you with the greatest magnanimity and fortitude, in the cause of outward liberty. *For the righteous are bold as a lion.*"[180]

So with their priorities in proper order, the Black Regiment emphasized spiritual and civil liberty at the same time and with the same vigor. An illustration of how they viewed the relationship between these two liberties can be seen in Jacob Duche's sermon mentioned before. Of all the sermons that dealt with both liberties, his is one of the best:

(Gal. 5:1) "Having thus briefly opened the occasion and meaning of the words, I shall proceed to show, in the first place, what we are to understand by that spiritual liberty 'wherewith Christ hath made us free,' and what kind of conduct that must be which is here expressed by the words 'stand fast.'

"However severe, my dear brethren, the loss of our temporal liberties may be, there is certainly a bondage far more severe than this; yea, far more cruel, than that of Israel under their Egyptian taskmasters—a bondage not only to men, but to the fallen spirits of darkness, seeking to exercise over us a joint power and dominion with our own irregular and corrupt passions—a bondage universal, from which no son of Adam hath ever been exempt—a tyranny whose baleful influences have been felt, from the fall of man down to this very day. It has seized not only upon the body, but upon the soul. It has erected its throne in the heart, and from thence imposes its arbitrary decrees. It is confined to no age or sex, no state or condition of human life. High and low, learned and unlearned, the savage and the sage, are alike victims of this despotic power—alike slaves by nature under this bondage of corruption.

"From hence, then, it appears that the liberty with 'which Christ hath made us free,' is nothing less than such a release from the arbitrary power of sin, such an enlargement of the soul by the efficacy of divine grace, and such a total surrender of the will and affections to the influence and guidance of the divine spirit ('for we are made a willing people in the day of God's power'), as will enable us to live in the habitual cheerful practice of every grace and virtue here, and qualify us for the free, full and uninterrupted enjoyment of heavenly life and liberty hereafter.

"Thus far have I travelled in a well-known path, and spoken a language familiar to most of you, and which you have long been accustomed to hear from this pulpit. I am now to strike into another path, which, though it may not always terminate in such glorious scenes of never-ending felicity as the former, yet, if steadfastly pursued, will conduct the sons of men to a happiness, of an inferior kind indeed, but highly necessary to their present temporary state of existence in this world.

"If *spiritual liberty* calls upon its pious votaries to extend their views far forward to a glorious hereafter, *civil liberty* must at least be allowed to secure in a considerable degree our well being here. And I believe it will be no difficult matter to prove that the latter is as much the gift of God in Christ Jesus as the former, and consequently, that we are bound to stand fast in our civil as well as our spiritual freedom.

"From what hath been said under my first head of discourse, I think it must appear, that liberty, traced to her true source, is of heavenly extraction, that divine virtue is her illustrious parent, that from eternity to eternity they have been and must be inseparable companions, and that the hearts of all intelligent beings are the living temples, in which they ought to be jointly worshipped.

"Gracious God, stop the precious effusion of British and American blood – too precious to be spared in any other cause than the joint interest of both against a common foe!

"Pained as I am at this melancholy prospect, I mean not, however, to decline addressing you in your military capacity, and suggesting such a conduct for the preservation of your temporal rights as, by the blessing of heaven, will be most likely to insure you success.

"'Stand fast,' then. 'Stand fast' by a strong faith and dependence upon Jesus Christ, the great Captain of your salvation. Enlist under the banner of his cross. And let this motto be written upon your hearts: '*In hoc signo vinces*' – 'Under this standard thou shalt overcome.'

"'Stand fast' by an undaunted courage and magnanimity. And here give me leave to remind you that there is a kind of courage which seems to be merely animal or constitutional. This may stand a soldier in good stead, perhaps, for a few moments, amid the heat and fury of a battle, when his blood and spirits are set on fire by the warlike sound of drums and trumpets. But I would have you possessed of more than this, even a courage that will prove you to be good Christians as well as good soldiers; a firm, invincible fortitude of soul, founded upon religion and the glorious hope of a better world; a courage that will enable you not only to withstand an armed phalanx, to pierce a squadron, or force an entrenchment, when the cause of virtue and your country calls you to such a service, but will support you likewise against the principalities and powers of darkness, will stand by you under the assaults of pain and sickness, and give you firmness and consolation amid all the horrors of a death-bed scene.

"Such a courage as this, too, will always be tempered with prudence, humanity, and greatness of soul. It will never degenerate into savage cruelty and barbarity.

"Nor let me dismiss this head of advice without reminding you of the glorious stand that hath been already made for us by our northern brethren, and calling upon you to thank Heaven for his great and gracious interposition. Surely 'the Lord of Hosts was with them;' surely 'the God of Jacob was their refuge.' Drop a pious tear to the memory of the illustrious slain, and let them yet live in the annals of American freedom.

"Lastly, 'stand fast' by a steady constancy and perseverance. Difficulties unlooked for may yet arise, and trials present themselves sufficient to shake the utmost firmness of human fortitude. Be prepared, therefore, for the worst.

"In a word, my brethren, though the worst should come—though we should be deprived of all the conveniences and elegancies of life—though we should be cut off from all our usual sources of commerce, and constrained, as many of our poor brethren have already been, to abandon our present comfortable habitations—let us, nevertheless, 'stand fast' as the guardians of Liberty.

"Even so grant, thou great and glorious God, that to thee only we may look, and from thee experience that deliverance which we ask, not for any merits of our own, but for the sake and through the merits of the dear Son of thy love, Christ Jesus our Lord! To whom, with thee, O Father, and thee, O blessed Spirit! Three persons in one eternal God, be ascribed all honor, praise, and dominion, now, henceforth, and forever!"[181]

"ELECTION" AND OTHER "POLITICAL" SERMONS

The preachers of the Black Robed Regiment seized every opportunity to speak out publically about the political environment in which they were living. These opportunities were not only provided each Sunday as they stood before their congregations, but were also created by special occasions throughout the year.

For example, in Boston, the Thursday or Fifth Day Lecture was established in 1633 by the Massachusetts preacher John Cotton as a special occasion when preachers were invited to expound on the biblical principles of government. This annual event was considered so vital and was so popular that it continued to be observed until the middle of the nineteenth century.[182] Additionally, special days of thanksgiving, fasting, and prayer were called regularly by governors of the individual colonies as well as by the Continental Congress, providing another opportunity for the patriot pastors to preach politics.

Pastors were also regularly invited to speak to military units in sermons appropriately called "Artillery Sermons." These times afforded them a prime opportunity to define, from a biblical perspective, the principles of liberty, government, and the need and godly responsibility to defend the rights of men against tyranny. In fact, there were few holidays throughout the year that did not give the preachers an opportunity to educate the people through biblical/political discourse. Commemorations of historic moments like the Boston Massacre, the battles of Lexington and Concord, the Fourth of July, the end of the war, the deaths of George Washington and other significant Founders, etc. were all employed for this purpose.

Of all the opportunities available to the pastors for preaching their "political theology," none was more important or more celebrated than the annual Election Sermon. These sermons occurred after the annual elections were completed and were preached before the lawmakers of the colonies/states as they began their new legislative year. The entire governing body of the colony/state, including such dignitaries as the governor, lieutenant governor, and the elected members of the legislature, would gather, along with local citizens, to listen to a leading pastor who had been given the extreme honor of speaking at this momentous occasion. His task: remind the newly seated legislators of what God required of government and that they would someday give an account to Him for the way they governed in the coming legislative year. In addition to sometimes being published in the newspapers, this important sermon was commonly immortalized by the legislature having it published and distributed throughout the area in pamphlet form.

The tradition of the election sermon can be traced all of the way back to the 1630s with the Connecticut election sermon of Rev. Thomas Hooker and the Massachusetts election sermon of Rev. Nathaniel Ward in 1641.[183] The delivery of the election sermon continued as a major part of the beginning of the legislative year in the colonies/states for decades. For example, Massachusetts observed the election sermon for some 250 years and Connecticut did so for approximately 150 years. As time passed, more and more of the colonies/states began the practice with such states as Vermont in 1778 and New Hampshire in 1784.[184]

In 1860, historian John Thornton said this about the election sermon:

"The annual 'Election Sermon,' a perpetual memorial, continued down through the generations from century to century, still bears witness that our fathers ever began their civil year and its responsibilities with an appeal to Heaven, and recognized Christian morality as the only basis of good laws."[185]

In 1862, historian Joel Headley wrote this about the election sermon:

"These sermons were as much a part of the stately and imposing ceremonies as the election itself. The ablest divines in the Colony were invited to deliver them — not as a mere compliment to religion, nor were they listened to simply with that quiet decorum and respectful attention, which is accorded in ordinary worship, but with the deep interest of those seeking light and instruction. The preachers did not confine themselves to a dissertation on doctrinal truths nor mere exhortation to godly behavior. They grappled with the great question of the rights of man, and especially the rights of the colonists in their controversy with the mother country.

"They dealt in no high sounding phrases of liberty and equality; they went to the very foundations of society, showed what the natural rights of man were, and how those rights became modified when men gathered into communities; how all laws and regulations were designed to be for the good of the governed; that the object of concentrated power was to protect not invade personal liberty, and when it failed to do this, and oppressed instead of protected, assailed instead of defended rights, resistance became lawful, nay, obligatory. They showed also the nature of compacts and charters, and applied the whole subject to the case of the Colonies. …

"The pulpit, therefore, was the most direct and effectual way of reaching the masses. The House of Representatives of Massachusetts knew this, passed resolutions requesting the clergy to make the question of the rights of the Colonies and the oppressive conduct of the mother country a topic of the pulpit on week days. They thus proclaimed to all future time their solemn convictions of their dependence on the pulpit for that patriotic feeling and unity of action, which they knew to be indispensable to success. Here, then, the historian can lay his hand on the deep, solid substratum that underlaid the Revolution."[186]

William Gordon, himself a member of the Black Regiment, noted the significance of the political preaching of the patriot pastors:

"[The] ministers of New England, being mostly Congregationalists, are, from that circumstance, in a professional way, more attached and habituated to the principles of liberty than if they had spiritual superiors to lord it over them, and were in hopes of possessing, in their turn, through the gift of government, the seat of power. They oppose arbitrary rule in civil concerns from the lover of freedom, as well as from a desire of guarding against its introduction into religious matters. The patriots, for years back, have availed themselves greatly of their assistance. Two sermons have been preached annually for a length of time, the one on general election day, the last Wednesday in May, when the new general court have been used to meet, according to charter, and elect counselors for the ensuing year; the other, some little while after, on the artillery election day, when the officers are reelected, or new officers chosen. On these occasions political subjects are deemed very proper; but it is expected that they be treated in a decent, serious, and instructive manner. The general election preacher has been elected alternately by the council and House of Assembly. The sermon is styled the Election Sermon, and is printed. Every representative has a copy for himself, and generally one or more for the minister or ministers of his town. As the patriots have prevailed, the preachers of each sermon have been the zealous friends of liberty; and the passages most adapted to promote the spread and love of it have been selected and circulated far and wide by means of newspapers, and read with avidity and a degree of veneration on account of the preacher and his election to the service of the day. Commendations, both public and private, have not been wanting to help on the design. Thus, by their labors in the pulpit, and by furnishing the prints with occasional essays, the ministers have forwarded and strengthened, and that not a little, the opposition to the exercise of that parliamentary claim of right to bind the colonies in all cases whatever.

"The clergy of this colony are as virtuous, sensible, and learned set of men, as will probably be found in any part of the globe of equal size and equally populous. The first settlers were early attentive to the providing of suitable persons to fill their pulpits with dignity. They saw the importance of it, and in 1636 the general court gave some hundred pounds toward a public school at Newton; but Mr.

John Harvard, a worthy minister of Charlestown, dying in 1638, and bequeathing between seven and eight hundred pounds to the same use, the school took the name of Harvard College by an order of court, and the town upon the occasion changed its name for that of Cambridge. – This college has been encouraged ever since, and is the first upon the continent. It is the *alma mater* to whom the youth of this colony in particular, are sent, whether designed for the pulpit, the bar, or other callings. Here they receive the rudiments of those qualifications by which they are enabled to serve their country in a civil or sacred department. The salaries of the ministers are moderate, but in general sufficient for their support, by the aid of good economy. They cannot approve of often bringing politics into the pulpit, yet they apprehend it to be right upon special occasions. Who but must admit, that 'it is certainly the duty of the clergy to accommodate their discourses to the times; to preach against such sins as are most prevalent, and to recommend such virtues as are most wanted. For example, if exorbitant ambition and venality are predominant, ought they not to warn their hearers against the vices? If public spirit is much wanted, should they not inculcate this great virtue? If the rights and duties of magistrates and subjects are disputed, should they not explain them, show their nature, ends, limitations, and restrictions?' You have frequently remarked, that though the partisans of arbitrary power will freely censure that preacher who speaks boldly for the liberties of the people, they will admire as an excellent divine, the parson whose discourse is wholly in the opposite strain, and teaches that magistrates have a divine right for doing wrong, and are to be implicitly obeyed; men professing Christianity, as if the religion of the blessed Jesus bound them tamely to part with their natural and social rights, and slavishly to bow their neck to any tyrant; as if Paul was faulty in standing up for his Roman privileges, that he might escape a scourging, or falling a sacrifice to the malice of his countrymen, when he appealed unto Caesar."[187]

THE DIFFERENCE IN "ESTABLISHING" AND "ENCOURAGING" RELIGION

Believing as they did that civil and religious liberties were strongly linked together, the patriot preachers believed that government should do more than simply "tolerate" religion – they believed government had an obligation to encourage it and even participate in it. For example, consider the preaching of Samuel

Stillman, pastor of the First Baptist Church of Boston. Stillman had the distinction of being one of the pastors who served as a delegate to the 1787 Constitutional Convention. In his sermon, *The Duty of Magistrates*, preached before the Supreme Court of Massachusetts on May 29, 1779, he juxtaposed the government's legal responsibility to encourage religion against its illegal attempt to "establish" religion:

"It may be said, that religion is of importance to the good of civil society; therefore the magistrate ought to encourage it under this idea. It is readily acknowledged that the intrinsic excellence and beneficial effects of true religion are such that *every man* who is favored with the Christian revelation ought to befriend it. It has the *promise of the life that now is, and of that which is to come.* And there are many ways in which the civil magistrate may encourage religion, in a perfect agreement with the nature of the kingdom of Christ, and the rights of conscience.

"As a *man*, he is *personally* interested in it. His everlasting salvation is at stake. Therefore he should search the Scriptures for himself, and follow them wherever they lead him. This right he hath in common with every other citizen.

"As the *head of a family*, he should act as a priest in his own house, by endeavoring to bring up his children in the nurture and admonition of the Lord.

"As a *magistrate*, he should be as a nursing father to the church of Christ, by protecting all the peaceable members of it from injury on account of religion; and by securing to them the uninterrupted enjoyment of equal religious liberty. The authority by which he acts he derives alike from *all the people;* consequently he should exercise that authority *equally* for the benefit of *all*, without any respect to their different religious principles. They have an undoubted right to demand it. …

"On the other hand, if the magistrate destroys the equality of the subjects of the state on account of religion, he violates a fundamental principle of a free government, establishes separate interests in it, and lays a foundation for disaffection to rulers and endless quarrels among the people.

"Happy are the inhabitants of that commonwealth, in which every man sits under his vine and fig tree, having none to make him afraid; in which all *are protected* but none *established.* Permit me, on this occasion, to introduce the words of the Rev. Dr. Chauncey, whose age and experience add weight to his sentiments. 'We are,' says this gentleman, 'in principle against all civil establishments in religion. We desire not, and suppose we have no right to desire, the interposition of the state to establish our sentiments in religion, or the manner in which we would express them. It does not, indeed, appear to us, that God has entrusted the state with a right to make religious establishments.' And after observing that if one state has this right, all states have the same right, he adds: 'And as they must severally be supposed to exert this authority in establishments conformable to their own sentiments in religion, what can the consequence be, but infinite damage to the cause of God and true religion? And such, in fact, has been the consequence of these establishments in all ages and in all places. What absurdities in sentiment, and ridiculous follies, not to say gross immoralities in practice, have not been established by the civil power, in some or other of the nations of the world?'

"To which I take the liberty to add the following passage of a very ingenious author:

"'The moment any religion becomes national, or established, its purity must certainly be lost, because it is impossible to keep it unconnected with men's interests; and if connected, it must inevitably be perverted by them. Again, that very order of men, who are maintained to support its interests, will sacrifice them to their own. By degrees knaves will join them, fools believe them, and cowards will be afraid of them; and having gained so considerable a part of the world to their interests, they will erect an independent dominion among themselves, dangerous to the liberties of mankind, and representing all those who oppose tyranny, as God's enemies, teach it to the meritorious in His sight to persecute them in this world, and damn them in another. Hence must arise hierarchies, inquisitions and Popery; for Popery is but the consummation of that tyranny which every religious system in the hands of men is in perpetual pursuit of.'

"It is well known to this respectable assembly, that Christianity flourished remarkably for the space of three hundred years after the ascension of Christ, amidst the hottest and most bloody persecutions, and when the powers of the world were against it, and began to decline immediately upon its being made a legal establishment by Constantine, the first Christian emperor, who heaped upon it his ill-judged favors and introduced a train of evils which he had not designed...

"Seeing, then, Christianity made its way in the beginning when the powers of the world were against it, let us cheerfully leave it to the force of its own evidence, and to the care of its adorable author; while we strictly attend to all those means which he hath instituted for the propagation of it. The ministers of Christ are particularly called upon to *preach the word, to be instant in season, out of season,* to teach the people *publicly and from house to house;* always encouraging themselves with that gracious promise, *Lo, I am with you alway, even unto the end of the world.*

"Upon the whole, I think it is a plain as well as a very important truth, that the *Church of Christ* and a *commonwealth are essentially different.* The one is a *religious* society, of which Christ is the sole head, and which he gathers out of the world, in common, by the dispensation of his gospel, governs by his laws in all matters of religion, a complete code of which we have in the sacred Scriptures; and preserves it by his power.

"The other is a *civil* society—originating with the people, and designed to promote their *temporal interests*—which is governed by men, whose authority is derived from their fellow-citizens, and confined to the affairs of this world.

"In this view of the matter, the line appears to me to be fairly drawn between *the things that belong to Caesar* and *the things* that belong to God. The magistrate is to govern the *state,* and Christ is to govern the *church.* The former will find business enough in the complex affairs of government to employ all his time and abilities. The latter is infinitely sufficient to manage his own kingdom without foreign aid.

"Thus have I considered the important principles of civil and religious liberty, according to that ability which God hath given; and with a freedom that becomes a citizen when called upon, at a most critical period, to address the rulers of a free people; whose patriotic minds, it is taken for granted, would at once despise the language of adulation."[188]

Stephen Peabody, the pastor of the First Congregational Church of Atkinson, New Hampshire, preached the June 11, 1797 New Hampshire election sermon. In it he pointed out how religion is a huge benefit to a nation and thus, why the government should encourage it:

"The ideas which have by some been adopted, that the civil authority should never interpose in matters of religion, are erroneous. It is granted by the most learned politicians, that the religious forms which have been established and supported, have had a powerful tendency to promote civility, to restrain vicious men, to protect the innocent, to countenance worthy pursuits, and to discountenance the immoralities which have contaminated mankind! Sentiments of this nature have flowed from knowledge and experience: And if they be well founded, is it not a truth, that establishments of this kind invite the attention of that civil policy which is the support of government? If, therefore, virtue and religion form the principal pillar which upholds the civil fabric, it is evidently a duty for wise rulers to contribute something for its support. Upon this principle, many professed deists contribute with cheerfulness and liberality to public teachers of morality; they are patrons to the worship of God in gospel order: They have considered it as a measure wisely adapted to uphold government – and in this they deserve an encomium."[189]

Even though the preachers and their congregations were adamantly against having a government-sponsored church, i.e. a state church, they certainly wanted Christianity to be the dominant faith in America. By insisting that religion be "encouraged" while not being "established," they assigned to their government a challenging but doable task, and the legislators of that day were definitely up to the challenge. Rather than shying away from religion, the legislators courageously and successfully ran toward it. It is at this point where many modern Americans make a huge error – they confuse "encouraging" religion with "establishing" it.

Although encouragement and establishment may seem the same, they are worlds apart. The Founders wanted a government that fostered religion – not a government that forced religion. They certainly did not want the same situation in America that existed in Great Britain with the Church of England. There, the king was not only the head of the government but was also the head of the church and could use his authority to force the citizens to embrace his religious faith. Americans did not want that and fought a war to keep from it!

To guard against repeating this fatal error, the Framers placed a limit on government in the First Amendment of the Constitution restricting Congress from "establishing" a state religion/church:

> "Congress shall make no law respecting an establishment of religion, or prohibiting the free exercise thereof ..."

Unlike today, people of that time understood the phrase "establishment of religion" to be a clear reference to the "government-established" Church of England. They understood that men's freedom to publicly practice their religion was an unalienable right given them by God – a right that government had no power to restrict. They did not believe that government "allowed" them to practice their religious beliefs publicly; they believed God gave them the "right" to do so. But equally important, they did not see public expression of religion to be an "establishment" of religion. They would never have understood "an establishment of religion" to mean what we interpret it to mean today. The Founders would be astonished and completely bewildered when today's courts interpret "establishment of religion" to mean:

- Reading the Bible aloud at school
- Praying at a school function such as a ballgame
- Hanging the Ten Commandments on the courthouse or schoolhouse walls
- Erecting a nativity scene on a courthouse lawn
- Singing Christmas carols at school

As was shown in chapter 10, the Founders clearly intended for America to be a "Christian" nation. Certainly they did not want the government to "establish" a state religion that the citizens could be forced to embrace, but they also believed men had the unalienable right to worship God as they saw fit, and to do so publicly. They would be appalled to learn that allowing Bible reading, prayer, Christmas carols, nativity scenes, and Ten Commandments displays in public buildings is considered by today's elites as "establishing" a state church/religion. Most reasonable people, given the proper information and time to think it through, agree that allowing the previously mentioned religious expressions does not come remotely close to "establishing" a state church/religion. Instead they understand that it is nothing more than the government's "recognizing" the right of citizens to freely express their religious beliefs.

The Founders' intent was clear – religion needed to be protected from government – government did not need to be protected from religion. So, even though the Founders believed government should be restricted from "establishing" a national religion, they and the Black Regiment pastors insisted that government encourage religion and they helped foster a healthy intercourse "between" government and religion.

RELIGION WAS CRITICAL TO LIBERTY AND FAIR GOVERNMENT

The Founders believed religion, Christianity specifically, were essential in insuring the liberty and success of a free society. Strongly convinced of this, the patriot preachers taught that government and religion were friends. As far as they were concerned, whatever promoted God's kingdom also promoted America.

John Witherspoon emphasized this in his sermon on May 17, 1776:

> "On the other hand, when the manners of a nation are pure, when true religion and internal principles maintain their vigor, the attempts of the most powerful enemies to oppress them are commonly baffled and disappointed. This will be found equally certain, whether we consider the great principles of God's moral government, or the operation and influence of natural causes. What follows from this? That he is the best friend to American liberty, who is most sincere and active in promoting true and undefiled religion, and who sets himself with the greatest firmness to bear down profanity and immorality of every kind. Whoever is an avowed enemy to God, I scruple not to call him an enemy to his country."[190]

On May 27, 1778, Phillips Payson, pastor in Chelsea, Massachusetts, addressed this same subject in his Massachusetts election sermon:

> "I must not forget to mention religion, both in rulers and people, as of the highest importance to the public. This is the most sacred principle that can dwell in the human breast. It is of the highest importance to men, — the most perfec-

tive of the human soul. The truths of the gospel are the most pure, its motives the most noble and animating, and its comforts the most supporting to the mind. The importance of religion to civil society and government is great indeed, as it keeps alive the best sense of moral obligation, a matter of such extensive utility, especially in respect to an oath, which is one of the principal instruments of government. The fear and reverence of God, and the terrors of eternity, are the most powerful restraints upon the minds of men; and hence it is of special importance in a free government, the spirit of which being always friendly to the sacred rights of conscience, it will hold up the gospel as the great rule of faith and practice. Established modes and usages in religion, more especially the stated public worship of God, so generally form the principles and manners of a people, that changes or alterations in these, especially when nearly conformed to the spirit and simplicity of the gospel, may well be esteemed very dangerous experiments in government. For this, and other reasons, the thoughtful and wise among us trust that our civil fathers, from a regard to gospel worship and the constitution of these churches, will carefully preserve them, and at all times guard against every innovation that might tend to overset the public worship of God, though such innovations may be urged from the most foaming zeal. Persons of a gloomy, ghostly, and mystic cast, absorbed in visionary scenes, deserve but little notice in matters either of religion or government. Let the restraints of religion once be broken down, as they infallibly would be by leaving the subject of public worship to the humors of the multitude, and we might well defy all human wisdom and power to support and preserve order and government in the state. Human conduct and character can never be better formed than upon the principles of our holy religion; they give the justest sense, the most adequate views, of the duties between rulers and people, and are the best principles in the world to carry the ruler through the duties of his station; and in case a series of faithful services should be followed with popular censure, as may be the case, yet the religious ruler will find the approbation of his conscience a noble reward."[191]

Two years later on May 31, 1780, Simeon Howard, pastor of the West Church in Boston, made this same point in that year's Massachusetts election sermon:

"Let me observe, once more, that it is of great importance to their happiness that religion and virtue generally prevail among a people; and in order to this, government should use its influence to promote them. Rulers should encourage them, not only by their example, but by their authority; and the people should invest them with power to do this, so far as is consistent with the sacred and inalienable rights of conscience, which no man is supposed to give up, or may lawfully give up, when he enters into society. But, reserving these, the people may and ought to give up every right and power to the magistrate which will enable him more effectually to promote the common good, without putting it in his power essentially to injure it. He ought, therefore, to have power to punish all open acts of profaneness and impiety, as tending, by way of example, to destroy that reverence of God which is the only effectual support of moral virtue, and all open acts of vice, as prejudicial to society. He should have power to provide for the institution and support of the public worship of God, and public teachers of religion and virtue, in order to maintain in the minds of the people that reverence of God, and that sense of moral obligation, without which there can be no confidence, no peace or happiness in society.

"Without such care in government, there is danger that the people will forget the God that is above, and abandon themselves to vice; or, to say the least, impiety and vice are much less likely to become general where such care is taken than where it is not. And God having, in the constitution of nature, made religion and virtue conducive, and even necessary, to the happiness of human society, he has thereby plainly taught us that it is the duty and business of society, as such, or of the civil magistrate, to do everything to promote them that may be done without injuring the rights of conscience. And no man who has full liberty of inquiring and examining for himself, of openly publishing and professing his religious sentiments, and of worshipping God in the time and manner which he chooses, without being obliged to make any religious profession, or attend any religious worship contrary to his sentiments, can justly complain that his rights of conscience are infringed. And such liberty and freedom every man may enjoy, though the government should require him to pay his proportion towards supporting public teachers of religion and morality.

"Taking this care of religion is so plain and important a duty, that the government which should wholly neglect it would not only act a very unwise and imprudent part with respect to themselves, but be guilty of base ingratitude and a daring affront to Heaven. By such conduct they would, as a community, in effect adopt the language of the profane fatalists mentioned by Job, who "say unto God, depart from us, for we desire not the knowledge of thy ways. What is the Almighty that we should serve him? And what profit shall we have if we pray unto him?" Now, although it is possible that rulers who have no religion themselves may enact proper laws to support it among the people, yet it is to be remembered that their example will have great influence, and, if that be irreligious and vicious, will in some measure defeat the good effects of their authority, and do more to spread corruption than that will to prevent it. It is therefore highly proper, in order to promote piety and good morals among the people, that rulers be men who fear God — who have a just sense of religion on their own minds, and conform to it in their lives.

"It may be proper to add, that though the fear of God may exist where there is no knowledge or belief of Christianity, yet that the scheme of doctrines contained in the gospel is much better calculated than any other known to the world to produce and strengthen that divine principle. The plan of redemption which it unfolds for the fallen race of men exhibits the Deity in the most amiable light, as the perfection of love and benevolence. "The solemn scenes which it opens beyond the grave; the resurrection of the dead; the general judgment; the equal distribution of rewards and punishments to the good and bad, and the full completion of divine wisdom and goodness in the final establishment of order, perfection, and happiness," afford such motives to the love and reverence of God, and to the practice of all holiness and virtue, as can be drawn from no other scheme of religion; and, therefore, a belief of the gospel of Christ may justly be considered as an important qualification for a civil ruler. …

"Finally, our political fathers will not fail to do all they can to promote religion and virtue through the community, as the surest means of rendering their government easy and happy to themselves and the people. For this purpose they will watch over their morals with the same affectionate and tender care that a pious and prudent parent watches over his children, and, by all the methods which love to God and man can inspire and wisdom point out, endeavor to check and suppress all impiety and vice, and lead the people to the practice of that righteousness which exalteth a nation. If any new laws are wanting, or more care in the execution of laws already made, for discouraging profaneness, intemperance, lewdness, extravagant gaming, extortion, fraud, oppression, or any other vice, they will take speedy care to supply this defect, and render themselves a terror to evil-doers, as well as an encouragement to such as do well. They will promote to places of trust men of piety, truth, and benevolence. Nor will they fail to exhibit in their own lives a fair example of that piety and virtue which they wish to see practiced by the people. They will show that they are not ashamed of the gospel of Christ, by paying a due regard to his sacred institutions, and to all the laws of his kingdom. Magistrates may probably do more in this way than in any other, and perhaps more than any other order of men, to preserve or recover the morals of a people. The manners of a court are peculiarly catching, and, like the blood in the heart, quickly flow to the most distant members of the body. If, therefore, rulers desire to see religion and virtue flourish in the community over which they preside, they must countenance and encourage them by their own example. And to excite them to this, I must not omit to observe that, though the fear of God, a regard to truth, and a hatred of covetousness, are necessary to form the character of a good ruler, they are, if possible, still more necessary to form the character of a good man, and secure the approbation of God, the Judge of all; for to him magistrates, in common with other men, are accountable. Nor does he regard the persons of princes any more than of their subjects. If they are impious and vicious, if they abuse their power, they may bring great misery upon other men, but they will surely bring much greater upon themselves. The eye of Heaven surveys all their counsels, designs, and actions; and the day is coming when these shall all be made manifest, and every one receive according to his works. Happy they who in that day shall be found faithful, for they shall lift up their heads with confidence, and, amidst applauding angels, enter into they joy of their Lord; while those who have oppressed and injured the people by their power, and corrupted them by their example, shall be covered with shame and confusion, and sentenced to that place of blackness and darkness, where there is weeping, and wailing, and gnashing of teeth!"[192]

On May 8, 1783, as the war was coming to a close, Ezra Stiles, president of Yale, preached the Connecticut election sermon in Hartford. In it, he emphasized that Christianity, what he called "true religion," was essential for America's success:

"That our system of dominion and civil polity would be imperfect without the true religion; or that from the diffusion of virtue among the people of any community would arise their greatest secular happiness: which will terminate in this conclusion, that holiness ought to be the end of all civil government. 'That thou mayest be a holy people unto the Lord thy God.' ...

"Liberty, civil and religious, has sweet and attractive charms. The enjoyment of this, with property, has filled the English settlers in America with a most amazing spirit, which has operated, and still will operate, with great energy. Never before has the experiment been so effectually tried of every man's reaping the fruits of his labor and feeling his share in the aggregate system of power. The ancient republics did not stand on the people at large, and therefore no example or precedent can be taken from them. Even men of arbitrary principles will be obliged, if they would figure in these states, to assume the patriot so long that they will at length become charmed with the sweets of liberty."

Then Stiles, after clarifying that government should not have the power to establish religion and that religion should not have the power to legislatively rule the people, emphasized the importance of religion and its contributions to the government and thus, the nation:

"Shall the Most High send down truth into this world from the world of light and truth, and shall the rulers of this world be afraid of it? Shall there be no intrepid Daniels, — great in magistracy, great in religion? How great was that holy man, that learned and pious civilian, when he shone in the supreme triumvirate at the head of an empire of one hundred and twenty provinces — venerable for political wisdom, venerable for religion!

"This was the system of theology brought over from the other side of the flood by our pious forefathers, now with God. The more this is realized in a state, the more will its felicity be advanced; for, certainly, the morals of Christianity are excellent. It enjoins obedience to magistracy, justice, harmony, and benevolence among fellow citizens; and, what is more, it points out immortality to man. Politicians, indeed, usually consider religion only as it may affect and subserve civil purposes, and hence it is mighty indifferent to them what the state of religion be, provided they can ride in the whirlwind and direct the storm. Nothing is more common than to see them in every country making use of sects, for their own ends, whom they in their hearts despise and ridicule with supreme contempt. Not so the Christian patriot, who from his heart wishes the advancement of Christianity much less for the civil good than for the eternal welfare of immortal souls. We err much if we think the only or chief end of civil government is secular happiness. Shall immortals, illuminated by revelation, entertain such an opinion? God forbid! Let us model civil society with the adoption of divine institutions so as shall best subserve the training up and disciplining innumerable millions for the more glorious society of the church of the first-born. Animated with the sublime ideas which Christianity infuses into a people, we shall be led to consider the true religion as the highest glory of a civil polity. The Christian institution so excelled in glory, that the Mosaic lost all its glory. So the most perfect secular polity, though very excellent, would lose all its glory when compared with a kingdom wherein dwelleth righteousness, a community wherein the religion of the divine Jesus reigns in vigor and perfection.

"Which of these governments is it probable would most contribute to the secular welfare, and be attended with the greatest dignity, and even the greatest worldly splendor? But, above all, which most subservient to eternity and its momentous concerns? In which, as a school of institution and discipline, should we enjoy the happiest advantages for immortality? Which of these empires would be the favorite of Jesus? Or is he indeed an unconcerned spectator of human affairs? If not, why should we doubt or hesitate to give the preference to the Christian Republic? If revelation be not true, it does us no hurt; we are as safe and as well off as others, having all their moral virtue. But if revelation be true, it is true exclusively, and therefore to be attended to at peril."[193]

CHRISTIANITY IS ESSENTIAL FOR GOOD GOVERNMENT

When the war was finally over and the Americans were getting down to the business of strengthening the union, the patriot pastors continued to emphasize the importance of religion. The following sermons illustrate how the preachers continued to stay engaged in the arena of government, reminding the people that, just as they had needed the Lord to help them win the war, they would need the Lord to help them establish a good and godly government upon which they could build a righteous nation.

On May 29, 1776, at the outset of the war, Samuel West had emphasized in his Massachusetts election sermon that religion was essential in making good citizens and only by supporting religion could America become a stable and law abiding society:

"And as nothing tends like religion and the fear of God to make men good members of the commonwealth, it is the duty of magistrates to become the patrons and promoters of religion and piety, and to make suitable laws for the maintaining public worship, and decently supporting the teachers of religion. Such laws, I apprehend, are absolutely necessary for the well being of civil society. Such laws may be made, consistent with all that liberty of conscience which every good member of society ought to be possessed of; for, as there are few, if any, religious societies among us but what profess to believe and practice all the great duties of religion and morality that are necessary for the well-being of society and the safety of the state, let every one be allowed to attend worship in his own society, or in that way that he judges most agreeable to the will of God, and let him be obliged to contribute his assistance to the supporting and defraying the necessary charges of his own meeting. In this case no one can have any right to complain that he is deprived of liberty of conscience, seeing that he has a right to choose and freely attend that worship that appears to him to be most agreeable to the will of God; and it must be very unreasonable for him to object against being obliged to contribute his part towards the support of that worship which he has chosen. Whether some such method as this might not tend, in a very eminent manner, to promote the peace and welfare of society, I must leave to the wisdom of our legislators to determine; be sure it would take off some of the most popular objections against being obliged by law to support public worship while the law restricts that support only to one denomination."[194]

In 1783, as the war was winding down, Ezra Stiles made this same point to the General Assembly of Connecticut:

"And while this honorable House is attending to the secular concerns of civil government, may we not humbly wish that you would not repudiate the idea of being nursing fathers to our spiritual Israel, the church of God within this state? Give us, gentlemen, the decided assurance that you are friends of the churches, and that you are the friends of the pastors, who have certainly in this trying warfare approved themselves the friends of liberty and government. Your predecessors, one hundred years ago, accounted this among their principal honors. They were solicitous to promote religion and learning, and to give suitable encouragement to both. ... without which we are left to perfect incertitude, if not totally in the dark, with respect to eternity and its vast concerns.

"... That our system of dominion and civil polity would be imperfect without the true religion; or that from the diffusion of virtue among the people of any community would arise their greatest secular happiness: which will terminate in this conclusion, that holiness ought to be the end of all civil government. 'That thou mayest be a holy people unto the Lord thy God.'"[195]

On June 3, 1784, on the occasion of the completion of the New Hampshire state constitution, Samuel McClintock preached this same theme to that state's Senate and House of Representatives:

"As religion has a manifest tendency to promote the temporal as well as eternal interests of mankind, it is the duty of rulers to give all that countenance and support to religion that is consistent with liberty of conscience. And it is perfectly consistent with that liberty and equal protection which are secured to all denominations of Christians, by our excellent constitution, for rulers in the exercise of their authority to punish profane swearing, blasphemy, and open contempt of the institutions of religion, which have a fatal influence on the interests of society, and for which no man, in the exercise of reason, can plead conscience; and by their example, to encourage the practice of those things which all denominations allow to be essential in religion. Even on the supposition that the Christian religion were, as its enemies would insinuate, a cunningly devised fable, yet as its genius and precepts are so friendly to civil government; as it contains a system of the most pure and sublime morality, and enjoins on its professors in the most express manner, and by the most powerful sanctions, subjection to the powers that are ordained of God, it would be sound policy in rulers to give all possible countenance and encouragement to this religion as the means of strengthening their own hands; and to treat it with neglect and contempt, and teach the people by their own example to do so likewise, would be undermining their own authority; cutting off the branch on which they themselves stand; for when men have cast off the fear of God, it is a natural consequence, that neither will they regard man. The religion of Christ, where it has its proper influence on the hearts and lives of men, will not fail to make the best rulers and the best subjects. It is unnecessary to enlarge before rulers, one requisite qualification in whom is, that they are of the protestant religion: They will surely encourage and promote their own religion."[196]

On May 12, 1785, Samuel Wales, Congregational pastor in Connecticut and professor of divinity at Yale, preached the sermon, *The Dangers Of Our National Prosperity; And The Way To Avoid Them*, to the General Assembly of the State of Connecticut in Hartford. In it, he declared that proper civil government must be founded on Christian principles:

"Indeed never should it be forgotten that all the measures of civil policy ought to be founded on the great principles of religion; or, at the least, to be perfectly consistent with them: otherwise they will never be esteemed, because they will be contrary to that moral sense of right and wrong which God has implanted in the breast of every rational being. ... The practice of religion must therefore be considered as absolutely essential to the best state of public prosperity, it must be so, unless we may expect happiness in direct opposition to the constitution of nature and of nature's God. 'Righteousness exalteth a nation: but sin is a reproach to any people.' This is the course of nature, this is the voice of heaven, this the decree of God. ... We cannot therefore do a more faithful or important service for our country than to pray fervently and perseveringly to the Father of mercies, that He would by the energy of the Holy Ghost, form the hearts of this people to an holy life, and thus 'Purify unto Himself a peculiar people, zealous of good works.'"[197]

Insisting that political liberty depended on national virtue, Joseph Lathrop, pastor of the Congregational Church in West Springfield, Massachusetts, preached this message on December 14, 1787:

"Civil liberty is a very valuable blessing. It was the professed object of the late dangerous war. It is secured to us, as far as success in the prosecution of the war, wisdom in the settlement of the peace, and deliberation in framing our government, could secure it. Our own virtue and prudence, under providence, must do the rest.

"This is a land, not only of civil, but religious liberty. The enjoyment of gospel privileges was a grand motive with our ancestors to enterprise on emigration to this distant world. They brought with them the sacred scriptures, early formed churches for divine worship, diligently instructed their children in the knowledge of religion, erected private schools for their education, and, as soon as the abilities of the country would permit, they established larger seminaries, in which youth might be trained up for public employments, especially for the ministry, that this important office might not become useless and contemptible by falling into the hands of illiterate men. ...

"Political liberty depends on national virtue. Prevailing vice sooner or later introduces national slavery. Under almost any form of government a virtuous people will be free and happy. But a people sunk in corruption must be wretched. Their government, however liberal in its principles, will be severe in its administration, because they can subsist under no other. If we would convey to our children the greatest possible freedom, we must train them up in virtuous sentiments and manners."[198]

Elizur Goodrich, pastor of the Congregational Church in Durham, Connecticut, preached this same principle to that state's General Assembly on May 10, 1787:

"The end therefore, and nature of civil government imply that it must have for its foundation, the principles and laws of truth, justice and righteousness, mercy and the fear of God; or it can never advance the happiness of mankind. For that mankind by uniting into society, and putting themselves under a common government, can promote their true interest, otherwise than by observing these laws, is as contrary to reason as, that a machine may be of great and beneficial use in human life, when its whole construction is contrary to all the principles, by which the world of nature is actuated and kept together.

"There can be no beneficial union among the members of a community, where these great principles of righteousness and truth integrity and the fear of God, are not maintained, both among themselves, and towards all mankind. Any number of men, confederated together in wickedness and injustice, can have no strength, but what they derive from being faithful to one another. Such a combination may exist among robbers and pirates: but their agreement ought not to be dignified by the name of civil union: it ought rather to be esteemed a wicked conspiracy against the rights of mankind, which can never be justified by number, nor on any pretense of public good. … The same virtue and integrity, truth, justice and honor, which we venerate in a private character, must be found in the public administration, and generally prevailing among a people, or a state, cannot be united, peaceful and happy in itself, and respectable in the world. …

"Although some exclude religion and the profession and worship of the gospel from having any concern in the happiness of civil society and in the choice of rulers among a free people, yet without religion, a people happily united in all other respects, want the bond, most essentially necessary to preserve the union, and to excite every one to faithfulness in his station.

"The blessed gospel is therefore the best privilege which a people can enjoy; and were its precepts duly observed, the civil state would be in the best order, and in the most excellent condition. Persons of all ranks, according to their abilities, would be blessings to the community. … But, if we forget the God of our salvation, and neglect the means of virtue and religion, with which we are favored above any people on earth – if we are divided, and contend about every plan devised for strengthening the national union, and restoring the national honor and safety – if the several states, losing sight of the great end of the confederation, are influenced by mere local and partial motives, and if, in their respective and distinct jurisdictions, they forsake the paths of righteousness, we shall become the scorn and contempt of foreign nations, a prey to every bold invader; or fall by intestine divisions, till we sink into general ruin, and universal wretchedness. … If any one doubt this, let him consult the history of nations, and especially of Israel …"[199]

Samuel Langdon, president of Harvard College and pastor of the Congregational Church in Hampton Falls, New Hampshire, delivered the 1788 New Hampshire election sermon on June 5. In *The Republic Of The Israelites An Example To The American States* Langdon warned that if Americans ever renounced Christianity, their freedom, peace, and happiness would be no more:

"I call upon you to preserve the knowledge of God in the land, and attend to the revelation written to us from heaven. If you neglect or renounce that religion taught and commanded in the Holy Scriptures, think no more of freedom, peace, and happiness; the judgments of heaven will pursue you. Religion is not a vain thing for you because it is your life: it has been the glory and defense of New England from the infancy of the settlements; let it be also our glory and protection. I mean no other religion than what is divinely prescribed, which God himself has delivered to us with equal evidence of his authority, and even superior to that given to Israel, and which he has as strictly commanded us to receive and observe. ... And if our religion is given up, all the liberty we boast of will soon be gone; a profane and wicked people cannot hope for divine blessings, but it may be easily foretold that '*evil will befall them in the latter days.*'"[200]

Declaring that only "real" Christianity would provide political liberty, Samuel Miller, Presbyterian minister in New York City, preached this sermon, *A Sermon On The Anniversary Of The Independence Of America,* on July 4, 1793:

"[M]y fellow citizens, that I propose, on the present occasion, to offer you a few general remarks on the important influence of the Christian religion in promoting political freedom. ... I am well aware, that these words, taken in their proper sense, have a principal reference to liberty of a different kind from that to which I would accommodate and apply them. They refer to that glorious deliverance from the power, and the ignoble chains of sin and Satan, which is effected by the Spirit of the Lord, in every soul, in which his special and saving influences are found. They point out, also, that release from the bondage of the legal administration, which the gospel affords to all who receive it in sincerity and truth. But, as I am persuaded the proposition contained in our text is equally true, whether we understand it as speaking of spiritual or political liberty, we may safely apply it to the latter, without incurring the charge of unnatural perversion.

"The sentiment, then, which I shall deduce from the text, and to illustrate and urge which, shall be the principal object of the present discourse, is, *That the general prevalence of real Christianity, in any government, has a direct and immediate tendency to promote, and to confirm therein, political liberty.*"...

"The truth is, that political liberty does not rest, solely, on the form of government, under which a nation may happen to live. It does not consist, altogether, in the arrangement or in the balance of power; nor even in the rights and privileges which the constitution offers to every citizen. These indeed, must be acknowledged to have a considerable effect in its promotion or decline. But we shall find, on a close inspection, that something else is of equal, if not of greater importance. ... When, therefore, that *perfect law of liberty,* which this holy religion includes, prevails and governs in the minds of all, their freedom rests upon a basis more solid and immoveable, than human wisdom can devise. For the obvious tendency of this divine system, in all its parts, is, in the language of its great Author, to bring *deliverance to the captives, and the opening of the prison to them that are bound; to undo the heavy burthens; to let the oppressed go free; and to break every yoke.*

"The prevalence of real Christianity, tends to promote the principles and the love of political freedom, by the doctrines which it teaches, concerning the human character, and the unalienable rights of mankind; and by the virtues which it inculcates, and leads its votaries to practice.

"Can oppression and slavery prevail among any people who properly understand, and are suitably impressed with, those great gospel truths, that all men are, by nature, equal – children of the same common Father – dependent upon the same mighty power, and candidates for the same glorious immortality? Must not despotism hide his head in those regions, where the relations of man to man are distinctly realized – where citizens, of every rank, are considered as a band of brethren, and where the haughty pretensions of family and blood, are viewed in all their native absurdity, and in those odious colors in which this sublime system represents them? In short, must not every sentiment, favorable to slavery, be forever banished from a nation, in which, by means of the benign light of the glorious sun of righteousness, all the human race are viewed as subject to the same great laws, and amenable to the same awful tribunal, in the end.

"Christianity, on the one hand, teaches those, who are raised to places of authority, that they are not intrinsically greater than those whom they govern; and that all the rational and justifiable power with which they are invested, flows from the people, and is dependent on their sovereign pleasure. There is a love of dominion natural to every human creature; and in those who are destitute of religion, this temper is apt to reign uncontrolled. Hence experience has always testified, that rulers, left to themselves, are prone to imagine, that they are a superior order of beings, to obey whom, the ignoble multitude was made, and that their aggrandizement is the principal design of the social compact. But the religion of the gospel, rightly understood, and cordially embraced, utterly disclaims such unworthy sentiments, and banishes them with abhorrence from the mind. It contemplates the happiness of the community, as the primary object of all political associations – and it teaches those, who are placed at the helm of government, to remember, that they are called to preside over equals and friends, whose best interest, and not the demands of selfishness, is to be the object of their first and highest care.

"On the other hand, Christianity, wherever it exerts its native influence, leads every citizen to reverence himself – to cherish a free and manly spirit – to think with boldness and energy – to form his principles upon fair enquiry, and to resign neither his conscience nor his person to the capricious will of men. It teaches, and it creates in the mind, a noble contempt for that abject submission to the encroachments of despotism, to which the ignorant and the unprincipled readily yield. It forbids us to call, or to acknowledge, any one master upon earth, knowing that we have a Master in heaven, to whom both rulers, and those whom they govern, are equally accountable. In a word, Christianity, by illuminating the minds of men, leads them to consider themselves, as they really are, all co-ordinate terrestrial princes, stripped, indeed, of the empty pageantry and title, but retaining the substance of dignity and power. Under the influence of this illumination, how natural to disdain the shackles of oppression – to take the alarm at every attempt to trample on their just rights; and to pull down, with indignation, from the seat of authority, every bold invader!

"But again – The prevalence of Christianity promotes the principles and the love of political freedom, not only by the knowledge which it affords of the human character, and of the unalienable rights of mankind, but also by the duties which it inculcates, and leads its votaries to discharge. …

"No less extensively beneficial in its effects on civil liberty, is that pure and refined benevolence, which the Christian system inculcates, and establishes in the minds of those who are under its government. Though the constitution of a country be ever so defective; yet if every rank of citizens be under the habitual influence of that universal charity and good will, which is one of the distinguished glories of our holy religion, there will freedom substantially flourish. To suppose that oppression, with the numerous hell-born woes, which follow in his train, can be cherished in regions, where the mild spirit of benevolence and love reigns, is to suppose that the most discordant principles are capable of uniting; that demons of darkness, and angels of light can dwell together in harmony. Impossible! Wherever that heavenly temper is found, which, like the Deity himself, delights in showering down blessings, both on enemies and friends; there will the unalienable rights of men be acknowledged, and every infringement of them will be viewed with abhorrence. …

"Christianity, more powerful than human strength, and more efficacious than human law, regulates the passions, and roots out the corruptions of men. It not only tames the savage breast, and gives a deadly blow to barbarity of manners; but also tends to quench every extravagant thirst for power; to beat down every high thought, that exalteth itself against the general good; and to render men contented with those rights which the God of nature gave them. While these dispositions prevail, slavery must stand at an awful distance, bound in chains … [T]here never was a government, in which the knowledge of pure and undefiled Christianity prevailed, in which, at the same time, despotism held his throne without control. …

"Again; if it be a solemn truth, that the prevalence of Christianity, has a natural and immediate tendency to promote political freedom, then, those are the truest and the wisest patriots, who study to increase its influence in society. Hence it becomes every American citizen to consider this as the great palladium of our liberty, demanding our first and highest care."[201]

On May 8, 1794, Jonathan Edwards, Jr., pastor of White Haven Church in New Haven, Connecticut, hammered the same point in his Connecticut election sermon, *The Necessity Of The Belief Of Christianity*:

"Therefore the subject, which I beg leave to propose from our text for present consideration, is this, The necessity of a belief of Christianity by the citizens of this state, in order to our public and political prosperity. For if that people only be happy or prosperous, whose God is the Lord; and if to believe and comply with Christianity be implied in having the Lord for our God; it follows, that the belief of Christianity by the citizens of this state, is necessary to our political prosperity.

"Political prosperity requires the general practice of a strict morality. But this cannot be so well secured by any other means, as by a belief of Christianity. Motives of a religious kind appear to be necessary to restrain men from vice and immorality. Civil pains and penalties alone are by no means sufficient to this end; nor are civil honors and rewards sufficient encouragements to the practice of virtue in general.

"The best and perhaps the only remedy for such diseases, is a full belief of the divine universal providence, of the accountableness of all men to God for all their conduct, and of a future equal retribution.

"Some religion then, and some belief of a future state is necessary to our political prosperity. But what religion shall we adopt? And what system concerning a future state is most useful to the state? It is not possible to introduce and give a general spread through the state, to Mahometanism or paganism; and it would be a work of time and of great difficulty, to lead the citizens in general into the belief of deism or what is called the philosophical religion. Therefore we seem necessitated to have recourse to Christianity: and this is most excellently adapted to the ends of restraining men from vice and promoting that general practice of strict morality, which is so essential to the political prosperity of any people. It is adapted to these ends by its precepts; by the moral character of the author of those precepts; by his absolute supremacy and sovereignty; by the motives of reward and punishment with which those precepts are enforced; by the facts which it relates, and by the examples which it exhibits. It is enforced not by the bare authority of our feeble reason, but by the authority of our creator, our judge, and our all-perfect God. It depends not on the obscure investigations, subtle refinements and uncertain conclusions of human intellect; but on the omniscience, the veracity, the justice, the goodness and the will of God: And thus it is excellently adapted to the principles and feelings which are common to human nature, and which exist in the weakest and most ignorant, as well as the most intelligent and learned. … Above all, the motives arising from the doctrines of the final judgment and a future state, lay an inconceivably greater restraint on the depravity of human nature, than any thing that is or can be suggested by the philosophical religion.

"Agreeably to the gospel all men are to be rewarded according to their works done in the body, whether they be good or evil. Some are to be beaten with few stripes, some with many stripes, according to their several aggravations of guilt. But in the future punishment which infidels admit, there is nothing vindictive, nothing therefore which is intended to support law and government. The only punishment which they admit, is that which is designed for the good of the person punished; and therefore as soon as the person punished repents, he is released. Now it is manifest on the slightest reflection, that the motive to avoid sin and vice on this plan, is exceedingly diminished from what it is on the plan of the gospel. On the plan of the gospel the motive is endless misery, proportioned in degree to the demerit of the person punished. On the infidel plan it is a merciful chastisement, which is to continue no longer than till the subject shall repent. And as every sinner will naturally flatter himself, that he shall repent as soon as he shall find his punishment to be intolerable; so all the punishment, which on this plan he will expect, is one that shall continue but for a moment, after it shall have become extreme or intolerable.

"[S]ince Christianity appears to be necessary to the public good of the state, it ought to be encouraged by magistrates and rulers of every description. They are appointed to be the guardians of the public good; of course it is their duty to protect and promote every thing tending to it, and especially every thing necessary to it. Therefore as Christianity is necessary to the public good, they are bound to encourage, promote and inculcate that, by their example and profession, by speaking and acting in favor of it both in public and private, by supporting Christian ordinances and worship, and by promoting to places of trust and profit those who profess it and live agreeably, and who are otherwise properly qualified.

"For the same reasons the citizens in general are obligated to encourage and promote Christianity, by being themselves Christians and that not only in profession, but in heart and life, and by giving their suffrages for those who are of the same character. It is indeed to be confessed, that not all professed Christians are good men or real Christians; yet among professed Christians are many men, who possess good abilities and a proper share of information, who are strictly moral and upright, and who expect to give an account of their conduct to God. Such are the men to be promoted in the state; and the citizens by promoting such men, will encourage and promote Christianity, and at the same time promote the good of the state.

"Since the belief and practice of Christianity are so necessary to the political good of our state, and since you are appointed to be the guardians of our political good, I thought it not impertinent to suggest to you some important means, by which you may obtain the end for which you are appointed. Opposition to Christianity both in faith and practice was never, at least in our country, so great and so increasing, as at the present day. It lies with you, gentlemen, by a steady belief, profession and practice of Christianity; by your conversation and weight; by the appointments which you shall make to the various offices, civil and military, and by all your public proceedings, to withstand this opposition, and to guard against the danger to the public good, arising from the depravity of manners which opposition to Christianity naturally induces. It is your province, in conjunction with his Excellency the Governor, to appoint all our executive civil authority and to confer the higher military honors. When men of licentious principles and practice are promoted either in the civil or military line, it gives a dignity and an influence to vice and irreligion. And "one sinner destroys much good," especially when exalted to a high station of honor and authority. Now, if you give this advantage to vice, you will thereby injure the state; but more immediately you will injure religion and the kingdom of Christ. And let me beseech you to remember, that you also have a master in heaven, to whom you, as well as the rest of men, must give an account. The only way to gain his approbation is, to keep a conscience void of offense, and in your political transactions not to act from party attachments and private connections, not to practice intrigue to serve your own interests or those of your friends; but to endeavor to serve the public in the best manner according to your capacity and opportunity. In so doing you will appoint to the several executive offices, men of knowledge and discretion; men that fear God and hate covetousness; men who will be just and rule in the fear of God. By the promotion of such men, virtue will be encouraged and vice will be restrained; by their official proceedings, law and justice will be executed, and "judgment will run down as waters, and righteousness as a mighty stream," even that righteousness which exalteth a nation. Then shall our political interests be in a prosperous state; then shall we be that happy people whose God is the Lord. ... Of all forms of government a republic most essentially requires virtue and good morals in the great body of the people, in order to its prosperity and even its existence."[202]

February 19, 1795 was declared by President George Washington as a day of national thanksgiving and prayer. On that day, Bishop James Madison, Episcopal Bishop and president of the College of William and Mary, preached *Manifestations Of The Beneficence Of Divine Providence Towards America* in Richmond, Virginia. In it, he declared,

"[V]irtue is the vital principle of a republic, that unless a magnanimous spirit of patriotism animates every breast, unless a sincere and ardent love for justice, for temperance, for prudence, for fortitude, in short, for all those qualities, which dignify human nature, pervades, enlivens, invigorates the whole mass of citizens, these fair superstructures of political wisdom must soon crumble into dust. Certainly, my brethren, it is a fundamental maxim, that virtue is the soul of a republic. But, zealous for the prosperity of my country, I will repeat, and in these days, it is of infinite moment to insist, that without religion, I mean *rational religion*, the religion which our Savior himself delivered, not that of fanatics or inquisitors, chimeras and shadows are substantial things compared with that virtue, which those who reject the authority of religion would recommend to our practice. Ye then who love your country if you expect or wish, that real virtue and social happiness should be preserved among us, or, that genuine patriotism and a dignified obedience to law, instead of that spirit of disorganizing anarchy, and those false and hollow pretenses to patriotism, which are so pregnant with contentions, insurrections and misery, should be the distinguishing characteristics of Americans; or, that, the same Almighty arm which hath hitherto protected your country, and conducted her to this day of glory, should still continue to shield and defend her, remember, that your first and last duty is "to fear the Lord and to serve him"; remember, that in the same proportion as irreligion advances, virtue retires; remember, that in her stead, will succeed factions, ever ready to prostitute public good to the most nefarious private ends, whilst unbounded licentiousness, and a total disregard to the sacred names of liberty and of patriotism will here once more, realize that fatal catastrophe, which so many free states have already experienced. Remember, the law of the Almighty is, they shall expire, with their expiring virtue. God of all nature!

"And hath it not been generally true, that ignorance, a neglect of God and his worship, idleness, luxury, dissolute manners, and factions, have been certain preludes to the destruction of states and empires? Is not this abundantly proved by the histories of ancient times? Was not this verified in the destruction of Sparta, Athens, Rome? And if we may reason from past events, we may safely presume, that like causes will produce similar effects, however we may be involved in the issue.

"Though it pleases God not to reward or punish individuals in this life, according to their merit or demerit, as appears by the histories of the prophets and apostles, by the parable of Dives and Lazarus, by the prosperity of Nero, and the misfortunes of Louis; yet heaven hath balanced national virtue by affluence, and vice by a counterpoise of adversity. Nothing, then, can be a greater stimulus to a virtuous government, to adopt the most energetic measures, that religion and every species of virtue may be encouraged: On the other hand, that vice, with its baneful retinue, and whatever may be derogatory to the citizen, the statesman, or the Christian, may be discountenanced, and meet with an exemplary punishment! The officers of government have a price put into their hands, to promote the interest of their brethren, and the common cause of virtue. And when they are repeatedly, by the suffrages of their country, called into office, it is an evidence in their favor, and a public declaration, that their past conduct hath been approved."[203]

WHAT THEY ACTUALLY PREACHED IN THOSE ELECTION SERMONS

Many of the sermon excerpts cited thus far are actually from election sermons, so the following will simply serve to provide extra examples of the content of this type of sermon. The following examples present the range of subjects covered in these election sermons. (These excerpts are taken from election and artillery sermons and one Boston Thursday Lecture sermon by Rev. Benjamin Coleman.)

- The power of government lies with the people:

Thomas Hooker's sermon delivered in Hartford, Connecticut on May 31, 1638 (One of the earliest election sermons preached in America on record):

> "That the choice of public magistrates belongs unto the people by God's own allowance. The privileges of election which belong to the people therefore must not be exercised according to their humors but according to the blessed will and law of God. ... They who have power to appoint officers and magistrates, it is in their power also, to set the bounds and limitations of the power and place unto which they call them. ... Because the foundation of authority is laid, firstly, in the free consent of the people. ... As God has given us liberty let us take it."[204]

John Davenport's Massachusetts Election Sermon preached before the General Court in Boston on May 19, 1669:

> "[Civil rule is] God's Ordinance. It is from the Light and the Law of Nature and the Law of Nature is God's Law ... it is necessary that they [men] be joined in a Civil-Society; ... the power of making Laws, followeth naturally, though the manner of Union, in a Political Body, is voluntary ... the designation of these or those to be Civil Rulers, leaving out others is from God, by the People's free Choice, at least by the Suffrages of the major part of them, wherein the rest must acquiesce. This Power of Rulers of the Common-wealth is derived from the People's free Choice ... for the Power of Government is originally in the People ... the People so give the Magisterial Power unto some, as that they still retain in themselves these three Acts, 1. That they may measure out so much Civil Power, as God in his Word Alloweth to them, and no more, nor less. 2. That they may set bounds and banks to

the exercise of that Power, so as it may not be exuberant, above the laws, and due Rights and Liberties of the People. 3. That they give it out conditionally, upon this or that condition; so as, if the condition is violated, they may resume their power of choosing another."[205]

- Government is subordinate to the laws of God:

Ebenezer Pemberton's Massachusetts election sermon, *On the Powers and Limitations of Magistrates*, preached on May 31, 1710:

"The Power of the greatest Potentate on Earth is not Inherent in him, but is a Derivative. ... For God is the Source and Original of all Power; there is no Power but what is derived from him, depends on him, is limited by him, and is subordinate to him, and accountable ... Rulers are to be the Guardians of their Peoples' Religion and Property, their Liberties, Civil & Sacred. ... Hence Rulers, of all Orders, ought to conform to and regulate them- selves in all their Administrations, by this Divine Standard. ... They must govern themselves by unalterable principles, and fixed Rules, and not by unaccountable humors, or arbitrary will. ... It is a Statute of the Great Law-giver of the World, that they which Rule over Men be Just. ... Rulers have Power, but it is a limited Authority; limited by the Will of God, and Right Reason, by the General Rules of Government, and the particular Laws Stated in a Land ... 'Hence, this Character of Rulers [Gods] requires ... That they take care that Righteous Laws be Enacted, none but such, and all such, as are necessary for the Safety of the Religion & Liberties of a People. ... Rulers must be. ... Just to the Laws and the Established Constitution they are under: ... God Himself has called you Gods; but those that are not skillful, thoughtful vigilant and active to promote the Public Safety and Happiness, are not Gods but dead Idols. ... it can never go well with a People, when Government is brought into Contempt. Government has something too Divine in it to be insulted, and rudely treated. ... I am not Ignorant to what an extravagant height the Doctrine of Submission to Rulers has been carried by some, and I wish I could see no danger of the Contrary Extreme of depressing it to a mere Nullity. Extremes on both hands are to be avoided; for both are dangerous to a State. The One may Expose a People to the Oppression of Sullen Tyranny; the Other to the Confusions of Lawless Anarchy: ... Doubtless God has not left a State without a Regular Remedy to Save itself, when the Fundamental Constitution of a People is overturned; their Laws and Liberties, Religion and Properties are openly Invaded, and ready to be made a Public Sacrifice. But on the other side it is beyond me to imagine that the God of Order has ever invested any men of a Private Station, who can with a Nod inflame and raise the Multitude with a Lawless Power, on pretense of Public Mismanagements, to Embroil the State, Overturn the Foundations of Government."[206]

John Bulkley's Connecticut election sermon, *The Necessity of Religion in Societies*, preached before the Connecticut General Court in Hartford on May 14, 1713:

"It's not in the Power of Rulers to make what Laws they please, Suspend, Abrogate or Disannul them at pleasure.... As for Men's Civil Rights, as Life, Liberty, Estate, &c. God has not Subjected these to the Will & Pleasure of Rulers. They may not Enact any Laws to the Prejudice of them, nor Disanul such Laws of the State as tend to Secure these Interests.... Tis already Determin'd in the Divine Law (with relation to these Interests of a People) that the Enjoyment of them be free & undisturb'd and Rulers may not make any Determinations repugnant here to: Or, if they do, they are of no force. No Law of the Civil Magistrate can bind in Opposition to the Divine.... And as to such things being indifferent in their own Nature, and not already Determin'd in the Law of God, nor by Principle deducible therefrom, altho' they are subject to the Determination of Humane Authority, yet all must be done in due Subordination to those Laws of God that have made it a Sin in any to invade these Rights of a People. ... In elective states, where Persons are Advanc'd by the Suffrage of others to Places of Rule, and vested with Civil Power, the Persons Chosing give not the Power, but God .... And hence it is, that Humane Laws bind the Conscience; Not simply as Humane, but as made by that Authority which is Divine in its Original, and to which Obedience is Commanded in the Divine Law."[207]

Nathaniel Appleton's Massachusetts election sermon, *The Great Blessing of Good Rulers, Depends Upon God's Giving His Judgments And His Righteousness To Them*, preached in Boston on May 26, 1742:

"The Grand charter which the Sovereign of the World has given to Magistrates, empowers them to make Orders and By-Laws (for human Laws are no other) for the well-ordering and governing civil Societies, but it is with this Limitation and Proviso, that they be not repugnant to the Law of God, which is the Law of Justice, Truth, Mercy and Goodness, your Laws then must be tempered after the same Manner."[208]

- Abusive government:

John Hancock's Massachusetts election sermon, *Rulers Should Be Benefactors*, preached in Boston on May 30, 1722:

"[Abusive rulers are] the greatest Burdens unto Mankind, and the greatest Plagues and punishments to the World. … if you should abuse your Power, and go over all the bounds of your Duty & Obligations; oppress & vex this People, and lay heavy burdens upon them, and grievous to be born; you'd forfeit the gratitude and regard due to Benefactors; and become obnoxious not only to the resentments of the People groaning under their burdens, but also to the Divine Displeasure; … As Oppression makes a wise man mad, so it makes a righteous God angry."[209]

- The purpose of government is the public good:

Azariah Mather's Connecticut election sermon, *Good Rulers A Choice Blessing*, preached in Hartford on May 13, 1725:

"The great subordinate End is the Publick good; the Means and Laws of Government must be calculated to work and bring about that End and Effect. And a good Ruler knows these Maxims are not only founded in Nature, but expressly asserted in God's Word: … All shall be Sacrificed to subserve the Publick."[210]

- Human government was instituted by God:

Benjamin Coleman's Thursday Lecture sermon preached in Boston on August 13, 1730:

"The order and happiness of this lower world, the peace and weal of it, depend on the civil government which God has ordained in it. All this is very elegant and rhetorical, a high and noble strain of speech, upon the highest subject that belongs to this our earth. The Great God has made the governments and rulers of the earth its pillars, and has set the world upon them. … The governments and rulers of the earth are its pillars in respect of strength to uphold and support the virtue, order and peace of it. … Both the order & the persons are of the Lord's ordering, constituting and appointing. Civil government is of divine institution, and God commissions and entrusts with the administration whom he pleases. The great King of the World has order'd a government in it, and he raises up governors, supreme and subordinate. There is no Power but of God; the Powers that be are ordained of Him. He puts the scepter into the hand, and the spirit of government into the heart. … The virtue and religion of a people, their riches and trade, their power, honor and reputation; and the favor of God toward them, with his blessing on them; do greatly depend on the pious, righteous and faithful government which they are under. … Government is not a creature of man's lust and will, but of divine constitution, and from a necessity in the nature of things. The very being and weal of society depends thereon.

"Government was not in the original of it assumed or usurped by any one man. For instance, not by Lamech before the Flood, nor by Nimrod after it. Indeed the spirit of tyranny, and the lust of dominion, seem to have began in them; but order & rule was before them. Mankind naturally went into that, and these were the men who made the first breaches on it; the one being of the race of Cain, the other of Ham; who have had some of their likeness in every place, and thro' all generations; that would turn the world upside down and overthrow the foundations which God has laid.

"In a word, magistracy, like the other ordinances of heaven, stands by the power and blessing of God; who effectually owns it and works by it, establishes the earth and it abideth. He has graven it deep in the hearts of men, even as the desire of happiness and self-preservation. He has as much ordained, that while the earth remaineth civil order and government shall not cease; as he has sworn that seed time and harvest, cold and heat, summer and winter, day and night, shall not. Both the one and the other equally continue to the world's end, absolutely necessary to the life, comfort and welfare of mankind. … See the divine wisdom and goodness in ordaining and establishing a magistracy and government in the world. It is one of the many great instances, wherein the Supreme Governor of the world has taken care for the universal and perpetual weal of it. And they that would be lawless and ungoverned, despising dominion and speaking evil of dignity, distinction, authority and rule among men, act as madly and mischievously as one would do, that should go into a house and sap the foundation of it, till it fall upon him and crush him to death."[211]

- Government must act according to the Constitution and its laws:

John Barnard's Massachusetts election sermon, *The Throne Established By Righteousness,* preached in Boston on May 29, 1734:

"It is certain, (with a proper Salvo to the natural Rights of Mankind, which it is the End of all Government to preserve,) none can have any Right to act contrary to the fundamental Laws of that State, till all Parties concerned agree upon such Alterations as are thought needful, and then those Alterations become wrought into the Constitution, and are a certain Rule for all the Parts of the Government to go by, in their future Administrations. … For where, (as in mixed Government especially,) there are peculiar Rights and Powers belonging to the Throne, and some peculiar Rights and Privileges belonging to the People; and where, again, the Rights and Powers of the Throne are branched out, and divided among the several Partners in Rule, to each their proper Portion; nothing is more plain than that, Righteousness requires, that no one invade the Right that peculiarly belongs to another. ... So that it is the first Point of Righteousness in a State, to act upon the Constitution; because every Part of the Government, … have as full and just Right ... in and to that Part of Power, or to those Privileges, which are assigned and made over to them, in the very Foundation of the Government, as any Man has, or can have, to what he calls his own; … the Rulers are to govern according to Law. When the Kingdom was founded in Israel, Samuel wrote the Manner of the Kingdom in a Book, and laid it up before the Lord, … that it might be their Magna Charta, the fundamental Constitution of the Kingdom, and the standing Rule of their Government for the future. … Thus it will be found, ... an equal departure from the Rule of Righteousness, to wrest the Sword out of the Hand of him to whom the Constitution has committed it, as to snatch the Purse from those that have the keeping of it. … Thus Righteousness in Rulers requires them to adjust all the Parts of their Administration to the true Rights, Liberties, and Privileges of the Subject. These are various in their Kind, and more or less, in Number, and Degree, according to the Nature of the Constitution, and are in wrought into it; … There is nothing a people are more tender of than These. … will not be persuaded easily to part with them. … No Sum would be tho't too much to be given for the peculiar Privileges of some People, nor can they be defended at too dear a Rate; and therefore These ought to be preserved inviolate, … Hence it is the highest Point of Righteousness, in the Rulers of a People, the primary Design of whose Institution was to secure the Community in their Rights, to be very careful to maintain entire, and untouched, those natural and civil, Liberties, and Privileges, which are the Property of every Member of the Society."[212]

- The definition of despotic government:

Jared Eliot's Connecticut Election Sermon, *Give Caesar His Due,* preached in Hartford on May 11, 1738 clearly defined the difference between despotic and legal government:

"Arbitrary Despotic Government, is, When this Sovereign Power is directed by the Passions, Ignorance & Lust of them that Rule. And a Legal Government is, When this Arbitrary & Sovereign Power puts itself under Restraints, and lays itself under Limitations, in all Instances where they see it Either possible or probable, that the Exercise of this Sovereign Power may prove or have proved Prejudicial or Mischievous to the Subject: Even this is an Act of Sovereign Power. This is what we call a Legal Limited & well Constituted Government. Under such a Government only there is true Liberty."[213]

- Principles of good government are found in Scripture:

Solomon William's Connecticut election sermon preached in Hartford in 1741 pointed out that the source of government that respects the rights of men can be found only in Scripture:

"In the Law of God they will find the best Maxims and Rules of Government they can ever be furnish'd with .... There never was nor can be any wisdom among men, but what is communicated from God; nor is there any Law of Nature, or Rule of Natural & Moral wisdom, which we speak of, as implanted in the Mind of man, but what is found in the Bible, and cultivated and improved by that Revelation ... Here you learn, That every man has an indisputable right to all the good things which God gives him by Nature and Providence, his own Labor or regular Compacts, Agreements and Constitutions made between men; and that these are to be inviolably secured to every man till he forfeits them. Here Rulers are taught to seek the virtue and happiness of their People, as the end of Government ... Besides, it teaches them the just measures of their authority & all the true Uses of it, as 'tis derived from the Supreme Lord for the good of the People, and to be used for Him, to promote their Felicity, according to the just, natural & covenanted Rights of the people ..."[214]

- Man's sinful nature makes government necessary:

Preaching to the Supreme Court of Massachusetts in 1779, Samuel Stillman said,

"Such an instance affords us many important lessons, and calls upon us to guard as much as possible in *our beginning*, against the corruption of human nature. We should leave nothing to human virtue, that can be provided for by law or the constitution. The more we trust in the hands of any man, the more we try his virtue, which, at some fatal hour, may yield to a temptation; and the people discover their error, when it is too late to prevent the mischief."[215]

Charles Chauncy's Massachusetts election sermon preached in Boston on May 27, 1747 stressed that it was because of man's sin that God ordained human government:

"The present circumstances of the human race are therefore such, by means of sin, that 'tis necessary they should, for their mutual defense and safety, combine together in distinct societies, lodging as much power in the hands of a few, as may be sufficient to restrain the irregularities of the rest, and keep them within the bounds of a just decorum. Such a superiority in some, and inferiority in others, is perfectly adjusted to the present state of mankind. Their circumstances require it. They could not live, either comfortably or safely without it.

"And from hence, strictly and properly speaking, does that civil order there is among men take rise. Nor will it from hence follow, that government is a mere humane constitution. For as it originates in the reason of things, 'tis, at the same time, essentially founded on the will of God. For the voice of reason is the voice of God: And he as truly speaks to men by the reason of things, their mutual relations to and dependencies on each other, as if he uttered his voice from the excellent glory. And in this way, primarily, he declares his will respecting a civil subordination among men. The suitableness of order and superiority, both to the nature of man, and his circumstances in the world, together with its necessary connection, in the nature of things, with his safety and happiness, is such an indication of the divine pleasure, that there should be government, as cannot be gainsay'd nor resisted. …

"If the prerogatives of the King are sacred, so also are the rights of Lords and Commons." If either oversteps its rights or invades those of another part "the law of righteousness is violated: ... if one part of the government is really kept from exerting itself, according to the true meaning of the constitution, … the designed balance is no longer preserved; and which side soever the scale turns, whether on the side of sovereignty, or popularity, 'tis forced down by a false weight, which by degrees, will overturn the government, at least, according to this particular model." And the case is the same in dependent governments, especially where the derived constitution is divided into several ruling parts. Here also the constitution is evidently the 'grand rule to all clothed with power, or claiming privilege, in either branch of the government.'"[216]

Eventually, as the war with Britain became more probable, the content of the election sermons began to shift from the subject of government to the defense of liberty. Dim foreshadowings of the impending clash can be seen in these sermons as the patriot preachers used them to issue a clarion call to arms using their sizeable influence to rally the colonists to the cause of liberty and independence. Consider:

- The defense of liberty is God's will:

James Cogswell's artillery sermon, *God the Pious Soldier's Strength And Instructor*, preached in Pomfret, Connecticut on April 13, 1757 to a company of soldiers under the command of Capt. Israel Putnam:

"There is a Principle of Self-Defense and Preservation, implanted in our very Natures, which is necessary to us almost as our Beings, and which no positive Law of God ever yet contradicted. … When our Liberty is invaded and struck at, 'tis sufficient Reason for our making War for the Defense or Recovery of it. Liberty is one of the most sacred and inviolable Privileges Mankind enjoy; … what Comfort can a Man take in Life when at the Disposal of a despotic and arbitrary Tyrant, who has no other law but his Will: ... To live is to be free: Therefore when our Liberty is attacked, and clandestine, underhand Machinations, or open Violence threaten us with the loss of so dear a Blessing, 'tis Time to rouse, and defend our undoubted and invaluable Privileges … When our Religion is in danger ... it will warrant our Engaging in War … Religion is a treasure never to be parted with … we fight for our Properties, our Liberties, our Religion, our Lives"[217]

Samuel Cook's election sermon to the Massachusetts General Court preached on May 30, 1770:

"America now pleads her right to her possessions, which she cannot resign while she apprehends she has truth and justice on her side. Americans esteem it their greatest infelicity that, through necessity, they are thus led to plead with their parent state, the land of their forefathers nativity, whose interest has always been dear to them, and whose wealth they have increased by their removal more than their own. They have assisted in fighting her battles, and greatly enlarged her empire, and, God helping, will yet extend it through the boundless desert, until it reaches from sea to sea. They glory in the British constitution, and are abhorrent, to a man, of the most distant thought of withdrawing their allegiance from their gracious sovereign and becoming an independent state. And though, with unwearied toil, the colonists can now subsist upon the labors of their own hands, which they must be driven to when deprived of the means of purchase, yet they are fully sensible of the mutual benefits of an equitable commerce with the parent country, and cheerfully submit to regulations of trade productive of the common interest. These their claims the Americans consider not as novel, or wantonly made, but founded in nature, in compact, in their right as men and British subjects; the same which their forefathers, the first occupants, made and asserted as the terms of their removal, with their effects, into this wilderness and with which the glory and interest of their king and all his dominions are connected. May these alarming disputes be brought to a just and speedy issue, and peace and harmony be restored!

"But while, in imitation of our pious forefathers, we are aiming at the security of our liberties, we should all be concerned to express by our conduct their piety and virtue, and in a day of darkness and general distress carefully avoid everything offensive to God or injurious to men. It belongs not only to rulers, but subjects also, to set the Lord always before their face, and act in his fear. While under government we claim a right to be treated as men, we must act in character by yielding that subjection which becometh us as men. Let every attempt to secure our liberties be conducted with a manly fortitude, but with that respectful decency which reason approves, and which alone gives weight to the most salutary measures. Let nothing divert us from the paths of truth and peace, which are the ways of God, and then we may be sure that he will be with us, as he was with our fathers, and never leave nor forsake us."[218]

John Tucker's Massachusetts election sermon preached in Cambridge on May 29, 1771:

"[T]he people as well as their rulers are the proper judges of the civil constitution they are under and of their own rights and principles. … Unlimited submission is not due to government in a free state. There are certain boundaries beyond which submission cannot be justly required, and should not be yielded. [The people] have an undoubted privilege to complain of unconstitutional measures in government, and of unlawful encroachments upon their rights, and may, while they do it with becoming decency, do it with that noble freedom and firmness which a sense of wrong joined with the love of liberty will inspire. … Sirs, it is not necessary if our constitutional rights and privileges should be demanded, we should readily yield to the unrighteous claim. Should we thus meanly resign them up, and take in exchange the chains of slavery for ourselves and children, could we forgive ourselves? Would our unhappy posterity forgive us? Would we not deserve the punishment while we felt the guilt of assassins, for having stabbed the vitals of our country?"[219]

Gad Hitchcock's Massachusetts election sermon preached on May 25, 1774:

"Our danger is not visionary but real; our contention is not about trifles, but about liberty and property, and not ours only, but those of posterity to the latest generation. ... If I am mistaken in supposing plans are formed and executing, subversive of our natural and chartered rights and privileges, and incompatible with every idea of liberty, all America is mistaken with me. Our continued complaints, our repeated humble, but fruitless, unregarded petitions and remonstrances, and, if I may be allowed the sacred allusion, our groanings that can not be uttered, are at once indications of our sufferings, and the feeling sense we have of them. ... King George may say the evils that produce this state of things are imaginary, but I tell you and I tell the tyrant to his face, it is because the wicked bear rule."[220]

John Lathrop's artillery sermon preached to the Ancient and Honorable Artillery Company in Boston on June 6, 1774:

"[The] original compacts ... which lie in the foundation of all civil societies, may not be disturbed. A single article may not be altered but with the consent of the whole body. — Whoever makes an alteration in the established constitution, whether he be a subject or a ruler, is guilty of treason. Treason of the worst kind: Treason against the state.... That we may and ought, to resist, and even make war against those rulers who leap the bounds prescribed them by the constitution, and attempt to oppress and enslave the subjects, is a principle on which alone the great revolutions which have taken place in our nation can be justified."[221]

Jonas Clark's Massachusetts election sermon preached in Boston on May 31, 1781:

"'Tis not indeed pretended that any one man or number of men have any natural right or superiority, or inherent claim of dominion or governmental authority over any other man or body of men. All men are by nature free and equal and independent in this matter. It is in compact, and in compact alone, that all just government is founded. The first steps in entering into society, and towards the establishment of civil government among a people, is the forming, agreeing to, and ratifying an original compact for the regulation of the state — describing and determining the mode, departments, and powers of the government, and the rights, privileges and duties of the subjects." This must be done by the whole body of the people, or by leaders or delegates of their choice. This right of the people, whether emerging from a state of nature, or the yoke of oppression, is an unalienable right. It cannot be disposed of or given up by a people, even though ever so much inclined to sell or sacrifice their birthright in this matter.

"While the social compact exists, the whole state and its members are bound by it; and a sacred regard ought to be paid to it. No man, party, order, or body of men in the state have any right, power, or authority to alter, change, or violate the social compact. Nor can any change, amendment, or alteration be introduced but by common consent. It remains, however, with the community, state or nation, as a public, political body, at any time, a.t pleasure, to change, alter, or totally dissolve the constitution, and return to a state of nature, or to form a new government as to them may seem meet. These principles being admitted, it is evident that no man or body of men, however great or good — no nation, kingdom or power on earth, hath any right to make or impose a constitution or government upon a free people.

"Equality and independence are the just claim — the indefeasible birthright of men. In a state of nature, as individuals, in society, as states or nations, nothing short of these ever did or ever will satisfy a man or a people truly free — truly brave. When opportunity offers, and power is given, it is beyond dispute the duty of the subjected nation to assert its liberty; to shake off the foreign yoke, and maintain its equality and independence among the nations.

"The principles of reason, the laws of nature, and the rules of justice and equity, give men a right to select their form of government. Even God himself, the supreme ruler of the world, whose government is absolute and uncontrollable, hath ever paid a sacred attention to this important right — hath ever patronized this interesting claim in the sons of men. The only constitution of civil government that can plead its origin as direct from heaven, is the theocracy of the Hebrews; but even this form of government, though dictated by infinite wisdom, and written by the finger of God, was laid before the people for their consideration, and was ratified, introduced, and established by common consent."[222]

Just imagine the impact it would have on our government today if, at the beginning of the legislative sessions in each of the states and at the beginning of each new Congress in Washington D.C., all of the legislators gathered together to listen to sermons like the ones you have just read. The effect would no doubt be the same as it was in the 1770s – our government would be more godly and far more constitutional.

Believing that government was as much an institution of God as the family and the church, many of the sermons of the Black Robed Regiment focused on the biblical definition and grounds of good government. Their sermons could have been used as civics lessons in school …

Chapter 14

THEIR SERMONS WERE "CIVICS LESSONS"

"I must study Politicks and War that my sons may have liberty to study Mathematics and Philosophy. My sons ought to study Mathematics and Philosophy, Geography, natural History, Naval Architecture, navigation, Commerce and Agriculture, in order to give their Children right to study Painting, Poetry, Music, Architecture, Statuary, Tapestry and Porcelain."[223]

John Adams to Abigail Adams, May 12, 1780

"They were legally-minded men. Their theology and church polity were legalistic and had a large share in determining the character of their political thinking. The law of God did not concern religious and ecclesiastical matters alone, but affected politics as well. They conceived the universe to be a great kingdom whose sovereign was God, whose relations with His Son and with men were determined by covenant or compact, 'covenant-constitutions', which were always conditional and implied strict obligations on each side."[224]

Historian Alice Baldwin, 1918, referring to the patriot preachers

"Governments are instituted among men, deriving their just powers from the consent of the governed … it is the right of the people to alter or abolish it, and to institute a new government, laying its foundations on such principles, and organizing its powers in such form, as to them shall seem most likely to effect their safety and happiness."

The Declaration of Independence, July 4th, 1776

"Justice is the end of government. It is the end of civil society. It ever has been, and ever will be pursued, until it be obtained, or until liberty be lost in the pursuit."[225]

James Madison, *Federalist No. 51*, February 6, 1788

From the earliest days in America, the citizens intended to institute governments firmly founded on what they had learned from God's Word. Their legal documents, their colonial compacts, their state constitutions – even their town covenants, "dripped" with biblical principles. The town covenant of Exeter, New Hampshire, signed on July 4, 1639, serves as a good example of this fact and gives keen insight into how the colonists viewed God's laws as the only basis of good and legitimate government:

> "Whereas it hath pleased the Lord to move the heart of our dread sovereign Charles, by the grace of God, king, &c. to grant license and liberty to sundry of his subjects to plant themselves in the western parts of America. We his loyal subjects brethren of the church in Exeter, situate and lying upon the River Pascataqua, with other inhabitants there, considering with ourselves the holy will of God and our own necessity that we should not live without wholesome laws and civil government among us, of which we are altogether destitute; do in the name of Christ and in the sight of God, combine ourselves together to erect and set up among us such government as shall be to our best discerning agreeable to the will of God, professing ourselves subjects to our sovereign lord king Charles according to the liberties of our English colony of Massachusetts, and binding of ourselves solemnly by the grace and help of Christ, and in his name and fear to submit ourselves to such godly and Christian laws as are established in the realm of England to our best knowledge, and to all other such laws which shall upon good grounds be made and enacted among us according to God, that we may live quietly and peaceably together in all godliness and honesty."[226]

From whence did they learn these concepts? From their preachers.

It is undeniable that the Black Regiment believed the Word of God gave instructions about every area of life and that nothing was excluded – including government. Believing Scripture taught that government was as much from God as the family and the church, they felt an obligation to preach about it and they did so with equal vigor. Their messages about government were not only sermons; they were Civics lessons as well.

A great example is Benjamin Colman's sermon preached at the Thursday Lecture in Boston on August 13, 1730. Colman was the first pastor of the Brattle Street Church in Boston and served as a trustee of Harvard, having turned down the presidency of that institution. In *Government The Pillar Of The Earth*, Colman said,

"The things said of these pillars [government and rulers] of the earth are also very great: 'They are the Lord's, and He has set the World upon them.' That is to say, The order and happiness of this lower world, the peace and weal of it, depend on the civil government which God has ordained in it. ... The Great God has made the governments and rulers of the earth its pillars, and has set the world upon them. ...

"I. *The governments and rulers of the earth are its pillars.*

"The pillar is a part of great use and honor in the building: So is magistracy in the world. One style in scripture for it is, foundations and cornerstones. Where we read of *the Chief of the People,* in the Hebrew it is the corners. We read also of the *Foundations of the Earth being out of Course.* The meaning is, the government of it was so. Kings bear up and support the inferior pillars of government, and a righteous administration restores a dissolving state: Psalm 75:3, *The Earth and all the Inhabitants thereof are dissolved: I bear up the Pillars of it.* ... Now the design and use of pillars in a building is one of these two, or both together: For strength to uphold it or for beauty to adorn it.

"The governments and rulers of the earth are its pillars in respect of strength to uphold and support the virtue, order and peace of it. Pillars should be made strong, and commonly are so; of stone and marble, iron and brass. ... Magistrates need be strong, for government is a great weight; and it is *laid upon their shoulders.*

"The governments and rulers of the earth are its pillars for ornament, to adorn it. Pillars in a fine building are made as beautiful as may be; they are planed and polished, wrought and carved with much art and cost, painted and gilded, for sight as well as use. As the legs are to a body, comely in its goings: Such are pillars in a stately structure for beauty to the eye. ... So those in power and magistracy are to be supposed, men adorned with superior gifts, powers and beauties of mind: Men that adorn the world wherein they live, and the offices which they sustain. And then their office adorns them also, and sets them in conspicuous places, where what is great and good in them is seen of all. To be sure, government and magistracy adorn the world as well as preserve it. ... Magistrates uphold and adorn the world, as pillars do a fabric, by employing their superior wisdom and knowledge, skill and prudence, discretion and judgment for the public good. …

"Integrity, uprightness, faithfulness added to knowledge and wisdom, makes men strong and beautiful pillars, whether in church or state. … All that rule over men should be like … *just men ruling in the fear of the Lord,* and then they are to the world as the light and rain, without which the earth must perish. As darkness vanishes before the light, so *a King that sitteth upon the Throne of Judgment scattereth away all Evil with his Eyes.* … God's righteousness and faithfulness, justice and judgment, are the foundation of his everlasting government … Nor can the kingdoms and provinces on the earth stand, but on the like basis of a just and righteous humane government. … 'Both the superior and inferior magistrates shall minister abundantly to the stability and tranquility of the state.'

"A pillar implies fortitude and patience; resolution, firmness and strength of mind, under weight and burden: Not to be soon shaken in mind, nor moved away from what is right and just; but giving our reason in the meekness of wisdom, and hearing the reasons of others in the same spirit of meekness, to form an impartial judgment, and abide by it; But yet with submission to the public judgment and determination. … There is a passive courage, ever necessary in an accomplish'd ruler, as much it may be as an active. The pillar stands regardless thro' the weather beat on it, or tho' dirt be cast on it. True it will wear under the injuries of time, but it looks still great, and stands while it wears away.

"II. *These pillars of the earth are the Lord's.*

"The earth is the Lord's and the fullness thereof; the world and they that dwell therein. All are God's rightful propriety & dominion. The shields of the earth belong to him. These are the same with the pillars of it. …

"The Lord makes these pillars, forms fashions'em, polishes and adorns 'em. He gifts, qualifies and furnishes all whom he calls out to public service. He makes the more plain and rough, and he orders the carved work and gilding in his house. He, the Father of Light & Glory, gives men their natural powers and excellencies; and all their acquired gifts are from him.

"Civil government is of divine institution, and God commissions and entrusts with the administration whom he pleases. The great King of the World has order'd a government in it, and he raises up governors, supreme and subordinate. *There is no Power but of God; the Powers that be are ordained of Him.* He puts the scepter into the hand, and the spirit of government into the heart. …

"The pillars are the Lord's, for he disposes of them as he pleases; places and fixes them where he will; rears 'em when he sees fit; and when he will removes, or takes 'em down: Or if he has no pleasure in them, breaks 'em to pieces and throws 'em away. …

"III. *God hath set the world upon the governments and rulers, whom he has made the pillars of it.*

"The natural world is in the hand of God, and is upheld in its being and order by his power. The moral world is most upon his heart, and govern'd in a way and manner suited to the nature and present state of man. And as he governs the spirits of men when he pleases by immediate impressions on them; so as more proper to the present order and happiness of mankind, he has appointed the government of men to be by men. So the peace, tranquility and flourishing of places are made to depend on the wisdom and fidelity of their rulers, in the good administration of the government. … The virtue and religion of a people, their riches and trade, their power, honor and reputation; and the favor of GOD toward them, with his blessing on them; do greatly depend on the pious, righteous and faithful government which they are under. …

"Government is not a creature of man's lust and will, but of divine constitution, and from a necessity in the nature of things. The very being and weal of society depends thereon. Government was not in the original of it assumed or usurped by any one man. For instance, not by Lamech before the Flood, nor by Nimrod after it. Indeed the spirit of tyranny, and the lust of dominion, seem to have began in them; but order & rule was before them. Mankind naturally went into that, and these were the men who made the first breaches on it; the one being of the race of Cain, the other of Ham; who have had some of their likeness in every place, and thro' all generations; that would turn the world upside down and overthrow the foundations which GOD has laid.

"In a word, magistracy, like the other ordinances of heaven, stands by the power and blessing of GOD; who effectually owns it and works by it, establishes the earth and it abideth. He has graven it deep in the hearts of men, even as the desire of happiness and self-preservation. He has as much ordained, that while the earth remaineth civil order and government shall not cease; as he has sworn *that seed time and harvest, cold and heat, summer and winter, day and night,* shall not. Both the one and the other equally continue to the world's end, absolutely necessary to the life, comfort and welfare of mankind.

"See the divine wisdom and goodness in ordaining and establishing a magistracy and government in the world. It is one of the many great instances, wherein the Supreme Governor of the world has taken care for the universal and perpetual weal of it. And they that would be lawless and ungoverned, despising dominion and speaking evil of dignity, distinction, authority and rule among men, act as madly and mischievously as one would do, that should go into a house and sap the foundation of it, till it fall upon him and crush him to death. …

"Let people reverence & honour their worthy rulers, and let the highest among men be very humble before God. They are pillars, but of the earth. The earth and its pillars are dissolving together. Government abides, in a succession of men, while the earth endures, but the persons, however good & great, must die like other men. We must not look too much at the loftiness of any, nor lean too much on any earthly pillar: Put not your Trust in Princes, nor in the Son of Man in whom there is no Help: His Breath goeth forth, he returneth to his Dust. Nor may the highest among mortals behold themselves with elation & security, as the vain king of Babylon once; but let them fear and tremble before the God of heaven, who inherits all nations, and stands in the congregation of the mighty, and judgeth among the gods. …

"Let rulers consider what they owe to GOD, who has rear'd and set 'em up; and to the public which GOD has set upon them. Let 'em seek wisdom & strength, grace and conduct from GOD, that they may answer the title given 'em in my text. Let 'em stand, and bear, and act for GOD; whose they are, and who has set 'em where they are. Let the public good be their just care; that it may be seen that GOD has set the world in their heart, as well as laid it on their shoulders. Let 'em act uprightly, that they may stand secure and strong. Let 'em fear GOD, and rule by his word, that they may be approved by GOD, and accepted always by men with all thankfulness.

"As government is the pillar of the earth, so religion is the pillar of government. Take away the fear of GOD's government & judgment, and humane rule utterly falls, or corrupts into tyranny. But if religion rule in the hearts and lives of rulers, GOD will have glory, and the people be made happy.

"Fathers of our country, let me freely say to you, that the devotion and virtue of our humble, but illustrious ancestors (the first planters of New-England), laid the foundation of our greatness among the provinces: And it is this that must continue and establish it under the divine favor & blessing. Emulate their piety and godliness, and generous regards to the public, and be acknowledged the pillars, the strength and ornament of your country!"[227]

By preaching sermons like this, the patriot preachers played a major role in helping the colonists to form their beliefs about government. For example, Timothy Cutler poignantly pointed out in his Connecticut election sermon in Hartford on May 9, 1717 that man's understanding of government came from God. Cutler said: "God having made Man a Rational Creature, hath (as it were) Twisted Law into the very Frame and Constitution of his Soul."[228]

To the majority of those living in colonial America, the Bible was the supreme arbiter of all truth and anything that conflicted with God's Word was rejected as false. It was, therefore, upon this strong biblical foundation that Americans formed their political beliefs. To state it plainly – the Bible was their law book. As Alice Baldwin observed, "If his [Americans'] ideas of government and the rights of man were in part derived from other sources, they were strengthened and sanctioned by Holy Writ."[229]

The early arrivers to America, like the Pilgrims, used the principles they found in their Bibles to govern their society so law and order could be established for the good of all. As the colonies began to grow, the colonists generally embraced the principles of government originally used by the Pilgrims and Puritans.

On Sunday, the patriot preachers often taught the principles of government and law right from their pulpits. So, to a great degree, the churches in early America were not only mission sights for proclaiming the gospel; they also served as classrooms for government and civics. Historian John Wingate Thornton wrote,

> "The result of all this was, a new community, voluntarily gathered in New England, primarily for religion, organized into many 'independent' churches, each of them a petty democracy, electing its officers and minister, making its own laws, and regulating its own affairs, so far as possible, by the system of polity indicated with more or less distinctness in Holy Scripture. Out of this condition of things the state was gradually developed. Here was individualism, an admirable system for making good full-blooded Puritan citizens, but very poor and unmanageable subjects.'"[230]

As we have already seen, the impact of the Black Regiment's sermons on the Founders was so significant that the Declaration of Independence contains sentences that are almost literal quotations from their sermons. The historian Alice Baldwin wrote,

> "By the time the Declaration of Independence was signed, in 1776, Puritan preachers had taught the right to life, liberty, and property for more than one hundred years." ...
>
> "To the men of New England who had been nourished from their youth on the election sermons and who had been thoroughly enlightened by their pastors in theoretical and practical politics, it was but natural to turn to the ministers when they needed some one to express their ideas of government. ... the surprisingly large number of pastors who were chosen to assist in committee work and in constitution making is a striking testimony to the faith of the people in their knowledge and sympathy.
>
> "It would be hard to measure the value of their [patriot preachers] service in the war. But of equal value was their help in constitution making. These ministers believed in the theories they preached and intended to see that the unique opportunity before them was not lost. That the new governments should be formed according to right principles they were determined. The only way in which they could conceive of government set up by compact was through the calling of the constitutional convention. To define the natural rights retained by the people meant a bill of rights. To separate and limit the powers of each part of the government so that the rights of each should be exactly determined and carefully preserved meant the drawing up of a written constitution which could be changed only by the people themselves. The insistence of the ministers on these and other points seems to have had a decided influence on the course of events. A few years later, when Massachusetts was in the throes of adopting the Federal Constitution, General Lincoln wrote to Washington, 'It is very fortunate for us, that the clergy are pretty generally with us. They have in this State a very great influence over the people.' So might the leaders of the Revolution have said not only in Massachusetts but in all the New England Colonies."[231]

Of course, all of this makes perfect sense, since the pastors were some of the more educated of the citizens. Given that the pastors had been previously called upon to write the local town covenants and government documents, it seemed obvious to the colonists to choose those same men to serve as members of their respective state constitutional conventions. As delegates to these conventions, the pastors had strong input in designing the governments of the individual states and were thus provided with a perfect opportunity to infuse their biblical convictions into the framework of those governments.

Once these individual state constitutional conventions began to meet and craft constitutions for their respective states, it was the pastors who kept a close eye on the proceedings. If they believed the constitutions did not sufficiently protect the people's rights, it was common for them to speak out and push for the rejection of those constitutions. For example, Massachusetts pastors like William Gordon, Samuel Cooper, Peter Thacher, Thomas Allen, and Jonas Clark, who had been so outspoken against Great Britain at the beginning of the war, when the Massachusetts constitution was first proposed (without a Bill of Rights), were just as outspoken against it as they had been the British. Gordon objected so strongly that he decried the new state constitution in articles that were published in newspapers like the Boston *Independent Chronicle.* In 1778, because of his open criticism of the Assembly, he was removed as chaplain of that body – but not before his stand for liberty had accomplished its desired effect.

Joining Gordon in his dissent was Jonas Clark, the famed pastor of the Lexington Minutemen. In June 1778, writing for the citizens of Lexington and expressing their disapproval of the proposed constitution for the state of Massachusetts, Clark wrote,

> "It may be observed that it appears to us that into a state of well-regulated society, mankind gave up some of their natural rights in order that others of greater importance to their well-being, safety and happiness, both as societies and individuals, might be the better enjoyed, secured and defended. That a civil Constitution or form of government is of the nature of a most sacred covenant or contract entered into by the individuals which form the society, for which such Constitution or form of government is intended, whereby they mutually and solemnly engage to support and defend each other in the enjoyment of those rights which they mean to retain. That the main and great end of establishing any Constitution or form of government among a people or in society, is to maintain, secure and defend those natural rights inviolate."[232]

Even with the attention the patriot pastors paid to the writing of the state constitutions, they paid even more careful attention when it came time to adopt a constitution for the whole nation. As odd as it may seem, when the Constitution of the United States was first presented to the individual states for ratification, it was the Black Regiment that vehemently spoke out against it. Their objection – it contained no Bill of Rights for the people.

The patriot preachers who had struggled so hard and long for freedom, now that the war had been fought and won, had no intention of exchanging British tyranny for an American version of the same thing. Even though they strongly believed that the Constitution should explain what the government could do, they believed even more strongly that it should clearly delineate what the government could not do. They wanted a national constitution that gave government very limited powers – one that granted "negative" powers (what government could not do) rather than one that granted "positive" powers (what government could do). Essentially, they wanted a government that defended their rights and provided for a lawful society in which liberty and free enterprise could prosper – and nothing more. They were much more fearful of what the government could do "to them" than they were interested in what the government could do "for them." As far as they were concerned, the government that governed least governed best.

According to Baldwin, the colonists believed,

> "… governments are limited by the purpose for which they were founded, viz. the good of the people. … A government which did not have the good of the people at heart did not have the sanction of God …"[233]

The citizens then reasoned that a government that did not have the sanction of God would not have the sanction of the people. Thankfully, their concerns and objections were heard and great limitations were placed upon the government by the codification of the people's specific rights in the first ten amendments to the Constitution of the United States. In essence, the Bill of

Rights served as handcuffs for the federal government by restricting its ability to abuse men's rights. Then, and only then, did the pastors encourage their congregations to ratify the Constitution.

Clearly, we owe the patriot preachers a great deal of gratitude for the government we enjoy today. The key principles of human rights and proper government we treasure were preached and taught from the pulpits of America in the seventeenth and eighteenth centuries. Clinton Rossiter, historian, political scientist, and professor at Cornell University, put it this way:

> "Had ministers been the only spokesman of the rebellion–had Jefferson, the Adamses, and [James] Otis never appeared in print–the political thought of the Revolution would have followed almost exactly the same line.... In the sermons of the patriot ministers ... we find expressed every possible refinement of the reigning political faith."[234]

The patriot preachers made it clear in their sermons that men's rights are gifts from God, not endowments by a benevolent government. Because of this, they taught that government had the responsibility to protect and promote those rights – not restrict and remove them. The following sermon excerpts provide a sampling of what the people were hearing from the pulpit in those years.

1. LIBERTY & GOVERNMENT ARE GIFTS FROM GOD.

- John Davenport, Massachusetts Election Sermon, 1669: "the Law of Nature is God's law."[235]
- Ebenezer Pemberton, Massachusetts Election Sermon, May 31, 1710: "The Origin of Government is Divine. It is from God, by His Sovereign Constitution and Appointment."[236]
- John Barnard, Massachusetts Election Sermon, 1734: "This Voice of Nature is the Voice of God. Thus 'tis that vox populi est vox Dei."[237]

- Samuel Hall, Connecticut Election Sermon, 1746: "I think there can be no doubt about this; but that in all cases where the matter under Determination appertains to natural Right, the Cause is God's Cause."[238]
- Joseph Fish, Connecticut Election Sermon, 1760: "Every Man has a natural, unalienable Right to think and see for himself."[239]
- Benjamin Stevens, Massachusetts Election Sermon, 1761: "Liberty both civil and religious is the spirit and genius of the sacred writings."[240]
- Samuel Langdon, Massachusetts Election Sermon, May 31, 1775: "Thanks be to God that he has given us, as men, natural rights, independent on all human laws whatever"[241]
- Moses Mather's sermon, *America's Appeal To The Impartial World,* preached in Hartford, Connecticut in 1775:

"Free agency, or a rational existence, with its powers and faculties, and freedom of enjoying and exercising them, is the gift of God to man. The right of the donor, and the authenticity of the donation, are both incontestable; hence man hath an absolute property in, and right of dominion over himself, his powers and faculties; with self- love to stimulate, and reason to guide him, in the free use and exercise of them, independent of, and uncontrollable by any but him, who created and gave them. And whatever is acquired by the use, and application of a man's faculties, is equally the property of that man, as the faculties by which the acquisitions are made; and that which is absolutely the property of a man, he cannot be divested of, but by his own voluntary act, or consent, either expressed, or implied. ... Expressed, by actual gift, sale, or exchange, by himself, or his lawful substitute: implied, as where a man enters into, and takes the benefits of a government, he implicitly consents to be subject to its laws; so, when he transgresses the laws, there is an implied consent to submit to its penalties. And from this principle, all the civil exousiai, or rightful authorities, that are ordained of God, and exist in the world, are derived as from their native source. From whence are authorities, dominions and powers? From God, the sovereign ruler, as the fountain, *through the voice and consent of the people.* For what purpose are they erected? *for the good of the people.* Wherefore the sovereign ruler, condescends to clothe, with authority, the man who by the general voice, is exalted, from among the people, to bear rule; and to pronounce him his minister for their good. Hence, it is evident, that man hath the clearest right, by the most indefeasible title, to personal security, liberty, and private property. And whatever is a man's own, he hath, most clearly, a right to enjoy and defend; to repel force by force; to recover what is injuriously pillaged or plundered from him, and to make reasonable reprisals for the unjust vexation. And, upon this principle, an offensive war may sometimes be justifiable, viz. when it is necessary for preservation and defense."[242]

- Samuel Langdon's election sermon, *The Republic Of The Israelites: An Example To The American States*, preached at Concord, New Hampshire, to the honorable General Court on June 5, 1788:

"Wisdom is the gift of God, and social happiness depends on his providential government; therefore, if these states have framed their constitutions with superior wisdom, and secured their natural rights, and all the advantages of society, with greater precaution than other nations, we may with good reason affirm that God hath given us our government; that he hath taught us good statutes and judgments, tending to make us great and respectable in the view of the world."[243]

- Samuel Sherwood's sermon, *Scriptural Instructions To Civil Rulers,* preached in New Haven, Connecticut on August 31, 1774:

"What we have heard on this subject, should serve to excite our thankful acknowledgments to the supreme Ruler of the world for his great favor to us in the happy constitution of government we have hitherto lived under. The providence of God which rules the world (tho' it does not neglect the lesser affairs of men), especially concerns itself in more important things, which respect more large societies and communities of men. Civil government is one of the principal of these. *God is the judge; he setteth up one, and putteth down another;* and orders all the changes and revolutions that come to pass in the kingdoms and empires of the world: whose providence has been very extraordinary, and in a manner, miraculous, in conducting our fathers into this, once howling wilderness in preserving them in their weak, infant-state, when exposed to destruction many ways; and leading them to settle on such an excellent constitution of government; which affords such full protection, and ample security to the subjects, of their lives, liberties and properties; and in providing for us in succession down to this day, such a wise, virtuous and upright set of rulers who we have reason to think, have, in the main, ruled in the fear of the Lord. Our privileges in this respect are very great, beyond what any other people enjoy in any part of the earth. The bigger part of the world have had their liberties wrested out of their hands; been oppressed and enslaved by lawless and cruel tyrants: while we are yet in the possession of freedom. May God preserve it to us safe, and hand it down to the latest posterity! Our fathers went through the greatest perils and dangers to procure these privileges for us; and we ought to be willing to do our utmost to preserve them, and hand them down to our children and offspring. Our treasure, and our blood too, are not too dear and costly sacrifices for such valuable things.

"As there are certain rights of men, which are unalienable even by themselves; and others which they do not mean to alienate, when they enter into civil society. And as power is naturally restless, aspiring and insatiable; it therefore becomes necessary in all civil communities (either at their first formation or by degrees) that certain great first principles be settled and established, determining and bounding the power and prerogative of the ruler, ascertaining and securing the rights and liberties of the subjects, as the foundation stamina of the government; which in all civil states is called the constitution, on the certainty and permanency of which, the rights of both the ruler and the subjects depend; nor may they be altered or changed by ruler or people, but by the whole collective body, or a major part at least, nor may they be touched by the legislator; for the moment that alters essentially the constitution, it annihilates its own existence, its constitutional authority. Not only so, but on supposition the legislator might alter it; such a stretch of power would be dangerous beyond conception; for could the British parliament alter the original principles of the constitution, the people might be deprived of their liberties and properties, and the parliament become absolute and perpetual; and for redress in such case, should it ever happen, they must resort to their native rights, and be justified in making insurrection. For when the constitution is violated, they have no other remedy; but for all other wrongs and abuses that may possibly happen, the constitution remaining inviolate, the people have a remedy thereby."[244]

2. GOVERNMENT HAS A VERY SPECIFIC PURPOSE: GOD'S GLORY AND THE RESTRAINT OF EVIL.

"As near the law of God as they can be" was the advice given by the General Court of Massachusetts to the laymen and preachers of the committee who were writing the laws that would govern their Commonwealth. Interestingly, the first code of written laws in Massachusetts was penned by a preacher in 1629.[245]

The eighteenth century American possessed very strongly held beliefs about government. But unlike many of today's Americans who believe government should be involved in and control every area of their lives, early Americans believed government's role should be limited and specific. To them, government's primary purpose was to glorify God by guarding men's God-given rights by the enforcement of laws based upon biblical principles. They believed that because of man's sinfulness, government was essential to restrain the "sons of violence."

- John Allen's Massachusetts Election Sermon, 1744: "[The] great end of government is the good of the subject: This is the very design of Christ himself in his rule over us ..."[246]

- Jonathan Mayhew's Massachusetts Election Sermon, 1754: "After the glory of God there can be no other end of government than the good of man, the common benefit of society ... The end of government, then, as it is a divine ordinance, must be human felicity ... must be the common good of all, and of every individual, so far as consistent therewith ..."[247]

- Ezra Stiles's Connecticut election sermon, May 8, 1783:

"That her [American] system of dominion must receive its finishing from religion; or, that from the diffusion of virtue among the people of any community, would arise their greatest secular happiness: all which terminate in this conclusion, that Holiness ought to be the end of all civil government ... We err much, if we think the only or chief end of civil government is secular happiness. ... Animated with the sublime ideas which Christianity infuses into a people, we shall be led to consider the true religion as the highest glory of a civil polity. ... So the most perfect secular polity, though very excellent, would lose all its glory, when compared with ... a community wherein the religion of the divine Jesus reigns in vigor and perfection. ... Nor are we to conceive that civil virtue is the only end of civil government. As the end of God's government is his declarative glory in the holiness and happiness of the universe, so all civil government ought to subserve the same end. ... But I must desist, with only observing that the United States are under peculiar obligations to become a holy people unto the Lord our God, on account of the late eminent deliverance, salvation, peace, and glory, with which he hath now crowned our new sovereignty.

"And while this honorable house is attending to the secular concerns of civil government, may we not humbly wish that you would not repudiate the idea of being nursing fathers to our spiritual Israel, the church of God within this state? Give us, gentlemen, the decided assurance, that you are friends of the churches, and that you are the friends of the pastors, who have certainly, in this trying warfare, approved themselves the friends of liberty and government. Your predecessors 100 years ago accounted this among their principal honors. They were solicitous to promote religion and learning and to give suitable encouragement to both."[248]

- Charles Chauncy's Massachusetts election sermon, *Civil Magistrates Must Be Just, Ruling In The Fear Of God,* May 27, 1747:

"The present circumstances of the human race are therefore such, by means of sin, that 'tis necessary they should, for their mutual defense and safety, combine together in distinct societies, lodging as much power in the hands of a few, as may be sufficient to restrain the irregularities of the rest, and keep them within the bounds of a just decorum."[249]

- Samuel Cooke's Massachusetts election sermon, *The True Principles of Government, Discourse III*, May 30, 1770:

"From this and many other passages in the sacred oracles, it is evident that the Supreme Ruler, though he has directed to no particular mode of civil government, yet allows and approves of the establishment of it among men.

"The ends of civil government, in divine revelation, are clearly pointed out, the character of rulers described, and the duty of subjects asserted and explained; and in this view civil government may be considered as an ordinance of God, and, when justly exercised, greatly subservient to the glorious purposes of divine providence and grace: but the particular form is left to the choice and determination of mankind.

"In a pure state of nature, government is in a great measure unnecessary. Private property in that state is inconsiderable. Men need no arbiter to determine their rights; they covet only a bare support; their stock is but the subsistence of a day; the uncultivated deserts are their habitations, and they carry their all with them in their frequent removes. They are each one a law to himself, which, in general, is of force sufficient for their security in that course of life.

"It is far otherwise when mankind are formed into collective bodies, or a social state of life. Here, their frequent mutual intercourse, in a degree, necessarily leads them to different apprehensions respecting their several rights, even where their intentions are upright. Temptations to injustice and violence increase, and the occasions of them multiply in proportion to the increase and opulence of the society. The laws of nature, though enforced by divine revelation, which bind the conscience of the upright, prove insufficient to restrain the sons of violence, who have not the fear of God before their eyes.

"A society cannot long subsist in such a state; their safety, their social being, depends upon the establishment of determinate rules or laws, with proper penalties to enforce them, to which individuals shall be subjected. The laws, however wisely adapted, cannot operate to the public security unless they are properly executed. The execution of them remaining in the hands of the whole community, leaves individuals to determine their own rights, and, in effect, in the same circumstances as in a state of nature. The remedy in this case is solely in the hands of the community.

"A society emerging from a state of nature, in respect to authority, are all upon a level; no individual can justly challenge a right to make or execute the laws by which it is to be governed, but only by the choice or general consent of the community. The people, the collective body only, have a right, under God, to determine who shall exercise this trust for the common interest, and to fix the bounds of their authority; and, consequently, unless we admit the most evident inconsistence, those in authority, in the whole of their public conduct, are accountable to the society which gave them their political existence. This is evidently the natural origin and state of all civil government, the sole end and design of which is, not to ennoble a few and enslave the multitude, but the public benefit, the good of the people; that they may be protected in their persons, and secured in the enjoyment of all their rights, and be enabled to lead quiet and peaceable lives in all godliness and honesty. While this manifest design of civil government, under whatever form, is kept in full view, the reciprocal obligations of rulers and subjects are obvious, and the extent of prerogative and liberty will be indisputable.

"The people, the collective body only, have a right, under God, to determine who shall exercise this trust [make and execute laws] for the common interest, and to fix the bounds of their authority; and, consequently, unless we admit the most evident inconsistence, those in authority, in the whole of their public conduct, are accountable to the society which gave them their political existence. This is evidently the natural origin and state of all civil government, the sole end and design of which is, not to ennoble a few and enslave the multitude, but the public benefit, the good of the people; that they may be protected in their persons, and secured in the enjoyment of all their rights, and be enabled to lead quiet and peaceable lives in all godliness and honesty."[250]

- Samuel West's Massachusetts election sermon, *Natural Law: The True Principles of Government*, May 29, 1776:

"The necessity of forming ourselves into politic bodies, and granting to our rulers a power to enact laws for the public safety, and to enforce them by proper penalties, arises from our being in a fallen and degenerate state. The slightest view of the present state and condition of the human race is abundantly sufficient to convince any person of common sense and common honesty that civil government is absolutely necessary for the peace and safety of mankind; and, consequently, that all good magistrates, while they faithfully discharge the trust reposed in them, ought to be religiously and conscientiously obeyed. An enemy to good government is an enemy not only to his country, but to all mankind; for he plainly shows himself to be divested of those tender and social sentiments which are characteristic of a human temper, even of that generous and benevolent disposition which is the peculiar glory of a rational creature. …

"Men of unbridled lusts, were they not restrained by the power of the civil magistrate, would spread horror and desolation all around them. This makes it absolutely necessary that societies should form themselves into politic bodies, that they may enact laws for the public safety, and appoint particular penalties for the violation of their laws, and invest a suitable number of persons with authority to put in execution and enforce the laws of the state, in order that wicked men may be restrained from doing mischief to their fellow-creatures, that the injured may have their rights restored to them, that the virtuous may be encouraged in doing good, and that every member of society may be protected and secured in the peaceable, quiet possession and enjoyment of all those liberties and privileges which the Deity has bestowed upon him; *i.e.*, that he may safely enjoy and pursue whatever he chooses, that is consistent with the public good. This shows that the end and design of civil government cannot be to deprive men of their liberty or take away their freedom; but, on the contrary, the true design of civil government is to protect men in the enjoyment of liberty.

"From hence it follows that tyranny and arbitrary power are utterly inconsistent with and subversive of the very end and design of civil government, and directly contrary to natural law, which is the true foundation of civil government and all politic law. Consequently, the authority of a tyrant is of itself null and void; for as no man can have a right to act contrary to the law of nature, it is impossible that any individual, or even the greatest number of men, can confer a right upon another of which they themselves are not possessed; *i.*e., no body of men can justly and lawfully authorize any person to tyrannize over and enslave his fellow-creatures, or do anything contrary to equity and goodness. As magistrates have no authority but what they derive from the people, whenever they act contrary to the public good, and pursue measures destructive of the peace and safety of the community, they forfeit their right to govern the people. Civil rulers and magistrates are properly of human creation; they are set up by the people to be the guardians of their rights, and to secure their persons from being injured or oppressed, — the safety of the public being the supreme law of the state, by which the magistrates are to be governed, and which they are to consult upon all occasions. The modes of administration may be very different, and the forms of government may vary from each other in different ages and nations; but, under every form, the end of civil government is the same, and cannot vary: it is like the laws of the Medes and Persians — it altereth not."[251]

- Samuel McClintock's New Hampshire election sermon, *A Sermon On Occasion Of the Commencement Of The New Hampshire Constitution,* June 3, 1784:

"Government is necessary, and must be supported; and it ought to be a humiliating consideration that the necessity and expenses of this divine institution, is founded in the corruption and vices of human nature; for if mankind were in a state of rectitude there would be no need of the sanctions of human laws to restrain them from vice or to oblige them to do what is right. They would be deterred from the former by a sense of its deformity, and led to practice the latter by a view of its intrinsic beauty. But in the present disordered state of our nature there would be no safety of life or property without the protection of law. A state of nature would be a state of continual war and carnage. The weak would be devoured by the strong, and every affront avenged with the death of the offender. Even under the best governments, we see the human passions often break through all the restraints of law in acts of violence and outrage! Which shows what reason we have to be thankful to God for that excellent Constitution we live under, and how incumbent it is on every one who is a friend to the order, peace and happiness of society, or who even regards the safety of his own life and property, to support and maintain it."[252]

3. GOVERNMENT'S POWER COMES FROM THE PEOPLE.

- Roger Williams's *The Bloudy Tenent of Persecution*, 1643-44:

"The sovereign, original, and foundation of civil power lies in the people; and it is evident that such governments as are by them erected and established, have no more power, nor for no longer time, than the civil power or people consenting and agreeing shall betrust them with. This is clear, not only in reason, but in the experience of all commonweals, where the people are not deprived of their natural freedom by the power of tyrants."[253]

- John Barnard's Massachusetts Election Sermon, 1734:

"So that after all is said, the Right to rule takes its Rise from the Consent, and Agreement, that is the Choice and Election, of the Community, State, or Kingdom ... and He, and He only, has the Right to rule, to whom the Government commits the Power, and Authority."[254]

- Jonathan Mayhew's Massachusetts Election Sermon, 1754:

"... from man, from common consent, it is that lawful rulers immediately derive their power."[255]

- James Lockwood's Connecticut Election Sermon, 1759:

"[T]his colony was made and constituted a Body Corporate or Politick, with all the Rights and Immunities of a Free People. ... The Laws we are under ... are not the Sovereign Injunctions of an arbitrary Ruler, but they are all Laws of our own making ... Our Lives and Limbs, our Property and Estates, our Rights and Liberties, our Characters and good Names lie at no Man's Mercy."[256]

- Andrew Eliot's Massachusetts Election Sermon, 1765:

"All power has its foundation in compact and mutual consent, or else it proceeds from fraud or violence:... When government is founded in mutual consent, it is the undoubted right of the community to say who shall govern them; and to make what limitations or conditions they think proper." He emphasized the great privilege of electing the councillors and exclaimed: "God grant that the privilege may never be wrested from us!"[257]

- William Patten's Massachusetts Thanksgiving Sermon, 1766:

"Whoever in his senses, (unless he had the temper of a slave) ever submitted his liberty; to the absolute disposal of others, under the notion of their being the sole judges of right and wrong?"[258]

- Elisha Williams's *A Seasonable Plea, Essential Rights And Liberties Of Protestants* in 1774:

"[R]eason teaches men to join in society, to unite together into a commonwealth under some form or other, to make a body of laws agreeable to the law of nature, and institute one common power to see them observed. It is they who thus unite together, viz. the people, who make and alone have right to make the laws that are to take place among them; or which comes to the same thing, appoint those who shall make them, and who shall see them executed. For every man has an equal right to the preservation of his person and property; and so an equal right to establish a law, or to nominate the makers and executors of the laws which are the guardians both of person and property. ... Hence then the fountain and original of all civil power is from the people, and is certainly instituted for their sakes; or in other words, which was the second thing proposed, The great end of civil government, is the preservation of their persons, their liberties and estates, or their property. … That greater security therefore of life, liberty, money, lands, houses, family, and the like, which may be all comprehended under that of person and property, is the sole end of all civil government. …

"Reason teaches us that all men are naturally equal in respect of jurisdiction or dominion one over another. … So that we are born free as we are born rational. … This natural freedom is not a liberty for every one to do what he pleases without any regard to any law; for a rational creature cannot but be made under a law from its Maker: But it consists in a freedom from any superior power on earth, and not being under the will or legislative authority of man, and having only the law of nature (or in other words, of its Maker) for his rule. … And as reason tells us, all are born thus naturally equal, i.e. with an equal right to their persons; so also with an equal right to their preservation; and therefore to such things as nature affords for their subsistence. …

"What liberty or power belonging to man as he is a reasonable creature does every man give up to the civil government whereof he is a member. Some part of their natural liberty they do certainly give up to the government, for the benefit of society and mutual defense (for in a political society every one even an infant has the whole force of the community to protect him), and something therefore is certainly given up to the whole for this purpose. Now the way to know what branches of natural liberty are given up, and what remain to us after our admission into civil society, is to consider the ends for which men enter into a state of government. For so much liberty and no more is departed from, as is necessary to secure those ends; the rest is certainly our own still. …

"The members of a civil state or society do retain their natural liberty in all such cases as have no relation to the ends of such a society. … From whence can such a society derive any right to hinder them from doing that which does not affect the ends of that society? Should a government therefore restrain the free use of the scriptures, prohibit men the reading of them, and make it penal to examine and search them; it would be a manifest usurpation upon the common rights of mankind, as much a violation of natural liberty as the attack of a highwayman upon the road can be upon our civil rights. And indeed with respect to the sacred writings, men might not only read them if the government did prohibit the same, but they would be bound by a higher authority to read them, notwithstanding any humane prohibition. The pretense of any authority to restrain men from reading the same, is wicked as well as vain. But whether in some cases that have no relation to the ends of government and wherein therefore men retain their natural liberty;

if the civil authority should attempt by a law to restrain men, people might not be oblig'd to submit therein, …

"The members of a civil state do retain their natural liberty or right of judging for themselves in matters of religion. Every man has an equal right to follow the dictates of his own conscience in the affairs of religion. Every one is under an indispensable obligation to search the scripture for himself (which contains the whole of it) and to make the best use of it he can for his own information in the will of God, the nature and duties of Christianity. And as every Christian is so bound; so he has an unalienable right to judge of the sense and meaning of it, and to follow his judgment wherever it leads him; even an equal right with any rulers be they civil or ecclesiastical. This I say, I take to be an original right of the human nature, and so far from being given up by the individuals of a community that it cannot be given up by them if they should be so weak as to offer it. Man by his constitution as he is a reasonable being capable of the knowledge of his Maker; is a moral & accountable being: and therefore as every one is accountable for himself, he must reason, judge and determine for himself. … the rights of conscience are sacred and equal in all, and strictly speaking unalienable. This right of judging every one for himself in matters of religion results from the nature of man, and is so inseparably connected therewith, that a man can no more part with it than he can with his power of thinking: … And it is the sacred scriptures alone which have this right to our entire submission, as now described: and no other authority which has yet been or ever shall be set up, has any manner of right at all to govern and direct our consciences in religious matters. …

"Every society ought to be subject only to its own proper legislature. The truth of this is evident at the first view; and civil societies readily adhere to this as an inviolable principle. …

"Whenever the power that is put in any hands for the government of any people is applied to any other end than the preservation of their persons and properties, the securing and promoting their civil interests (the end for which power was put into their hands), I say when it is applied to any other end, then (according to the great Mr. Lock) it becomes tyranny. And since their power would be as truly applied to another end, in making such laws as I have above hinted at, as in making those that are notoriously unjust and oppressive (tho' the latter is worse); then it truly becomes tyranny. …

"And every man having a property in his own person, the labor of his body and the work of his hands are properly his own, to which no one has right but himself; it will therefore follow that when he removes any thing out of the state that nature has provided and left it in, he has mixed his labor with it and joined something to it that is his own, and thereby makes it his property. He having removed it out of the common state nature placed it in, it hath by this labor something annexed to it that excludes the common right of others; because this labor being the unquestionable property of the laborer, no man but he can have a right to what that is once joined to, at least where there is enough and as good left in common for others. Thus every man having a natural right to (or being the proprietor of) his own person and his own actions and labor and to what he can honestly acquire by his labor, which we call property; it certainly follows, that no man can have a right to the person or property of another: And if every man has a right to his person and property; he has also a right to defend them, and a right to all the necessary means of defense, and so has a right of punishing all insults upon his person and property. ..."[259]

- Samuel Sherwood's Connecticut election sermon, August 31, 1774:

"Government originates (under God) from the people; as from its native source; centers in them, their good is its ultimate object; and operates by securing to them, the enjoyment of their natural rights and civil privileges ... That form of government that is adapted to the genius and circumstances of the governed, affords them the greatest security, and places the authority of the governing most out of the reach of the former ..."[260]

- Moses Mather's Connecticut election sermon, *America's Appeal To The Impartial World,* 1775:

"By nature, every man (under God) is his own legislator, judge, and avenger, and absolute lord of his property. In civil government, rightly constituted, every one retains a share in the legislative, taxative, judicial, and the vindictive powers, by having a voice in the supreme legislature, which enacts the laws, and imposes the taxes, and by having a right, in all cases wherein he is injured, to resort to, and demand redress, in a course of law, from the tribunal of the public, and the sword of state."[261]

- Samuel West's Massachusetts election sermon, May 29, 1776:

"Reason and equity require that no one be obliged to pay a tax that he has never consented to, either by himself or by his representative. But, as Divine Providence has placed us at so great a distance from Great Britain that we neither are nor can be properly represented in the British Parliament, it is a plain proof that the Deity designed that we should have the powers of legislation and taxation among ourselves; for can any suppose it to be reasonable that a set of men that are perfect strangers to us should have the uncontrollable right to lay the most heavy and grievous burdens upon us that they please, purely to gratify their unbounded avarice and luxury? Must we be obliged to perish with cold and hunger to maintain them in idleness, in all kinds of debauchery and dissipation? But if they have the right to take our property from us without our consent, we must be wholly at their mercy for our food and raiment, and we know by sad experience that their tender mercies are cruel."[262]

One of the best sermons by the Black Regiment addressing government and the believer's responsibility to it was the sermon, *The Duty Of Magistrates,* preached by Samuel Stillman before the Supreme Court of Massachusetts on May 29, 1779:

(Matthew 22:21) "Render therefore to Caesar, *the things that are Caesar's*" That is, those things which he may lawfully claim. What these were, our Lord does not ascertain. Nor is it necessary that we should, as they relate to Caesar and his subjects. I shall therefore proceed to apply this sacred passage to ourselves, in our present situation, by considering:

I. What those duties are which the people owe to the civil magistrate.

II. The duties of the magistrate to the people. And then,

III. Endeavor to draw the line between the things that belong to Caesar, and those things that belong to God.

"I. We are first to inquire, what those duties are which the people owe to the civil magistrate.

"I apprehend that this question implies another, which is previously necessary to be determined, viz.: How came the men whom we call magistrates with any power at all over the people? Were they born to govern? Have they a higher original than other men? Or do they claim the sovereignty *jure divino?*

"The time has been when the divine right of kings sounded from the pulpit and the press; and when the sacred name of religion was brought in to sanctify the most horrid systems of despotism and cruelty. But, blessed be God, we live in a more happy era, in which the great principles of liberty are better understood. With us, it is a first and fundamental principle, that God made all men equal.

"'Nothing is more evident,' says Locke, 'than that creatures of the same species and rank, promiscuously born to all the same advantages of nature, and the use of the same faculties, should also be equal one amongst another, without subordination or subjection, unless the Lord and Master of them all should, by any manifest declaration of his will, set one above another, and confer on him, by evident and clear appointment, an undoubted right to dominion and sovereignty.'

"Until such a declaration of the divine will shall be produced, we ought firmly to maintain the natural equality of all men.

"And as they are equal, so they are likewise in a state of entire freedom. Whatever they possess is their own, to be disposed of solely agreeably to their own will. None have a right to claim any part of their property, to disturb them in their possessions, or to demand subjection in any degree whatever, while they act consistently with the laws of nature. He who attempts to do either is an usurper; puts himself into a state of war, and may be opposed as a common highwayman.

"If we admit the truth of these principles, we come, by an easy transition, to the foundation of civil society, viz., the consent of the people. For, if all men are equal by nature, it must depend entirely upon themselves whether they will continue in their natural condition, or exchange it for a state of civil government. Consequently the sovereignty resides originally in the people.

"As their leaving a state of nature for a state of civil society is a matter of their own choice, so they are equally free to adopt that form of government which appears to them the most eligible, or the test calculated to promote the happiness of themselves and of their posterity.

"Which is the best form of civil government, is a question of the first magnitude to any people; and particularly to us who have lately considered this weighty matter; and who expect, at some future period, finally to determine it. May that God by whom all human events are controlled, inspire my fellow-citizens with that wisdom that shall be profitable to direct!

"From the premises, the following is a natural conclusion—*That the authority of the civil magistrate is, under God, derived from, the people.*

"In order therefore to determine with accuracy, what the powers of the civil magistrate are, and also the duties that the people owe him, we must have recourse to the constitution; by which, in all good governments, the authority of the former, and the rights of the latter are determined with precision.

"That it should be so, is a dictate of common sense. For upon a supposition of the contrary, how shall the rulers or subject determine their respective obligations?

"From hence arises, in my view, the indispensable necessity of a Bill Of Rights drawn up in the most explicit language, previously to the ratification of a constitution of government; which should contain its fundamental principles, and which no poison in the state, however dignified, should dare to violate but at his peril.

"As we are at present without a fixed form of government, I shall treat the subject rather according to my wishes, than the present state of things. For the constitution ought at least to have a general existence in idea before the reciprocal duties of magistrates and people can be ascertained.

"Some of those principles which, I apprehend, may be called *fundamental*, have been mentioned; to which I beg leave to subjoin:

"That the great end for which men enter into a state of civil society is *their own advantage*.

"That civil rulers, as they derive their authority from the people, so they are accountable to them for the use they make of it.

"That elections ought to be *free* and *frequent*.

"That representation should be as equal as possible.

"That as all men are equal by nature, so, when they enter into a state of civil government, they are entitled *precisely* to the same rights and privileges, or to an *equal degree* of political happiness.

"That some of the natural rights of mankind are unalienable, and subject, to no control but that of the Deity. Such are the Sacred Rights of Conscience; which, in a state of nature and of civil society, are exactly the same. They can neither be parted with nor controlled by any human authority whatever.

"Attempts of this kind have been repeatedly made by an ambitious clergy, assisted by rulers of despotic principles; the consequence of which has been, that crowds of the best members of society have been reduced to this dreadful alternative, either to offend God and violate the dictates of their own minds, or to die at a stake.

"That the right of trial by jury ought to be perpetual.

"That no man's property can, of right, be taken from him without his consent, given either in person or by his representative.

"That no laws are obligatory on the people but those that have obtained a like consent. Nor are such laws of any force, if, proceeding from a corrupt majority of the legislature, they are incompatible with the fundamental principles of government, and tend to subvert it.

"Upon the truth of the principles advanced, I observe, that the authority of the magistrate is derived from the people by consent—that it is limited and subordinate—and that so long as he exercises the power with which he is vested, according to the original compact, the people owe him *reverence, obedience* and *support.*

"Inspiration teaches us to *give honor to whom honor, fear to whom fear.*

"When any men are taken from the common rank of citizens, and are entrusted with the powers of government, they are by that act ennobled. Their election implies their personal merit, and is a public declaration of it. For it is taken for granted, that the people have been influenced in their choice by worthiness of character, and not by family connections, or other base motives. They are, therefore, entitled to a certain degree of respect from their constituents—who, while they pay them due reverence, will feel it reflected upon themselves, because they bear their commission. Both interest and duty oblige them to reverence the powers that be. It is their duty in consequence of their own appointment. And their interest, because the good of the community depends much upon it. For as far as any of the citizens unjustly depreciate the merit of rulers, so far they lessen the energy of government, and put it out of their power to promote the public good.

"It is the duty of the people to *support the magistrate, in the due execution of the laws against such, and all other offenders.* To choose men to office, and not to support them in the execution of it, is too great an absurdity, one would think, to find any abettors.

"It is taken for granted, that the rulers of the people will not forget the source of their power, nor the design of their appointment to office—that they have no authority but what they derived from the people; who, from a confidence in them that reflects great honor on them, have put it into their hands, with this sole view—that they might thereby promote the good of the community.

"Whether this great end is accomplished, by the exercise of the authority of civil rulers, the people are to judge; with whom the powers of government originate, and who must know the end for which they entrusted them in the hands of any of their fellow-citizens. This right of judging of their conduct implies, that it lies with them either to *censure* or *approve it.*

"These considerations are happily calculated to prevent the abuse of power, which has already happened in repeated instances. And of which there ever will be danger, while mankind remain in their present state of corruption.

"A faithful ruler will consider himself as a trustee of the public, and that he is accountable both to God and to the people for his behavior in his office. He will, therefore, be very careful not to involve himself in more public business than he can perform with fidelity.

"It would have a happy tendency to render the duty of the magistrate easy and successful, were he to cultivate an intimate acquaintance with the genius and temper of the people over whom he presides. By such an acquisition if prudent, he would be capable of pursuing a mode of conduct that would not fail of gaining him the affections and confidence of his subjects. The importance of which is self-evident.

"'He *who ruleth over men' says David, 'must be just, ruling in the fear of God'* In his exalted station, he should go before the people as an example of every moral virtue; and as a hearty friend of that constitution of government which he hath sworn to protect. To the meanest of the people he should act the part of a political father, by securing to them the full enjoyment of life, liberty, and property. To him they are to look that justice is not delayed, nor the laws executed with partiality; but that all those who united in clothing him with the authority of the magistrate may uninterruptedly enjoy that *equal liberty,* for the security of which they entered into a state of civil society. Thus will he be *as the light of the morning when the sun riseth, even a morning without clouds.*

"III. To attempt to draw the line between the things that belong to Caesar, and those things that belong to God.

"The power which the people commit into the hands of the magistrate is wholly confined to the things of this world. Other power than this they have not. They have not the least authority over the consciences of one another, nor over their own consciences so as to alienate them or subject them to the control of the civil magistrate in matters of religion, in which every man ought to be fully persuaded in his own mind, and to follow its dictates at all hazards, because he is to *account for himself at* the judgment-seat of Christ.

"Seeing, then, that the people have no power that they can commit into the hands of the magistrate but that which relates to the good of civil society, it follows that the magistrate can have no other, because he derives his authority from the people. Such as the power of the people is, such must be the power of the magistrate."[263]

When the war was won, the patriot preachers continued right on preaching this message. For example, on June 5, 1788, Samuel Langdon reminded the people that the power of government was with the people:

"The power in all our republics is acknowledged to originate in the people: it is delegated by them to every magistrate and officer; and to the people all in authority are accountable, if they deviate from their duty, and abuse their power. Even the man, who may be advanced to the chief command of these United States, according to the proposed constitution; whose office resembles that of a king in other nations, which has always been thought so sacred that they have had no conception of bringing a king before the bar of justice; even he depends on the choice of the people for his temporary and limited power, and will be liable to impeachment, trial, and disgrace for any gross misconduct. On the people, therefore, of these United-States it depends whether wise men, or fools, good or bad men, shall govern them; whether they shall have righteous laws, a faithful administration of government, and permanent good order, peace, and liberty; or, on the contrary, feel insupportable burdens, and see all their affairs run to confusion and ruin."[264]

On June 11, 1797, Stephen Peabody, pastor of the First Congregational Church of Atkinson, New Hampshire, preached this same theme in his election sermon:

"This is the general principle which supports the government of united America, happily removed from that monarchy, aristocracy, or democracy, which have injured mankind. This form has the public good for its principal object: It rests primarily in the hands of the people; and when delegated, is exercised a limited period, and returns to its origin. A people with a good constitution, judicious laws, in the hands of an executive authority influenced by the maxims of wisdom and goodness, attentive to their true interest, will acquire strength and stability, as they improve in knowledge and virtue."[265]

And since they believed the government received its power from the people, the preachers taught that the people had a responsibility to engage in the process.

Samuel Cooper emphasized this point in his sermon, *A Sermon On The Day Of The Commencement Of The Constitution,* preached in Boston on October 25, 1780:

"We have now a government free indeed; but after all, it remains with the people, under God, to make it an honorable and happy one: This must ultimately depend upon the prudence of their elections, and the virtue of their conduct. A government framed by ourselves for our own benefit, and according to the fairest models of our own minds, and administered by men of our own choice, ought to be more deeply respected, and more religiously supported by us than any kind of imposed authority. … In a word, if the rulers and the people act throughout in this spirit; if they mutually watch over and sustain each other; and those virtues are cultivated among us which support and are supported by a free republic, our new government will then open with the most happy omens, and the commencement of it will be the era of our rising felicity and glory."[266]

4. MEN HAVE THE RIGHT TO FORM THEIR OWN GOVERNMENT.

Believing then, that the power of government resided with the people, the Black Regiment preached that men had the right to form their own government and/or abolish that government if it ever ceased to promote their general welfare. The following examples offer a glimpse of how the patriot preachers evangelized this concept.

- Samuel Langdon's Massachusetts election sermon, *Government Corrupted By Vice,* May 31, 1775 – declared that not only did men have the right to establish their own government, but also had the right to "put an end to" any government that did not answer to their "grand purpose":

"Every nation, when able and agreed, has a right to set up over itself any form of government which to it may appear most conducive to its common welfare. … Thanks be to God, that he has given us, as men, natural rights, independent of all human laws whatever; and these rights are recognized by the grand charter of British liberties. By the *law of nature* any body of people, destitute of order and government, may form themselves into a civil society according to their best prudence, and so provide for their common safety and advantage. When one form is found, by the majority, not to answer the grand purpose in any tolerable degree, they may by common consent put an end to it, and set up another; only as all such great changes are attended with difficulty, and danger of confusion, they ought not to be attempted without urgent necessity, which will be determined always by the general voice of the wisest and best members of the community. If the great servants of the public forget their duty, betray their trust and sell their country, or make war against the most valuable rights and privileges of the people; reason and justice require that they should be discarded, and others appointed in their room, without any regard to formal resignations of their forfeited power."[267]

- Moses Mather's Connecticut election sermon, 1775 – the original settlers in America had the right to form their own government:

"When our ancestors left the kingdom of England, they were subjects of that kingdom, and entitled to equal privileges with the rest of its subjects; when they came into America, where no civil constitutions were existing, they joined themselves to none: the lands which they entered and possessed, they acquired by purchase, or by conquest of the natives: they came over of themselves, viz. were not colonies sent out, to make settlements by government; not to mention the intolerable oppressions, by which they were driven out, crossed the Atlantic, and availed themselves of possessions, at their own risk and expense, and by their own sword and prowess. Now, in America, they were still subjects of the kingdom of England, or they were not; if the former, then they were entitled to enjoy, in America, the same or equal privileges, with those enjoyed by the subjects residing in England— if the latter, then that kingdom had no right of jurisdiction over them, and they were in a state of nature, at liberty to erect such a constitution of civil government as they should choose. … By nature, every man (under God) is his own legislator, judge, and avenger, and absolute lord of his property. In civil government, rightly constituted, every one retains a share in the legislative, taxative, judicial, and the vindictive powers, by having a voice in the supreme legislature, which enacts the laws, and imposes the taxes, and by having a right, in all cases wherein he is injured, to resort to, and demand redress, in a course of law, from the tribunal of the public, and the sword of state."[268]

- Samuel West's Massachusetts election sermon, May 29, 1776:

"In order to determine this point, we are to remember that all men being by nature equal, all the members of a community have a natural right to assemble themselves together, and act and vote for such regulations as they judge are necessary for the good of the whole. But when a community is become very numerous, it is very difficult, and in many cases impossible, for all to meet together to regulate the affairs of the state; hence comes the necessity of appointing delegates to represent the people in a general assembly. And this ought to be looked upon as a sacred and inalienable right, of which a people cannot justly divest themselves, and which no human authority can in equity ever take from them, viz., that no one be obliged to submit to any law except such as are made either by himself or by his representative."[269]

5. THE BEST FORM OF GOVERNMENT IS A REPUBLIC.

The Founders did not create our form of government in a vacuum. Their decision to create a republic rather than a pure democracy was not their idea alone. Having experienced first hand the dangers of a monarchy, the Founders knew that they did not want a monarchal form of government. But they also understood that a pure democracy could be just as brutal, so they did not want that for America either. The patriot preachers had been preaching individual rights for years and were calling for representative government long before the war began. They, along with the Founders, believed that liberty was God's "grand fountain" of all temporal blessings and they were convinced that a republic was the best form of government to guard that liberty.

- Abraham Keteltas's sermon preached in Newbury-port, Massachusetts, 1777:

"Liberty is the grand fountain, under God, of every temporal blessing, and what is infinitely more important, it is favorable to the propagation of unadulterated Christianity. Liberty is the parent of truth, justice, virtue, patriotism, benevolence, and every generous and noble purpose of the soul. Under the influence of liberty, the arts and sciences, trade, commerce, and husbandry flourish and the wilderness blossoms like the rose. …

"Under the auspicious smiles of Liberty, riches increase, industry strains every nerve, secure of property, and joy and plenty smile on every side. How inestimable a blessing then must liberty be, and how inconceivably great its loss!

"But if liberty is thus friendly to the happiness of mankind, and is the cause of the kind parent of the universe; certainly tyranny & oppression are the cause of the devil, the cause which God's soul hates. The Holy Scriptures abound with instances and prophecies of his judgments against tyrants and oppressors; and not only sacred, but profane history, prove the fulfillment of those prophesies."[270]

- Samuel West's Massachusetts election sermon preached, May 29, 1776:

"It becomes me not to say what particular form of government is best for a community – whether a pure democracy, aristocracy, monarchy, or a mixture of all the three simple forms. They have all their advantages and disadvantages, and when they are properly administered may, any of them, answer the design of civil government tolerably. Permit me, however, to say, that an unlimited, absolute monarchy, and an aristocracy not subject to the control of the people, are two of the most exceptionable forms of government: firstly, because in neither of them is there a proper representation of the people; and, secondly, because each of them being entirely independent of the people, they are very apt to degenerate into tyranny. However, in this imperfect state, we cannot expect to have government formed upon such a basis but that it may be perverted by bad men to evil purposes."[271]

- Enos Hitchcock, who had served as chaplain in the Continental Army, preached this sermon in the Baptist-meeting house in Providence, Rhode Island on July 4, 1793, declaring that a republic was superior to any other form of government:

"Every good government must exist somewhere between absolute despotism, and absolute democracy. In either of these extremes, neither liberty nor safety can be enjoyed. It will follow, that a constitution wherein the three powers, legislative, executive and judicial, are most perfectly combined for the prosperity of the people, is the best. Indeed, the great Montesquieu has made it appear, that these three powers exist, in some degree, in every form of government, even the most absolute. As these powers display their cooperative influence, in a greater or less degree, in the governmental machine, they have received their name or style. The name of aristocracy is given to the government of those states, where a permanent senate governs all, without ever consulting the people."[272]

- James Madison, Episcopal Bishop, preached *Manifestations Of The Beneficence Of Divine Providence Towards America* in Richmond, Virginia on February 19,

1795 in which he defended the "excellencies" of a representative republic:

"Fellow-citizens, it is an easy task for those who may have the honor of addressing an American audience this day, to point out the excellencies of our civil governments, to show their superior aptitude for the promotion of political happiness, to evince that obedience to laws, constitutionally enacted, is the only means of preserving liberty, and that every expression of the public will is obligatory upon every citizen; to prove, that representative republics, instead of being the prolific parents of anarchy and confusion, are, on the contrary, of all the forms of government, under which men have yet associated, either thro' compulsion or choice, the most promotive of private and public happiness, the most susceptible of that energy, which is equally capable of curbing the licentiousness of the multitude, or of frustrating the wicked designs of the ambitious ..."[273]

As the patriot preachers praised the virtues of the republican form of government, they also warned of its shortcomings – one of which was their relatively short life spans. Samuel McClintock pointed this out to the New Hampshire legislators on June 3, 1784:

"Republics, in their very constitution, are shorter lived than other governments: their foundation being laid in virtue, when the body of the people become corrupt, the enemy takes advantage while they are lulled into a fatal sleep on the soft lap of pleasure, to bind them with the cords of absolute power; so that when they awake, like Sampson, too late, they find themselves deprived of that in which their strength lay. This was formerly the fate of the Roman commonwealth, and is at present the case of Venice and the United Netherlands. All empires have had their period, and without doubt ours, like them, will also be lost in the lapse of time. We would fain place that event at a distant period. We cannot but hope that the Almighty has designed America as the stage on which he will make the most illustrious displays of his power and glory—let us unite our endeavors for its accomplishment. Let vice in every form be discountenanced, that, as ashamed, it may hide its head, and genius, merit and virtue, be encouraged and rewarded. Let wisdom guide our public councils, and equity and moderation mark our public measures."[274]

In addition to extolling the virtues of a republic, the patriot preachers also addressed other principles of government that we highly prize today:

— THE IMPORTANCE OF AN ARMED CITIZENRY:

The patriot preachers understood that only an armed populace was capable of defending its God-given rights. They boldly preached this concept which was ultimately enshrined in the U.S. Constitution in the Second Amendment. For example, consider the sermon preached by Ezra Stiles to the General Assembly of Connecticut on May 8, 1783:

> "Moreover, as we have seen the wisdom of our ancestors in instituting a militia, so it is necessary to continue it. The Game Act, in the time of James I., insidiously disarmed the people of England. Let us not be insidiously disarmed. In all our enlargements in colonization, in all our increasing millions, let the main body be exercised annually to military discipline, whether in war or peace. This will defend us against ourselves and against surrounding states. Let this be known in Europe, in every future age, and we shall never again be invaded from the other side of the Atlantic. 'The militia of this country,' says General Washington, 'must be considered as the palladium of our security and the first effectual resort in case of hostility.'"[275]

— TRIAL BY PEERS:

The patriot preachers understood that justice could prevail only where a fair and just judicial system was free to function. They knew that the best way to ensure citizens of a fair trial was to place their fate in the hands of fellow citizens rather than those of a single judge. Samuel Sherwood preached this principle on August 31, 1774, declaring,

> "As it is not the laws merely, that are made, considered in themselves, but the construction and sense put upon them, by the judges and triers, that falls upon the subject and affects him in his person and property; it was necessary that the constitution should guard the rights of the subject, in the executive as well as the legislative part of government: And no mode of trial would so effectually do this, be so unexceptionable, by reason of their equality, and the impartial manner

in which they are taken and impanelled; so advantageous, on account of their knowledge of the parties, the credibility of the witnesses, and what weight ought to be given to their testimony, as that by our peers, a jury of the vicinity: For very good and wholesome laws may be perniciously executed. Wherefore it is expressly provided and ordained, in the Great Charter, chap. 29, 'That no freeman shall be taken or disseized of his freehold, or liberties, or free customs, or be outlawed, or exiled, or any otherwise destroyed; and we will not pass sentence upon him, nor condemn him, but by lawful judgment of his peers; or by the laws of the land.' By this no freeman might be molested in his person, liberty or estate, but according to the laws of the land, by lawful warrant, granted by lawful authority, expressing the cause for which, the time when, and place where he is to answer or be imprisoned, with the terms of his enlargement; nor have sentence passed upon him in any case, but by lawful judgment of his peers; who, in the instance of giving their verdict, do unanimously declare and announce the law, with respect to themselves, in like circumstances. It is, says Dr. Blackstone, the most transcendent privilege which any subject can enjoy or wish for, that he cannot be affected in his property, his liberty or person, but by the unanimous consent of twelve of his neighbors and equals: And when a celebrated French writer concludes, that because Rome, Sparta, and Carthage, lost their liberties, therefore England must in time lose theirs, he should have recollected, that Rome, Sparta, and Carthage were strangers to trial by jury; and that it is a duty which every man owes to his country, his friends, his posterity and himself, to maintain, to the utmost of his power, this valuable constitution in all its parts, to restore it to its ancient dignity, if at all impaired, or deviated from its first institution, &c. and above all, to guard with the most jealous circumspection, against the introduction of new and arbitrary methods of trial, which, under a variety of plausible pretenses, may in time, imperceptibly undermine this best preservative of English liberties."[276]

— THE NECESSITY OF A GOOD PRESS:

Phillips Payson's Massachusetts election sermon, May 27, 1778:

"The full liberty of the press – that eminent instrument of promoting knowledge, and great palladium of the public liberty – being enjoyed, the learned professions directed to the public good, the great principles of legislation and government, the great examples and truths of history, the maxims of generous and upright policy, and the severer truths of philosophy investigated and apprehended by a general application to books, and by observation and experiment – are means by which the capacity of a state will be strong and respectable, and the number of superior minds will be daily increasing."[277]

— THE IMPORTANCE OF EDUCATION, ESPECIALLY RELIGIOUS EDUCATION:

- Phillips Payson's Massachusetts election sermon, May 27, 1778:

"The slavery of a people is generally founded in ignorance of some kind or another; and there are not wanting such facts as abundantly prove the human mind may be so sunk and debased, through ignorance and its natural effects, as even to adore its enslaver, and kiss its chains. Hence knowledge and learning may well be considered as most essentially requisite to a free, righteous government."[278]

- Simeon Howard's Massachusetts election sermon, May 31, 1780:

"Liberty and learning are so friendly to each other, and so naturally thrive and flourish together, that we may justly expect that the guardians of the former will not neglect the latter. The good education of children is a matter of great importance to the commonwealth. Youth is the time to plant the mind with the principles of virtue, truth and honor, the love of liberty and of their country, and to furnish it with all useful knowledge; and though in this business much depends upon parents, guardians, and masters, yet it is incumbent upon the government to make provision for schools and all suitable means of instruction."[279]

- Samuel Cooper's sermon delivered in Boston, October 25, 1780:

"Neither piety, virtue, or liberty can long flourish in a community, where the education of youth is neglected. How much do we owe to the care of our venerable ancestors upon this important object? Had not they laid such foundations for training up their children in knowledge and religion, in science, and arts, should we have been so respectable a community as we this day appear? Should we have understood our rights so clearly? or valued them so highly? or defended them with such advantage? Or should we have been prepared to lay that basis of liberty, that happy constitution, on which we raise such large hopes, and from which we derive such uncommon joy? We may therefore be confident that the schools, and particularly the university, founded and cherished by our wise and pious fathers, will be patronized and nursed by a government which is so much indebted to them for its honor and efficacy, and the very principles of its existence. The present circumstances of those institutions call for the kindest attention of our rulers; and their close connection with every public interest, civil and religious, strongly enforces the call.

"The sciences and arts, for the encouragement of which a new foundation hath lately been laid in this commonwealth, deserve the countenance and particular favor of every government. They are not only ornamental but useful: They not only polish, but support, enrich, and defend a community. As they delight in liberty, they are particularly friendly to free states. Barbarians are fierce and ungovernable, and having the grossest ideas of order, and the benefits resulting from it, they require the hand of a stern master; but a people enlightened and civilized by the sciences and liberal arts, have sentiments that support liberty and good laws: They may be guided by a silken thread; and the mild punishments proper to a free state are sufficient to guard the public peace."[280]

- ## Samuel McClintock's New Hampshire election sermon, June 3, 1784:

"The education of youth in useful knowledge and the principles of virtue, being essential to the preservation of a free government, and the public welfare, should be a main object of every wise government. The faculties of the human mind, in their natural state, are like precious metal in the ore, which must be refined and polished by the hand of education to make them useful. Knowledge is not only necessary in rulers to qualify them to fill public posts with dignity and reputation; but also in the people to make them good subjects. A wise and knowing people will think it no less their interest than duty to support government and yield obedience to the laws; whereas the ignorant being governed wholly by their passions, are dangerous subjects of any government, especially a free one. They are mere machines, and ever liable to be excited by an artful designing demagogue, to such acts of violence and outrage, as have sometimes brought the public to the brink of ruin. Witness the frequent revolutions in the Ottoman government, where sometimes a sultan is deposed and strangled by a sudden insurrection, while the grand seignior sits trembling in his palace. It would then render a most essential service to the public, and be a happy mean of securing to distant posterity the blessings of that free and wise government we are placed under, if rulers would take effectual measures for the instruction of the rising generation in useful knowledge—posterity will rise up and call them blessed. … The worthy framers of our constitution have expressed their sense of it, when they say, that 'Knowledge and learning generally diffused through a community are essential to the preservation of a free government,' and when they add, that "it shall be the duty of the legislators and magistrates, in all future periods of this government, to cherish the interest of literature and the sciences, and all seminaries and public schools."[281]

- ## Elizur Goodrich's Connecticut election sermon, May 10, 1787:

"I shall only add, that as the best and most useful laws can be of no use, unless subjects be trained up and educated in a manner of living conformable to them, every wise state will pay great attention to the education of children, and to all such regulations, as are necessary for the instruction of the people in the principles of piety and virtue. The best security men can have, of living together in harmony and love, is from the prevalence of true religion, and a due regard to the will and authority of the Supreme Being. Religion and virtue, are the strongest bond of human society, and lay the best foundation of peace and happiness in the civil state."[282]

- ## Samuel Langdon's New Hampshire election sermon, June 5, 1788:

"I call upon you also to support schools in all your towns, that the rising generation may not grow up in ignorance. Grudge not any expense proportionate to your abilities. It is a debt you owe to your children, and that God to whom they belong; a necessary evidence of your regard for their present and future happiness, and of your concern to transmit the blessings you yourselves enjoy to future generations. The human mind without early and continual cultivation grows wild and savage: knowledge must be instilled as its capacities gradually enlarge, or it cannot expand and extend its sphere of activity. Without instruction men can have no knowledge but what comes from their own observation and experience, and it will be a long time before they can be acquainted even with things most necessary for the support and comfort of the present life. Leave your children untaught to read, write, cypher, &c. teach them no trade, or husbandry; let them grow up wholly without care; and they will be more fit for a savage than civil life, and whatever inheritance you may think to leave them will be of no advantage. But, on the contrary, train them up in the fear of God, in an acquaintance with his word, and all such useful knowledge as your abilities will allow, and they will soon know how to provide for themselves, perhaps may take care of their aged parents, and fill the various stations in life with honor and advantage. Look round and see the growing youth: they are to succeed in your stead; government and religion must be continued by them; from among these will shortly rise up our legislators, judges, ministers of the gospel, and officers of every rank. Can you think of this, and not promote schools, academies, and colleges? Can you leave the youth uninstructed in any thing which may prepare them to act their part well in the world? Will you suffer ignorance to spread its horrid gloom over the land? An ignorant people will easily receive idolatry for their religion, and must bow their necks to the tyrant's yoke, because they are incapable of using rational liberty. Will you then consign over your posterity to foolish and abominable superstitions instead of religion, and to be the slaves of despotism, when a small proportion of the produce of your labors will make them wise, free, and happy?"[283]

- Enos Hitchcock's Independence Day sermon, July 4, 1793:

"Our attention now returns with delight to contemplate that portion of religious and scientific freedom which our country enjoys. To the early care of our ancestors to establish literary, and encourage religious institutions, are we much indebted for the accomplishment of the late revolution, which shows us the vast importance of paying great attention to the rising sons and daughters of America, by giving them an enlightened and a virtuous education. Here the human mind, free as the air, may exert all its powers towards the various objects laid before it, and expand its faculties to an extent hitherto unknown. It has been the policy of all monarchical governments, and of some religious institutions, to keep the people in ignorance, the more easily to dazzle them into obedience by external marks of greatness, and of native superiority. Knowledge and true religion go hand in hand. When the former is obscured, the latter is mutilated, and enveloped in the shades of superstition and bigotry. And whenever the civil power has undertaken to judge and decide concerning truth and error, to oppose the one, while it protected the other, it has invariably supported bigotry, superstition and nonsense."[284]

- Stephen Peabody's New Hampshire election sermon, June 11, 1797:

"A foundation placed in the minds of youth, is like "good seed sown in good ground," in its proper season; and gives the fairest prospects of a happy increase to the well being of society. The principles of virtue and knowledge early implanted, naturally take root, and produce a luxuriant harvest. Those who are thus favored, are "trained up in the way they should go," the best prompter on life's devious journey. Hence the propriety of having able instructors, whose morals and language are worthy of imitation: And hence the necessity of giving ample encouragement, in a business so important and laborious. Though honorable donations have been made for the promotion of literature, yet the fostering hand of our civil fathers may be required for bringing to maturity. May it not then be expected, that every aid and encouragement will be given to education? The views of such as are young, are hereby extended; they are raised above the groveling vulgarisms too common to that age, which will have a happy influence upon society, in preparing the rising generation to fill with honor the most dignified stations, when they may be called to act upon the theatre of life."[285]

— SECURE NATIONAL BORDERS:

Although many modern Americans do not understand the importance of secure borders, the patriot pastors did. John Smalley's May 8, 1800 Connecticut election sermon illustrates this fact:

"A nation that has an extended coast, and an extensive commerce to defend, had better be at immense charges for the security of these, than lie open to those spoliations and invasions, to which, without arming, when all the world is at war, they might inevitably be exposed."[286]

— INTERNATIONAL TRADE:

The pastors also understood the importance of balanced trade with foreign countries. This can be seen in Samuel Wales's May 12, 1785 Connecticut election sermon, *The Dangers Of Our National Prosperity; And The Way To Avoid Them*:

"After all that has been said in favor of foreign trade and foreign luxuries, it still remains a demonstration in politics, that when our imports exceed our exports, the course of trade is against us, and we are constantly growing poor."[287]

— UNFAIRNESS OF GOVERNMENT-FORCED WELFARE:

Even though the pastors believed Scripture taught that it was the responsibility of Christians to help those who could not help themselves, they also took to heart the admonition of the Apostle Paul in 2 Thessalonians 3:10 where he said, "if any would not work, neither should he eat." John Smalley's Connecticut election sermon on May 8, 1800 provides a perfect example:

"Liberality to the poor, out of one's own proper goods, is a capital Christian virtue; but of the property of other people, judges and law-givers, may possibly be over liberal. The persons even of the poor, are not to be respected in judgment. Making provision by law, for supporting such as are unable to support themselves, is doubtless very commendable; but why those who happen to be the creditors of the poor; who have helped them much already, and suffered much by their slackness and breach of promise, should be still obliged to lose ten times more for their relief, or for the relief of their families, than others equally able, it is not easy to conceive. And should courts of law, or courts of equity, cancel the debts of men, whenever they plead a present incapacity to pay them, whether such clemency might not too much weaken government, as a security to every one in his rightful claims, may be a question. Indeed, in any case, to give an insolvent debtor a final discharge from all he owes, without the consent of his creditors, looks like giving him a license to be an unrighteous man. For can it ever be right, or can any court under heaven make it right, for a man not to pay his promised debts, for value received, when now he has money enough, because once, the payment of them was not in the power of his hands.

"Thus to exonerate of a heavy load of old debts, one deeply insolvent, is necessary, it will be said; as without this he could have no courage to commence business anew. And, no doubt, such expected exoneration, will be a mighty encouragement to extravagant adventurers, who have nothing to lose, since, by running the greatest hazards, with the slenderest chance of immense gain, they risk only the property of others. If successful, the profit is their own; if unsuccessful, the loss is their neighbor's. But if the tendency of being thus merciful, were much better than it is; or the urgency for it far greater; would it not be doing evil that good may come. "He that ruleth over men must be just." The laws of truth and righteousness, are not noses of wax; to be bent any way, as will suit present convenience. It is dangerous to break down, or break over, the fixed barrier of eternal justice, on any pretense of temporary necessity."[288]

— THE IMPORTANCE OF PERSONAL HARD WORK AND THE RESPONSIBILITY OF LIVING WITHIN ONE'S MEANS:

This principle was also addressed by the patriot preachers. A perfect example is John Witherspoon's sermon preached at Princeton on May 17, 1776:

"I exhort all who are not called to go into the field, to apply themselves with the utmost diligence to works of industry. It is in your power by this mean not only to supply the necessities, but to add to the strength of your country. Habits of industry prevailing in a society, not only increase its wealth, as their immediate effect, but they prevent the introduction of many vices, and are intimately connected with sobriety and good morals. Idleness is the mother or nurse of almost every vice; and want, which is its inseparable companion, urges men on to the most abandoned and destructive courses. Industry, therefore is a moral duty of the greatest moment, absolutely necessary to national prosperity, and the sure way of obtaining the blessing of God. I would also observe, that in this, as in every other part of God's government, obedience to his will is as much a natural mean, as a meritorious cause, of the advantage we wish to reap from it. Industry brings up a firm and hardy race. He who is inured to the labor of the field, is prepared for the fatigues of a campaign. The active farmer who rises with the dawn and follows his team or plow, must in the end be an overmatch for those effeminate and delicate soldiers, who are nursed in the lap of self-indulgence, and whose greatest exertion is in the important preparation for, and tedious attendance on, a masquerade, or midnight ball. …

"In the last place, suffer me to recommend to you frugality in your families, and every other article of expense. This the state of things among us renders absolutely necessary, and it stands in the most immediate connection both with virtuous industry, and active public spirit. Temperance in meals, moderation and decency in dress, furniture and equipage, have, I think, generally been characteristics of a distinguished patriot. And when the same spirit pervades a people in general, they are fit for every duty, and able to encounter the most formidable enemy."[289]

— NATIONAL DEBT:

Not only did the pastors believe that individuals should live within their means, they also believed that nations should do the same. Samuel Cooper's Boston sermon on October 25, 1780 made this point:

"An established honor and fidelity in all public engagements and promises, form a branch of righteousness that is wealth, is power, and security to a state: It prevents innumerable perplexities: It creates confidence in the government from subjects and from strangers: It facilitates the most advantageous connections: It extends credit; and easily obtains supplies in the most pressing public emergencies, and when nothing else can obtain them: While the want of it, whatever benefits some shortsighted politicians may have promised from delusive expedients, and deceitful arts, renders a state weak and contemptible; strips it of its defense; grieves and provoke[s] its friends, and delivers it up to the will of its enemies. Upon what does the power of the British nation chiefly rest at this moment? That power that has been so unrighteously employed against America? Upon the long and nice preservation of her faith in all monied matters. With all her injustice in other instances, mere policy hath obliged her to maintain a fair character with her creditors. The support this hath given her in frequent and expensive wars, by the supplies it has enabled her to raise upon loan, is astonishing. By this her government hath availed itself of the whole immense capital of the national debt, which hath been expended in the public service, while the creditors content themselves with the bare payment of the interest. It may be demonstrated that the growing resources of these states, under the conduct of prudence and justice, are sufficient to form a fund of credit for prosecuting the present war, so ruinous to Britain, much longer than that nation, loaded as she now is, can possibly support it.

"But need I urge, in a Christian audience, and before Christian rulers, the importance of preserving inviolate the public faith? If this is allowed to be important at all times, and to all states, it must be peculiarly so to those whose foundations are newly laid, and who are but just numbered among the nations of the earth. They have a national character to establish, upon which their very existence may depend. Shall we not then rely that the present government will employ every measure in their power, to maintain in this commonwealth a clear justice, an untainted honor in all public engagements; in all laws respecting property; in all regulations of taxes; in all our conduct towards our sister states, and towards our allies abroad."[290]

Clearly, the patriot preachers believed that Scripture had a great deal to say about government and that any just and equitable government was one that was squarely founded on biblical principles. But the preachers also believed that good government was impossible without good leaders. These preachers found in the Bible very specific qualifications for good leaders. The following chapter lays out exactly what the patriot preachers taught their people to expect and demand in the leaders they chose.

Chapter 15

THE BIBLICAL QUALIFICATIONS OF GOOD LEADERS

When People are put to unnecessary charge, they are Oppressed, and when they are Oppressed, they are abused; it is directly contrary to the Office of Rulers, to lay heavy burdens on the People ..."[291]

Solomon Stoddard, 1703 Massachusetts Election Sermon

"... [Abusive rulers are] the greatest Burdens unto Mankind, and the greatest Plagues and punishments to the World.... if you should abuse your Power, and go over all the bounds of your Duty & Obligations; oppress & vex this People, and lay heavy burdens upon them, and grievous to be born; you'd forfeit the gratitude and regard due to Benefactors; and become obnoxious not only to the resentments of the People groaning under their burdens, but also to the Divine Displeasure; ... As Oppression makes a wise man mad, so it makes a righteous God angry."[292]

John Hancock, 1722 Massachusetts Election Sermon

"When a government is in its prime, the public good engages the attention of the whole; the strictest regard is paid to the qualifications of those who hold the offices of the state; virtue prevails; everything is managed with justice, prudence, and frugality; the laws are founded on principles of equity rather than mere policy, and all the people are happy. But vice will increase with the riches and glory of an empire; and this gradually tends to corrupt the constitution, and in time bring on its dissolution. This may be considered not only as the natural effect of vice, but a righteous judgment of Heaven, especially upon a nation which has been favored with the blessings of religion and liberty, and is guilty of undervaluing them, and eagerly going into the gratification of every lust."[293]

Samuel Langdon, 1775 Massachusetts Election Sermon

The Black Regiment preachers knew that, next to the political involvement of the citizens, good rulers were essential to creating and maintaining a good government. Consequently, they had much to say about the qualifications, duties, and accountability of those entrusted with the power of government. As they saw it, government existed for the good of the people – not the other way around. Samuel West communicated this in his 1776 Massachusetts election sermon:

> "Though magistrates are to consider themselves as the servants of the people, seeing from them it is that they derive their power and authority, yet they may also be considered as the ministers of God ordained by him for the good of mankind; for, under him, as the Supreme Magistrate of the universe, they are to act: and it is God who has not only declared in his word what are the necessary qualifications of a ruler, but who also raises up and qualifies men for such an important station. The magistrate may also, in a more strict and proper sense, be said to be ordained of God, because reason, which is the voice of God, plainly requires such an order of men to be appointed for the public good. Now, whatever right reason requires as necessary to be done is as much the will and law of God as though it were enjoined us by an immediate revelation from heaven, or commanded in the sacred Scriptures.
>
> "From this account of the origin, nature, and design of civil government, we may be very easily led into a thorough knowledge of our duty; we may see the reason why we are bound to obey magistrates, viz., because they are the ministers of God for good unto the people. While, therefore, they rule in the fear of God, and while they promote the welfare of the state, — *i.e.*, while they act in the character of magistrates, — it is the indispensable duty of all to submit to them, and to oppose a turbulent, factious, and libertine spirit, whenever and wherever it discovers itself. When a people have by their free consent conferred upon a number of men a power to rule and govern them, they are bound to obey them. Hence disobedience becomes a breach of faith; it is violating a constitution of their own appointing, and breaking a compact for which they ought to have the most sacred regard."[294]

Elizur Goodrich echoed these same sentiments in Hartford, Connecticut in his May 10, 1787 election sermon:

"All the qualifications of a good administration may be summed up in two heads, the ability and faithfulness of those, who are entrusted with the weighty concerns of the state: To one or the other of these two things may be referred, whatever can be desired or expected in a good ruler. These qualifications are of the highest importance, in every administration. A free people, under God, may justly put confidence in such an administration, and not find themselves disappointed, as they must unavoidably be if they commit themselves into the hands of weak or wicked men. The former, though they mean never so well, are unable to do good; the latter may improve their great talents, to do mischief: Neither of them are fit to be entrusted with the great affairs of state. Who, on the one hand, would willingly trust his whole interest to the power and disposal of a man of the greatest abilities, but destitute of honor and conscience; or on the other hand, who would undertake a dangerous voyage, on the boisterous ocean, under the command of the most upright and honest man, who had no knowledge of the art of navigation, nor any acquaintance with the seas. In common affairs no honest man will undertake any business for which he knows he is unfit, though he should be solicited to do it: The same should be observed by men, invited to serve the public. When a people have raised men of weak abilities to posts of honor, it may seem hard to neglect them; and it must, indeed, be ungrateful, if in any good degree, they maintain the dignity of their stations, and advance the public good; and especially, if the posts they hold, were unsought, and conferred without solicitation. Nevertheless it should be considered, that those, who undertake the affairs of the public, are as answerable for their abilities, as the soldier for his courage, when he enlists into the service of his country. The safety of the public is to be preferred to the honor of an individual.

"It is therefore, of the highest importance to the being, happiness and peace of free republics, to show a fixed and unalterable regard to merit in the choice of their rulers: The next thing is to discover a deference and submission to authority, obedience to the laws, a spirit of righteousness and peace, and a disposition to promote the public good."[295]

To ensure that Americans chose men fit for leadership; those who would strive to keep the government honorable and lawful, the patriot preachers taught their people to use the following principles when selecting their leaders:

1. Rulers should be men of strong Christian character.

Believing that magistrates were the "ministers of God" appointed for the good of the people (Romans 13), the patriot preachers emphasized how important it was for the people to carefully consider the character of the men they chose to govern. The preachers taught that leaders should be Christians, men who feared God and respected the law. John Jay, Founding Father, president of the Continental Congress from December 10, 1778 to September 28, 1779, and first Chief Justice of the U.S. Supreme Court, gave this advice concerning the kind of men Americans should select for public office:

> "Providence has given to our people the choice of their rulers, and it is the duty, as well as the privilege and interest of our Christian nation, to select and prefer Christians for their rulers."[296]

(*Note: It is important to note that the first Chief Justice of the U.S. Supreme Court called America a "Christian" nation.)

CHARACTER COUNTS

The patriot preachers placed character at the top of their list of qualifications for good government and government officials. (I believe if the patriot preachers and Founders were alive today, they would be saying, "It's the character, stupid!" This is a lesson Americans should have learned well over the past few years from the moral scandals associated with President Clinton and the extremely questionable positions and executive actions of President Obama.) The following sermon excerpts perfectly illustrate this:

- Charles Chauncy's Massachusetts election sermon preached in Boston on May 27, 1747:

> "To be sure, 'tis the truth of the thing. Civil rulers ought to be possessed of a principle of religion, and to act under the direction of it in their respective stations. This is a matter of necessity. I don't mean that it is necessary in order to their having a right to rule over men. *Dominion is not founded in grace*: Nor is every pious good man fit to be entrusted with civil power. 'Tis easy to distinguish between

government in it's abstracted notion, and the faithful advantageous administration of it. And religion in rulers is necessary to the latter, tho' not to the former.

"Not but that they may be considerably useful in their places, if the religious fear of God does not reign in their hearts. From a natural benevolence of temper, accompanied with an active honest turn of mind, they may be instrumental in doing good service to the public: Nay, they may be prompted, even from a view to themselves, their own honour and interest, to behave well in the posts they sustain, at least, in many instances. But if destitute of religion, they are possessed of no principle that will stimulate a care in them to act up to their character steadily and universally, and so as fully to answer the ends of their institution.

"'Tis a principle of religion, and this only, that can set them free from the unhappy influence of those passions and lusts, which they are subject to, in common with other men, and by means whereof they may be betrayed into that tyranny and oppression, that violence and injustice, which will destroy the peace and good order of society. These, 'tis true, may be under some tolerable check from other principles, at least, for a while, and in respect of those actings that are plainly enormous. But no restraints are like those, which the true fear of God lays upon men's lusts. This habitually prevailing in the hearts of rulers, will happily prevent the out-breaking of their pride, and envy, and avarice, and self-love, and other lusts, to the damage of society; and not only so, but it will weaken, and gradually destroy, the very inward propensities themselves to the various acts of vice. It naturally, and powerfully, tends to this: And this is the effect it will produce, in a less or greater degree, according to the strength of the religious principle, in those who are the subjects of it.

"And a principle of religion also, and this only, will be effectual to excite rulers to a uniform, constant and universal regard to truth and justice, in their public conduct. Inferior principles may influence them in particular cases, and at certain seasons: But the fear of God only will prompt them to every instance of right action, and at all times. This will possess them of such sentiments, give such a direction to their views, and fix such a happy bias on their minds, as that their chief concern and care will be, to behave in their offices so as to answer the good ends for which they were put into them. In one word, they will now be the subjects of that divine and universal principle of good conduct, which may, under God, be depended on, to carry them thro' the whole of their duty, upon all occasions, under all difficulties, and in opposition to all temptations, to the rendering the people, over whom they bear rule, as happy as 'tis in their power to make them.

"To be sure, without a principle of religion, none of their services for the public will meet with the divine approbation. 'Tis therefore, in respect of themselves, a matter of absolute necessity that they be possess'd of the true fear of God. It won't suffice, should they behave well in their places, if they have no higher view herein than their own private interest; if they are influenced, not from a due regard to God, his honor and authority, but from love to themselves. This will spoil their best services, in point of the divine acceptance: Whereas, if they act from a principle of religion, what they do in a way of serving their generation will be kindly taken at the hands of a merciful God, and he will, thro' Jesus Christ, amply reward them for it, in the great day of retribution.

"The opinion we have of your Excellency's integrity and justice, forbids the least suspicion of a design in you to invade the civil charter-rights of this people. And tho' you differ in your sentiments from us, as to the model of our church-state, and the external manner of our worship; yet we can securely rely on the generosity of your principles to protect us in the full enjoyment of those ecclesiastical rights we have been so long in possession of: And the rather, because your Excellency knows, that our progenitors enterprised the settlement of this country principally on a religious account; leaving their native land, and transporting themselves and their families, at a vast expense, and at the peril of their lives, into this distant, and then desolate wilderness, that they might themselves freely enjoy, and transmit to us their posterity, *that manner of worship and discipline,* which we look upon, as they did, most agreeable to the purity of God's word. ...

"You all know, from the oracles of God, how men must be furnished, in order to their being fit to be chosen into places of such important trust; that they must be wise and understanding, and known to be so among their tribes; that they must be *able men, and men of truth, men that fear God, and hate covetousness.* And 'tis to be hoped, we have a sufficiency of such, in the land, to constitute his majesty's council. It would be lamentable indeed, if we had not. 'Tis your business, gentlemen, to seek them out. And with you will the fault principally lie, if we have not the best men in the country for councilors; men of capacity and knowledge, who are well acquainted with the nature of government in general, and the constitution, laws, privileges and interests of this people in particular: Men of known piety towards God, and fidelity to their king and country: Men of a generous spirit, who are above acting under the influence of narrow and selfish principles: Men of unquestionable integrity, inflexible justice, and undaunted resolution, who will dare not to give their consent to unrighteous acts, or mistaken nominations; who will disdain, on the one hand, meanly to withdraw, when speaking their minds with freedom and openness may expose them to those who set them up, and may have it in their power to pull them down, or, on the other, to accommodate their conduct, in a servile manner, to their sentiments and designs; in fine, who will steadily act up to their character, support the honor of their station, and approve themselves invariably faithful in their endeavors to advance the public weal.

"These are the men, 'tis in your power, my honorable fathers, to choose into the council; and these are the men for whom, in the name of God, and this whole people, I would earnestly beg every vote this day: And suffer me to say, these are the men you will all send in your votes for, if you are yourselves men of integrity and justice, and exercise your elective-power, not as having concerted the matter beforehand, in some party-juncto, but under the influence of a becoming awe of that omnipresent righteous God, whose eye will be upon you, to observe how you vote, and for whom you vote, and to whom you must finally render an account, before the general assembly of angels and men, for this day's transaction."[297]

- Samuel Cooke's Massachusetts election sermon, May 30, 1770:

"Justice and judgment are the habitation of the throne of the Most High, and he delighteth to honor those who rule over men in his fear. ... This is his support under the weight of government, and fixes his dependence upon the aid of the Almighty, in whose fear he rules. How excellent in the sight of God and man are rulers of this character! ...

The advantages of civil government, even under the British form, greatly depend upon the character and conduct of those to whom the administration is committed. When the righteous are in authority, the people rejoice; but when the wicked beareth rule, the people mourn. The Most High, therefore, who is just in all his ways, good to all, and whose commands strike dread, has strictly enjoined faithfulness upon all those who are advanced to any place of public trust. Rulers of this character cooperate with God in his gracious dispensations of providence, and under him are diffusive blessings to the people, and are compared to the light of morning, when the sun riseth, even a morning without clouds. ...

"This fear of God is the beginning and also the perfection of human wisdom; and, though dominion is not absolutely founded in grace, yet a true principle of religion must be considered as a necessary qualification in a ruler. ... Justice and judgment are the habitation of the throne of the Most High, and he delighteth to honor those who rule over men in his fear. ... This is his support under the weight of government, and fixes his dependence upon the aid of the Almighty, in whose fear he rules. How excellent in the sight of God and man are rulers of this character!"[298]

- Samuel Sherwood's Connecticut sermon, August 31, 1774:

"He that ruleth over men, must be just: And that he may be so, he must rule in the fear of the Lord. If we consider human nature, as vitiated by the apostasy; we shall find, that hardly any thing but the fear of punishment, is able to keep men in awe, and due subjection. That it is thus with subjects, is evident from the many severe laws, and terrible executions of them, which the wisest and most merciful rulers in all nations, have found necessary to preserve the peace, and promote the happiness of civil society. Now, 'tis certain that the essential principles of human nature are the same in all men, whatever external relations they sustain. There is therefore great danger, that rulers will degenerate into tyrants; and of blessings, become plagues and curses to mankind; unless there be some way to keep them in awe, some principle to excite their fears, and by that means, keep them within their proper sphere, and engage them to the observation of justice. Now, this is not always to be done by a fear of men. Sovereigns are exempted from the common power of human laws; there is no ordinary authority that may judge them; and this their security may prove a strong temptation to them, to neglect the proper duties of their exalted stations. They may trust in their forces and armies to defend them from the resentment of an injured and oppressed people; and so imagine themselves perfectly secure from punishment at present; and the nearer any subordinate ruler approaches to sovereignty, the less has he to fear from men, and consequently, the greater prospect has he, of indemnification in acting unjustly. There is therefore the utmost need and necessity, that those who rule over men, should rule in the fear of the Lord; that they should have a firm belief of the being, perfections and providence of God; that they should not only fear his vindictive punishing justice, but beyond this, as the text requires, maintain an holy awe and reverence of him upon their minds; and consider him as that righteous judge to whom they must at last, give an account of the discharge of the great trust reposed in them; and from whom they shall receive a righteous sentence of absolution or condemnation. ...

"Of what importance is it, that civil rulers be men of uprightness and integrity; men of real piety and religion; who fear the Lord, and keep up a proper awe and reverence of him upon their minds? This is necessary to their own comfort and happiness; to the peace of their consciences; and to their having a well-grounded hope of a future crown of glory in the coming world. It is likewise necessary to the good and happiness of the society, over which they are appointed to rule. If a sovereign prince or ruler be destitute of integrity and justice; and has not the fear of the great God before his eyes: all inferior motives which might have influence on men in lower stations, will be insufficient to restrain him from wicked nets of tyranny and oppression, and keep him to his duty. As such cannot well be arraigned before any human tribunal on earth, to account for their conduct; if they have no fear and dread on their minds, of appearing before, and accounting to their supreme Judge, the sovereign ruler of the world; they will be in the utmost danger, not only of ruining themselves both for time and eternity; but also, of ruining their subjects in all their dear and valuable interests; and of involving them in the greatest conceivable distresses and troubles. This is so far from being true, *That such can do no wrong*; that on the contrary, the experience of all ages testifies, that they are capable, when they lose the principles of justice and religion, of doing the greatest mischief and wrong, of any men in the world. *As a roaring lion, and a raging bear,* says Solomon, *So is a wicked ruler over a poor people.* He adds further, *The prince that wanteth understanding is also a great oppressor.* ... the fear of the Lord is the proper, effectual principle to influence civil rulers to the exact observance of justice."[299]

- Samuel West's Massachusetts election sermon, May 29, 1776:

"From this account of civil government we learn that the business of magistrates is weighty and important. It requires both wisdom and integrity. When either are wanting, government will be poorly administered; more especially if our governors are men of loose morals and abandoned principles; for if a man is not faithful to God and his own soul, how can we expect that he will be faithful to the public? There was a great deal of propriety in the advice that Jethro gave to Moses to provide able men, — men of truth, that feared God, and that hated covetousness, — and to appoint them for rulers over the people. For it certainly implies a very gross absurdity to suppose that those who are ordained of God for the public good should have no regard to the laws of God, or that the ministers of God should be despisers of the divine commands. David, the man after God's own heart, makes piety a necessary qualification in a ruler: "He that ruleth over men (says he) must be just, ruling in the fear of God." It is necessary it should be so, for the welfare and happiness of the state; for, to say nothing of the venality and corruption, of the tyranny and oppression, that will take place under unjust rulers, barely their vicious and irregular lives will have a most pernicious effect upon the lives and manners of their subjects: their authority becomes despicable in the opinion of discerning men. And, besides, with what face can they make or execute laws against vices which they practice with greediness? A people that have a right of choosing their magistrates are criminally guilty in the sight of Heaven when they are governed by caprice and humor, or are influenced by bribery to choose magistrates that are irreligious men, who are devoid of sentiment, and of bad morals and base lives. Men cannot be sufficiently sensible what a curse they may bring upon themselves and their posterity by foolishly and wickedly choosing men of abandoned characters and profligate lives for their magistrates and rulers. ...

"Honored fathers of the House of Representatives: We trust to your wisdom and goodness that you will be led to appoint such men to be in council whom you know to be men of real principle, and who are of unblemished lives; that have shown themselves zealous and hearty friends to the liberties of America; and men that have the fear of God before their eyes; for such only are men that can be depended upon uniformly to pursue the general good."[300]

- Simeon Howard's Massachusetts election sermon, May 31, 1780:

"It is of great importance that civil rulers be possessed of this principle [fear of God]. It must be obvious to all that a practical regard to the rules of social virtue is necessary to the character of a good magistrate. Without this a man is unworthy of any trust or confidence. But no principle so effectually promotes and establishes this regard to virtue as the fear of God. A man may, indeed, from a regard to the intrinsic amiableness and excellency of virtue, from a mere sense of honor, from a love of fame, from a natural benevolence of temper, or from a prudent regard to his own temporal happiness, follow virtue when he is under no strong temptation to the contrary. But suppose him in a situation where he apprehends that temporal infamy and misery will be the certain consequence of his practicing virtue, and temporal honor and happiness the consequence of his forsaking it, without any regard to God, as his ruler and judge, and can we expect that he will adhere to his duty? Will he sacrifice everything dear in this life in the cause of virtue, when he has no expectation of any reward for it beyond the grave? Will he deny himself a present gratification, without any prospect of being repaid either here or hereafter? Will he expose himself to reproach, poverty, and death, for the sake of doing good to mankind, without any regard to God as the rewarder of virtue or punisher of vice? This is not to be expected. We all love, and we ought to love, ourselves; and all wish to be happy. Why, then, should a man give up present ease and happiness for suffering and death in the cause of virtue, if he has no expectation that God will reward virtue? This would be acting against the principle of self-love, which is generally too powerful to be counteracted.

"But suppose a man to be habitually under the influence of this principle, — that is, to believe and duly consider God as his ruler and judge, who will hereafter reward virtue and punish vice with happiness and misery respectively, unspeakably greater than any to be enjoyed in this world – and he may then, upon rational principles, and in consistency with his self-love, forego the greatest temporal good, and expose himself to the greatest temporal evil, in the cause of virtue; and we may reasonably expect that he will. Virtue will be his chief good; he will be attached to it as to his very being, with all the strength and ardor of his love and desire of happiness. The fear of God, therefore, is the most effectual and the only sure support of virtue in the world.

"Men invested with civil powers are not, to be sure, less, but generally much more, exposed to temptations to violate their duty than other men. They have more frequent opportunities of committing injuries, and may do it with less fear of present punishment; and therefore stand in need of every possible restraint to keep them from abusing their power by deviating into the paths of vice. …

"There is, I apprehend, nothing in this supposition inconsistent with the principles of rational theology and natural religion. Nor, without supposing that God does thus interpose, is it easy to conceive how that part of the divine government which is in the hands of civil rulers should in all cases be adapted to the various circumstances of particular persons. But there is little reason to think that this light and direction will be granted to men who have no fear of God before their eyes, because, though they lack wisdom, they will not ask it of God, who giveth to all men liberally, and upbraideth not. And rulers being without this divine counsel, it will not be strange if, merely for this reason, their conduct is wrong and ill-judged, calculated in many instances not for the good, but the hurt of the people, and, it may be, at a critical time, for their utter destruction. …

"A man of truth will not undertake an office for which he thinks himself incapable, because this would be promising to do what he is conscious he is incapable of doing; nor will he be instrumental of appointing others to offices for which he thinks them unqualified: this would be acting falsely; because, by the appointment, he declares that he thinks them qualified."[301]

- Samuel Cooper's sermon delivered in Boston, October 25, 1780:

"Our civil rulers will remember, that as piety and virtue support the honor and happiness of every community, they are peculiarly requisite in a free government. Virtue is the spirit of a republic; for where all power is derived from the people, all depends on their good disposition. If they are impious, factious and selfish; if they are abandoned to idleness, dissipation, luxury, and extravagance; if they are lost to the fear of God, and the love of their country, all is lost. Having got beyond the restraints of a divine authority, they will not brook the control of laws enacted by rulers of their own creating."[302]

- Ezra Stiles's Connecticut election sermon, May 8, 1783:

"If men, not merely nominally Christians, but of real religion and sincere piety, joined with abilities, were advanced and called up to office in every civil department, how would it countenance and recommend virtue!"[303]

- Elizur Goodrich's Connecticut election sermon, May 10, 1787:

"Here I might delineate more fully the character of an able and faithful administration; but I will not enlarge, and shall say only in a few words, that the principal lines of it, are knowledge, wisdom, and prudence, courage and unshaken resolution, righteousness and justice, tempered with lenity, mercy, and compassion, and a steady firmness of public measures, when founded in wisdom and the public good, together with inflexible integrity, the fear of God, and a sacred regard to the moral and religious interests of the community. These are the great characteristics of an administration, which will procure respect and confidence; and has the best tendency to promote the happiness, union and strength of a people, and to render them as a "city, that is compact together. …

"If a virtuous people venerate rulers of this character, and unite their endeavors with them in advancing all the noble ends of society, they will have the fairest prospect of peace and prosperity; which was the last thing, I proposed to be considered.

"Let the first object, exciting the attention of a free people, be the character of those, whom they introduce into public offices; and, the next, that they reverence the worthy magistrate, support him in his office and dignity, and show a ready obedience to the laws of the state. …

"Hear all the equitable petitions of the people; but should they ask you to be unrighteous, stop your ears: Be merciful and compassionate; but maintain a conduct consistent with the dignity, faith and honor of government, and with those fixed rules and everlasting maxims, by which it is to be administered. …

"I shall add only in a few words, that while in all other ways, you endeavor the good of this people, and expect from them a reverential regard for magistracy, and a peaceable behavior in the state, you will, gentlemen, appoint men of virtue and religion to all important offices of executive trust: And be yourselves the best examples of righteousness and the fear of God. Show yourselves friends to religion and virtue—to the church of Christ, and the worship of God—to the ministers of the gospel—and to the great and important interests of education and learning in the state: By this you will do honor to yourselves, and essential service to your country, merit the esteem and gratitude of good men, and meet the approbation of God. If religion and good manners be legible, not only in your laws, but in your lives, rendering you conspicuous for piety and mercy, justice and sobriety, your authority will be strengthened, and your administration supported. The attractive force of your examples, will engage your people to that behavior, which is necessary to the peace and prosperity of the state; and the endeavors of good citizens will be united in procuring and advancing the noble and beneficial ends of society. Thus you will be the lights of the world, the ornaments of mankind; and having with eminent usefulness served your generation according to the will of God, may you finally enjoy the rewards of faithful servants."[304]

2. Wicked rulers bring great harm to government.

The opposite of righteousness is wickedness. The patriot preachers were far more concerned about the threat wicked rulers posed to the country than they were of the benefits produced by righteous ones. So in their sermons, they warned their people of the sin of choosing men of questionable character as leaders.

- Charles Chauncy's Massachusetts election sermon, May 27, 1747:

"Religion is not in such a flourishing state, at this day, but that it needs the countenance of your example, and the interposition of your authority, to keep it from insult and contempt. We thankfully acknowledge the pious care, the legislature has lately taken to restrain the horrid practice of cursing and swearing, which so generally prevailed, especially in this, and our other sea-port towns, to the dishonor of God, and our reproach as wearing the name of Christians. And if laws still more severe are necessary, to guard the day and worship of God from [being profaned], we can leave it with your wisdom to enact such, as may tend to serve so good a design. And tho' we would be far from desiring, that our rulers should espouse a party in religion; yet we cannot but hope, they will never do any thing to encourage those, who may have arrived at such an height in spiritual pride, as to say, in their practice, to their brethren as good as themselves, 'stand by thy self, come not near me; for I am holier than thou:' Concerning whom the blessed God declares, 'These are a smoke in my nose, a fire that burneth all the day.' …

"And as for those, be their character, persuasion, or party, what it will, who, under the notion of appearing zealous for God, his truths or ways, shall insult their betters, vilify their neighbors, and spirit people to strife and faction, we earnestly wish the civil arm may be stretched forth to chastise them: And if they suffer, 'twill be for disturbing the peace of society; the evil whereof is rather aggravated than lessened, by pretenses to advance the glory of God and the interest of religion."[305]

Samuel Sherwood's Connecticut election sermon, August 31, 1774:

"There are certain duties required of rulers, as well as of subjects; and their obligations faithfully and punctually to fulfill them, rise in proportion to the dignity and importance of their high and elevated stations; and the effect and influence which their conduct has on the rest of the body. A man's being raised to honor and promotion above others, is so far from releasing him from, or lessening his duty, that every step he takes in his advancement, proportionally enlarges it, and adds a new and powerful obligation to the performance of it. … Subjects have rights, privileges and properties; and are countenanced and supported by the law of nature, the laws of society, and the law of God; in demanding full protection in the enjoyment of these rights, and the impartial distribution of justice, from their rulers. And when rulers refuse these, and will not comply with such a reasonable and equitable demand from the subject; the society is dissolved; and its fundamental laws violated and broken; and the relation between the ruler and the subject ceases, with all the duties and obligations that arose from it. … The good of society in all its individual members, is the end for which it is formed; and for which government is instituted and appointed. And this cannot be obtained, unless rulers exert their power, influence and authority to protect their subjects in all their valuable rights and privileges; defend them against their enemies, both from without, and within; and administer impartial justice among them. …

"Public good is the end of government of every sort. … When civil rulers, forgetting the end of their institution, and the proper duties of their station, neglect and trample upon the rules of justice; and consult only to gratify their own pride and ambitious humor and passion: when they consider their subjects as an inferior species of beings, made as beasts of burden, for their pleasure or profit; when, instead of observing the reason and nature of things, they make their own mere will and pleasure, the rule of acting; and govern in an arbitrary, tyrannical manner; 'tis impossible to describe the evils and mischiefs they bring on mankind. These have been so great and terrible, that some have been ready to question, whether civil rulers have not done more hurt than good, in the world."[306]

- Samuel West's Massachusetts election sermon, May 29, 1776:

"It is our duty to endeavor always to promote the general good; to do to all as we would be willing to be done by were we in their circumstances; to do justly, to love mercy, and to walk humbly before God. These are some of the laws of nature which every man in the world is bound to observe, and which whoever violates exposes himself to the resentment of mankind, the lashes of his own conscience, and the judgment of Heaven. This plainly shows that the highest state of liberty subjects us to the law of nature and the government of God. The most perfect freedom consists in obeying the dictates of right reason, and submitting to natural law. When a man goes beyond or contrary to the law of nature and reason, he becomes the slave of base passions and vile lusts; he introduces confusion and disorder into society, and brings misery and destruction upon himself. This, therefore, cannot be called a state of freedom, but a state of the vilest slavery and the most dreadful bondage. The servants of sin and corruption are subjected to the worst kind of tyranny in the universe. Hence we conclude that where licentiousness begins, liberty ends."[307]

- John Smalley's Connecticut election sermon, May 8, 1800:

"One way more was hinted, in which those who govern, may weaken government; and that is, by being men of a vicious character; or by not paying a due attention to the strict regularity of their own lives. Indeed, 'a wicked ruler' is often strong, and fierce, and active, as 'a roaring lion and a ranging bear;' but rarely for the benefit of 'the poor people.' He will not be eager to pluck the spoil out of the mouth of the fraudulent villain, or the violent oppressor; unless that he may get it into his own. Nor will authority, in the hands of libertine men, however it may terrify, be much revered. When the makers or judges of laws, are themselves notorious breakers of them, or of the laws of heaven, government will necessarily fall into contempt. It is also to be observed, that advancing to posts of honor, men of loose principles and morals, gives reputation to licentiousness, and stamps it as the current fashion. Their example will encourage evil doers, more than all the punishments they are likely to inflict, will be a terror to them. 'The wicked walk on every side when the vilest men are exalted.' …"

Smalley then attacked the vice of alcohol and condemned its use by those entrusted with the reins of government:

"But rulers may be far from being the vilest men, they may be very good men; and yet, by an incautious conformity to common practices, supposed to be innocent, they may too much countenance some things which are of very hurtful tendency. Permit me to instance in one particular. 'It is not for kings,' we read, 'to drink wine, nor for princes strong drink.' And certainly, it is not for the lower classes to drink so much of these as many of them do, if they regard their health, or competence, or peace. I select this instance, because it is directly pertinent to the main subject in hand. Nothing is a greater weakener of government—nothing makes the multitude more heady and high-minded—nothing raises oftener or louder, the cry of liberty and equality—nothing more emboldens and inflames that little member, which boasteth great things, and setteth on fire the whole course of nature—nothing, in a word, makes men more incapable of governing themselves, or of being governed, than strong drink. Now, if rulers drink, though not to drunkenness; not so as quite to 'forget the law,' or greatly to 'pervert the judgment of any;' if they only drink as much as is very universally customary, in polite circles, on great occasions; though they do not hurt themselves, they may too much sanction that which will hurt their inferiors. That divine injunction, 'Thou shalt not follow a multitude to do evil,' lies with peculiar weight on civil rulers, as well as religious teachers. They, more than others, are under obligation to lead the multitude, in whatsoever things are sober, wise and good. They, of all men, are bound in duty to abstain from all appearance of any thing, which, improved upon by bungling eager imitators, might grow into a practice pernicious to society. Nor should it be forgotten, that every deviation from rectitude of conduct, lessens the dignity, and lowers the authority of great men. 'Dead flies cause the ointment of the apothecary to send forth a stinking savor: so doth a little folly, him that is in reputation for wisdom and honor.'"[308]

- ## Simeon Howard's Massachusetts election sermon, May 31, 1780:

"I might observe further, under this particular, that impious, immoral men at the head of government, and having authority to appoint subordinate officers, will probably make choice of men of their own character, and in this way be a means of spreading corruption, and of much injury to society. But I must pass on to consider another qualification of rulers. …

"'Hating covetousness.' Covetousness, you all know, is an inordinate desire of riches, — such a desire as will make a man pursue them by unlawful means, and prevent his using them in a right manner. Hating covetousness is a strong expression to denote a freedom from this vicious temper, and a sense of its unreasonableness and turpitude.

"A civil ruler, under the direction of this principle, will oppress and defraud his subjects whenever he has it in his power; he will neglect the duties of his office whenever he can promote his private interest by the neglect; he will enact laws to serve himself, not the community; and he will enact none that he thinks would be prejudicial to his private interest, however beneficial they might be to the public, however necessary for the support of justice and equity between man and man; he will pervert justice, and rob the innocent for bribes; he will discourage every measure that would occasion expense to himself, however salutary to his country. Rather than part with his money, he will see the arts and sciences, which are so ornamental and friendly to a community, languish, erudition starve, and the rising genius which promised glory to his country nipped in the bud by the cold hand of poverty; yea, religion itself, the greatest honor and blessing of society, he will see languish and die, rather than impart anything to support its cause. And having long looked upon riches in the same light that good men do upon religion, as his chief good, and feeling the same attachment to them which they do to that, he may, if required by laws already made to pay anything for its support, absurdly plead that it is against his conscience, strangely mistaking his love of money for the love of God, and his covetousness for his conscience; supposing, with those corrupters of religion mentioned by the apostle, 'that gain is godliness.'"[309]

3. Wicked rulers are God's judgment on a nation.

Accountability and responsibility were major issues for the Black Regiment. They preached that all people, citizens and legislators alike, were accountable first to God, and then to their fellow man. The preachers warned that if the people disregarded God's Word and His will, He could discipline them by allowing wicked men to be elevated to positions of authority over them. Simply stated, in God's providential economy, the people received the kind of government they deserved and a nation's leaders were a reflection of the people (a lesson we are painfully learning in our nation today).

- Samuel Sherwood's Connecticut election sermon, August 31, 1774:

"When we see an haughty and ambitious monarch, or corrupt ministry spending the blood and treasure of their subjects, in carrying on an unrighteous quarrel and contention with them, or against their neighbors; from a mistaken notion of glory; distressing their towns and cities with their troops and armaments, depopulating their country, and seeming to aim at the universal destruction of mankind; we may well be shock'd at the sight, and look on such a lawless, arbitrary ruler, as the heaviest calamity and judgment, that a righteous God can send upon a sinful people. But notwithstanding the dark and dismal prospect which a scene of tyranny and oppression affords; 'tis undoubtedly true, that civil government is designed for the good of men; and when administered with justice and mercy, it does excellently well answer this design. As tyrants are the greatest of temporal judgments, as being the cause of all the most distressing evils that can be imagined; so good rulers are the greatest blessings to the world, and the instruments in God's hand, of securing all our other good things. But then, to render them such, they must be just, considered both in a legislative and executive capacity."[310]

- Simeon Howard's Massachusetts election sermon, May 31, 1780:

"There can be no doubt but God often brings distress and ruin upon a sinful people through the ill management of their rulers, given up to error and blindness. In the nineteenth chapter of Isaiah we have a prophecy of the overthrow of the kingdom of Egypt; and the infatuation of their rulers is mentioned as one of the immediate causes of this calamity. ... therefore, if a people desire to have rulers of wise and understanding hearts, counseled and directed by Heaven, they should take care that they be men who fear God."[311]

- Elizur Goodrich's Connecticut election sermon, May 10, 1787:

"Not only may a people be delivered into the hands of tyrants, as the rod and scourge of heaven for their impiety and madness; but through their own folly, "children may be their princes, and babes rule over them." Such a "people shall be oppressed every one by another, and every one by his neighbor."[312]

4. Rulers must obey the law as well as the citizens.

One of the primary reasons the colonists felt driven to fight for independence was the hypocrisy of the King and the Parliament in the way they governed the colonies. The fact that the King made compacts and agreements with the colonies and then ignored them and that the Parliament seemed bent on passing laws to control and dominate the colonies greatly infuriated and frustrated the Americans. The colonists grew weary of rulers who disregarded and disobeyed the very laws they enacted. In response, the patriot preachers taught that the same laws that bound the citizens bound the rulers as well.

- Stephen Peabody's New Hampshire election sermon, June 11, 1797:

"There can be no greater burlesque upon the character of rulers, than when, under binding obligations to God, and their constituents, they are making laws which they are the first in violating! But how agreeable are the prospects, when judicious laws are made, are esteemed sacred; and are punctually observed by the enactors! A sanction is hereby placed upon them, which impresses every mind. And societies having their eye upon their rulers, observing their consistency, are led to follow their example, which naturally tends to rectify the vices and to reform the manners of the community. When precept and example are harmonious in rulers, every observer is charmed with the character; when they are at variance, they cannot fail to produce contempt. Of great importance then it must appear, for those who are clothed with authority, to have the qualifications described in my text, to be themselves exemplary, and let their light shine before men, who, aiming at one great object, the best interest of the public, are filled with present animation; and their views, not confined to this life, are extended, and terminate in immortality."[313]

- Samuel Cooke's Massachusetts election sermon, May 30, 1770:

"Rulers are appointed guardians of the constitution in their respective stations, and must confine themselves within the limits by which their authority is circumscribed. A free state will no longer continue so than while the constitution is maintained entire in all its branches and connections. If the several members of the legislative power become entirely independent of each other, it produceth a schism in the body politic; and the effect is the same when the executive is in no degree under the control of the legislative power, the balance is destroyed, and the execution of the laws left to arbitrary will. The several branches of civil power, as joint pillars, each bearing its due proportion, are the support, and the only proper support, of a political structure regularly formed. A constitution which cannot support its own weight must fall; it must be supposed essentially defective in its form or administration. Military aid has ever been deemed dangerous to a free civil state, and often has been used as an effectual engine to subvert it. …

"Justice also requires of rulers, in their legislative capacity, that they attend to the operation of their own acts, and repeal whatever laws, upon an impartial review, they find to be inconsistent with the laws of God, the rights of men, and the general benefit of society. This the community hath a right to expect. …

"The just ruler will not fear to have his public conduct critically inspected, but will choose to recommend himself to the approbation of every man. As he expects to be obeyed for conscience sake, he will require nothing inconsistent with its dictates, and be desirous that the most scrupulous mind may acquiesce in the justice of his rule."[314]

- Samuel Sherwood's Connecticut election sermon, August 31, 1774:

"Rulers are obliged to be just, on account of the great trust reposed in them. Sovereign authority is the greatest trust that can be reposed in any man. The power of making laws is very great, and extensive in its nature, and of the utmost importance in the exercise of it. And next to this, is that of putting laws in execution. The man that is appointed to judge another, with authority to decide all controversies among his fellow-subjects: to determine and pass sentence upon the lives and properties of such vast numbers of men; has a very great and important trust reposed in him. And the weight and importance of the trust reposed in any inferior executive officer, is proportioned to the authority vested in him. Now, the receiving such a trust lays a man under very great obligations to faithfulness in the discharge of it. Men in such high places of trust and authority, instead of being released from the laws of God, and having their obligations to faithfulness in the discharge of duty, lessened and diminished; have them increased, in proportion to their advancement; and it is not beneath the dignity of their stations, to attend very seriously to the advice and exhortation of the Psalmist, *Be wise now therefore, O ye kings; be instructed ye judges of the earth. Serve the Lord with fear; kiss the son, lest he be angry, and ye perish from the way, when his wrath is kindled but a little.* 'Tis of importance, if men have but one talent, that they improve it: but if they have ten, and neglect and refuse so to do; the punishment will be tenfold greater. If a private man neglects his duty, he, and others connected with him, may suffer. But if a chief ruler is unjust and unfaithful, the whole community or body politic suffers. As much therefore as the welfare and happiness of such a community, or body, is to be valued above, and preferred to the happiness of an individual; so much higher and greater are his obligations to faithfulness, than the obligations of a private member of society; and if he refuses to discharge them uprightly and conscientiously, as in the fear of God; a proportionally heavy and aggravated punishment must he expect to receive, when judged by him.

"The exercise of justice is necessary in civil rulers, to their own present comfort, and future happiness. 'Tis a common observation, that the greatest tyrants are the greatest and most miserable slaves. Those rulers who invade the rights and liberties of their own subjects, in an arbitrary, tyrannical manner, and seek to oppress and enslave them; are always in fear of being themselves destroyed by them. They are obliged, at vast expense, to keep up large armies to distress and enslave their peaceable subjects; who, under such a grievous yoke of bondage, cannot be easy and satisfied; but will be naturally struggling after liberty; and be ready, when it galls their necks, to turn against and depose such oppressing tyrants; and sometimes, to imbrue their hands in their blood: of which, many instances are to be found in the histories of the Roman, and of the Turkish empire. Whereas, when princes rule in a just and constitutional way, with mildness and benignity; and seek the good and welfare of their subjects; they may always put full, unreserved confidence in them, and depend on being supported and defended by them, at the expense of all that is dear and valuable to them; yea, at the expense of their lives, which will not be thought too dear a sacrifice for the safety and honor of such a worthy prince.

"Again. This justice and faithfulness in rulers is necessary to their having peace in their own minds and consciences. Such have consciences as well as other men, accusing or else excusing; who, upon the faithful discharge of the high trust reposed in them, will have inward peace, security and joy, and heart-felt satisfaction such as the world can neither give, nor take away. But on the other hand; if the rules of justice and righteousness be neglected and trampled upon by them, and they practice high handed tyranny and oppression: and seek to enslave and destroy their subjects; what dreadful horrors of conscience must they necessarily feel when awakened to any serious reflections on their wicked, guilty conduct, which has been so distressing and ruinous to thousands more innocent and righteous than themselves."[315]

- Elizur Goodrich's Connecticut election sermon, May 10, 1787:

"Remember, gentlemen, that while you are examining the rights of individuals, and their claims on one another, or on the public, you drop the character of legislators, and should act by the same fixed rules of law and equity, as the judge on the bench. In causes of a judicial kind, your high character of sovereignty will not excuse an arbitrary decision, or denial of justice, any more than the same may be excused in the lowest executive court."[316]

5. Rulers have certain duties they are bound to fulfill.

The patriot preachers believed men were not elevated to places of leadership and authority simply to satisfy their own selfish desire for power and fame or to further their political careers. The patriot preachers believed leaders were empowered to fulfill two basic duties:

- To obey and honor God by doing that which was right and just.
- To serve the people by ensuring that their rights and liberties were protected.

Samuel Langdon best summed up what the Black Regiment believed about a ruler's duties in his June 5, 1788 New Hampshire election sermon:

"You will consider that you assemble from time to time as fathers of the large family, which depends on you to take care of its general welfare, and that no local views ought to govern you, nor partial instructions of your constituents bind you to act contrary to the clear conviction or your own minds. You will be cautious of forming parties for any selfish purposes, and of being too hasty in determining important matters, or too slow in your proceedings when business is urgent. In order to form a wise judgment of every thing that comes before you, you are sensible of the propriety of examining things to the bottom, attending patiently to every argument on both sides, and asking conscience, rather than any friend, what ought to be done. Like frugal householders you will save all unnecessary expenses, and take good care of the treasury; but not suffer the faithful servants of the state to be so stinted in their reward as to discourage them from their duty. Lay no grievous burdens on the people beyond their abilities; but take the earliest, easiest, and most righteous methods to reduce and pay off the public debt, unhappily involved in all the perplexities occasioned by boundless emissions of depreciating paper notes. Be liberal, yet frugal in grants of money, according to the exigencies of the public. Let no laws be wanting which good order, and the proper administration of government and justice require; but make no law which establisheth iniquity. And may I propose it, as worthy of your consideration, whether some reformation may not be necessary as to processes in our courts of justice: whether appeals from court to court are not allowed beyond reason and equity, in the plainest cases, and of too trivial value: by which some of our courts are made mere vehicles, justice is delayed, and the law made unnecessarily expensive, tedious and vexatious; and whether some method may not be thought of to determine the judgment of causes in lower or higher courts in proportion to their value and importance. I beg leave to say one word as to religion. With respect to articles of faith or modes of worship, civil authority have no right to establish religion. The people ought to choose their own ministers, and their own denomination, as our laws now permit them; but as far as religion is connected with the morals of the people, and their improvement in knowledge, it becomes of great importance to the state; and legislators may well consider it as part of their concern for the public welfare, to make provision that all the towns may be furnished with good teachers, that they may be empowered to make valid contracts, and that the fulfillment of such contracts should be secured against the fickle humors of men, who are always ready to shift from sect to sect, or make divisions in parishes that they may get free from all legal obligations to their ministers. Perhaps a little addition to the law already in force in this state might sufficiently secure the continuance of religious instruction, enlarge rather than diminish liberty of conscience, and prevent envyings, contentions, and crumbling into parties. Will you permit me now to pray in behalf of the people, that all the departments of government may be constantly filled with the wisest and best men; that his excellency the president may have the assistance of an able and faithful council; that the administration of justice may be in the hands of judges and justices well qualified for their offices, who will not take bribes, or in any manner pervert judgment; in a word, that the constitution established may in every respect be well supported by your care, and that the people may know the blessings of good government by the union of your counsels, and the wisdom of your proceedings. May the Almighty King of kings always be in the midst of you, direct and assist you, impress your hearts with his fear, and grant present and future blessings in reward of your fidelity."[317]

6. Rulers will give an account to God for the way they govern.

As Christians, the patriot preachers believed that an ultimate day of reckoning was coming for every person at the final judgment of God. But the preachers pointed out that, because of a ruler's high position and great authority, he was even more accountable to God and would not only have to answer to the people but would, even more importantly, have to answer to God for his actions. The following excerpts are examples of how the preachers warned those in power to keep the final judgment of God in mind and govern accordingly:

- Charles Chauncy's Massachusetts election sermon, May 27, 1747:

"You are, my fathers, accountable to that God whose throne is in the heavens, in common with other men. And his eyes behold your conduct in your public capacity, and he sees and observes it, not merely as a spectator, but an almighty righteous judge, one who enters all upon record in order to a reckoning another day. And a day is coming, it lingers not, when you shall all stand upon a level, with the meanest subjects, before the tremendous bar of the righteous judge of all the earth, and be called upon to render an account, not only of your private life, but of your whole management as entrusted with the concerns of this people.

"Under the realizing apprehension of this, suffer me, in the name of God, (tho' the most unworthy of his servants) to advise you to review the public conduct, respecting the passing bills, and to do whatever may lay in your power to prevent their being the occasion of that injustice, which, if continued much longer, will destroy the small remains of common honesty that are still left in the land, and make us an abhorrence to the people that delight in righteousness."[318]

- Samuel Sherwood's Connecticut election sermon, August 31, 1774:

"Lastly. This justice and faithfulness is necessary to their future happiness. Tho' civil rulers are stiled *gods*, yet must they die like men; and at last, give an account of themselves to the judge of the quick, and the dead. …

"He that ruleth over men, must be just: And that he may be so, he must rule in the fear of the Lord. If we consider human nature, as vitiated by the apostasy; we shall find, that hardly any thing but the fear of punishment, is able to keep men in awe, and due subjection. That it is thus with subjects, is evident from the many severe laws, and terrible executions of them, which the wisest and most merciful rulers in all nations, have found necessary to preserve the peace, and promote the happiness of civil society. Now, 'tis certain that the essential principles of human nature are the same in all men, whatever external relations they sustain. There is therefore great danger, that rulers will degenerate into tyrants; and of blessings, become plagues and curses to mankind; unless there be some way to keep them in awe, some principle to excite their fears, and by that means, keep them within their proper sphere, and engage them to the observation of justice. Now, this is not always to be done by a fear of men. Sovereigns are exempted from the common power of human laws; there is no ordinary authority that may judge them; and this their security may prove a strong temptation to them, to neglect the proper duties of their exalted stations. They may trust in their forces and armies to defend them from the resentment of an injured and oppressed people; and so imagine themselves perfectly secure from punishment at present; and the nearer any subordinate ruler approaches to sovereignty, the less has he to fear from men, and consequently, the greater prospect has he, of indemnification in acting unjustly. There is therefore the utmost need and necessity, that those who rule over men, should rule in the fear of the Lord; that they should have a firm belief of the being, perfections and providence of God; that they should not only fear his vindictive punishing justice, but beyond this, as the text requires, maintain an holy awe and reverence of him upon their minds; and consider him as that righteous judge to whom they must at last, give an account of the discharge of the great trust reposed in them; and from whom they shall receive a righteous sentence of absolution or condemnation."[319]

- Elizur Goodrich's Connecticut election sermon, May 10, 1787:

"With deference to your high stations, I am warranted with all freedom to assure you, in the fear of God, the almighty and eternal Judge, that the consideration of not being accountable to an higher court on earth, should be one of the most forcible motives, to engage you to the greatest uprightness and impartiality, not only between subject and subject, but especially the subject and the public. Remember, that as in this world, there is an appeal from a lower to an higher court, so when the most sovereign and uncontrollable court on earth, gives an unrighteous sentence, and wickedly perverts judgment, there is immediately entered in the high court of heaven, an appeal, which, in the great day of general assise, will be called, and must be answered. Then you, my honorable auditors, and all the kings and judges of the earth shall appear, and give an account for your conduct, while you acted in the character of gods, on earth."[320]

Chapter 16

THEY PREACHED REPENTANCE, TOO

In the midst of the War Between the States, Joel Tyler Headley warned his readers in the preface to his book, *The Chaplains and Clergy Of The Revolution*, that repentance was America's only hope in the midst of their crisis. He urged the government to once again turn to the church for assistance as it had some ninety years before:

> "This diversion of the mind from armies to the God of armies is especially needed in our present crisis. Enthusiasm and numbers will not deliver us from the troubles that now overwhelm us. Penitence and humility will go farther than either, and whether the State turns as it did in the Revolution to the Church as its strongest support or not, we may rest assured, if its prayers do not save us, whatever success we may achieve will in the end prove a sad failure."[321]

In his Thanksgiving sermon delivered on December 14, 1787, Massachusetts preacher, Joseph Lathrop, declared,

> "No attempts hitherto made, to subvert our liberties, has been successful. They will probably be preserved, until the people themselves, sunk in vice and corruption, destroy them with their own hands. How near we are to this fatal period, heaven knows!"[322]

Even though the Black Regiment valued liberty so much that they were willing to fight for it, they valued the "Kingdom of God and His righteousness" even more. To them, civil liberty was always trumped by spiritual liberty. Believing that "heaven and earth would pass away," they knew that even their blessed America would someday pass from the scene. The one kingdom they knew would last forever was the Kingdom of God. This was what prompted Samuel Langdon on May 31, 1775, only weeks after the battles of Lexington and Concord, to preach to the Massachusetts lawmakers:

"We must keep our eyes fixed on the supreme government of the ETERNAL KING, as directing all events, setting up or pulling down the kings of the earth at his pleasure, suffering the best forms of human government to degenerate and go to ruin by corruption; or restoring the decayed constitutions of kingdoms and states, by reviving public virtue and religion, and granting the favorable interpositions of his providence. …

"Oh, may our camp be free from every accursed thing! May our land he purged from all its sins! May we be truly a holy people, and all our towns cities of righteousness! Then the Lord will be our refuge and strength, a very present help in trouble; and we shall have no reason to be afraid though thousands of enemies set themselves against us round about, though all nature should be thrown into tumults and convulsions. He can command the stars in their courses to fight his battles, and all the elements to wage war with his enemies. He can destroy them with innumerable plagues, or send faintness into their hearts, so that the men of might shall not find their hands. In a variety of methods he can work salvation for us, as he did for his people in ancient days … May the Lord hear us in this day of trouble, and the name of the God of Jacob defend us, send us help from his sanctuary, and strengthen us out of Zion! We will rejoice in his salvation, and in the name of our God we will set up our banners. Let us look to him to fulfill all our petitions."[323]

In the Cambridge, Massachusetts meetinghouse on October 22, 1774, the members of the First Continental Congress gave evidence of their conviction that the sins of America were the primary cause for the calamity they faced and that the only remedy was the people's repentance and God's forgiveness. On that day, they voted to "observe a day of public Thanksgiving throughout the same." The actual proclamation signed by John Hancock, president of the Congress, read,

"From a consideration of the continuance of the gospel among us, and the smiles of Divine Providence upon us with regard to the seasons of the year, and the general health which has been enjoyed; and in particular, from a consideration of the union which so remarkably prevails, not only in this province, but throughout the continent, at this alarming crisis, it is resolved, as the sense of this Congress, that it is highly proper that a day of public thanksgiving should be observed throughout this province; and it is accordingly recommended to the several religious assemblies in the province, that Thursday, the fifteenth day of December next, be observed as a day of thanksgiving, to render thanks to Almighty God for all the blessings we enjoy. And, at the same time, we think it incumbent on this people to humble themselves before God, on account of their sins, for which he hath been pleased, in his righteous judgment, to suffer so great a calamity to befall us as the present controversy between Great Britain and the colonies; as also to implore the Divine blessing upon us, that, by the assistance of his grace, we may be enabled to reform whatever is amiss among us; that so God may be pleased to continue to us the blessings we enjoy, and remove the tokens of his displeasure, by causing harmony and union to be restored between Great Britain and these colonies, that we may again rejoice in the smiles of our sovereign, and in possession of those privileges which have been transmitted to us, and have the hopeful prospect that they shall be handed down entire to posterity under the Protestant succession in the illustrious House of Hanover. John Hancock, President."[324]

Just weeks before, on August 31, 1774, Samuel Sherwood, convinced that the colonists were guilty of "turning their backs upon the ordinances of God," boomed out these words in his "Address to the Freemen of the Colony" in Newhaven, Connecticut:

"That our having neglected the worship and turned our backs upon the ordinances of God; our distrusting and despising the grace of the gospel, and trifling away the day of salvation; are to be numbered among those sins by which we have awfully provoked a righteous God to anger against us. That omissions and neglects of this kind, have abounded to an unusual, and indeed, to an astonishing degree, cannot be denied. That such sins are provoking to God, and that especially, in a country which, like this, was originally settled principally for the purposes of reformation and religion, cannot reasonably be doubted."[325]

Sounding that same note, William Gordon preached in his Thanksgiving Sermon in Boston on December 15, 1774:

"Do we join piety to our prudence and fortitude; do we confess and repent of our sins, justify God in his so trying us, accept of our punishment at his hands without murmuring or complaining; do we humble ourselves, amend our ways and doings, give up ourselves to God, become a holy people, and make the Most High our confidence, — we may hope that he will be on our side; and 'if the Lord is for us, what can men do unto us?' Have we the God of hosts for our ally, we might bid adieu to fear, though the world was united against us."[326]

John Joachim Zubly also joined this chorus in his sermon, *The Law of Liberty*, preached at the opening of the Provincial Congress of Georgia in 1775:

"One thing more. Consider the extreme absurdity of struggling for civil liberty, and yet to continue slaves to sin and lust. 'Know ye not to whom ye yield yourselves servants to obey? His servants ye are to whom ye obey, whether of sin unto death, or of obedience unto righteousness.' Cease from evil, and do good; seek peace and pursue it: who will hurt you while you follow that which is good? Become the willing servants of the Lord Jesus Christ; hearken to and obey the voice of His gospel, for 'where the spirit of the Lord is, there is liberty;' and 'if the Son makes you free,' then, and not till then, 'shall you be free indeed.'"[327]

Three years after preaching his Boston Thanksgiving sermon (mentioned above), William Gordon preached an election sermon to the General Court of Massachusetts on July 4, 1777 in which he stressed the need for the colonists to repent:

"I might enlarge, but must forbear. 'Tis expedient and opportune, however, to mention that, would we have our independency perpetuated, let us repent of our sins, attend to religion, and live the doctrines of Christianity; then may we reasonably expect that future generations will joyfully commemorate this anniversary, and that the names of those who boldly stood forth in the cause of liberty, and acted a consistent and uniform part, will be blessed."[328]

THE PATRIOT PREACHERS GREW UP IN A TIME OF GREAT REPENTANCE

The Black Robed Regiment did not simply appear out of thin air. Men who possess convictions so deep that they are willing to die for them do not just happen – they are made. The patriot preachers of the eighteenth century were actually the spiritual offspring of a major move of God's Spirit that had occurred in the previous generation.

Like a raging prairie fire, a spiritual revival had swept across the colonies during the 1730s, '40s, and '50s. Historian James Adams wrote that this revival left behind "ecstatic converts, bitter critics, and divided churches. ... Ironically, the revival that split churches united the colonies into a mass Jesus movement."[330] This mass movement came to be known as the First Great Spiritual Awakening in American history.

This "great awakening" came at a time of great spiritual deadness and darkness in the colonies. Even though the colonies had been firmly founded on biblical principles by such devout Christians as the Puritans, Baptists, Congregationalists, Lutherans, Dutch Reformed, other Protestants, and Catholics, amazingly, in seventy-five years or less, the people had backslidden into a state of spiritual apathy and carnality. Again, historian James Adams offers an amazing insight into the spiritual climate of the colonies during that time:

"By the time the Great Awakening began to change the spiritual landscape of colonial America, Puritanism on the Atlantic seaboard had developed a strong rationalistic streak. Slowly reason began to replace revelation. Puritan divines preached that God could be known as well through His works as through His Word ... [so] the piety of this people eventually began to cool. In the last third of the seventeenth century, old-line Puritan leaders detected a diminishing of zeal and spiritual energy. Urian Oakes pinpointed the problem: The faithful had become 'sermon proof.' Inoculated with so many doses of orthodox sermons, they had become immune to catching the real thing – orthodox Christianity. A 'cooling of former life and heat in spiritual communion' occurred. Religious formality, high morals, and intellectual assent to orthodox beliefs replaced experiential piety. The beat was missing in the religion of the heart. Souls were not being stirred. 'There is risen up a generation' lamented Increase Mather, in 1764, 'who give out, as if saving grace and Morality were the same.' The regenerative power of the Holy Spirit experienced by the fathers was not being visited on the second generation – and who would dare predict what would happen in the third and fourth generations!...

"The concept that God had entered into a covenant with the saints in the colonies also began to break down. The Half-Way Covenant, which lowered the requirements for church membership, failed to achieve its goal of adding more members. In fact, it had just the opposite effect. Religion had become formal and void of emotional content. As a result, interest in things of the spirit diminished. More and more emphasis was placed on morality and less and less attention given to life-changing personal conversion. The Age of the Enlightenment took its toll in the colonial churches.

"Many settlers, living long distances from any church and seldom hearing a sermon or partaking of the sacraments, became indifferent and secularized. 'Times were thus ripe for some new emphasis in religion as well as a new type of religious leadership to meet the peculiar situation which the American colonies presented.'"[330]

Then, when all seemed hopeless for the church, God sovereignly began to move in the hearts of men. By pouring out His Spirit on men like Jonathan Edwards, George Whitefield, John Wesley, and others, a whole army of preachers was mobilized and delivered volley after volley of power-packed sermons downrange to huge crowds of spiritually thirsty seekers who enthusiastically drank in the water of life. Thousands of people were stirred in their spirits, and multitudes were swept into the army of God. As Adams put it:

"The rivulets of revival spread across the spiritually parched countryside, then merged into a mighty stream to sweep thousands into the Kingdom of God. … What the colonies had awakened to in 1740 was none other than independence and rebellion. … Until Betsy Ross could get around to sewing the American flag, the colonists would rally around the Christian banner."[331]

It was from this "spiritual hotbed" that the Black Robed Regiment was forged. In fact, many of the men who would eventually make up the Black Regiment were young boys when the waves of the Great Awakening broke upon the colonies. One can only imagine the tremendous impression the whole scene made on these young men.

So, in addition to leading a massive revival that birthed thousands into God's Kingdom and served to prepare the colonists for the coming war with Great Britain, the Great Awakening also produced the next generation of preachers, the Black Robed Regiment. This new crop of patriotic prophets would provide the vital service of leading Americans through the struggle for independence, liberating thousands from British tyranny, and securing religious/civil liberty for a new nation. And just like their Great Awakening predecessors, the Black Regiment understood that the key to a right relationship with God and to victory over their enemies was a repentant heart. Accordingly, they belted out sermon after sermon, calling for Americans to repent and seek God if they ever hoped to win their independence from Great Britain.

Samuel Langdon was one of these fiery prophets. On May 31, 1775, he preached the Massachusetts election sermon in which he declared that the colonists' sins had caused the war and that, short of repentance, they could never hope for victory and freedom:

> "We have rebelled against God. We have lost the true spirit of Christianity, though we retain the outward profession and form of it. We have neglected and set light by the glorious gospel of our Lord Jesus Christ, and his holy commands and institutions. The worship of many is but mere compliment to the Deity, while their hearts are far from him. By many the gospel is corrupted into a superficial system of moral philosophy, little better than ancient Platonism; and, after all the pretended refinements of moderns in the theory of Christianity, very little of the pure practice of it is to be found among those who once stood foremost in the profession of the gospel. In a general view of the present moral state of Great Britain it may be said, 'There is no truth, nor mercy, nor knowledge of God in the land. By swearing, and lying, and killing, and stealing, and committing adultery,' their wickedness breaks out, and one murder after another is committed, under the connivance and encouragement even of that authority by which such crimes ought to be punished, that the purposes of oppression and despotism may be answered. As they have increased, so have they sinned; therefore God is changing their glory into shame. The general prevalence of vice has changed, the whole face of things in the British government.

"Let us consider—that for the sins of a people God may suffer the best government to be corrupted, or entirely dissolved; and that nothing but a general reformation can give ground to hope that the public happiness will be restored, by the recovery of the strength and perfection of the state, and that divine Providence will interpose to fill every department with wise and good men. …

"But, alas! Have not the sins of America, and of New England in particular, had a hand in bringing down upon us the righteous judgments of Heaven? Wherefore is all this evil come upon us? Is it not because we have forsaken the Lord? Can we say we are innocent of crimes against God? No, surely. It becomes us to humble ourselves under his mighty hand, that he may exalt us in due time. However unjustly and cruelly we have been treated by man, we certainly deserve, at the hand of God, all the calamities in which we are now involved. Have we not lost much of that spirit of genuine Christianity which so remarkably appeared in our ancestors, for which God distinguished them with the signal favors of providence when they fled from tyranny and persecution into this western desert? Have we not departed from their virtues? Though I hope and am confident that as much true religion, agreeable to the purity and simplicity of the gospel, remains among us as among any people in the world, yet in the midst of the present great apostasy of the nations professing Christianity, have not we likewise been guilty of departing from the living God? Have we not made light of the gospel of salvation, and too much affected the cold, formal, fashionable religion of countries grown old in vice, and overspread with infidelity? Do not our follies and iniquities testify against us? Have we not, especially in our seaports, gone much too far into the pride and luxuries of life? Is it not a fact, open to common observation, that profaneness, intemperance, unchastity, the love of pleasure, fraud, avarice, and other vices, are increasing among us from year to year? And have not even these young governments been in some measure infected with the corruptions of European courts? Has there been no flattery, no bribery, no artifices practiced, to get into places of honor and profit, or carry a vote to serve a particular interest, without regard to right or wrong? Have our statesmen always acted with integrity, and every judge with impartiality, in the fear of God? In short, have all ranks of men showed regard to the divine commands, and joined to promote the Redeemer's kingdom and the public welfare? I wish we could more fully justify ourselves in all these respects. If such sins have not been notorious among us as in older countries, we must nevertheless remember that the sins of a people who have been remarkable for the profession of godliness, are more aggravated by all the advantages and favors they have enjoyed, and will receive more speedy and signal punishment; as God says of Israel: 'You only have I known of all the families of the earth, therefore will I punish you for all your iniquities.'

"My brethren, let us repent and implore the divine mercy. Let us amend our ways and our doings; reform every thing which has been provoking to the Most High, and thus endeavor to obtain the gracious interpositions of Providence for our deliverance.

"If true religion is revived by means of these public calamities, and again prevails among us; if it appears in our religious assemblies, in the conduct of our civil affairs, in our armies, in our families, in all our business and conversation, we may hope for the direction and blessing of the Most High, while we are using our best endeavors to preserve and restore the civil government of this colony, and defend America from slavery."[332]

Just one year later on May 29, 1776, Pastor Samuel West reminded the Massachusetts legislators again of this same truth as he delivered that year's election sermon:

"Our cause is so just and good that nothing can prevent our success but only our sins. Could I see a spirit of repentance and reformation prevail through the land, I should not have the least apprehension or fear of being brought under the iron rod of slavery, even though all the powers of the globe were combined against us. And though I confess that the irreligion and profaneness which are so common among us gives something of a damp to my spirits, yet I cannot help hoping, and even believing, that Providence has designed this continent for to be the asylum of liberty and true religion; for can we suppose that the God who created us free agents, and designed that we should glorify and serve him in this world that we might enjoy him forever hereafter, will suffer liberty and true religion to be banished from off the face of the earth? But do we not find that both religion and liberty seem to be expiring and gasping for life in the other continent? — where, then, can they find a harbor or place of refuge but in this?

"To conclude: While we are fighting for liberty, and striving against tyranny, let us remember to fight the good fight of faith, and earnestly seek to be delivered from that bondage of corruption which we are brought into by sin, and that we may be made partakers of the glorious liberty of the sons and children of God: which may the Father of Mercies grant us all, through Jesus Christ. Amen."[333]

Even the British understood that a right standing before God and the subsequent blessings that followed were contingent on the people's repentant attitude. On December 6, 1776, English pastor John Fletcher rebuked the British for their sinfulness. In his sermon, *The Bible And The Sword,* Fletcher rebuked the English people for their unwillingness to repent and seek God and for their refusal to "mix" religion into their politics like the Americans were doing. In this excerpt, Fletcher quotes Welsh preacher, Dr. Richard Price, who was supportive of American independence:

"In a late publication, too large and too dear for common readers, we find the following observations. Dr. Price, the champion of the American patriots, has advanced an argument, which deserves the attention of all, who wish well to church and state: Take it in his own words.

"'In this hour of tremendous danger, it would become us to turn our thoughts to heaven. This is what our brethren in the colonies are doing. From one end of North America to the other, they are fasting and praying. But what are we doing? Shocking thought! We are ridiculing them as fanatics, and scoffing at religion. We are running wild after pleasure, and forgetting every thing serious and decent at masquerades. We are gambling in gaming houses; trafficking for boroughs; perjuring ourselves at elections; and selling ourselves for places. Which side then is Providence likely to favor? In America we see a number of rising states in the vigor of youth, and animated by piety. Here we see an old state, inflated and irreligious, enervated by luxury, and hanging by a thread. Can we look without pain on the issue?'

"There is more solidity in this argument, than in all that Dr. Price has advanced. If the colonists throng the houses of God, while we throng play-houses, or houses of ill fame; if they crowd their communion-tables, while we crowd the gaming table or the festal board; if they pray, while we curse; if they fast, while we get drunk; and keep the Sabbath, while we pollute it; if they shelter under the protection of heaven, while our chief attention is turned to our troops; we are in danger—in great danger. Be our cause ever so good, and our force ever so formidable; our case is bad, and our success doubtful. Nay, *the Lord of hosts,* who, of old, sold his disobedient people into the hands of their unrighteous enemies, to chastise and humble them, this righteous Lord, may give success to the arms of the colonies, to punish them for their revolt, and us for our profaneness. A youth that believes and prays as David, is a match for a giant that swaggers and curses as Goliath. And they that, in the name of the Lord, enthusiastically encounter their enemies in a bad cause, bid fairer for success than they that, in a good cause, profanely go into the field; trusting only in the apparent strength of an arm of flesh. To disregard the king's righteous commands, as the colonists do, is bad: But to despise the first-table commandments of the King of kings, as we do, is still worse. Nor do I see how we can answer it, either to reason or our own consciences, to be so intent on forcing British laws, and so remiss in yielding obedience to the laws of God.

"Is it not surprising, that amidst all the preparations, which have been made to subdue the revolted colonies, none should have been made to check our open rebellion against the King of kings; and that in all our national applications to foreign princes for help, we should have forgotten a public application to *the Prince of the kings of the earth?* Many well-wishers to their country flattered themselves, that at a time, when the British empire stands, as Dr. Price justly observes, 'on an edge so perilous,' our superiors would have appointed a day of humiliation and prayer; a day to confess the national sins, which have provoked God to let loose a spirit of political enthusiasm and revolt upon us; a day to implore pardon for our past transgressions, and to resolve upon a more religious and loyal course of life; a day to beseech the Father of lights and mercies to teach at this important juncture, our senators wisdom in a peculiar manner; and to inspire them with such steadiness and mildness, that by their prudence, courage, and condescension, the war may be ended with little effusion of blood; and, if possible, without shedding any more blood at all. Thousands expected to see such a day; thinking that it becomes us, as reformed Christians, nationally to address the throne of grace, and entreat God to turn the hearts of the colonists towards us, and ours towards them, that we may speedily bury our mutual animosities in the grave of our common Savior. And not a few supposed, that humanity bids us feel for the myriads of our fellow-creatures, who are going to offer up their lives in the field of battle; and that charity and piety require us to pray that they may penitently part with their sins, and solemnly prepare themselves for a safe passage, I shall not say from Britain to America; but, if they are called to it, from time into eternity. Such, I say were the expectations of thousands, but hitherto their hopes and wishes have been disappointed.

"Dr. Price knows how to avail himself of our omission or delay in this respect, to strengthen the hands of the American patriots, by insinuating, that heaven will not be propitious to us; and that *'our cause is such, as gives us [no] reason to ask God to bless it.'* None can tell what fuel this plausible observation of his, will add to the wild fire of political enthusiasm, which burns already too fiercely in the breasts of thousands of injudicious religionists. I therefore humbly hope, that our governors will consider Dr. Price's objection taken from our immorality and profaneness; and that they will let the world see, we are neither ashamed nor afraid to spread the justice of our cause before the Lord of hosts, and to implore his blessing upon the army going to America, to enforce gracious offers of mercy, and reasonable terms of reconciliation.

"... the best way to counter-work the enthusiasm of patriotic religionists, is to do constitutional liberty and scriptural religion full justice; by defending the former against the attacks of despotic monarchs on the right hand, and despotic mobs on the left; and by preserving the latter from the opposite onsets of profane infidels on the left hand, and enthusiastic religionists on the right. I humbly hope, that our governors will always so avoid one extreme, as not to run into the other; and that, at this time, they will so guard against the very appearances of irreligion and immorality ... What we owe to God, to ourselves, and to the colonists, calls upon us to remove whatever may give any just offence to those who seek occasion to reflect upon us. ...

"Righteousness exalteth a nation, says the wise man, but sin is a reproach to any people, and may prove the ruin of the most powerful empire. Violence brought on the deluge. Luxury overthrew Sodom. Cruel usage of the Israelites destroyed Egypt. Complete wickedness caused the extirpation of the Canaanites. Imperiousness, and an abuse of the power of taxation, rent ten tribes from the kingdom of Judah. Pride sunk Babylon. Nineveh and Jerusalem, by timely repentance, once reversed their awful doom; but returning to their former sins, they shared at last the fate of all the states, which have filled up the measure of their iniquities. And have we taken so few strides towards that awful period, as to render national repentance needless in this day of trouble? ...

"Let our devotion be improved by the American controversy, as well as our morals. Instead of 'scoffing at religion,' ... let us honor the piety of the colonists. So far at least, as their religious professions are consistent, sincere, and scriptural, let them provoke us to a rational concern for the glory of God, and our eternal interests. ... Have we forgotten that many of the first colonists crossed the Atlantic for conscience' sake; seeking in the woods of America, some, a shelter against our once persecuting hierarchy; and others, a refuge from our epidemical profaneness? And does not their offspring look upon us in the same odious light? Do they not abhor or despise us, as impious, immoral men, 'enervated by luxury;'—men, with whom it is dangerous to be connected, and who *'may expect calamities, that shall recover to reflection' [perhaps to devotion] 'libertines and atheists'* themselves?

"And is it only for God's sake, for the sake of our own souls, and for the sake of the colonists, that we should look to our conduct and Christian profession?"[334]

On April 19, 1781 at the sixth commemoration of the Battle of Lexington, Henry Cumings warned the Americans that sin, not the redcoats, was the greatest threat to their success:

"And here, let me observe, that nothing darkens our prospects more, or gives us more reason to be fearful, as to the event of the present contest, than the great and general prevalence of unrighteousness among us. He must have been very unobserving, who does not know, that by means of unrighteousness, the body-politic has been, and still is, laboring under a dangerous disease, *the whole head being sick and the whole heart faint,* and there being but little *soundness, from the crown of the head to the sole of the foot.*

"The goodness of our cause does not make success certain. A good cause often suffers, and is sometimes lost, by means of the sin and folly of those, who are engaged in it. This is a consideration, which ought to lie with weight on our minds, at the present day, and engage us to *put away the evil of our doings, and keep ourselves from every wicked thing.*

"When Solomon says, *righteousness exalteth a nation,* he asserts no more, than what the experience of all ages has found to be true. For righteousness not only procures the smiles of a propitious Providence upon a people; but also tends, in the natural course of things, to promote their prosperity; being adapted to prevent dissentions and discords among them, to cement them together in the firmest union, and, by preserving public and private credit, to enable them to collect their force and strength, when the case requires, for repelling an invading enemy, and defending themselves against all the hostile attempts of aspiring ambition. The effects of unrighteousness are very different; for unrighteousness not only provokes God to withhold his blessings from a people; but it also tends, in its own nature, to entangle and perplex their affairs, and to render them weak, and unable to oppose any violent assaults of arbitrary power, by creating among them internal strife and contention; by dividing them into angry parties; by destroying mutual trust and confidence; and so rendering it extremely difficult, and next to impossible, to unite them in measures, necessary for their safety and defense against a common enemy, or the despotic views of designing ambition.

"We have therefore reason to fear, if unrighteousness should continue to abound, that the righteous Judge of the world, will cease to restrain the wrath of our enemies, and, leaving us in the hands of our own folly, permit them to execute the dreadful purposes of their furious resentments, as a just punishment for our obstinate perseverance in our evil ways. But if we will put away our unrighteousness, *cease to do evil, and learn to do well,* we shall have grounds to hope, that *the righteous Lord, who loveth righteousness,* will still be our friend and patron, and enable us to maintain our cause, against the utmost force of our enraged enemies, until they are brought to reason or ruin. For, to the righteous, God is near, and never will their cause forsake.

"Though God is pleased to employ the wrath of our enemies, as a rod of correction, to punish us, for our sins; and may permit them to proceed to great lengths, in the prosecution of their arbitrary and unrighteous schemes, in order to teach us righteousness, and make us pious and virtuous; yet their conduct is nevertheless odious and abominable in his sight, and will not (as we have reason to believe) pass unpunished. We may therefore assure ourselves, that when we leave our sins, and become an obedient people, God will bring to naught all their mischievous designs, either by disposing them to peace, or by leaving them to follow the lead of their own haughty temper, until they plunge themselves into destruction. For God often turns the oppression of the oppressor upon his own head and causes him, in the end, to fall into the pit which he digged for others. And a people, who have smarted under the cruel rod of oppression, may rationally expect this, when they are suitably prepared for salvation by repentance and reformation. For the most powerful and successful oppressors, are only rods of God's school (like the proud Assyrian before mentioned) and when he has answered the designs of his providence by them, he usually lets loose his wrath upon them, and punishes them for their arrogance, pride and mischievous ambition."[335]

When the long and costly war was finally at an end and the immediate danger had passed, the Americans were tempted to lower their guard, both physically and spiritually. They were weary. The war had lasted longer and had cost more than they had ever imagined. But even though they were inclined to let up, the patriot pastors were not about to let that happen. They knew that the only way to preserve the liberties that had been so hard won was to see to it that the spiritual vitality of the new nation was maintained. Samuel McClintock, himself a member of the Continental Army and a veteran of the Battle of Bunker Hill, said this to the New Hampshire legislature on June 3, 1784:

"But it is to be considered, that its (America's prosperous future) being realized, depends on the practice of that righteousness which alone exalteth a nation…

"It is laid down in the text, as the rule of the divine government over the nations of the earth, to deal with them according to their moral character. Tho' God is an absolute, yet he is a holy and righteous sovereign. Such is the perfection of his nature, that he never can do any thing but what is fit and right. … But with regard to nations, God hath always made a distinction between the righteous and the wicked, and in plucking up and destroying, or building up and planting them, has ever treated them according to the rule of justice laid down in the text. … This is the constitution of God—the immutable law of his kingdom, founded in the infinite perfection of his nature, so that unless God should change, that is, cease to be God, we cannot be a happy, unless we are a virtuous people. … but as virtue is the basis of republics, their existence depends upon it, and the moment that the people in general lose their virtue, and become venal and corrupt, they cease to be free. This shows of what importance it is to preserve public virtue under such a constitution as ours, and how much it becomes all who have any regard to the good of their country, and of posterity, and who wish the scenes of future happiness and grandeur, which present themselves to the imagination, may be realized to do every thing in their power, to promote that virtue upon which this depends. …

"The Almighty Ruler of nations and kingdoms sets before us this day, life and death, blessing and cursing, and leaves it to ourselves which we will chose. Altho' true religion, the religion of the heart, consisting in faith and love unfeigned, and a real conformity to the divine character, is necessary in all who on good grounds would hope for eternal life; yet those who are wholly destitute of this religion, have it in their power to practice, on natural principles, that virtue, which according to the constitution of the divine government over nations, will ensure their temporal prosperity and glory.

"While we are obedient and do that which is right, we have the highest assurance that our tranquility shall be lengthened, and the increase of our happiness and glory like the light of the morning; but if we do evil and fall into the vices and corruptions that have ever brought ruin on other nations, we may assuredly expect that we shall meet with their doom. Our situation, and the constitution of our government makes this warning peculiarly necessary."[336]

So even though the war of bullets and bombs was over, the Black Robed Regiment would fight on. They would reclaim their pulpits and wage war on the real enemy – sin and apathy. For them, the war would never be over, at least not until the Lord called them home.

Chapter 17

WE'LL ANSWER TO GOD FOR THE WAY WE VOTE!

"We electors have an important constitutional power placed in our hands: we have a check upon two branches of the legislature, as each branch has upon the other two; the power I mean of electing at stated periods, one branch, which branch has the power of electing another. It becomes necessary to every subject then, to be in some degree a statesman: and to examine and judge for himself of the tendencies of political principles and measures. Let us examine, then, with a sober, a manly … and a Christian spirit; let us neglect all party virulence and advert to facts; let us believe no man to be infallible or impeccable in government, any more than in religion; take no man's word against evidence, nor implicitly adopt the sentiments of others, who may be deceived themselves, or may be interested in deceiving us."[337]

John Adams, August 29, 1763

"Let each citizen remember at the moment he is offering his vote that he is not making a present or a compliment to please an individual—or at least that he ought not so to do; but that he is executing one of the most solemn trusts in human society for which he is accountable to God and his country."[338]

Samuel Adams, April 16, 1781

"In selecting men for office, let principle be your guide. Regard not the particular sect or denomination of the candidate—look to his character as a man of known principle, of tried integrity, and undoubted ability for the office. When a citizen gives his suffrage to a man of known immorality he abuses his trust; he sacrifices not only his own interest, but that of his neighbor, he betrays the interest of his country."[339]

Noah Webster, 1823

"Impress upon children the truth that the exercise of the elective franchise is a social duty of as solemn a nature as man can be called to perform; that a man may not innocently trifle with his vote; that every elector is a trustee as well for others as himself and that every measure he supports has an important bearing on the interests of others as well as on his own."[340]

Daniel Webster, October 5, 1840

Liberty and the right to self-government was the prize for which the patriot preachers fought. But they knew that self-government was meaningless if the people did not engage in the political process. For the first time since God had established the government of Israel, another people, this time on the North American continent, were attempting to build a government squarely on biblical principles. The choice of who would rule them, a choice afforded to few nations in history, was now within the grasp of Americans. But with great opportunity also came great responsibility, a responsibility the people would have to take seriously. So the Black Regiment wasted no time in adamantly preaching that voting was the most sacred of all civic responsibilities, one that could not be faithfully executed without God's guidance.

The patriot preachers took it even further than voting. The Black Regiment taught that Americans, to fulfill their responsibility to their country, were bound by God to vote for men of strong Christian character.

What a grave departure from the way many Americans, especially Christians, think and vote today. Most studies show that some fifty percent of self-professed evangelicals do not even vote. Of the other fifty percent who do vote, some twenty-five percent often vote for candidates who embrace values that are diametrically opposed to what evangelicals claim to believe. As was asked earlier, how is it that so many Christian voters can disconnect how they vote from what they believe? For example, how do pro-lifers vote for pro-abortion candidates, how do supporters of traditional marriage vote for those who promote same-sex marriage, and how do free market capitalists vote for socialists who promote a welfare state?

There can be only a few answers to this paradox:

1. Many evangelicals do not actually believe what they claim to believe.

2. They blindly follow a particular political party, regardless of the positions of that party and its candidates.

3. They have never been taught from the pulpit the biblical principles of government, so they do not know how to "connect the dots" between what they claim to believe and how they actually vote.

Although some certainly fall into the first two categories, I believe the vast majority of conservatives fall into the third category. The reason is quite simple: few pastors in America are willing to preach what the Bible says about government. The reason for this was stated earlier and is quite simple: most modern pastors grew up hearing the lie of separation of church and state and have come to believe that politics is a worldly, unspiritual enterprise, one that should not be addressed from the pulpit. In addition, these pastors do not want to be accused of preaching politics over the Gospel and certainly do not want to run afoul of irate church members who threaten to take their tithes elsewhere if the preacher gets "political" in the pulpit. But the "mother of all fears" is the prospect of incurring the wrath of the IRS who threatens to take away their church's non-profit status if they preach politics in the pulpit.

In stark contrast, when the preachers of the Black Robed Regiment became convinced that their liberties were at stake, they were willing to make any sacrifice necessary to preserve them, even if it meant incurring the wrath of the government. In the process, these preachers lost much more than their "non-profit status" or a few ministerial tax breaks. Many lost everything, including their lives – everything, that is, but their sacred honor.

One thing is certain; they did not hesitate to instruct their congregations about whom they should elect to office. The following sermon excerpts not only illustrate what the patriot preachers had to say about the Christian's privilege and responsibility to vote, but they also show how the preachers pointed out the kind of candidate deserving of a Christian's vote:

- Samuel Sherwood's Connecticut sermon, August 31, 1774:

"There is but one general distinction that is of essential importance in the cause now depending, and that is to be made by drawing the dividing line between the true friends to the rights of humanity, our dear country, and constitutional liberties and privileges, civil and religious: And the base, traitorous and perfidious enemies thereto. Let the first sort of such an amiable character be honored and beloved, and promoted to all public offices and employments in the state: let the latter sort have a public brand of infamy put upon them, to mark them out as the worst of villains, the open and avowed enemies of mankind, and traitors of their country, who are secretly hoping for ministerial favors. If any under pretense of great moderation, or a pacific disposition, stand as neuters in this important cause, skulking as behind the door, and undetermined on which side they can serve themselves to best advantage, sometimes appearing friendly to this party, and sometimes to that; we can have no safe dependence on them in a day of extremity. He that will not stand forth firmly and boldly for this country, when exposed so as to need his help; is no true friend to it. And as there may possibly be some such secret dissembling enemies acting in disguise, among us; it might be well for you, gentlemen freemen, to be cautiously on your guard against them: they cannot safely be trusted with the lowest office in the state. As you have it in your power to choose your own rulers and officers ... the present state of these times makes it requisite and necessary that you be very vigilant and watchful, and get a thorough knowledge of men's political principles, before you advance them to any seat in government, or any office in the state."[342]

- Samuel Stillman's sermon to the Supreme Court of Massachusetts, May 29, 1779:

" … every elector, before he gives his vote for any person to sit in council, will take pains to satisfy himself whether he possesses the qualifications that are necessary for so exalted a station – such as wisdom, virtue, firmness, and an unfeigned love of his country. Tried friends deserve the preference – an experience of whose capacity and fidelity in times past, recommends them as worthy of our present confidence. …"[342]

- Simeon Howard's Massachusetts election sermon, May 31, 1780:

"The people's appointing their own rulers will be no security for their good government and happiness if they pay no regard to the character of the men they appoint. A dunce or a knave, a profligate or an avaricious worldling, will not make a good magistrate because he is elected by the people. To make this right of advantage to the community, due attention must be paid to the abilities and moral character of the candidate. This is a consideration that concerns this people at large, as all have a voice in the election of our rulers, either personally or by their representatives. But upon this occasion it is proper to observe that it especially concerns the members of the honorable Council and House of Representatives here present, by whom the councilors for the ensuing year are this day to be elected. And I shall not, I hope, be thought to go beyond my line of duty if I say that the electors ought not to give their votes at random, or from personal or private views. They act in this business in a public character, by virtue of power delegated to them by the people, to whom, as well as to God, the origin of all power, they are accountable for the use they make of it. Nor can they answer it to either, or even to their own consciences, if, through interested or party views, they advance to the council-board men unqualified for the important duties of that station. At such a critical time as the present, the want of wisdom or integrity in that House may be attended with the most fatal consequences."[343]

- Elizur Goodrich's Connecticut election sermon, May 10, 1787 – warning voters that they should never commit the government into the hands of men destitute of true godliness and patriotism:

"Happy the people who have wisdom to discern the true patriot of superior abilities, in all his counsels ever manifesting a sincere regard to the public good, and never with a selfish view attempting to deceive them, into hurtful measures; and happy the people who distinguish him from the designing demagogue, who, while he sooths them in their vices, and flatters them with high notions of liberty, and of easing their burdens, is plunging them into the depths of misery and bondage. … It is essentially necessary in all good governments, but especially the life and spirit of a happy, free and republican state, which subsists on the virtues of its citizens, and can never, while any sound wisdom is left to direct the public choice, by design commit the civil administration into the hands of men destitute of political abilities, or who are the patrons of vice. …

"Make it your constant aim to choose able and faithful men, who fear God and hate covetousness, to be your rulers; honor and encourage them in all their endeavors to make you a virtuous, prosperous and happy people, and apply yourselves with diligence to your own business, that in your several stations, you may contribute to the public good."[344]

- Samuel Langdon's New Hampshire election sermon, June 5, 1788 – encouraging the people to preserve their government by electing men who feared God and loved truth and righteousness:

"Preserve your government with the utmost attention and solicitude, for it is the remarkable gift of heaven. From year to year be careful in the choice of your representatives, and all the higher powers of government. Fix your eyes upon men of good understanding, and known honesty; men of knowledge, improved by experience; men who fear God, and hate covetousness; who love truth and righteousness, and sincerely wish the public welfare. Beware of such as are cunning rather than wise; who prefer their own interest to every thing; whose judgment is partial, or fickle; and whom you would not willingly trust with your own private interests. When meetings are called for the choice of your rulers, do not carelessly neglect them, or give your votes with indifference, just as any party may persuade, or a sordid treat tempt you; but act with serious deliberation and judgment, as in a most important matter, and let the faithful of the land serve you. Let not men openly irreligious and immoral become your legislators; for how can you expect good laws to be made by men who have no fear of God before their eyes, and who boldly trample on the authority of his commands? And will not the example of their impiety and immorality defeat the efficacy of the best laws which can be made in favor of religion and virtue? If the legislative body are corrupt, you will soon have bad men for counselors, corrupt judges, unqualified justices, and officers in every department who will dishonor their stations; the consequence of which will be murmurs and complaints from every quarter. Let a superior character point out the man who is to be your head; for much depends on his inspection and care of public affairs and the influence of his judgment, advice and conduct, although his power is circumscribed: in this choice therefore be always on your guard against parties, and the methods taken to make interest for unworthy men, and let distinguished merit always determine your vote. And when all places in government are filled with the best men you can find, behave yourselves as good subjects; obey the laws; cheerfully submit to such taxation as the necessities of the public call for; give tribute to whom tribute is due, custom to whom custom, fear to whom fear, and honor to whom honor, as the gospel commands you. Never give countenance to turbulent men, who wish to distinguish themselves, and rise to power, by forming combinations and exciting insurrections against government: for this can never be the right way to redress real grievances, since you may not only prefer complaints and petitions to the court, but have the very authority, which you think has been misused, in your own power, and may very shortly place it in other hands. How happy was it for this state, that the insurrection, attempted here two years ago, was so seasonably and with so little difficulty suppressed, when the neighboring state was brought into such a difficult and critical situation by the distracted populace, and has now scarcely recovered from that violent political paroxysm."[345]

- Jonathan Edwards, Jr.'s Connecticut election sermon, May 8, 1794:

"But the way to virtue and good morals is to choose the Lord for your God. Nor is this all; you not only have to choose and serve the Lord yourselves, but by the same reasons by which you are obligated to choose the Lord for your God, you are obligated to seek out and by your suffrages to promote to legislative authority, such as are of the same character. In a republic all authority is derived from the people: and such as they generally are, we may expect their representatives, legislators and all their civil authority will be. If you have the Lord for your God, you will elect those of the same character with yourselves, to be your legislators; you will encourage and support them and other faithful rulers in the thorough discharge of their duties of civil government, and you will withhold your suffrages from those who acknowledge not the Lord as their God and regard not his law. Nor can you consistently and innocently give your suffrages to men of this last description: for thus you would give a sanction and influence to sin and vice, would be partakers of their wickedness and would do an injury to the state.

"But if you and the good people of the state in general shall unite to practice virtue and Christianity, and to promote the wisest and best men among us, we shall doubtless be that happy people described in the text, and as so many instances of our happiness 'judgment shall dwell in the wilderness and righteousness remain in the fruitful field. And the work of righteousness shall be peace, and the effect of righteousness quietness and assurance for ever.'"[346]

- Stephen Peabody's New Hampshire election sermon, June 11, 1797:

"When we act as electors, our eyes should ever be upon the 'faithful of the land.' We shall, no doubt, have frequent calls for elections to the most important offices. … Calls of this nature should be improved to awaken our vigilance, that we may obtain a true knowledge of the most deserving, and of those of a contrary description; that our future proceedings may be consonant to the principles of reason and sound policy. …

"Such as fully believe the Christian religion, and receive the scriptures as the word of God, have additional motives for their utmost exertions that sobriety and goodness may be promoted. It is indisputable, that the more a society live in the practice of virtue, the greater prosperity they enjoy: The more they are under the influence of vicious principles, the more unhappiness they will experience. The sacred oracles give us the best directions: In them, no unreasonable restraints are imposed, no rational enjoyments are forbidden: Excess alone is transgression. So far as the scriptures are strictly regarded, so far every member of the community conducts with propriety: The various propensities and passions peculiar to human nature, are directed to right objects: And there, Christ, a most faithful and compassionate legislator, stands, giving law to his subjects. In those records, his character is exhibited, his maxims are registered, his example left for our imitation; and the whole perfectly reconcilable to virtue, religion, and the best policy: Thence may be extracted wisdom and instruction to guide us into the paths of rectitude;

to save us from destructive courses of error and delusion: Here is a constitution worthy the particular notice of every man who holds an office in government; that under the influence of its rules, he may be instrumental in diffusing virtuous and benevolent principles: Directed by this, he will give his public testimony in favor of those who are engaged professionally to prepare mankind for blessings in this life, and a glorious future reward."[347]

- John Smalley's Connecticut election sermon, May 8, 1800 (bad government is the people's fault and they get the kind of government they deserve):

"… the people may always have good rulers, unless it be their own fault. … That weakness of government which is a calamity to any people, is often principally the fault of the people themselves. It may be owing to their negligence, or to their caprice and folly, in the choice of their rulers; or it may be owing to their ill- treatment of them when chosen. A government most excellent in its constitution, and most wise, just and firm, in its administration, may be enervated, or rendered inadequate, by the ungovernableness of the people: By their revilings and slanders—their haughtiness and insolence—their factions and tumults. David once said, 'I am this day weak, though anointed king; and these men, the sons of Zeruiah, are too hard for me.'

"Nor must it be omitted, that, besides the immediate natural causes of a weak government, the irreligion, or general wickedness of a people, may be its procuring cause, as a judgment of heaven. 'The most High ruleth in the' nations of men; 'and giveth' the dominion over them, 'to whomsoever he will.' 'For promotion cometh neither from the east, nor from the west, nor from the south; but God is the judge; he putteth down one, and setteth up another.' When the ways of a people please the Lord—when they fear him, and work righteousness; among other blessings, he gives them good governors, under whose able and equitable administration, they lead quiet and peaceable lives. On the contrary, when they forget him, neglect his worship, and disregard his word; among other modes of punishment, he takes away their wise and faithful magistrates, and gives them weak or wicked ones in their stead; or leaves them to trample all authority under foot. …

"One advantage is, that the people may always have good rulers, unless it be their own fault. … in elective governments, where the people at large are the electors, and especially where the elections are frequent, they may always have wise and faithful men in all places of authority; if such are to be found, and if such they choose. ...

"If the freemen – the fountain of power, would strengthen government, or guard against its being farther weakened; they should be very punctual in attending their legal meetings, and very careful for whom they give in their suffrages, as members of Assembly, or of Congress. They should see that they do not vote for weak men, however honest; nor for vicious men, however capable; nor for intriguing men, who are crowding themselves forward, by every popular artifice: who understand perfectly all the duties and faults of their superiors, but see no beam in their own eye, and never mind their own business. Men of real abilities, are generally unassuming and self-diffident. Men sensible of the difficulties and responsibility of important posts of trust, are generally backward to undertake them. Men restless where they are, and troublesome to those above them, are generally haughty and overbearing, if advanced to higher stations. Nor should the freemen be too much given to change; unless they mean to weaken government. Bad men, if in office, cannot be too soon turned out; but those who have ruled well, ought not to be dropped, merely that every man may have his turn; nor merely to show the great power of the people, and to keep their servants, who govern them, more in fear of them."[348]

THE PATRIOT PREACHERS WERE NOT BASHFUL ABOUT TELLING THEIR PEOPLE HOW TO VOTE

Once again, unlike most modern preachers, the Black Regiment did not beat around the bush, speak in vague generalities, or drop hints using coded language about whom or for what their church members should vote – they came right out and told them. Certainly they expected their people to make up their own minds in the end, but the patriot preachers believed they had not done their duty unless they had made it clear which candidate(s) they thought were deserving of elected office. Consider these examples:

William Linn was a Presbyterian minister in Pennsylvania. During the War of Independence, he served as a chaplain to the Continental Army, after the war he became the first chaplain of the United States House of Representatives in 1789, and later served as the president of Queens College (later named Rutgers University) from 1791 to 1795. During the U.S. presidential campaign of 1800, Linn boldly told his listeners in his *Serious Considerations on the Election of a President* that, based upon his assessment of Thomas Jefferson's character, it would be better to throw away their votes than to cast them for Jefferson:

"… rather than be instrumental in the election of Mr. Jefferson, it would be more acceptable to God and beneficial to the interests of your country, to throw away your vote. … Let me further repeat, the single thing intended, is to show that … he ought not to be honored and entrusted with the Presidency of the United States of America."[349]

During that same presidential campaign, another Presbyterian preacher, John Mitchell Mason, who ministered in New York (chapter 13), also spoke out against Jefferson. In his 1800 sermon, *The Voice Of Warning To Christians,* Mason, believing Thomas Jefferson to be an atheist, declared him to be unfit for the presidency of the United States:

"Fellow Christians, A crisis of no common magnitude awaits our country. The approaching election of a president is to decide a question not merely of preference to an eminent individual, or particular views of policy, but, what is infinitely more, of national regard or disregard to the religion of Jesus Christ. Had the choice been between two infidels or two professed Christians, the point of politics would be untouched by me. Nor, though opposed to Mr. Jefferson, am I to be regarded as a partisan; since the principles which I am about to develop, will be equally unacceptable to many on both sides of the question. I dread the election of Mr. Jefferson, because I believe him to be a confirmed infidel: you desire it, because, while he is politically acceptable, you either doubt this fact, or do not consider it essential. Let us, like brethren, reason this matter."[350]

Whether or not we agree with Linn's and Mason's assessment of Jefferson's character and fitness for the presidency, there is no denying their boldness to unashamedly declare what they believed – and these preachers certainly had no reservations about preaching their convictions about which candidates were worthy of Christians' votes.

Almost a century later in 1884, preachers were still instructing their congregations from the pulpit about voting. In the presidential election of that year, George Ball, D.D., pastor of Hudson Street Baptist Church in Buffalo, New York, spoke out against the candidacy of New York Governor Grover Cleveland. Among numerous allegations that Cleveland possessed less than honorable morals, it was believed that, in 1874, Gov. Cleveland had fathered an illegitimate son with a 36-year-old widow, Maria Halpin. Pastor Ball concluded that Mr. Cleveland was unqualified for the presidency of the United States:

> "... [Gov. Grover Cleveland is a] champion libertine, and artful seducer, a foe to virtue, an enemy of the family, a snare to youth and hostile to true womanhood. ... Since he has become governor of this great state, he has not abated his lecheries."[351]

(Note: Even though some believed the allegation was untrue, the fact that Cleveland was never able to determine whether or not the child was his and never denied the affair, provides strong evidence that Pastor Ball's low assessment of Cleveland's character was probably accurate.)

Again, whether we agree with the outspokenness of the Black Regiment or not, it cannot be denied that for the first one hundred fifty years of our nation's history, the patriot preachers did not hesitate to state publicly from their pulpits exactly how they believed their congregations should vote. Even if their congregations did not completely agree or heed their advice, they did not have to speculate about what their preachers believed or thought about politics. Just imagine how this would impact the way today's church votes, if their pastors were as outspoken about political issues as were the preachers of the eighteenth century.

Chapter 18

GOD GAVE THE VICTORY!

On November 20, 1794, David Osgood, pastor of the First Parish Church in Medford, Massachusetts, declared to a crowd in Boston:

"The honor of God, the interests of religion, and the comfort and consolation of good men, being all promoted by the memory of the divine dispensations; it is highly agreeable to reason, and consonant to scripture, that public days should be set apart, on which a whole people may unite in celebrating the goodness of God; recollecting the instances of his providential care of, and kindness towards, them; and talking of his wonderful works in their favor. Such institutions serve as *pillars of remembrance,* to revive and perpetuate a sense of our obligations to heaven. The thoughts of the great body of the people are so taken up about their own private affairs, that they are prone to pay but little attention to the concerns of the public. After the first impression is worn off, they soon forget, at least practically, national mercies and deliverances, as well as national judgments. They need to have their minds stirred up by way of remembrance. And when God, by a long and continued series of remarkable interpositions, has multiplied, blessed, and prospered any people—has, on one occasion and another, repeatedly rescued them from great and threatening dangers—put them in full possession of their rights and liberties, laws and religion; and from year to year continues them in the quiet enjoyment of these privileges, together with the usual bounties of his munificent providence; they cannot too frequently recollect, nor too fervently and gratefully acknowledge, these signal instances of the divine benignity. It surely becomes Christian magistrates, and is a duty they owe to God, to call upon their subjects to unite in commemorating these wonderful works of heaven in their favor."[352]

The Black Regiment was just as quick to give God the praise for victory when the war was over as they had been to seek His assistance when it began. From the very beginning of the struggle, they had known that the odds were stacked against them. They knew and preached that unless God was their defense and strength, their army would be destroyed and America's hopes for liberty and independence would be crushed.

On July 24, 1766, almost ten years before the war, Charles Chauncy preached this message on a "Day of Thanksgiving to Almighty God" to an excited audience in Boston celebrating the repeal of the Stamp Act:

"Though our civil joy has been expressed in a decent, orderly way, it would be but a poor, pitiful thing should we rest here, and not make our religious, grateful acknowledgments to the Supreme Ruler of the world, to whose superintending providence it is principally to be ascribed that we have had 'given us so great deliverance.' Whatever were the means or instruments in order to this, that glorious Being, whose throne is in the heavens, and whose kingdom ruleth over all, had the chief hand herein. He sat at the helm, and so governed all things relative to it as to bring it to this happy issue. ... In short, it was ultimately owing to this influence of the God of Heaven that the thoughts, the views, the purposes, the speeches, the writings, and the whole conduct of all who were engaged in this great affair were so overruled to bring into effect the desired happy event. ...

"Let us be ambitious to make it evident, by the manner of our conduct, that we are good subjects and good Christians. So shall we in the best way express the grateful sense we have of our obligations to that glorious Being, to the wisdom and goodness of whose presidency over all human affairs it is principally owing that the great object of our fear and anxious concern has been so happily removed. And may it ever be our care to behave towards him so as that he may appear on our behalf in every time of danger and difficulty, guard us against evil, and continue to us all our enjoyments, both civil and religious. And may they be transmitted from us to our children, and to children's children, as long as the sun and the moon shall endure. Amen."[353]

Even before American soldiers were engaged on actual battlefields, the patriot preachers had already been thanking God for thwarting Great Britain's attempts to undermine their liberties. A good example is William Gordon's December 15, 1774 sermon in Boston:

"Though, when we survey the country, we bemoan the attempts that have been made upon the ancient foundations of its civil government, which, if successful, will in all probability, after a time, undermine and destroy its religious liberties; yet we are thankful that no dwelling has been destroyed, that none of any party have as yet perished by the shocks they have occasioned in the state, that the sword hath not been commissioned by Heaven to destroy, and the way to an accommodation been rendered still more inaccessible through the shedding of blood. We adore the goodness of God, which has kept us from being consumed by the ravages of war. It is of the Lord's mercies that we are not consumed, because his compassions fail not. And much more so that, in the distressing and alarming situation of our public affairs, there have been so many favorable circumstances to preserve us from fainting, to hearten us up, and to encourage our hopes in expecting that we shall at length, in the exercise of prudence, fortitude, arid piety, get well through our difficulties."

Gordon went on to predict a time when America would win the war and be able to give God the glory for the victory:

"Let us, then, be pious, brave, and prudent, and we shall — some of us, at least — have room for thanksgivings, not merely for promising appearances, but for actual deliverance out of present difficulties, though it should not be till we have been conversant with the din of arms and the horrors of war. But should the country be wasted for a few years, and a number of its inhabitants be destroyed, ere the wished-for salvation is granted, how soon, after having secured its liberties, will it regain its former prosperity; yea, become far more glorious, wealthy, and populous than ever, through the thousands and ten thousands that will flock to it, with riches, arts, and sciences, acquired by them in foreign countries! And how will the surviving inhabitants and their posterity, together with refugees who have fled from oppression and hardships, whether civil or sacred, to our American sanctuary, daily give thanks to the Sovereign of the universe that this general asylum was not consumed! How oft will they, with raptures, think upon that noble exertion of courage that prevented it, celebrate the praises of those that led and suffered in the common cause, and with glowing hearts bless that God who owned the goodness of it, and at length crowned it with success! Hallelujah. The Lord God omnipotent reigneth."[354]

Once the fighting had commenced and the Americans had experienced a measure of success early on, the preachers were faithful to give God the praise. On May 31, 1775, just weeks after the battles of Lexington and Concord, Samuel Langdon was singing God's praises for His protection at the Battle of Chelsea, Massachusetts in his sermon delivered in Watertown, Massachusetts:

"Let us praise our God for the advantages already given us over the enemies of liberty, particularly that they have been so dispirited by repeated experience of the efficacy of our arms; and that, in the late action at Chelsea, when several hundreds of our soldiery, the greater part open to the fire of so many cannon, swivels, and muskets, from a battery advantageously situated, from two armed cutters, and many barges full of marines, and from ships of the line in the harbor, not one man on our side was killed, and but two or three wounded ; when, by the best intelligence, a great number were killed and wounded on the other side, and one of their cutters was taken and burnt, the other narrowly escaping with great damage. ... "[355]

That same year Moses Mather published his sermon, *America's Appeal To The Impartial World,* praising God for His provision in those early days of the conflict:

"Providence has furnished us with resources for defense; numbers to constitute armies, materials for constructing a navy, for making of powder, ball, cannon, mortars, arms, &c. and all kinds of ordnance and military stores. Our threatened situation demands, that we immediately take every precaution, and use all the means in our power for our preservation & defense, and with noble and valiant exertions, withstand and repel the attacks of tyranny."[356]

In his Thanksgiving Sermon preached at Roxbury, Massachusetts later that year on November 23, 1775, Isaac Mansfield also gave God the praise for His amazing protection of the American soldiers who had undergone tremendous bombardments from the British:

"Providence has likewise smiled upon the camp, in permitting so few fatal accidents, and evidently been its safeguard. I am informed that by means of upwards two thousand balls that have been thrown from the opposite lines, five men only have been taken off! I perceive likewise that by means of about three hundred balls, etc., thrown into this place in the course of one month, viz., from September 3 to October 3, but two were wounded (one but slightly; the other died, after some time, of his wound), and no man was immediately killed! It is to be remarked further, that not one person was hurt, in the course of above three hundred shells being thrown to a fortress erected upon Ploughed Hill in Charlestown."[357]

On May 17, 1776, John Witherspoon reminded a crowd at Princeton how God had favored the Americans up to that point. He then warned of the dangers of presumptuous pride and assured them of God's continued blessings as long as they pursued the path of righteousness:

"From what has been said upon this subject, you may see what ground there is to give praise to God for his favors already bestowed on us, respecting the public cause. It would be a criminal inattention not to observe the singular interposition of Providence hitherto, in behalf of the American colonies. It is however impossible for me, in a single discourse, as well as improper at this time, to go through every step of our past transactions, I must therefore content myself with a few remarks. How many discoveries have been made of the designs of enemies in Britain and among ourselves, in a manner as unexpected to us as to them, and in such season as to prevent their effect? What surprising success has attended our encounters in almost every instance? Has not the boasted discipline of regular and veteran soldiers been turned into confusion and dismay, before the new and maiden courage of freemen, in defense of their property and right? In what great mercy has blood been spared on the side of this injured country? Some important victories in the south have been gained with so little loss, that enemies will probably think it has been dissembled; as many, even of ourselves thought, till time rendered it undeniable. But these were comparatively of small moment. The signal advantage we have gained by the evacuation of Boston, and the shameful flight of the army and navy of Britain, was brought about without the loss of a man. To all this we may add, that the counsels of our enemies have been visibly confounded, so that I believe that I may say with truth, that there is hardly any step which they have taken, but it has operated strongly against themselves, and been more in our favor, than if they had followed a contrary course.

"While we give praise to God the supreme disposer of all events, for his interposition in our behalf, let us guard against the dangerous error of trusting in, or boasting of an arm of flesh. I could earnestly wish, that while our arms are crowned with success, we might content ourselves with a modest ascription of it to the power of the Highest. …

"From what has been said you may learn what encouragement you have to put your trust in God, and hope for his assistance in the present important conflict. He is the Lord of hosts, great in might, and strong in battle. Whoever hath his countenance and approbation, shall have the best at last. I do not mean to speak prophetically, but agreeably to the analogy of faith, and the principles of God's moral government. Some have observed that true religion, and in her train, dominion, riches, literature, and arts, have taken their course in a slow and gradual manner, from east to west, since the earth was settled after the flood, and from thence forebode the future glory of America. I leave this as a matter rather of conjecture than certainty, but observe, that if your cause is just, if your principles are pure, and if your conduct is prudent, you need not fear the multitude of opposing hosts. … If your cause is just – you may look with confidence to the Lord and entreat him to plead it as his own."[358]

In Boston on April 20, 1778, Jacob Cushing preached that, in light of the brutality of the British, God had been incredibly gracious to the Americans. He encouraged their continued supplication for God's blessings and the "hope of a happy conclusion":

"Finally, let us all devoutly worship and honor, fear and serve the Lord of hosts, and God of armies; hearken to his word, and seriously attend to every providence. Let us continue our fervent cries to God, and offer up importunate, unceasing supplications to the most High, to 'avenge the blood of his servants,' and be 'merciful to' this 'his land, and to his people.' We are encouraged to this from the providence and promises of a powerful and faithful God. The repeated successes during this calamitous war, from its beginning to the present day, have been great and wonderful; and give us confidence in God, and hope of a happy conclusion, if we amend our ways and doings. Our enemies, indeed, have been permitted to make great destruction in divers parts of our land (in their rage and cruelty unequall'd) who have attempted, with fire and sword, to spread desolation far and wide. For as they began the war with a mean, dastardly spirit, so they have prosecuted it, in all their measures, with a rigor and barbarity, exceeding the savages of the wilderness; yet, through the interposition of heaven, they have been frustrated in their grand design, defeated and disgraced. In various instances, particularly in the last campaign, a merciful God hath crowned our arms, with singular success and victory; enabling us to destroy and break up a whole army, under one of the greatest generals, perhaps, that Britain can boast of. This is the Lord's doing, and 'tis marvelous in our eyes."[359]

On April 19, 1781, Henry Cumings added his voice of praise to God for His providential assistance to the American cause:

"And as the wrath of Great Britain, under the overruling providence of God, first occasioned this great revolution, so her wrath has hitherto been defeated in all its powerful efforts to reduce us back to a state of dependence; which can be ascribed to nothing but the interposition of a powerful Providence, laying restraints upon her, and weakening her hands, so that she could not perform her enterprises. For if we look back, and consider the strength of our enemies, and our own weak condition, when the awful scenes of war first opened upon us, we cannot but acknowledge it to be owing to the special interposing power of the supreme Disposer of all things, that we were not soon overcome, but have been enabled to maintain our cause hitherto, in many severe conflicts, through several bloody campaigns.

"When we consider how unprepared and unprovided we were for the contest, when hostilities first commenced; that we were without money, without ammunition, without magazines, without clothing for soldiers; that we had neither military discipline nor any regular settled civil government; that we were destitute of that assistance from foreign powers, which we have had since; and, in short, that under the greatest disadvantages, being deficient in all military preparations, we were forced into a war, with an enemy, well prepared and well provided with all essentials for the conflict, having a numerous and well-disciplined army, commanded by skillful and experienced officers, who had been bred to arms; and a navy superior to any in Europe, which gave them the empire of the seas, and rendered their resources almost inexhaustible; when we consider these things, what reason have we to adopt the language of the psalmist, and say, *If it had not been the Lord, who was on our side, our enemies would have swallowed us up quick*? Especially, when we consider further, the peculiar hazards and difficulties we were subjected to, from internal enemies, who under the pretext of neutrality, or the disguise of friendship, were constantly plotting mischief against us, and doing all that they could, with safety, to weaken our hands; to discourage and dishearten us; to obstruct our operations; to perplex and entangle our affairs; and to aid and assist the British forces. The principal advantages gained, at one time or another, by our professed enemies, who have openly waged war against us, have been greatly owing to assistances afforded them, by secret enemies among ourselves, who, had not the mercy of God prevented, would, before now, have ruined their country. We have therefore abundant reason to be thankful to the sovereign Ruler of the world, not only that he hath hitherto protected us against the open violence of our avowed foes; but also that he hath guarded us against the treacheries and treasonable conspiracies, of false and disaffected persons, whom we have harbored in our own bosoms; and defeated those hidden and mischievous artifices, which they have used to work our destruction. …

"And, on the whole, we have great reason to adore the providence of God, who has hitherto remarkably restrained the wrath of our enemies; mercifully defended and protected us; and supported our righteous cause, by many signal interpositions.

"To every attentive observer, it must be obvious, that the wrath of Great Britain, so far as it has been permitted to exert itself, has contributed to bring about and establish our independency. It has evidently been the occasion of events, which have raised us to an honorable consideration among the European powers, and induced some of them openly to espouse our cause, and aid us by a friendly alliance. It is also worthy of observation, that the wrath, which has been enkindled in American breasts, has been overruled for the promotion of the same great ends. Great Britain first prepared fuel, and then put fire to the combustibles, which she had prepared, for setting the passions of America into a flame. And the wrath, which she has thus roused in America, has been wisely managed by Providence, for checking and restraining her rage and vengeance. Her conduct has not only been the occasion of stirring up a noble spirit of liberty throughout America, and kindling into a blaze every spark of virtuous patriotism, and true courage; but of firing the mind with honest indignation and resentment; yea, of transporting the passions, in some instances, among individuals, into criminal excesses. But even these excesses of the passions, have, by Providence, been made to conspire with better principles, and more laudable springs of action, to strengthen the opposition to British tyranny, and check the career of British rage and cruelty."[360]

In addition to fighting the British, the colonists were also busy creating a new government. Not only did the Black Regiment find cause to praise God for victories on the battlefront, they also found reason to be thankful for the progress on the legislative front. On October 25, 1780, with the war still raging, Samuel

Cooper honored God for the completion of Massachusetts's new constitution in this prayer he offered during his sermon:

"O thou supreme Governor of the world, whose arm hath done great things for us, establish the foundations of this commonwealth, and evermore defend it with the saving strength of thy right hand! Grant that here the divine constitutions of Jesus thy Son may ever be honored and maintained! Grant that it may be the residence of all private and patriotic virtues, of all that enlightens and supports, all that sweetens and adorns human society, till the states and kingdoms of this world shall be swallowed up in thine own kingdom: In that, which alone is immortal, may we obtain a perfect citizenship, and enjoy in its completion, 'the glorious Liberty of the Sons of God!' And let all the people say, Amen!"[361]

On May 31, 1780, Simeon Howard reminded his audience that they were indebted to God for bringing them to the place that they could govern themselves:

"This may also lead us to reflect, with pleasure and gratitude to God, upon the steps which have been taken by this people to frame a new constitution of government, and that a plan has been formed which appears, in general, so well calculated to guard the rights and liberties, and promote the happiness of society, and which, it is to be hoped, will soon be the foundation of our government, instead of that insecure basis upon which it now rests. …

"We are reminded of the gratitude which we owe to God that he has not permitted the natural and important right which every society has of electing its own rulers to be wrested out of our hands, as is the case in some other countries. Had Great Britain carried on without opposition the measures she was pursuing with us, we should probably in a little time have been wholly deprived of this privilege. … It is therefore owing to the opposition which this people made to the measures of the British court, and to the blessing of God upon that opposition, that they have now a voice in appointing their own rulers; otherwise our government might now have been in the hands of the weakest and most profligate favorites of that corrupt and infatuated court."[362]

WHEN THE WAR WAS FINALLY OVER …

General George Washington knew well how miraculous the American victory had been. In a letter to Major General Nathaniel

Greene on February 6, 1783, Washington recalled how greatly the odds had been stacked against them and the providential way in which America had won its independence from a vastly superior force:

> "If Historiographers should be hardy enough to fill the page of History with the advantages that have been gained with unequal numbers [on the part of America] in the course of this contest, and attempt to relate the distressing circumstances under which they have been obtained, it is more than probable that Posterity will bestow on their labors the epithet and marks of fiction; for it will not be believed that such a force as Great Britain has employed for eight years in this Country could be baffled in their plan of Subjugating it by numbers infinitely less, composed of Men oftentimes half starved; always in Rags, without pay, and experiencing, at times, every species of distress which human nature is capable of undergoing."[363]

Washington knew well that of which he spoke. Throughout the war, time and time again, he had witnessed God's hand intervene and save his army from certain annihilation. For example:

- On August 27, 1776, Washington and his troops fought the British on Long Island but were overwhelmed and forced to retreat to the relative safety of Brooklyn Heights. On the Heights, trapped by the British, Washington and his army waited for the obvious knock-out blow that was certain to come – one that would probably destroy the Continental Army and end the war with an American defeat. But on the night of the 29th, under the cover of darkness, Washington and his army were able to board small vessels provided by the surrounding citizens to make their escape to Manhattan. Miraculously, a strong wind blew in a heavy fog that some referred to as a "pea soup" fog, which masked the movements of Washington and his army. Many of the eyewitnesses remarked that even more miraculously, the fog only appeared in the area where the Americans were crossing the river – there was no fog where the British troops were. Amazingly, the fog lasted late into the morning of the 30th, much later into the day than usual, providing the time necessary for Washington to evacuate his troops to Manhattan and out of harm's way so they could live to fight another day. Interestingly, General Cornwallis tried to execute a similar escape at Yorktown, but unfortunately for him and the British army, not only did no fog appear as it had for Washington, coincidentally, a storm also blew up from the Atlantic, making the ocean too rough for ships to aid the British in their escape, thus forcing Cornwallis to surrender.[364]

- On December 25, 1776, with the war going badly for the Americans, General Washington took a calculated risk that would either turn the tide of war in favor of America or most likely crush his army and force them to surrender to the British, effectively ending the war with an American defeat. With a huge body of Hessian soldiers numbering some 1,200 encamped across the Delaware River at Trenton, Washington determined to cross the river and execute a surprise attack. Against the advice of his officers who believed that the American soldiers were too ill and too ill equipped to pull off such a demanding maneuver, Washington gave the command anyway. In the twilight of Christmas Day, December 25, 1776, in a snow storm that turned into sheets of sleet, the Americans, many destitute of shoes with feet wrapped in burlap and leaving bloody footprints in the snow, marched down to the Delaware and boarded boats to cross the river, blocked with ice flows. Unknown to Gen. Washington, the Hessians, tipped off by local Tories, were expecting a surprise attack and had made the necessary preparations, which would have almost certainly allowed them to defeat the Americans. But earlier in the day of December 25, a small band of colonials (who have never been officially identified) attacked the Hessians and fought a small battle and then retreated back into the wilderness after sustaining a small number of casualties. Thinking this was the attack of which they had been warned, Colonel Rawl, commander of the Hessians, noted what a pitiful attack it was and then allowed his troops to resume their Christmas celebration. Around eight o'clock the next morning, December 26, Gen. Washington, now with all of his troops safely across the Delaware and ready to fight, ordered the attack. The Hessians were taken completely by surprise and the Americans won an overwhelming American victory. The Americans killed some twenty-two Hessians and captured over nine hundred while sustaining only two killed and five wounded. The victory did indeed change the direction of the war, and from that time until the British surrender at Yorktown, America never looked back. No one ever learned the identity of those who made the early attack on the Hessians on December 25, but that attack sufficiently deceived the Hessians into a false sense of security, allowing Washington's army to gain a critical victory that it would probably never have been able to achieve had the Hessians been on guard.[365]

- On January 17, 1781 at the Battle of Cowpens, the American militia, under the command of General Daniel Morgan, fired into the British and then retreated with the British in hot pursuit. As the British rushed over a hill, American soldiers waiting just beyond the crest, fired upon them with devastating effect, killing 110 Redcoats and capturing 830. Cornwallis regrouped his troops and then pursued the Americans to the Catawba River, where the Americans had crossed just two hours before. As the British prepared to cross the river, a storm made the crossing impossible. Finally crossing the Catawba, the British caught up with the Americans just as they were completing their crossing of the Yadkin River. Again, as the British prepared to cross, a storm dropped torrential rains, causing the river to flood, making it impossible for them to cross. This same scenario was repeated a third time at the Dan River. The British General, Henry Clinton, wrote concerning this situation: "Here the royal army was again stopped by a sudden rise of the waters, which had only just fallen (almost miraculously) to let the enemy over." In March of 1781, General Washington commented about this series of miraculous events to Chaplain William Gordon: "We have, as you very justly observe, abundant reason to thank Providence for its many favorable interpositions in our behalf. It has at times been my only dependence, for all other resources seemed to have failed us."[366]

With Providential interventions like these and many more, no American was more cognizant of and thankful for God's assistance than George Washington.

- On December 18, 1778, he wrote, "Providence has heretofore taken us up when all other means and hope seemed to be departing from us, in this I will confide."[367]

- On May 19, 1780, he wrote, "… providence, to whom we are infinitely more indebted than we are to our own wisdom, or our own exertions, has always displayed its power and goodness, when clouds and thick darkness seemed ready to overwhelm us. The hour is now come when we stand much in need of another manifestation of its bounty however little we deserve it."[368]

- Writing to Rev. John Rodgers on June 11, 1783, Washington said, "Dear Sir: I accept, with much pleasure your kind Congratulations on the happy Event of Peace, with the Establishment of our Liberties and Independence. Glorious indeed has been our Contest: glorious, if we consider the Prize for which we have contended, and glorious in its Issue; but in the midst of our Joys, I hope we shall not forget that, to divine Providence is to be ascribed the Glory and the Praise."[369]

- Writing to Rev. William Gordon, July 8, 1783, Washington said, "To say nothing of the invisible workings of Providence, which has conducted us through difficulties where no human foresight could point the way; it will appear to a close Examiner, that there has been a concatenation of causes to produce this Event; which in all probability at no time, or under any Circumstances, will combine again."[370]

On December 11, 1783, in his *Declaration of Peace* preached at the Third Presbyterian Church in Philadelphia, George Duffield praised God for the end of the war and the American victory:

"… we give thanks to our God. For, according to this time, shall it be said of these United States, What hath God wrought for them? Great indeed, is the salvation he hath shown! and great the obligations we are under to praise! For had we failed in our just attempt to secure our invaluable rights, America's choicest blood had flowed in liberal streams, and her most valuable citizens, throughout the states, had expired by halters, and on gibbets. The daring patriot, whose zeal for his country had led him, with his life in his hand, to take a scat; in the great council of the states, or in legislation, or in administering justice; or who had led in the field in his country's cause—these had been led forth the first, in haughty triumph, amidst ten thousand insulting scoffs, as the victims of insatiable vengeance. …

"Tis he, the sovereign-disposer of all events, hath wrought for us, and brought the whole to pass. It was he who led his Israel of old, by the pillar and the cloud, through their wilderness journey; wherein they also had their wanderings; 'twas he, the same, presided over our affairs, directed our councils, and guided our senators by the way. 'Twas he who raised a Joshua to lead the tribes of Israel in the field of battle; raised and formed a Washington to lead on the troops of his chosen states, to final conquest, and imbued him with all his military patience, perseverance, prowess and skill; and admirably preserved his life and health, through all the danger and toil. … O America, with an ardent glow through every rank, to assert the cause of freedom; and led forth the husbandman and mechanic, with those of every class, to offer themselves undaunted in the daring conflict. It was he who hid fear from their eyes of either the superior numbers or skill of the powerful foe they rose to withstand; and from him came down that firmness and fortitude that raised American officers, and soldiers, beyond all former example, through hunger, nakedness and cold, to fight the battles of their country, and never forsake its standard. It was he breathed from above, and fired their bosoms in the hour of action, to crop the laurels of triumph, or, having dearly sold their precious lives, to embrace death, in all his glory, on the bloody field! And he only inspired our generous seamen with invincible firmness to endure the horrors of prison-ships and jails, and expire by famine and British barbarity, rather than renounce the virtuous cause in which they embarked. It was he who … endued the monarch of France with an angel's mind, to assert and secure the freedom of his United American States. And by him were the hearts of other nations disposed to our aid. And he, and he alone, who saith to the proud waves of the sea: "Hitherto shall ye come, but no farther," restrained the councils and arms of Britain from improving against us many opportunities and advantages which evidently lay within the line of their power. Who can recollect the critical night of retreat from Long Island; the scene of retiring from New York; the day of Brandy wine; or the endangered situation of the arms of America on Trenton's ever-memorable night—and not be constrained to say: "If it had not been the Lord who was on our side, our enemy had swallowed us up; the waters had overwhelmed us; the proud stream had swept us away!" But, blessed be his name, our help was found in him who made the heavens and the earth. It was God who blasted the secret designs of enemies and traitors against us; and, by an admirable interposition, brought forth into light the dark and deep-stained villainy of an *Arnold*, cursed and detested of God and men. And converted our repeated misfortunes, and even mistakes, into singular mercies and peculiar advantages, that not more manifest was his voice on Sinai, or his hand in his affairs of his Israel of old, than we have seen the wisdom, the power, and the goodness of our God displayed through the whole of our arduous contest, from its earliest period down. We may, with emphatical propriety, say: It is He, the Almighty God, has accomplished the whole in every part, and by his kind care and omnipotent arm has wrought out our deliverance; cast forth our enemy; bestowed upon us a wide, extended, fruitful country; and blessed us with a safe and honorable peace; and has brought the whole to pass in so short a space of time, and with so few difficulties attending, in comparison with what we had reason to expect, that the establishment of these United States in the peaceful possession of their rights and privileges, stands, an instance of divine favor, unexampled in the records of time. …

"In whatever point of light we view this great event we are constrained to say: "It is the doing of the Lord, and marvelous in our eyes," and to him be rendered the thanks and the praise. *"Not unto us, not unto us, but unto thy name, O Lord, be the glory"* for thine is the power, and the victory, and the greatness; both success and safety come of thee, and thou reignest over all, and hast wrought all our works in us and for us. *Praise, therefore, thy God, O America, praise the Lord, ye, his highly favored United States.* Nor let it rest in the fleeting language of the lip; or the formal thanksgiving of a day. But, let every heart glow with gratitude: And every life, by a devout regard to his holy law, proclaim his praise. It is this, our God requires, as that wherein our personal, and national good, and the glory of his great name consist. And without which, all our professions will be but an empty name.

"But blessed be God, with Israel of old we may take up our song; 'blessed be the Lord who gave us not as a prey to their teeth. Blessed be the Lord, the snare is broken, and we are escaped.' We cried unto him in the day of our distress. He heard our entreaties; and hath brought us forth into a large place; and established our rights; and opened before us a glorious prospect."[371]

Six months later on June 3, 1784, preaching to the New Hampshire legislature at Portsmouth, New Hampshire, Samuel McClintock joined the cacophony of praise to God for His deliverance of America. Looking back, McClintock pointed out just how unprepared and inept the Americans had been at the beginning of the conflict, making the American victory even more miraculous and sweet:

"The several steps which led to this great event cannot be rationally accounted for from any other cause. Among these the general union of the people throughout these states is not the least remarkable.

"That people so widely separated from one another by their situation, manners, customs, and forms of government, should all at once be willing to sacrifice their private interests to the public good, and unite like a band of brothers, to make the cause of one state, and even of one town, a common cause; and that they should continue firm and united amidst the greatest discouragements and the most trying reverses of fortune.

"That an army of freemen, voluntarily assembling at the alarm of danger—men who had been nurtured in the bosom of liberty, and unused to slavish restraints, should be willing to submit to the severity of military government, for the safety of their country, and patiently endure hardships that would have overcome the fortitude of veterans, following their illustrious leader in the depths of winter, through cold and snow, in nakedness and perils, when every step they took was marked with the blood that issued from their swollen feet, and when they could not be animated to such patience and perseverance by any mercenary motives, was a rare spectacle, and for its solution must be traced to a higher source than mere natural causes—in a word, the hand of providence evidently appeared in the various incidents and secondary causes which concurred to secure to us success.

"In raising up, at the beginning of the contest a group of noble patriots to counteract the political maneuvers of the British administration, and expose to view their dark designs to enslave this country, and who with peculiar strength of argument and power of persuasion, so ably defended the cause of their country, as to engage the attention and approbation of all Europe, and gain immortal honor to themselves—in bringing on the stage a great military character, the American Fabius, to take the command of our armies, endowed with those qualities which in a peculiar manner fitted him for such a command, at such a time and in such circumstances—in overruling things, so that the very instruments of war which had been prepared for our destruction, should fall into our hands when they were most wanted, and be turned against the enemy in our own defense—in disposing the heart of the illustrious monarch of France to aid and assist us in our virtuous struggle—in sending divisions into the councils of the enemy, disconcerting their measures, and discovering their secret plans, at the critical moment, by a concurrence of incidents which no human wisdom could have foreseen—in the repeated signal instances of success, particularly the capture of two of the best armies of the enemy, in which we had a convincing demonstration that the race is not to the swift, nor the battle to the strong; but that the victory was of the Lord; and finally, in disposing the enemy to acknowledge our independence and sovereignty, and to withdraw their fleets and armies. …

"At that time our contest with Britain appeared, from a consideration of the difference between their circumstances and ours, as unequal, as that between the stripling David and the giant of Gath; and the improbability of our success as great, as that he with a sling and stone should overcome that proud and mighty enemy, clothed with armor from head to foot.

"They were men of war from their youth. They had regular troops, used to service, who had signalized their valor on the plains of Minden, and the heights of Abraham, commanded by able, experienced generals, amply furnished with all the terrible apparatus of death and destruction, and aided by mercenary troops, who had been bred to arms, and were versed in all the stratagems of war—add to this, they had a navy that ruled the ocean, and regular resources to supply their demands—on the other hand, we were inexperienced in the art of war, and had neither disciplined troops, nor magazines of provision and ammunition, nor so much as one ship of war to oppose to their formidable fleets, nor any regular resources, nor even so much as the certain prospect of any foreign aid—besides, all the civil governments were dissolved, and the people reduced back to a state of nature, and in danger of falling into anarchy and confusion. From this comparative view of their strength and our weakness, to what can our success be ascribed but to that omnipotent hand which directed the stone from the sling? The several steps which led to this great event, cannot be rationally accounted for from any other cause. Among these the general union of the people throughout these states is not the least remarkable. …

"By this revolution, we are not only delivered from the calamities of a long, expensive and bloody war, but may now sit quietly under our own vine and fig-tree, without any to make us afraid, and every man is left at full liberty to pursue the means of opulence and happiness, without the danger of being deprived of the fruits of his industry by the hand of rapine and violence, which is ever the case of those who are either the subjects of arbitrary power or exposed to the ravages of war. By this revolution, the rights and privileges of men in a state of civil society, are secured to us; and we have the precious opportunity, which few nations have ever enjoyed, to take up government on its first principles, and to choose that form which we judge best adapted to our situation, and most promotive of our public interests and happiness. America seems like a young heir, arrived to mature age, who, being freed from the restraints of tutors and governors, takes the management of his estate into his own hands, and makes such laws for the regulation of his domestic affairs, as he judges will be most conducive to establish peace, order and happiness in his family."[372]

As the new nation moved forward, the patriot preachers made certain that their fellow citizens were reminded to celebrate the great things God had performed on their behalf during the war. In his June 11, 1797 New Hampshire election sermon,

Stephen Peabody, reminded the New Hampshire legislators of God's incredible blessings on America:

"A propitious Providence, like the "pillar of a cloud and of fire to Israel," led the American armies. And not less apparent hath been the hand of God, in our civil operations. The organization of our governments, hath been attended with salutary effects in the increase of property and respectability. After our thankful acknowledgments to God, the great Superintendent, we should not neglect to express gratitude to a Washington, a Franklin, an Adams, a Jay, and to other heroes who have been instrumental in accomplishing those great purposes, so much for the honor and interest of the American states, and for the happiness of future generations."[373]

What a difference some two hundred and thirty years makes. Those who fought for and founded this country had no doubts about how and why it came to be. They knew that to have defeated the mighty British army on the field of battle had taken more than determination, courage, and sacrifice – it had taken a miracle of God. General Washington unashamedly admitted that the victory was due far more to God's intervention than it was to the efforts of his Continental Army. Consequently, Americans did not hesitate to give God the praise. What a contrast with today's America! Not only do we seem oblivious to the past blessings of God on our country, incredibly, we seem convinced that we have done it all ourselves and feel no obligation whatsoever to offer any thanksgiving to heaven. Some even go as far as to claim that God and Christianity played no part in the birth of America.

Centuries ago, King Solomon warned:

"Pride goeth before destruction, and an haughty spirit before a fall." Proverbs 16:18

"Wisdom crieth without; she uttereth her voice in the streets: [21]She crieth in the chief place of concourse, in the openings of the gates: in the city she uttereth her words, *saying*, [22]How long, ye simple ones, will ye love simplicity? and the scorners delight in their scorning, and fools hate knowledge? [23]Turn you at my reproof: behold, I will pour out my spirit unto you, I will make known my words unto you. [24]Because I have called, and ye refused; I have stretched out my hand,

and no man regarded; [25]But ye have set at nought all my counsel, and would none of my reproof: [26]I also will laugh at your calamity; I will mock when your fear cometh; [27]When your fear cometh as desolation, and your destruction cometh as a whirlwind; when distress and anguish cometh upon you. [28]Then shall they call upon me, but I will not answer; they shall seek me early, but they shall not find me: [29]For that they hated knowledge, and did not choose the fear of the LORD: [30]They would none of my counsel: they despised all my reproof. [31]Therefore shall they eat of the fruit of their own way, and be filled with their own devices. [32]For the turning away of the simple shall slay them, and the prosperity of fools shall destroy them. [33]But whoso hearkeneth unto me shall dwell safely, and shall be quiet from fear of evil." Proverbs 1:20-33

America has become arrogant, haughty, and self-sufficient. If we are ever going to restore our nation's greatness, we must look toward heaven again! We modern Americans owe an even greater debt of gratitude to God than did George Washington and the patriot preachers of the Revolution. God has so bountifully blessed America. How can we not show our gratitude to Him? We must rekindle the spirit of thankfulness possessed by the Black Robed Regiment or else we are doomed to drown in our own pride and self-worship. This spirit of thankfulness must be much more than the occasional "God bless America" thrown in at the end of some politician's speech. It will have to be truly heartfelt and lived out in our deeds. The solution is so simple. Psalm 33:12 declares:

"Blessed is the nation whose God is the Lord; and the people whom He hath chosen for His own inheritance." Psalm 144:15 adds, "… happy is that people, whose God is the Lord."

Chapter 19

THE CHURCH AND THE INTERNAL REVENUE SERVICE

Why are so many pastors AWOL in the fight to reclaim our government? I have asked myself this question again and again. No doubt there are many reasons.

Some just honestly do not believe pastors should get involved in politics. For them, it is a matter of conscience. Others are afraid of the criticism and conflicts that will come if they get political. Fearing that members of their own congregations may rise up against them, these pastors are concerned for their own jobs. But beyond these reasons, I contend there are two primary reasons why most modern pastors refuse to preach about politics and have disengaged from the political process:

1. They believe the "myth" of separation of church and state.
2. They fear the loss of their church's non-profit, tax-exempt status.

Having already shown that the Bible and the Constitution do not demand a "strict separation of church and state" (chapters 10-11), let us focus on a church's fear of losing its tax-exempt status.

First, it is important to understand that the common fear most pastors and congregations have of losing their church's tax-exempt status is completely unwarranted. For the record: during the entire history of the Internal Revenue Service, not one church has ever lost its tax-exempt status because of political speech! Not one.

The closest any church has ever come was when the Church at Pierce Creek in Binghamton, New York placed full-page advertisements in the October 30, 1992 issues of *USA Today* and the *Washington Times* encouraging Christians not to vote for Bill Clinton for President. Going even further, Pierce Creek even solicited donations within those ads – a step that even the most politically engaged churches would probably not have taken. But even then, Pierce Creek did not lose its tax-exempt status.

The IRS did successfully prosecute the church but the most they were able to do was to revoke the advance letter of tax-exempt status that the IRS had given to the church when it originally filed as a 501(c)(3) organization. Even though this advance letter was revoked, Pierce Creek never lost its tax-exempt status.

(Note: It is important to know that this advance letter of tax-exempt status is not required for a church to be tax-exempt. In fact, a church does not even have to officially file as 501(c)(3) to be tax-exempt – churches are automatically tax-exempt. Whether a church officially files as a 501(c)(3) organization or not, the IRS treats them as such.)

It is interesting to note that in its ruling against the church, the Federal Court of Appeals for the District of Columbia admitted:

> "... because of the unique treatment churches receive under the Internal Revenue Code, the impact of the revocation is likely to be more symbolic than substantial. ... All that will have been lost is the advance assurance of deductibility in the event a donor should be audited."[374]

The Court went on to state that it knew of no authority,

> "to prevent the Church from reapplying for a prospective determination of its tax-exempt status and regaining the advance assurance of deductibility ..."[375]

After the Federal Court's May 12, 2000 ruling, Matt Staver, attorney with the Liberty Counsel, noted,

"Understand that the only thing the Church lost in this case is its advance tax-exempt letter ruling. Contributions given prior to the revocation of the IRS letter are still deductible and are not taxable to the Church. After the letter ruling was revoked, the Church could continue as a church, continue receiving donations, and donors could continue to claim deductions on their income tax return, provided that the Church did not continue to endorse or oppose candidates. If the Church wants an advance letter ruling at some point in the future, it is free to ask for another one. Obviously in the case of the presidential election, the Church could easily cease endorsing or opposing a candidate since the election had transpired."[376]

So in other words, once the election was over, the church could reapply for its letter from the IRS and retain it until, at some time in the future, it decided to endorse another candidate. In which case the IRS would presumably prosecute to revoke that new letter also. If so, the church could simply reapply for another letter, and another, and another and apparently continue repeating the process indefinitely.

According to numerous attorneys, even if a church or its pastor endorses a candidate from the pulpit on a given Sunday, the worst conceivable action the IRS can take is to consider the donations given on that day only as non-deductible. The next day the church would return to its "tax exempt posture" since it conceivably would not be "officially" endorsing a candidate on that day.

Additionally, most church members are shocked to discover that, along with allowing political speech from their pulpits, the church can even participate in official lobbying efforts as long as those efforts do not represent a major part of the church's ministry time. In short, as long as the church does not make lobbying its primary function, the IRS cannot do anything about it.

The bottom line is this: the IRS has very little power to prosecute and take away a church's tax-exempt status. In very real terms, when it comes to limiting religious speech, the IRS is a "paper tiger" – one that pastors and congregations need not fear (At least for now; but if Christians remain politically disengaged, this could change soon). Therefore, pastors should feel free to boldly proclaim their biblical convictions from the pulpit – even when it comes to politics. Of course, many believe this is something preachers should do regardless of the actions of the government or the IRS. Like Peter and John, many believe preachers should speak boldly no matter the consequences:

> "And they called them, and commanded them not to speak at all nor teach in the name of Jesus. [19]But Peter and John answered and said unto them, 'Whether it be right in the sight of God to hearken unto you more than unto God, judge ye. [20]For we cannot but speak the things which we have seen and heard.' [21]So when they had further threatened them, they let them go, finding nothing how they might punish them, because of the people: for all men glorified God for that which was done." Acts 4:19-21

Many are quick to point out that in Acts 4, the apostles were in jail for preaching the gospel – not politics. Granted, this is true. But the question can justifiably be asked, "If pastors won't speak out on political and social issues because they're afraid of losing their church's tax-exempt status, what would make us think that they would actually be willing to go to jail for preaching the Gospel if that ever became illegal?" In addition, it is important to note that certain issues like homosexuality and traditional marriage that were once considered spiritual/biblical issues are now considered "political." So, if/when the government forbids preaching about these subjects because they are now considered "political," will preachers who insist that we should not preach politics knuckle under and become silent about those as well? Many subjects the Black Regiment considered fair topics for sermons are today considered political issues and are therefore off limits for modern pulpits. And since the list of what is spiritual and what is political is now a constantly moving target, who decides which issues are political and which are spiritual/biblical and thus proper for the pulpit? The potential end of this dilemma is evident: eventually, everything in Scripture that is deemed offensive by the politically correct crowd will be categorized as political or hate speech and will therefore be designated as inappropriate for the pulpit.

The bottom line is this: as followers of Christ, we cannot allow ourselves to be controlled by the fear of man. We must stand up for and preach what we know is right; regardless of what the government says. Like David in Psalms 56:11, we should say, "In God have I put my trust: I will not be afraid what man can do unto me." We must follow the admonition of Jesus in Matthew 10:28, "And fear not them which kill the body, but are not able to kill the soul: but rather fear him which is able to destroy both soul and body in hell." After all, as Paul declared in Romans 8:31, "What shall we then say to these things? If God be for us, who can be against us?"

We can take heart; this battle is not our battle. As David said to Goliath in 1 Samuel 17:47, "And all this assembly shall know that the Lord saveth not with sword and spear: for the battle is the Lord's, and he will give you into our hands."

THE CHURCH'S TAX-EXEMPT STATUS IS NOT A GIFT FROM GOVERNMENT!

I am often amazed as Christians speak in hushed tones, whispers, and innuendos about political issues when they are at church as if it is against the law to speak of such things there. They are obviously fearful that the government may hear and take away their tax-exempt status.

The church's tax-exempt status is not a "gift" bestowed by a benevolent government. From the very beginning of our nation, the church has been recognized as a sovereign entity that is exempt from taxation. This principle has been affirmed throughout our nation's history, and as recently as 1971, the U.S. Supreme Court affirmed it in *Lemon v. Kurtzman*. Writing for the majority, Chief Justice Warren Burger said,

"In Walz [*Walz v. Tax Commission*, 1970] it was argued that a tax exemption for places of religious worship would prove to be the first step in an inevitable progression leading to the establishment of state churches and state religion. That claim could not stand up against more than 200 years of virtually universal practice imbedded in our colonial experience and continuing into the present."[377]

From the time the early settlers landed on North America's shores until 1789 when the U.S. Constitution was ratified, the driving motivation for Americans was to found a nation where people would be free to worship God according to the dictates of their own consciences – not according to the dictates of a potentate or other government entity. As was discussed in chapter 10, this principle was first expressed in documents like the Mayflower Compact and was then ultimately officially codified into law in the First Amendment to the U.S. Constitution. It is, therefore, insane to believe that these early Americans made the great sacrifices they made for liberty and freedom to then create a government with the power to limit their freedom of speech, especially religious, and severely punish those who did not comply with its restrictions. This would make absolutely no sense.

After all, as has been noted, our Founders believed that Christianity was a major part of America's footing and they made certain that it would receive the elevated position it deserved and the protection justice demanded. In his farewell address, President George Washington pointed out that "morality and religion" were the "two pillars" upon which our republic rests. This is the very reason why John Adams emphasized that our Constitution would "work" only in a nation dominated by the Christian faith and that it was "wholly inadequate for the government of any other." Understanding the central role of the church in America, historian John Wingate Thornton wrote in 1860, "The state was developed out of the church"[378] – not the other way around. Historian Alice Baldwin seconded Thornton's declaration when she wrote in 1918, "The Constitutional Convention and the written Constitution were the children of the pulpit."[379]

It is because the Founders believed the church to be so essential to the survival of the republic that they insisted on protecting it from governmental intrusion by taxation. So they ensured that the church would always be beyond government's reach by recognizing it as tax-exempt. Their reasoning was simple:

1. This principle is biblical.
2. The power to tax is the power to control and to ultimately destroy.

First, they found the church's right to tax-exemption taught in the Bible:

- In Genesis 47:26, the Pharaoh of Egypt, a pagan ruler, did not tax the priests in Egypt.
- In Ezra 7:24, Artaxerxes, the pagan king of Persia, decreed, "Also we certify you, that touching any of the priests and Levites, singers, porters, Nethinims, or ministers of this house of God, it shall not be lawful to impose toll, tribute, or custom, upon them."

A casual study of our early history reveals how this principle was applied throughout the colonies/states. For example, Virginia exempted churches from paying property taxes in 1777, New York did so in 1799, and Washington D.C. followed suit in 1802. That same year, the Seventh Congress exempted all churches in America from property taxes.[380]

(Note: Even today, parsonages are still exempt from property taxes in all 50 states. The minister's housing exemption, a principle first recognized in America in 1921, was modified in section 107(2) of the Internal Revenue tax code on August 11, 1953 by Representative Peter Mack allowing ministers of the gospel to designate a portion of compensation as a housing allowance and to exclude that amount from income to the extent that it is actually used to provide a home. In presenting the legislation, Rep. Mack declared, "Certainly, in these times when we are being threatened by a godless and antireligious world movement, we should correct this discrimination against certain ministers of the gospel who are carrying on such a courageous fight against this foe. Certainly this is not too much to do for these people who are caring for our spiritual welfare."[381] In 2000, the parsonage exemption was challenged when the IRS questioned the amount Rick Warren, pastor of Saddleback Church in southern California, claimed for his parsonage allowance on his tax returns. Whether or not every member of the court agreed that the amount Warren claimed was fair, they did uphold, in principle, that parsonages should be considered tax-exempt. Due to concerns generated by this challenge, two years later Congress passed the Clergy Housing Allowance Clarification Act of 2002 which was signed into law by President George Bush on May 20, 2002. Even though this act capped the parsonage exemption at the amount of a home's fair rental value, including furnishings and appurtenances such as a garage, plus the cost of utilities, it reaffirmed the principle of the church's tax-exempt status.)

In addition to believing that Scripture established the church as tax-exempt, the Founders also believed government had no authority or right to tax the church because they considered it a sovereign entity. Understanding that a sovereign entity such as the federal government had no authority to tax another sovereign entity such as an individual state, another country, or the church, the Founders considered the church outside the reach of governmental authority and taxation.

The article, "Churches Are Tax Exempt As A Matter Of Constitutional Right," published on OpposingViews.com, clearly explained the issue of the sovereign status of the church:

> "There is a distinction between constitutionally separate 'sovereigns.' For one sovereign entity to tax another leaves the taxed one subservient to that authority. This is true both in the symbolic statement of paying the tax and in the practical effect of supporting the sovereign party. So, in our constitutional structure, states may not tax each other, and they may not tax property of the federal government.

The District of Columbia_does not tax the property owned by foreign governments, and New York does not tax the property owned by the United Nations.

"So, too, churches in America are not subservient to the government. The First Amendment to the Constitution requires that 'Congress shall make no law respecting an establishment of religion or prohibiting the free exercise thereof.' The Constitution prevents the government from wielding its authority to control churches. Churches in this way differ from all other businesses and organizations. They are a unique institution whose existence is not derived from government authority, nor even from governmental acknowledgment. Churches preceded the birth of our nation and will remain long after its death. They transcend geographic and ethnic boundaries.

"In the 1970 opinion in *Walz vs. Tax Commission* of the City of New York, the high court stated that a tax exemption for churches 'creates only a minimal and remote involvement between church and state and far less than taxation of churches. [An exemption] restricts the fiscal relationship between church and state, and tends to complement and reinforce the desired separation insulating each from the other.'

"In *Walz v. Tax Commission*, the Supreme Court noted that the church's "uninterrupted freedom from taxation" has 'operated affirmatively to help guarantee the free exercise of all forms of religious belief.' The much misunderstood 'separation between church and state' is in truth designed to restrict the sovereignty of each over the other. That is, it is designed to achieve a position for each that is neither master nor servant of the other. Exemption from income taxation is essential for respect of the church as a separate sovereign entity. Otherwise the government has the power to encumber and even terminate churches if such taxes are not punctually paid or cannot be so paid in full."[382]

The Founders and those who immediately followed them also viewed government's power to tax as a huge threat to liberty – especially religious liberty. In 1819, while arguing the case of *McCulloch v. Maryland*, a case that determined whether or not an individual state could tax the First Bank of the United States, Daniel Webster said, "An unlimited power to tax involves, necessarily, a power to destroy."[383] In the Supreme Court's decision in that case, Chief Justice John Marshall wrote: "That the power of taxing it [First Bank of the United States] by the States may be exercised so as to destroy it, is too obvious to be denied … the power to tax involves the power to destroy."[384]

Believing that religion, i.e. the Christian Church, was essential to the survival of our republic, the Founders did not grant the federal government the power to tax the church because they believed that power could be used to threaten the free exercise of religion. Concerning this, Erik Stanley, senior legal counsel for the Alliance Defending Freedom, wrote,

> "With all of the discussion swirling about whether church leaders can speak freely about electoral candidates from the pulpit, one question frequently comes to the fore: If a church wants to talk about the positions of electoral candidates, it can just give up the 'gift' of tax-exempt status 'bestowed' by the government. That would be simple enough — if it wasn't so completely wrong.
>
> "That's because churches receive a tax exemption as a matter of constitutional right, not legislative grace. The U.S. Supreme Court stated decades ago that the power to tax involves the power to destroy, and no surer way to destroy the free exercise of religion exists than to tax it out of existence.
>
> "Therefore, tax-exempt status for churches has existed independent of any special grant of privilege from the IRS. Some assume that any tax exemption is a government subsidy. That would be true if the government owned all property and income, but in America, it doesn't. Americans have always placed a high value on the importance of private property. That's a big difference between the United States and many other nations.
>
> "Churches derive their tax exemption from the Constitution, and it is therefore not something the government can withdraw without serious damage to the Constitution, itself. For almost the first 200 years of our country's history, that tax exemption was recognized without any stipulations or conditions. Pastors spoke freely from the pulpit, both endorsing and opposing candidates for office without anyone questioning whether they should be tax exempt."[385]

Therefore, since the Founders believed that attacking the church through taxation was necessarily striking at the very foundation of America; they recognized the church as tax-exempt. They considered taxation of the church a violation of the First Amendment since it could prohibit the free exercise of religion. If America began to tax the church, we would be ignoring the original intent of the Founders and more than 236 years of accepted legal thought and practice.

THE JOHNSON AMENDMENT – THE REASON PASTORS FEAR THE IRS

Even when they are armed with this information, many pastors still remain reluctant to speak about politics from their pulpits. With judicial history on their side and the reality that the IRS is a "paper tiger" when it comes to interfering with religious expression, what could possibly continue to intimidate these men of God? The answer is: the Johnson Amendment.

For the first two hundred years of America's existence, pastors were free to endorse and oppose candidates without fearing resistance from their people or intimidation from their government. In fact, their congregations expected them to address political issues and no one during that time suggested that a church should lose its tax-exempt status because its pastor did so. But all of this changed in 1954.

In 1954, then Senator Lyndon Baines Johnson was running for reelection as senator from Texas. Johnson's first victory in 1948 was so razor thin, with a margin of only 87 votes, that Coke Stevenson, his challenger, was able to present credible evidence that Johnson had probably stolen the election through fraud. But with some "creative" judicial wrangling, Johnson had been able to use court injunctions to retain his victory. So six years later, when Johnson was running against Dudley Dougherty, a Texas State Representative, he had good reason to fear defeat. Johnson actually was in jeopardy of losing his bid for reelection due to the efforts of two conservative non-profit organizations: Facts Forum and the Committee for Constitutional Government. These groups were making a convincing claim that Johnson was, at the very least, soft on Communism.

Desperately needing to censor these groups or likely lose the race, Johnson, on July 2, 1954, with the assistance of a complicit senate, successfully inserted language into the IRS tax code that silenced these groups and swept him into the senate once more. Known since as the "Johnson Amendment," the new language read:

"Non-profit entities, including churches, cannot participate in, or intervene in (including the publishing or distributing of statements), any political campaign on behalf of *or in opposition to* (italicized words added in 1984) any candidate for public office"[386]

Even though the amendment flew in the face of the Constitution by violating the section of the First Amendment that reads, "Congress shall make no law respecting an establishment of religion, or prohibiting the free exercise thereof; or abridging the freedom of speech," that did not seem to matter to the senators in 1954. It is difficult to understand how they did not see that this new law was a frontal attack on Americans' fundamental right to free speech, but they pushed it right through Congress anyway. More appalling is the relatively little discussion and debate that occurred on the senate floor concerning this far-reaching change to the tax law. After Senator Johnson had been recognized from the senate floor, the following is the only discussion that took place:

Mr. Johnson of Texas: "Mr. President, I have an amendment at the desk, which I should like to have stated."

"The Presiding Officer: "The Secretary will state the amendment."

The Chief Clerk: "On page 117 of the House bill, in section 501(c)(3), it is proposed to strike out 'individuals, and' and insert 'individual,' and strike out 'influence legislation.' And insert 'influence legislation, and which does not participate in, or intervene in (including the publishing or distributing of statements), any political campaign on behalf of any candidate for public office.'"

Mr. Johnson of Texas: "Mr. President, this amendment seeks to extend the provisions of section 501 of the House bill, denying tax-exempt status to not only those people who influence legislation but also to those who intervene in any political campaign on behalf of any candidate for any public office. I have discussed the matter with the chairman of the committee, the minority ranking member of the committee, and several other members of the committee, and I understand that the amendment is acceptable to them. I hope the chairman will take it to conference, and that it will be included in the final bill which Congress passes."[387]

With that brief discussion, the Johnson Amendment became the law of the land and the club with which the IRS has intimidated pastors and churches for some fifty-eight years since. Commenting on the Johnson Amendment, Erik Stanley of Alliance Defending Freedom wrote,

> "Scholars attest to the fact that the Johnson Amendment was not intended in any way to restrict the free speech of churches on the subject, but it has been used in that manner ever since. It is patently unconstitutional.
>
> "If one doubts the impact of this ill-advised piece of legislation, passed by Congress without debate or analysis, one only need take a peek at the activity of organizations like Americans United for Separation of Church and State to see how they wield it as a weapon to keep churches (at least the ones they disagree with) from having a voice. This 'keep your opinions to yourself or else' threat has got to go."[388]

Ironically, the Johnson Amendment does not even mention pastors; it only restricts "churches" from participating in political campaigns – not pastors. So in a technical sense, the pastor's right to freely express himself from the pulpit is unaffected by the amendment. Unfortunately, that is not how the amendment has been understood and, instead, it has been used to muzzle pastors and prevent them from speaking their convictions from their pulpits. Some make the argument that since the pastor is a paid employee of the church, when he speaks from the pulpit he speaks officially for his church. On some occasions this may indeed be true, but normally it is not. Ask any preacher and he will tell you that quite often what he says does not necessarily reflect the opinions of those in his church. In fact, as a pastor I have found that I can pontificate with great emphasis from the pulpit only to discover that members of my congregation can go out on Monday and do the exact opposite of what I told them just the day before.

The fact is most pastors do not understand themselves to be articulating the opinions and positions of their churches when they preach. Instead, most believe they are articulating the opinions and positions of God recorded in His Word, as they understand them. Unlike CEOs, pastors are not called to be corporate spokesmen for their churches – they are called to be spokesmen for God.

If a pastor is sincerely concerned about appearing to speak for his whole congregation when he preaches about some particularly controversial subject, all he need do is simply preface his message with the statement that his comments may not necessarily reflect the opinions or positions of all those in his church. In short, just because the pastor takes a position on a particular subject does not necessarily mean that his church takes the same position. Obviously, those who attend a particular church normally do so because they believe what is preached from the pulpit is the truth, but they do not perceive the pastor to be speaking primarily on behalf of the church but on behalf of God.

Additionally, what does speaking out on political/legislative issues have to do with the non-profit status of the church? What do political activism and the profit motive have in common? Someone has yet to adequately explain why a church ceases to be a non-profit organization simply because it speaks out on a particular candidate or political issue.

ENTER THE ADF AND THE "PULPIT FREEDOM INITIATIVE"

So in light of fifty-eight years of unconstitutional tyranny from the IRS and the Johnson Amendment, what is a preacher/pastor to do? That is easy – join the growing number of preachers/pastors who are taking a stand against the Johnson Amendment.

One such effort is the "Pulpit Freedom Initiative" coordinated by the Alliance Defending Freedom. Recently having changed its name from the Alliance Defense Fund to the Alliance Defending

Freedom in order to better reflect the goals of the organization, ADF is an alliance of attorneys who are committed to keeping the door open for the spread of the Gospel. In 1994, recognizing the need for a strong and coordinated legal defense against growing attacks on religious freedom, more than thirty prominent Christian leaders, including Dr. James Dobson, Dr. Bill Bright, and Dr. James Kennedy, originally founded ADF. Their goal was, and continues to be, to transform the legal system by advocating for religious liberty, the sanctity of life, marriage, and the family.

ADF has brought together thousands of Christian attorneys and like-minded organizations that, for the past nineteen years, have worked tirelessly to advocate for the right of people to freely live out their faith in America and around the world. ADF is comprised of 300 allied organizations and some 2,200 allied attorneys who represent 52 states/territories and 31 countries and who are ready to come to the defense of any Christian whose religious liberties have been infringed.

The success of ADF's efforts has been truly incredible: winning some 80% of the cases they have litigated, including thirty-eight cases before the Supreme Court of the United States. As a result, the God-given, constitutionally protected right to religious freedom has been restored for thousands of Christians. Students, parents, business owners, employees, pastors, and community members who were previously censored or punished for their religious convictions and/or speech are now free to live out their faith.

In 2008, to strengthen the rights of pastors, ADF launched an effort they called the "Pulpit Freedom Initiative." This initiative was designed to educate the pastors of America about their freedom and right to speak their consciences from their pulpits. The primary target of this initiative is the Johnson Amendment.

Realizing that the IRS has used the Johnson Amendment since 1954 to intimidate pastors into believing that they must set aside their First Amendment rights when they step into their pulpits, ADF designed the Pulpit Freedom Initiative to take away this fear by educating and helping pastors to organize and challenge the Johnson Amendment's constitutionality. Of course this Amendment is completely unconstitutional, and as we have seen, the courts have time and time again reaffirmed Americans' freedom of speech – especially religious speech. In addition, even though many American Christians are unaware, history has shown that churches have broad rights to engage in political discourse without the fear of governmental interference. Even so and even though pastors have no reason to be afraid of their government (at least not yet), they seem fear-stricken at the mere suggestion that they say something about politics from their pulpits. So, the Pulpit Freedom Initiative was designed to take away this fear.

Some ask, "Why not just sue the IRS over the Johnson Amendment rather than go to all of the trouble of promoting an effort like the Pulpit Freedom Initiative?" The answer is simple: because of the way tax laws are written. Citizens cannot simply sue the IRS; they can only countersue once the IRS has initiated legal actions against them. Therefore, in order to challenge the Johnson Amendment, someone must defy it and in so doing, invite prosecution by the IRS. In such an instance, if the IRS chose to prosecute, the Alliance Defending Freedom would step in and defend the pastor(s) and officially challenge the Johnson Amendment's constitutionality.

(Note: For those concerned about being civilly disobedient, it is important to remember that the Apostles practiced civil disobedience. In addition, our Founders, the Black Robed Regiment preachers, and generations of Americans have always understood that a law that is unconstitutional is no law at all. Consequently, breaking an unconstitutional law is by definition not an unlawful act. Therefore preachers need not be concerned about "breaking the law" when defying the Johnson Amendment since we believe it to be unconstitutional and therefore "not a law" in the first place.)

In 2008, thirty-three pastors from across America, of which I was honored to be a part, officially participated in Pulpit Freedom Initiative's first "Pulpit Freedom Sunday." On that Sunday, we stood in our pulpits and used the Scriptures to instruct our congregations how we believed they should vote in that general election. Many of us, based upon our understanding of Scripture and the positions of the candidates, actually chose to endorse a particular candidate in our sermons. After we had preached our messages, we mailed a letter to the IRS informing them of what we had done, including a sermon manuscript and/or an audio/video recording of the message, so the IRS would know exactly what we had said. The goal was to force the IRS to "put up or shut up" concerning the restrictions of the Johnson Amendment. Had the IRS chosen to prosecute us, the ADF was prepared to spring into action and defend us. Our hope was to get the Amendment before the courts for a constitutional challenge to prove once and for all its unconstitutionality.

Having successfully completed our task in the fall of 2008, we waited to see what the IRS would do. Unfortunately, the IRS chose not to respond.

So in the general election of 2009, we repeated the process – only this time approximately eighty pastors participated. Again we heard nothing from the IRS. We did it again in 2010 with about one hundred pastors participating, but once again, the IRS did not respond. Pulpit Freedom Sunday 2011 saw a significant increase in participation, as over five hundred pastors officially joined our effort – with many more participating unofficially. Once again, the IRS said nothing.

On Pulpit Freedom Sunday 2012, almost sixteen hundred pastors stood in their pulpits and with their Bibles held high, defied the government's censorship of the pulpit! Regardless of how many Pulpit Freedom Sundays it takes, we intend to continue to defy the unconstitutional Johnson Amendment until the IRS attempts to stop us or admits, either by official statement or by silence, that the Amendment is truly unconstitutional. If the IRS continues to ignore our efforts, at some point we will declare victory and spread the news to America that preachers/pastors have the right to freely speak their minds from their pulpits without any fear of governmental interference or retribution, thus putting an end to the tyranny of the Johnson Amendment.

So pastor/preacher, you are free to speak out, loudly and boldly, without fear. You have the Lord, His Word, His people, and the Constitution on your side. The fight for our independence is not over; and it never will be. Eternal vigilance is the price of liberty. So pastor/preacher, are you ready for the fight?

Chapter 20

WHERE IS TODAY'S BLACK ROBED REGIMENT?

When the political institutions of our fathers cease to be animated by their spirit and virtues, the forms only will remain, monuments of their wisdom, and not less of our folly."[389]

Historian John Wingate Thornton, 1860

In chapter two we discussed how Pastor Peter Muhlenberg traded his clerical robe for a colonel's uniform. But Peter was not the only member of the Muhlenberg family who was in the ministry – in addition to his father, Henry, his brother, Frederick Augustus, was also a Lutheran preacher. In 1774, Frederick became the pastor of Christ's Church, first known as the Old Swamp Church, located at the southeast corner of Frankfort and William streets in New York City.

Unlike his brother Peter who left his pulpit to lead his 8th Virginia Regiment against the Redcoats, Frederick was much like many of today's pastors and believed that a preacher should not get involved in politics and war. He had even written to his brother rebuking him for his political involvement: "You have become too involved in matters with which, as a preacher, you have nothing whatsoever to do and which do not belong to your office."[390] But as we saw, John sent a stinging response back to

Frederick emphatically declaring that a Christian could not help but get involved – it was the Lord's own work (Vol. 1, Chapter 2).

As this heated exchange between brothers took place, a mighty storm was brewing; a storm that ultimately would break upon Frederick and his church in a mighty cataclysm when the British invaded New York City. In May 1776, perceiving this invasion as imminent, Frederick sent his wife, Cathy, who was pregnant at the time, and their two children to stay with her parents in Philadelphia, while he remained in New York City to continue ministering to his shrinking congregation. But when rumors began to circulate that the British were planning on hanging Muhlenberg if they caught him, Frederick's church urged him to flee for his own safety.[391] On July 2, 1776, Frederick Muhlenberg left New York City "looking over his shoulder at a city soon to be paralyzed by war."[392] Just hours later, General Howe landed on Staten Island and the British occupation of New York City had begun. As the Redcoats entered New York City, they came burning and pillaging along the way. Of the nineteen churches in New York City, they burned ten.[393]

It was a greatly changed Frederick Muhlenberg who arrived in Philadelphia to join his refugee family. Practically destitute, with no church, no house, and no way to support his family, Frederick began to rethink his position on pastors being involved in politics. On March 2, 1779, Frederick Muhlenberg, the preacher who insisted that preachers should not get involved in politics, became a member of the Continental Congress. One year later he became a member of the Pennsylvania General Assembly (House of Representatives) where he served from 1780 to 1783, serving as the Speaker the entire time. Later Frederick served as the president of the Pennsylvania Constitutional Convention where he pushed for the ratification of the U.S. Constitution. Significantly, he is one of only two people who signed the Bill of Rights. He served as a member of the U.S. House of Representatives from 1789-1797, and the preacher who said that preachers should not get involved in politics became the first Speaker of the House of Representatives of the United States of America.

So what changed Frederick's mind about preachers and politics? Simple: he was "pinched," pinched hard enough that he felt it. Though he may not have seen the light initially, he definitely felt the heat. The question is how hard will today's preachers have to be "pinched" before they will speak out? Will they, like Frederick Muhlenberg, have to lose practically everything before they are willing to stand up and speak out?

EVEN WHEN IT WAS OVER, IT WAS NOT OVER

In the waning days of 1783, Americans were ecstatic with joy – and with good reason. They had just won a brutal, painful, and costly eight-year war. Having defeated the most powerful army in the world, they were now breathing the fresh air of freedom. On December 11, 1783, George Duffield, preached the following sermon in the Third Presbyterian Church of Philadelphia on a day of thanksgiving to God:

> "Here has our God erected a banner of civil and religious liberty: And prepared an asylum for the poor and oppressed from every part of the earth. Here, if wisdom guide our affairs, shall a happy equality reign; and joyous freedom bless the inhabitants wide and far, from age to age. Here, far removed from the noise and tumult of contending kingdoms and empires; far from the wars of Europe and Asia, and the barbarous African coast; here shall the husbandman enjoy the fruits of his labor; the merchant trade, secure of his gain; the mechanic indulge his inventive genius; and the sons of science pursue their delightful employment, till the light of knowledge pervade yonder, yet uncultivated, western wilds; and form the savage inhabitants into men. Here also, shall our Jesus go forth conquering and to conquer; and the heathen be given him for an inheritance; and these uttermost parts of the earth, a possession. Zion shall here lengthen her cords, and strengthen her stakes; and the mountain of the house of the Lord be gloriously exalted on high. Here shall the religion of Jesus; not that, falsely so called, which consists in empty modes and forms; and spends its unhallowed zeal in party names and distinctions, and traducing and reviling each other; but the pure and undefiled religion of our blessed Redeemer: here shall it reign in triumph, over all

opposition. Vice and immorality shall yet here, become ashamed and banished; and love to God, and benevolence to man, rule the hearts and regulate the lives of men. Justice and truth shall here yet meet together, and righteousness and peace embrace each other: And the wilderness blossom as the rose, and the desert rejoice and sing. And here shall the various ancient promises of rich and glorious grace begin their complete divine fulfillment; and the light of divine revelation diffuse its beneficent rays, till the gospel of Jesus have accomplished its day, from east to west, around our world."[394]

As is evident from Duffield's message, Americans believed their prospects for a happy and prosperous future were bright and they were expecting great things. But they also knew that liberty and independence, as wonderful as they were, could not be taken for granted. The fight for liberty was not over – and it never would be. Enemies still lurked in the darkness that, if given the opportunity, would snatch away their new won freedom in a moment. The Black Regiment was not about to let that happen. They had fought hard to earn their freedom and they were prepared to fight just as hard to keep it.

In a speech in Dublin, Ireland in 1790, John Philpot Curran, Irish orator and politician, perfectly articulated what it took to preserve liberty:

> "It is the common fate of the indolent to see their rights become a prey to the active. The condition upon which God hath given liberty to man is eternal vigilance; which condition if he break, servitude is at once the consequence of his crime and the punishment of his guilt."[395]

Later Curran's words were morphed into the now famous phrase, "Eternal vigilance is the price of liberty" – a quote often erroneously attributed to Thomas Jefferson. Even though Jefferson was not the origin of that statement, he did write in a November 13, 1787 letter to William S. Smith that, "The tree of liberty must be refreshed from time to time, with the blood of patriots and tyrants. It is its natural manure."[396]

Both Curran and Jefferson were articulating a fact that the patriot preachers knew well: freedom is not free; it comes at a high price, and once purchased, must forever be guarded and defended.

If history had taught the preachers anything, it had taught them that wherever good men were enjoying their God-given liberty, there were always bad men who wanted to steal it away. They also knew that this problem reached all of the way back to the Garden of Eden, where, because of Adam's fall, envy, strife, conquest, and death had been the dominant theme of the sad story of mankind. The patriot preachers taught that, short of a right relationship with God, man was lost in an endless quest to satisfy his insatiable spiritual hunger by grabbing for more power, popularity, and things.

St. Augustine had articulated this dilemma way back in the late 4th century, when he said, "Thou hast made us for Thyself, O Lord, and our hearts are restless until they rest in Thee."[397] Almost thirteen hundred years later, Blaise Pascal, the Christian Frenchman, scientist, and writer, expanded upon Augustine's declaration:

> "What else does this craving, and this helplessness, proclaim but that there was once in man a true happiness, of which all that now remains is the empty print and trace? This he tries in vain to fill with everything around him, seeking in things that are not there the help he cannot find in those that are, though none can help, since this infinite abyss can be filled only with an infinite and unchangeable object; in other words by God himself."[398]

Now that they had won the war, the patriot preachers renewed their efforts to deliver this message to America. While helping build the new union they had just helped to birth, the preachers reminded Americans of their need to find satisfaction in Christ, not success and material prosperity – things that could, if allowed, become an even greater enemy to all they had accomplished than the Redcoats themselves had been.

AN ENEMY MORE DANGEROUS THAN THE REDCOATS

In the early days when the war was first upon them and victory was far from certain, Americans had been keenly aware of their dependence on God and had fervently sought His aid. Now that He had granted them victory and peace, and prosperity had come, the patriot preachers knew that to sustain their liberty and the success of their infant republic, it was essential that they not allow the red-hot spiritual fervency that had inspired and empowered them during the war to cool off.

So for the preachers, the war was not over – only the phase that required bullets and bombs. They knew that America was not yet out of the woods. Even though evil forces from "without" posed no immediate threat, evil forces from "within" did. Affluence, arrogance, and spiritual apathy were internal foes more deceptive and destructive than ones the American army had just defeated in the field of battle. And having just made incalculable sacrifices to "insure the blessings of liberty to themselves and their posterity" the patriot preachers had no intention of now allowing these enemies to destroy all they had accomplished.

Unfortunately, it did not take long before the very sins that the Black Regiment warned of began to seep back into the hearts and minds of the American people. With liberty came prosperity and with that prosperity came pride and arrogance. Americans were beginning to believe the false notion that they were self-sufficient and had no need of God's help – certainly not nearly as much as they had during the war. Knowing well the warning in Proverbs 16:18, "Pride goeth before destruction, and an haughty spirit before a fall," the patriot preachers began attacking America's new enemy.

This new threat prompted Samuel Wales, pastor of the First Congregational Church in Milford, Connecticut and professor of Divinity at Yale, to preach this Connecticut election sermon,

The Dangers Of Our National Prosperity; And The Way To Avoid Them, on May 12, 1785. In it, Wales outlined, as well as any of that time, the new danger Americans faced and the strategy necessary to defeat it.

First, he reminded Americans that they were just as dependent upon God now that things were going well as they had been when all seemed hopeless during the war:

"The greatest evil by which we are endangered, and which indeed is the source of all others, is the want of true religion. It is true, the superior blessings which we enjoy are well calculated to promote religion, to promote each of its essential branches, piety and charity. And such affects would those blessings naturally produce, did we improve them as we ought. But through the perverseness of our nature there is much danger that we shall use them for very different purposes. When we are favored with a profusion of earthly good, we are exceedingly prone to set our hearts upon it with an immoderate affection, neglecting our bountiful Creator from whom alone all good is derived. We bathe and bury ourselves in the streams, forgetting the fountain whence they flow. This is indeed a very disingenuous behavior towards the Father of mercies. It certainly discovers a very sordid disposition, a depraved and contracted mind. Such a disposition, however, is but too natural to man in his present degenerate state.

"We are much more inclined to murmur at God's justice in adversity than to acknowledge his goodness in prosperity; more ready to view God as the author of evil than as the author of good. In the distresses of the late war, though they were most evidently brought upon us by the instrumentality of men, we were nevertheless much more ready to impute them to the hand of God, than we now are to acknowledge the same hand in the happiness of peace, and the other rich blessings of his providence and grace. When our wants are very pressing, we are willing, or pretend to be willing to apply to God for relief. But no sooner is the relief given than we set our hearts upon the gift, and neglect the giver; or rather make use of his own bounty in order to fight against him. The reason is, because we are more inclined to love the creature than the Creator, to be *lovers of pleasure rather than lovers of God*. On this account, Moses with peculiar emphasis warns the Israelites to stand on their guard against such impiety in the days of their prosperity: *Beware that thou forget not the Lord thy God.*"

Second, he declared that prosperity, if allowed, could be as fatal to a nation as an armed enemy; especially to a nation like America that owed so much to God's providential care:

"Nor was this pernicious effect of abused prosperity peculiar to the people of Israel. It has, in one degree or another, been common to all people in every age of the world. It has been the case even with the Christian church. The consequences of outward prosperity have been often more fatal to the Christian cause than those of adversity. Indeed the distresses and persecutions of the church have often produced a very happy effect in the advancement of true Christianity. Hence that observation in primitive times: *"The blood of the Martyrs is the seed of the Church."* But the like happy effect has seldom if ever followed from a state of external peace and opulence. The first great instance of signal prosperity granted to the Christians in the beginning of the fourth century under Constantine the great, was soon followed by a great loss of fervent piety, and a sad corruption both of doctrines and morals. And the same sad effect has followed from many instances of their prosperity in succeeding ages; particularly from the flourishing state of many protestant churches since the grand emancipation from the papal See. Indeed wealth and power have been and still are the great supporters of that *man of sin who opposeth and exalteth himself above all that is called God, or that is worshipped.* …

"While prosperity is dangerous to a people in general, it is peculiarly so to those who are elevated above the common walks of life. Honor, power and wealth are attended with strong temptations, temptations which in most instances have proved too powerful for man. Indeed they have been and always will be too powerful for him, unless when he calls in foreign aid, even the aid of almighty grace. They who are possessed of these worldly goods, those envied distinctions, it is to be feared, often have their portion in this life only, and are therefore of all men the most miserable. …

"Wealth, with its common attendants, idleness and pleasure, were the ruin of Sodom and Gomorrah. 'Behold, this was the iniquity of Sodom, pride, fullness of bread, and abundance of idleness was in her and in her daughters.' These same things were the ruin of mighty Babylon. *'Thou that art given to pleasures,* said the prophet, *that dwellest carelessly, that sayest in thine heart, I am, and none else besides me.'"*

Third, he rebuked his fellow Americans for allowing their fervor for Christ to wane:

"Is it not a sad truth, that since the commencement of the late war, and especially since the restoration of peace, the holy religion of Jesus, that brightest ornament of our world, is, by many less regarded than it was before? And are not the sacred institutions of the gospel more neglected and despised? Are not the friends of Christianity treated with more disregard? Are not infidelity and profligacy of manners, viewed with less concern, and by many considered as matters of trivial consequence? Still, we ought with the highest gratitude to acknowledge the sovereign grace of Almighty God, which has, in some places, been manifested in the support of his own cause. In several of our states he has been pleased to excite in the minds of many individuals, here and there, an unusual attention to divine and eternal things. He saw us unpurified by the furnace of affliction: He saw us disregarding him while he spake to us in the whirlwind, the earthquake, and the fire. Yet has he been pleased to speak to us not only by the still voice of peace after war, but also by the omnipotent voice of his holy Spirit; inviting us to become the subjects of the Prince of peace, and making numbers in one place and another, as we trust, the actual possessors of that peace which the world can neither give nor take away. To his great name be all the glory ascribed.

"But notwithstanding some pleasing appearances of true religion, in several places, we have too much reason to fear that "the unthinking many" are abusing our present prosperity in such a manner as to produce a very different effect. We have reason to fear that they are fast growing into that state of irreligion which has been noticed already. The symptoms and effects of this evil are already too manifest; and will probably continue and increase unto more ungodliness, unless vigorous measures be taken to prevent them. Some few of these evils which may be called symptoms and effects of irreligion I beg leave particularly to mention."

Last, Wales concluded by reminding his audience that the truest kind of patriotism produced faithful and fervent followers of the Lord:

"Another particular evil by which we are endangered, is the want of true patriotism. By true patriotism I mean a real concern for the welfare of our whole country in general. This patriotism is a branch of that extensive benevolence which is highly recommended by our holy religion, and is at the same time most evidently consentaneous to the dictates of sound reason. While the war lasted our patriotism was eminent and produced the most happy effects.

"This same selfish spirit, when it possesses the minds of the common people, has this bad consequence, among many others, that it subjects them to an undue influence in the choice of civil rulers. Possessed of this spirit, they will not regard the probity or abilities of the candidates for office; but will be very ready to give their voice for those to whom they happen to be particularly attached by any private and sinister motives; for those by whom they are most humored in their prejudices and follies; and especially for those who most loudly exclaim against the payment of public debts and most vigorously oppose taxation however just or necessary.

"The practice of religion must therefore be considered as absolutely essential to the best state of public prosperity, it must be so, unless we may expect happiness in direct opposition to the constitution of nature and of nature's God. *'Righteousness exalteth a nation: but sin is a reproach to any people.'* This is the course of nature, this is the voice of heaven, this is the decree of God.

"We cannot therefore do a more faithful or important service for our country than to pray fervently and perseveringly to the Father of mercies, that he would by the energy of the Holy Ghost, form the hearts of this people to an holy life, and thus *'Purify unto himself a peculiar people, zealous of good works.'*

"So, although we have gained that for which we most ardently wished, an happy period to the late war, yet we can by no means be certain but that some far greater evils are now before us. We may be over-run and ruined both for time and eternity by a torrent of vice and licentiousness, with their never-failing attendants, infidelity and atheism. We may be left to destroy ourselves by intestine divisions and civil wars: or we may be visited with such sickness and pestilence as would soon produce a far greater destruction than any war of what kind so ever. God has many ways, even in the present world, to punish the sins both of individuals and of nations. He has ten thousand arrows in his quiver, and can always direct any or all of them unerring, to the victims of his wrath. No possible concurrence of circumstances can screen us from the notice of his eye or the power of his hand. Never, never, can we be secure but in the practice of true virtue and in the favor of God."[399]

THE CONSTITUTION HAD TO BE PRESERVED

In addition to the spiritual challenges young America faced, the patriot preachers had another concern: a fear that the nation might, in time, deviate from the Constitution and the principles enshrined therein. They knew that if this ever happened, the nation's destruction would be sealed. To guard against this hideous possibility, they reminded their congregations of the Founders' wisdom and of the need to preserve the godly, constitutional government they had designed.

On July 5, 1802, William Emerson, pastor of the First Church of Boston, preached a sermon dealing with this very subject. Although a theological liberal and a Unitarian, Emerson was spot on in his sermon, *An Oration In Commemoration Of The Anniversary Of American Independence.* In it, he warned Americans of the terrible consequences the country would experience if it ever strayed from the Constitution:

"Should it be the fate of America to drink still deeper of the inebriating bowl, its government, whose existence depends on the public sentiment, must fall a victim to the draught. Should the rulers of our country, especially, ever become intoxicated with the poison; should they deviate from the course prescribed by their wise predecessors, incautiously pulling down what had been carefully built; should they mutilate the form, or impair the strength of our most excellent constitution; should they amuse themselves with ephemeral experiments, instead of adhering to principles of certain utility; and should they despise the religion and customs of our progenitors, setting an example of impiety and dissipation, deplorable will be the consequences. From an head so sick, and an heart so faint, disease will extend to the utmost extremities of the political body. As well may you arrest the flight of time, or entice the moon from her orbit, as preserve your freedom under atheistical rulers, and amidst general profligacy of habit. Libertinism and lethargy, anarchy and misrule will deform our once happy republic; and its liberties will receive an incurable wound. The soil of America will remain; but the name and glory of the United States will have perished forever. This lovely peninsula will continue inhabited; but "the feelings, manners, and principles" of those Bostonians, who nobly resisted the various acts of British aggression, will be utterly changed. The streams of Concord will flow as formerly, and the hills of Charlestown grow verdant with each return of spring; but the character of the men, who mingled their blood with those waters, and who eternized those heights, will be sought for, but shall not be found."[400]

THEIR FEARS ARE BEING REALIZED TODAY

Although the patriot preachers did not live to see Emerson's fears realized, unfortunately, we twenty-first century Americans have. We are experiencing the horror of watching America do the very things the Black Regiment warned early Americans to avoid.

We modern Americans have become arrogant in our prosperity and comfort, we no longer honor the Lord who gave us the very liberties we abuse, and true patriotism which seeks the welfare of the county by seeking the will of God is becoming a rare commodity. Thinking we are too sophisticated for a religion as archaic and exclusive as Christianity, we have expelled God from school and banished Him from the public square.

In addition, those who insist that the Constitution is an archaic document and one that cannot possibly mean today what it meant in the eighteenth century are busy attempting to run it through a paper shredder. Arrogantly convinced that the Constitution is inadequate for the governance of a people as advanced and enlightened as we, our elected officials and judges are trashing it.

For example, in his 2006 book, *The Audacity of Hope: Thoughts on Reclaiming the American Dream,* Barack Obama wrote that if he ever became President he would not appoint any judge who was a strict constructionist – one who would interpret the Constitution according to the original intent of the Founders. As he put it:

> "Ultimately, though, I have to side with Justice Breyer's view of the Constitution — that it is not a static but rather a living document, and must be read in the context of an ever-changing world."[401]

In other words, he prefers judges who rewrite the Constitution to say whatever they want it to say. Tragically, the belief that the Constitution is antiquated and inadequate for today is becoming more and more popular. The idea of "original intent" is quickly becoming passé in most American law schools. For instance, in his book, *A Constitution of Many Minds: Why the Founding*

Document Doesn't Mean What It Meant Before, Cass Sunstein, Harvard Law Professor and "Regulation Czar" for the Obama administration claims that because the Constitution was written over two hundred years ago, it simply cannot be understood in its original context. He contends that it must be interpreted in light of contemporary public opinion and the rulings of foreign courts.

Why not? After all, on June 2, 1992 in *Lee v. Weisman*, Supreme Court Justice Douglas Souter essentially accused the authors of the Constitution of not really understanding what they had written:

> "… the Framers simply did not share a common understanding of the Establishment Clause, and, at worst, that they, like other politicians, could raise constitutional ideals one day and turn their backs on them the next."[402]

So America has Supreme Court justices who claim that the authors of the Constitution did not understand what they wrote, a U.S. Senator and later President of the United States who believes that the Constitution should morph with an ever-changing world, and a Harvard law professor and presidential "czar" who believes the Constitution should conform to the vastly divergent political philosophies of other nations.

And what do we have to show for all of this? An epidemic of divorce and broken homes, alarming numbers of one-parent families, condoms dispensed in public schools, rampant pre-marital sex, unwed pregnancies, an epidemic of venereal diseases, school violence and shootings, out of control drug abuse and addiction, underage alcohol use, random shootings in public places, graft and corruption in business and government, runaway government debt, hatred of our Founders, rejection of our founding principles, elected officials and judges who despise the Constitution and our American traditions, Occupy Wall Street riots, a coarsening society, disrespect and disdain for organized religion – especially Christianity, and the list goes on and on. Seems to be working out just fine.

In light of this moral meltdown, one question screams out for an answer: "Where are the patriot preachers of today?" Sadly, most of them are missing from action.

THE WAR OF INDEPENDENCE IS NOT OVER

Although it was won some two hundred and thirty years ago, our War of Independence is not over. In fact, today it is being waged with ever increasing intensity as we draw nearer to the return of Christ. Never before have the forces marshaled to destroy America seemed so formidable. Never before has America been closer to the brink of disaster. Never before have the stakes been higher.

But unfortunately, never before has America been more godless and defenseless. Never before has the church in America seemed less prepared for battle. Anemic, worldly, disengaged, and silent, the church seems completely satisfied with things the way they are. Rather than "fighting the good fight" as Paul admonished, modern Christians, for the most part, seem consumed with "success" and are demanding that God give them "their best lives now!" Rather than heeding Jesus' command not to "lay up treasures on earth" but to "lay up treasures in heaven," today's Christians are busy accumulating as much earthly treasure as possible. Like Nero, they seem content to fiddle while their country goes up in flames.

But there is hope. God has an army sufficient to fight against these dark forces. But unfortunately, that army suffers from a huge deficiency – it has too few generals to lead it. Of course, there are plenty of preachers/pastors/spiritual leaders in America, but so far, most of them have been unwilling to engage in the fight for religious liberty. Whatever their reasons, they have chosen to desert their nation in its present crisis. They desperately need to hear again the words of Black Regiment preacher William Smith spoken in 1775:

"[W]e know that our civil and religious rights are linked together in one indissoluble bond, we neither have, nor seek to have, any interest separate from that of our country; nor can we advise a desertion of its cause. Religion and liberty must flourish or fall together in America. We pray that both may be perpetual."[403]

How tragic that many of today's preachers do not seem to believe this.

Consequently, right now, the American church sits largely idle and as it does, it becomes increasingly soft and fat. Choosing to ignore the determined and highly organized enemy closing in around them, believers seem convinced they are safe within the walls of their churches. Of course, they are well aware of what the Scriptures say about spiritual warfare, they know they are called to be soldiers of Jesus Christ, they understand that God has provided all of the spiritual armor they need (Ephesians 6), and most importantly, they know that the Lord has promised them the victory. The only thing they do not seem to know is the location of the battlefield.

American pastors appear to have forgotten, or maybe they never learned, the lesson of the pastors in Germany in the years prior to WWII. As Hitler rose to power, he was friendly with the pastors and feigned alliances with them. As he spun his web with talk of peace and cooperation, he was busy behind the scenes building his military machine that would eventually entrap these spiritually blind pastors and launch one of the worst wars in history; a war that would kill millions and destroy Germany in the process. Few pastors saw through the ruse. A small number did, they spoke out, and it cost some of them their lives.

One of those pastors was Dietrich Bonhoeffer. Bonehoffer, a Lutheran pastor, was a powerful preacher and prolific writer. His book, *The Cost of Discipleship,* has become a Christian classic on what it means to "truly" follow Christ, and his book, *Life Together*, is still widely used as a textbook for living in community with other believers. Bonhoeffer staunchly resisted the work of the Nazis, even going as far as to participate in an attempt to assassinate Adolph Hitler. He was arrested by the Gestapo on April 5, 1943, imprisoned at the Tegel military prison, and was finally executed by hanging on April 9, 1945, just two weeks before the prison was liberated by American forces.

During his courageous stand against Nazi tyranny, Bonhoeffer famously said,

> "Silence in the face of evil is itself evil: God will not hold us guiltless. Not to speak is to speak. Not to act is to act."[404]

Today's pastors may believe that by their silence they are staying out of the fray but Bonheoffer was right. By not speaking, these pastors are speaking and by not acting, these pastors are acting. American pastors must not allow what happened in Germany to happen in America. Pastors must speak loudly and act boldly!

WHERE HAVE ALL THE WARRIORS GONE?

America exists because previous generations were willing to give more to their country than they received. They were willing to sacrifice their fortunes, their lives, and their sacred honor to gain something greater, something nobler: liberty, both spiritual and civil. Today, most Americans are becoming increasingly more interested in what they can "get from" their country than what they can "give to" it. We need to hear again John Fitzgerald Kennedy's challenge he gave to the country in his inaugural speech on January 20, 1961, "Ask not what your country can do for you; ask what you can do for your country." Unfortunately, more and more Americans, including Christians, are asking the exact opposite question.

How strange that a nation so willing to sacrifice so much throughout its history to liberate so many is now so willing to sell its liberties and soul for so little. Are we now prepared to passively accept the chains of socialism and slavery? "Is life so dear, or peace so sweet, as to be purchased at the prices of chains and slavery? Forbid it, Almighty God." Are there any today who will stand up and carry the torch that Patrick Henry and his compatriots carried so faithfully so long ago? Are there any "truth warriors" left in America?

Ezekiel, the Jewish prophet, lived in the late sixth century B.C. during a time when truth warriors were in short supply in Israel. In Ezekiel 22:23-31, the prophet wrote:

"And the word of the Lord came unto me, saying, [24]'Son of man, say unto her, Thou art the land that is not cleansed, nor rained upon in the day of indignation. [25]There is a conspiracy of her prophets in the midst thereof, like a roaring lion ravening the prey; they have devoured souls; they have taken the treasure and precious things; they have made her many widows in the midst thereof. [26]Her priests have violated my law, and have profaned mine holy things: they have put no difference between the holy and profane, neither have they showed difference between the unclean and the clean, and have hid their eyes from my sabbaths, and I am profaned among them. [27]Her princes in the midst thereof are like wolves ravening the prey, to shed blood, and to destroy souls, to get dishonest gain. [28]And her prophets have daubed them with untempered mortar, seeing vanity, and divining lies unto them, saying, Thus saith the Lord God, when the Lord hath not spoken. [29]The people of the land have used oppression, and exercised robbery, and have vexed the poor and needy: yea, they have oppressed the stranger wrongfully. [30]And I sought for a man among them, that should make up the hedge, and stand in the gap before me for the land, that I should not destroy it: but I found none. [31]Therefore have I poured out mine indignation upon them; I have consumed them with the fire of my wrath: their own way have I recompensed upon their heads, saith the Lord God.'"

It is significant that God blamed Israel's spiritual leaders for the nation's deplorable condition. The leaders had devoured souls, taken treasures and precious things, caused many women to become widows, violated God's laws, profaned holy things, lost the ability to discern between the holy and the profane, ignored the holy Sabbaths, and had spoken for God when He had not spoken. They had shed the blood of the people like ravenous wolves and had profited dishonestly. Following their example, the people had oppressed one another, practiced robbery, mistreated the poor and needy, and had abused and taken advantage of foreigners. Sound familiar?

Consequently, Israel was about to face God's judgment. Incidentally, for those who do not believe that God judges His own, consider Hebrews 10:30-31, "For we know him that hath said, Vengeance belongeth unto me, I will recompense, saith the Lord. And again, The Lord shall judge his people. [31]It is a fearful thing to fall into the hands of the living God."

But even though the Jews deserved judgment, as a beautiful expression of His grace, God was searching for a reason to withhold that judgment:

> "And I sought for a man among them, that should make up the hedge, and stand in the gap before me for the land, that I should not destroy it: but I found none." Ezekiel 22:30

> *(See Genesis 18 where God was willing to forego judging Sodom and Gomorrah if only ten righteous people could be found there.)

In Ezekiel 22:30, there are at least four noteworthy points that apply to America today as much as they did to Israel in the sixth century:

1. The Search

God was performing a massive search in Ezekiel's day. Actually, God had been searching since Adam's fall in the Garden: "And the Lord God called unto Adam, and said unto him, 'Where art thou?'" (Gen 3:9). Before judging Sodom and Gomorrah, God had searched for enough righteous people to prevent that judgment:

> "And he said, Oh let not the Lord be angry, and I will speak yet but this once: Peradventure ten shall be found there. And he said, I will not destroy it for ten's sake. [33]And the Lord went his way, as soon as he had left communing with Abraham: and Abraham returned unto his place." Genesis 18:32-33

In the days of King Asa Baasha, God was searching for the righteous in Israel:

> "For the eyes of the Lord run to and fro throughout the whole earth, to show himself strong in the behalf of them whose heart is perfect toward him." 2 Chronicles 16:9

So in Ezekiel's day, God was carrying out another search. How amazing that the infinite God who spoke the universe into existence and who lacks or wants for nothing would be searching for anything.

2. The Subject

Of all things, God was searching for a man. To prevent Israel's impending judgment, God was searching for a leader who would stand up and speak out for the truth. The call Ezekiel heard was similar to the one the prophet Isaiah had heard:

> "Also I heard the voice of the Lord, saying, 'Whom shall I send, and who will go for us?'" Isaiah 6:8

God's plan has always been a man – a man bold enough to stand and say what is right. This was the object of God's search.

3. The Situation

Ezekiel's time was a dark time for Israel, and without divine intervention, judgment was certain. Like a wall surrounding a fortified city, obedience to God had created a spiritual "hedge of protection" around Israel in the past. But the absence of strong spiritual leaders had created a gap in that hedge and this breach was being exploited by the powers of darkness. Now God, as He often did, was about to use foreign armies to punish Israel. The spiritual "gap" in Israel's defenses was about to be exploited by their physical enemies.

So, God's message to Ezekiel was Israel's final warning. Just as God had warned Sodom and Gomorrah of imminent judgment, He was now warning Israel that they, too, were running out of time and that, short of repentance, they were doomed. The gap had to be filled – and quickly.

4. The Sorrow

Tragically, at the end of God's search, He found no one to stand in the gap. It's not that He found a few or even one – He found none! What a sad commentary on God's people that the One who had done so much for them was unable to find anyone among them willing to take a stand for truth.

It is noteworthy that the Lord was not searching for a large number of warriors. In fact, Scripture teaches that God normally prefers to use a small remnant to accomplish His great deeds. Consider the story of Gideon and his three hundred soldiers in the book of Judges, chapters 6-7. Although Gideon's forces had initially numbered in the thousands, God wanted only those who were faithful, brave, and prepared to fight, so He whittled down Gideon's army to three hundred men.

Amazingly, the remnant God uses is usually comprised of helpless people who face hopeless circumstances. The reason is simple – if men accomplish great deeds in their own strength, they get the glory, but if a small, helpless remnant trusting in God, wins the victory against impossible odds, God gets the glory. And when God gets the glory, men and women are drawn to Him and are saved. Paul confirmed this principle when he wrote,

> "For ye see your calling, brethren, how that not many wise men after the flesh, not many mighty, not many noble, are called: 27But God hath chosen the foolish things of the world to confound the wise; and God hath chosen the weak things of the world to confound the things which are mighty; 28And base things of the world, and things which are despised, hath God chosen, yea, and things which are not, to bring to nought things that are: 29That no flesh should glory in his presence." 1 Corinthians 1:26-29

Unfortunately, in Ezekiel's situation, no small remnant was found to stand in the gap for Israel so judgment fell:

> "Therefore have I poured out mine indignation upon them; I have consumed them with the fire of my wrath: their own way have I recompensed upon their heads, saith the Lord God." Ezekiel 22:31

Now let us apply Ezekiel 22 to our present situation in America. Sadly, America's predicament is quite similar to that of Israel. Many of our spiritual leaders have failed miserably. Today's church is filled with compromise and liberalism. Those congregations that actually believe the Bible is God's inspired, inerrant, unchanging Word are becoming a minority. Even among these churches, many are led by pastors who have lost their will to defend liberty and, unlike their patriot preacher ancestors, seem willing to allow America to go down the tubes without a fight.

Like Israel, Americans have followed their leaders' example. The old adage, "As goes the church, so goes the nation," has been validated right before our very eyes. In the process, America slides further down the slippery slope of socialism and the church slips deeper into self-centeredness, spiritual compromise, and apathy. Today, we need truth warriors more than ever. But where are they? As God searches for those who are willing to "stand in the gap" for America, how many He is finding? Are there any who will boldly declare as Isaiah, "Here am I; send me?"

REPORTING FOR DUTY

Remember that Samuel Adams said, "If ever a time should come, when vain and aspiring men shall possess the highest seats in Government, our country will stand in need of its experienced patriots to prevent its ruin." If we ever hope to win the culture war in America, our "experienced patriots" must report for duty NOW!

But because this modern culture war is an unconventional type of fight, without bullets and bombs, some find it difficult to know how to report for duty and are asking, "How can I make a difference?" Let me suggest a few things we can do to actively engage in this culture war, defend our God-given liberties, and save our union.

1. Honor Jesus First.

In 1787, when Benjamin Franklin reminded the deadlocked Constitutional Convention that God was their only hope, he was speaking to those of us in the twenty-first century as much as he was to his fellow delegates in the eighteenth century. As Franklin quoted from Psalms 127:1 which declares, "Except the Lord build the house, they labour in vain that build it: except the Lord keep the city, the watchman waketh but in vain," whether he believed it or not, he was expressing the truth that unless God holds first place in our lives, everything else becomes moot. Jesus made this abundantly clear when He said,

> "But seek first the kingdom of God and His righteousness, and all these things shall be added to you." Matthew 6:33

> "For what profit is it to a man if he gains the whole world, and loses his own soul? Or what will a man give in exchange for his soul?" Matthew 16:26

Unfortunately, many people mistake sincerity and religiosity for true spiritual transformation. This fact prompted Jesus to give this warning:

> "Not every one that saith unto me, Lord, Lord, shall enter into the kingdom of heaven; but he that doeth the will of my Father which is in heaven. [22]Many will say to me in that day, Lord, Lord, have we not prophesied in thy name? and in thy name have cast out devils? and in thy name done many wonderful works? [23]And then will I profess unto them, I never knew you: depart from me, ye that work iniquity." Matthew 7:21-23

Jesus told Nicodemus that a "spiritual" birth is necessary for entrance into God's Kingdom. Without this spiritual birth, a person remains a "son of Adam" with the "sins of Adam" separating them from God. For this reason Jesus gave Himself as a sacrifice on the cross, thus paying the penalty for man's sins. Having paid the penalty with His death, He then rose again to guarantee forgiveness and redemption to all who will trust Him. It is crucial that each person make certain that he/she has "personally" experienced this new birth. The Apostle Paul warned everyone to make certain that they were truly "in the faith":

> "Examine yourselves as to whether you are in the faith. Test yourselves. Do you not know yourselves, that Jesus Christ is in you? – unless indeed you are disqualified." 2 Corinthians 13:5

So if we desire to make a difference for Christ, we must first genuinely know Him as Savior and Lord and then determine to place Him first in every area of our lives. With Jesus first, life takes on a special spiritual quality that gives us eternal purpose in everything that we do, including politics, and empowers us to bear fruit for Him.

2. Live out your faith.

There is a reason that the Lord leaves us here on this earth after we come to know Him – He intends for us to grow in faith and grace, and in the process, lead others to a saving knowledge of Him. People are looking for an authentic faith and are hungry to see Christianity authentically "lived out" in real life. So, after coming to Christ, it is critical that believers "walk" their faith. This can literally change the world. Jesus made this quite plain when He said,

> "You are the light of the world. A city that is set on a hill cannot be hidden. [15]Nor do they light a lamp and put it under a basket, but on a lampstand, and it gives light to all who are in the house. [16]Let your light so shine before men, that they may see your good works and glorify your Father in heaven." Matthew 5:14-16

According to Jesus, authentic faith enables God's Spirit to work through us and produces such spiritual transformation that others are drawn to Him. In John 12:32, Jesus said, "And I, if I be lifted up from the earth, will draw all men unto me." Although He was directly referring to His eventually being "lifted up" on the cross, indirectly He was referring to our "lifting Him up" as we are spiritually "crucified with Christ" and live out our faith before others. Paul told the believers at Philippi:

> "… that you may become blameless and harmless, children of God without fault in the midst of a crooked and perverse generation, among whom you shine as lights in the world, [16]holding fast the word of life" Philippians 2:15-16

Peter said in 1 Peter 2:15 that by living out their faith, believers actually validate the claims of Scripture, "For this is the will of God, that by doing good you may put to silence the ignorance of foolish men."

Those who are truly born again, willingly and enthusiastically "go public" with their faith. There are no "secret" Christians. The story is told of a man who was admiring a young boy's dog and asked him what kind of dog it was. The boy responded that his pet was a German Police dog. The man, realizing the dog was just a mutt, told the boy that his dog did not look like any German Police dog he had ever seen. The little boy responded that his dog was in the secret service!

Of course, there is no such thing as a secret service Christian. Jesus had stern words for those reluctant to take their faith public:

> "For whoever is ashamed of Me and My words in this adulterous and sinful generation, of him the Son of Man also will be ashamed when He comes in the glory of His Father with the holy angels." Mark 8:38

One of the greatest services a believer can perform for his country is to live out his faith passionately and publicly. By bringing the "salt and light" into normal, everyday life situations, believers not only provide a vibrant example of authentic Christianity, but they also inject kingdom principles into an otherwise godless culture. As "ambassadors for Christ," believers are to be a slice of heaven here on this earth as we reflect heaven's values down here.

3. Fulfill the responsibilities of your dual citizenship.

Often, Christians excuse themselves from being politically active by claiming that they are citizens of heaven and therefore cannot bother themselves with their U.S. citizenship as we discussed in

Vol. 1, Chapter 3. They are partially right. Believers are citizens of heaven. Paul reminded believers in Philippians 3:20, "For our citizenship is in heaven." Citizenship in God's Kingdom is certainly the most important of any citizenship believers will ever possess. Believers live on this earth as strangers and pilgrims here and are, like Abraham, seeking for a city whose builder and maker is God.

But in addition to their heavenly citizenship, American Christians are also citizens of the United States and must fulfill those obligations as well. It was Evangelist Charles Finney who said:

> "Politics are part of a religion in such a country as this and Christians must do their duty to the country as a part of their duty to God."[405]

American Christians have the privilege of living in the greatest country on earth. Even though America is certainly not perfect and has made many mistakes, it offers the greatest liberty we will ever experience this side of heaven. Privileged to live in the "land of the free and the home of the brave," we Christians should be America's best citizens. Remember, it was Daniel Webster who said that what makes men good Christians also makes them good citizens as well.

It is also important to remember that in Matthew 22:21, Jesus commanded His followers to be faithful to God and their government: "Render therefore to Caesar the things that are Caesar's and to God the things that are God's." Notice Jesus did not teach obedience to God "or" Caesar, but to God "and" Caesar. Philosophically, God and Caesar are not enemies. Under most circumstances (especially in America), a believer can fulfill both obligations without compromising his faith or his patriotism. Not only is it "not a sin" for Christians to be involved in government, it is a sin for them not to be involved. But how does a believer successfully balance his obligations to God and country?

- Respect and obey the government.

Paul taught the Christians in Rome that government was not a "bad" thing but was an institution designed and ordained of God:

"Let every soul be subject to the governing authorities. For there is no authority except from God, and the authorities that exist are appointed by God. … [5]Therefore you must be subject, not only because of wrath but also for conscience' sake." Romans 13:1

Therefore, if human government is God's idea and has His blessing, then it is a safe bet He wants His people to respect it, obey it, and ultimately participate in it. Peter echoed Paul's instructions when he wrote,

"Honor all people. Love the brotherhood. Fear God. Honor the king." 1 Peter 2:17

Notice, Peter told his readers to honor the king in the same verse in which he reminded them to fear God. Certainly there are times when someone who holds a position in government is unworthy of our respect and obedience at a personal level, but we are to honor him because of the respect due to the position. We must submit to authority as long as doing so does not force us to compromise our commitment to Christ.

- Pray for those in authority and in government.

Paul told Timothy, his young pastor protégé:

"Therefore I exhort first of all that supplications, prayers, intercessions, and giving of thanks be made for all men, [2]for kings and all who are in authority, that we may lead a quiet and peaceable life in all godliness and reverence. [3]For this is good and acceptable in the sight of God our Savior," 1 Timothy 2:1-3

Leadership comes with incredible pressures and heavy responsibilities so Christians should pray for God's influence in the lives of their leaders. Admittedly, it is difficult to pray for a leader who is dishonoring God but it is these leaders who need our prayers the most. Although it may seem a vain exercise, God reminds us that:

"The king's heart is in the hand of the LORD, as the rivers of water: he turneth it whithersoever he will." Proverbs 21:1

"… for the LORD had made them joyful, and turned the heart of the king of Assyria unto them, to strengthen their hands in the work of the house of God, the God of Israel." Ezra 6:22

Since it is never wrong to do the right thing, seek the Lord on behalf of those who are in authority; whether you agree with them or not.

- Register to vote and then vote biblical values!

With almost 50% of self-proclaimed born again evangelicals not voting (mostly because they are not registered to vote), it is no wonder why we have such godless government in America today. Christians have no right to complain about their government if they do not participate in it. Additionally, if we have the opportunity to vote and do not do so, we are as responsible for the kind of government our country has as if we voted for it. Neglecting to vote does not absolve us of our responsibility. A huge step toward fixing things in America would take no more effort from Christians than their registering and voting godly principles. Scripture warns that if we do not do what we know to do, we have sinned.

Of course the only thing worse than Christians not voting is Christians who do vote but vote for candidates who do not embrace or champion biblical values. Some 25% of born again evangelicals in America who do vote actually vote for candidates who do not share their biblical values. Regardless of party affiliation, a believer cannot honor God and knowingly vote for candidates who will, if elected, govern contrary to God's principles.

- Familiarize yourself with America's "true" history.

Americans are grossly ignorant of their history – especially when it comes to understanding the role Christianity played in birthing and building America. One of the greatest things Christians can do is educate themselves about the "true" history of America. Even though revisionist historians have been busy rewriting the story of America, thankfully, there are numerous sources available to uncover America's "actual" history.

The quest to educate yourself about the true history of our nation will be one of the most exciting, fulfilling, and inspiring endeavors of your life. What you will learn about the Christian influence in our nation's history will motivate you to work even harder to help return America to its founding principles.

Warning: Those who acquire a good knowledge of the complete story of America will find it virtually impossible to sit idly by while their fellow citizens are deceived and their country is destroyed. Familiarizing yourself with our true history will make a radical patriot of you and will definitely give you something to do with your spare time.

- Join or at least attend conservative groups.

Another way a believer can fulfill their dual citizenship is by getting involved in conservative groups. Most communities across the nation offer a wide range of groups that are dedicated to the restoration of America. Most communities have local tea parties, 912 groups, John Birch Society groups, conservative think tanks, etc. These groups offer a perfect opportunity for like-minded patriots to network with one another and participate in "hands on" projects to take our country back from the statists/socialists. You may not agree with every single issue these groups champion, but 100% agreement is not the goal. The goal is to find others with whom you agree on the core issues and then work to promote those.

By getting involved in these groups, patriots not only find an outlet for their patriotism, they also find the camaraderie and encouragement that is essential to keep morale healthy in the darker, more defeating times that inevitably come. If you find yourself in a community where none of these groups exist, then you have an excellent opportunity to start one. Most people are normally shocked to find many other like-minded patriots close by who are simply waiting for someone to step forward and lead.

- Encourage others to participate.

Reporting for duty also involves encouraging and inspiring others to get engaged in the fight. Everyone lives in the center of a circle of an amazingly large number of people with whom they have significant influence – from immediate family, to more distant relatives, to close friends, to work/school mates, to casual acquaintances. Among these are those who have become disillusioned with government and the direction it is taking our country. But with a little nudge from someone they respect, they will get back into the fight.

Many of these people are unfamiliar with the "whole story" of our nation's history, but they are eager and willing to learn and embrace the truth if someone will only teach them. These people want to do something but they just do not know what to do or how to do it. In addition, they often are not certain if anyone around them sees the same problems they see, so they are hesitant to speak out. When they discover that someone close to them holds the same core values they do, they are normally overjoyed and are immediately reenergized to know there is someone they can work with on behalf of their country. Essentially, people just need to know that they are not alone.

- Pray about running for office.

Many today have been led to believe that they must have a college degree in political science or be an attorney to run for office. Nothing could be further from the truth. To ensure that our government accurately reflected the will of the people, the Founders intended for it to be led by "citizen legislators" – not lifetime, professional politicians. Of course there is nothing inherently wrong with someone spending his life in public service in government (many of our Founders such as George Washington and

John Adams did so), but our Founders believed that every day Americans were perfectly qualified to function as public servants.

Even though many politicians try to give the impression that they are the smartest people in the room, the fact is, they are not. After all, if they were as brilliant as they purport themselves to be, they would not have gotten our country into the mess it is in today. The very fact that they do not seem to know what got us into this fix or what to do to get us out is ample proof that they are no smarter than any of the rest of us.

In fact, if a person spends even a small amount of time studying the true history of America, the Declaration of Independence, and the Constitution, he will be much more informed about America and its form of government than today's average politician. Astonishingly, many politicians have not read the Declaration or the Constitution in years; and some appear to have never read them at all. In addition, most politicians are woefully ignorant of Christianity's role in forming our country and its form of government. Those who have taken the time to learn this history are imminently more qualified to govern than those who have not, even if they have never set a foot on a law school campus.

Thankfully, with the recent birth of the tea party movement and other liberty groups, everyday citizens have become more involved in government and are stepping up to run for office; and what's even better, many of them are winning. This influx of regular, everyday citizens is slowly bringing some common sense back into our government, a commodity sorely missing from our halls of legislation for quite some time.

Even if you have never thought about running for office, you should. We Christians are fond of criticizing government for being anti-Christian, but few of us have been willing to throw our hats into the ring and take our Christian influence into the halls of government. Maybe you should run for Congress or your state legislature. Maybe you should run for a position in your county government, city council, or school board. Even if you are convinced that you are not cut out for service in government, then help someone else who is willing to do so. Believe me, they need the volunteers.

THE WAR RAGES ON

Even though our War of Independence was "officially" won some two hundred and thirty years ago, the war to maintain that independence is still raging. Since the price of freedom is eternal vigilance, we must remain engaged if we plan to win this culture war. We need every able-bodied man and woman.

On January 27, 1838, just fifty-five years after the War of Independence had ended, Abraham Lincoln, keenly aware of the continuing struggle for freedom, said this in a speech in Springfield, Illinois:

> "At what point then, is the approach of danger to be expected? I answer that if it ever reach us, it must spring from amongst us; it cannot come from abroad. If destruction be our lot, we ourselves must be the authors and finishers. As a nation of free men, we must live through our times or die by suicide. … Let us not be slandered from our duty by false accusations against us, nor frightened from it by menaces of destruction to the government, nor of dungeons to ourselves. Let us have faith that right makes might, and in that faith, let us, to the end, dare to do our duty as we understand it."[406]

Lincoln was right. Our real enemy is "amongst us." This is why we must be committed to …

BRINGING BACK THE BLACK ROBED REGIMENT

Having previously heard of King Solomon's wealth and splendor, the Queen of Sheba longed to see his kingdom. Once she had seen with her own eyes how lavishly God had blessed Solomon, the Queen exclaimed, "the half had not been told to me." The same could be said of this book's attempt to tell the rich and intriguing story of the lives and exploits of the Black Robed

Regiment; so much more could be said. One thing is undeniable; they understood that establishing a country that would honor God and prosper in the process would require a healthy respect for the principles of God's Word and the unalienable rights of men.

Restoring America to these principles will not be easy – it will require the same commitment from modern preachers as it did of Joab Trout, John Rosbrugh, Peter Muhlenberg, James Caldwell, and the other patriot preachers. Just as their leadership was required to give life to our nation, the leadership of today's preachers will be required to keep it from dying. As we appear to be swiftly approaching a constitutional crisis in America, we will not be able to preserve our liberty without a fierce fight. Preachers/pastors with strong spiritual mettle will have to lead that fight if we are to have a chance at saving our republic.

On July 4, 1777 on the first anniversary of the signing of the Declaration of Independence, William Gordon, himself a member of the Black Robed Regiment, made this very point. In his sermon to the Massachusetts General Assembly, Gordon reminded his audience that their liberties could not be secured without a great struggle:

> "And let me further tell you that I do not recollect reading of any people since the creation, that ever secured their liberties without undergoing far, far more than what we have experienced. I see, or fancy I see, a distant dawning that indicates we are not far from the end of our troubles. But if not, be of good courage, the horrors of slavery, after having exasperated our enemies by so animated and brave an opposition, are more to be dreaded than greater difficulties. Look upon your little ones, the darlings of your souls, and consider what will be their lot should the arms of Britain prevail. They will be forced to cry out: 'O that we had been born Africans instead of Americans!'"[407]

How we need to hear that message today! Without sermons like that, there probably would be no United States of America, and without sermons like that once again, there probably will not be a United States of America much longer. I simply do not know how to state it any clearer or more emphatically than that. If we ever needed the spirit of the Black Robed Regiment, we need it now. Christians must beseech God to move in the hearts of His prophets and pastors to raise up a new generation of patriot preachers.

WHAT IF YOUR PASTOR WILL NOT GET INVOLVED?

I regularly have believers tearfully share that their pastors refuse to speak out on political issues. Their question is always the same: "What can I do to get my pastor engaged?"

First, let me say that the demands and pressures of pastoring a church are immense. Most pastors are pulled in multiple directions by their people and are often expected to address or solve every problem. Believers must be cognizant of this fact and always be respectful when approaching their pastor – especially when it comes to politics. Remember that he has probably had the myth of the "separation of church and state" beaten into his head for most, or all, of his life and will need encouragement to go against the current.

Having said this, congregations must encourage, challenge, and pressure (if necessary) their pastors to lead the way and engage believers in the struggle before our opportunity to do so has passed and our liberties are lost forever. When a pastor does have the courage to speak out, believers should immediately show their support and cooperation. As a pastor who has done so, believe me when I say that he will most certainly hear from those who do not agree. He will desperately need to know that there are those in his church who agree with him, and he will need their vocal and visible support. A simple "I'm praying for you, brother" or "they needed to hear that" will not suffice; you will need to come in from the sidelines and join in the fight with him.

For those who find themselves in a church that their pastor simply refuses to engage in the debate, the options are much more difficult. These believers need to clearly articulate their belief to their pastor that he has a responsibility to preach the "whole counsel of God" and address every area of life. In the end, if he refuses to do so and they believe they have done all they can to help him understand their position, they should respectfully leave that church, find one where the pastor addresses these issues from the pulpit, and join him in his efforts. Believe me, he needs your help!

WHAT REALLY MATTERS IN THE END

On April 19, 1781, Henry Cumings offered a prayer in his sermon that needs to be prayed again in America:

> "O thou supreme Governor of the world, whose arm hath done great things for us, establish the foundations of this commonwealth, and evermore defend it with the saving strength of thy right hand! Grant that here the divine constitutions of Jesus thy Son may ever be honored and maintained! Grant that it may be the residence of all private and patriotic virtues, of all that enlightens and supports, all that sweetens and adorns human society, till the states and kingdoms of this world shall be swallowed up in thine own kingdom: In that, which alone is immortal, may we obtain a perfect citizenship, and enjoy in its completion, 'the glorious Liberty of the Sons of God!' And let all the people say, Amen!"[408]

As we struggle to restore America to its biblical foundations, we must keep the right priorities. Though we must fight to the last ounce of our courage to preserve liberty and truth, we must remember that countries and kingdoms pass away, people and places pass away, and national histories fade into the distant past, but God is eternal. Even if we are successful in returning America to its founding principles and see it restored to its former glory, eventually, it will pass away; but thankfully, God's kingdom will endure forever. The only thing in life that will remain is what we have done in obedience to Him. Evangelist C.T. Studd perfectly expressed this truth in his famous poem, "Only One Life":

"Two little lines I heard one day, Traveling along life's busy way;
Bringing conviction to my heart, And from my mind would not depart;
Only one life, 'twill soon be past, Only what's done for Christ will last.
Only one life, yes only one, Soon will its fleeting hours be done;
Then, in 'that day' my Lord to meet, And stand before His Judgment seat;
Only one life, 'twill soon be past, Only what's done for Christ will last.

Only one life, the still small voice, Gently pleads for a better choice
Bidding me selfish aims to leave, And to God's holy will to cleave;
Only one life, 'twill soon be past, Only what's done for Christ will last.

Only one life, a few brief years, Each with its burdens, hopes, and fears;
Each with its clays I must fulfill, living for self or in His will;
Only one life, 'twill soon be past, Only what's done for Christ will last.

When this bright world would tempt me sore, When Satan would a victory score;
When self would seek to have its way, Then help me Lord with joy to say;
Only one life, 'twill soon be past, Only what's done for Christ will last.

Give me Father, a purpose deep, In joy or sorrow Thy word to keep;
Faithful and true what e'er the strife, Pleasing Thee in my daily life;
Only one life, 'twill soon be past, Only what's done for Christ will last.

Oh let my love with fervor burn, And from the world now let me turn;
Living for Thee, and Thee alone, Bringing Thee pleasure on Thy throne;
Only one life, 'twill soon be past, Only what's done for Christ will last.

Only one life, yes only one, Now let me say, 'Thy will be done';
And when at last I'll hear the call, I know I'll say 'twas worth it all';
Only one life, 'twill soon be past, Only what's done for Christ will last."[409]

Only one life, and that life is short at its longest. In John 9:4, Jesus said, "I must work the works of him that sent me, while it is day: the night cometh, when no man can work." The same applies to us; we only have the small window of a lifetime in which to do what God has called us to do. It's time to get busy!

So, in our fight for right, God's Kingdom and His righteousness must remain job one (Matthew 6:33). In the end, what we are fighting for is the opportunity to freely and openly live and share the Gospel of Jesus Christ with a lost and dying world. As Jesus said, even if we gain the whole world, we accomplish nothing if we lose our souls in the process.

When time is no more and man's kingdoms are dust, all that will remain is God, His Kingdom, and those who have trusted His Son for salvation. In the Massachusetts election sermon delivered on May 31, 1780, Simeon Howard said it well:

> "But let every one remember that, whatever others may do, and however it may fare with our country, it shall surely be well with the righteous; and when all the mighty states and empires of this world shall be dissolved, and pass away 'like the baseless fabric of a vision,' they shall enter into the kingdom of their Father, which cannot be moved, and, in the enjoyment and exercise of perfect peace, liberty, and love, shine forth as the sun forever and ever."[410]

Until then, let us heed the 1776 challenge of Black Robed Regiment preacher William Gordon:

> "May heaven influence every one of us to contribute our best abilities, according to our several stations and relations, to the defense and support of the common weal [good]."[411]

… And let us pray that God will Bring Back the Black Robed Regiment!"

"Great Father, we bow before thee, we invoke thy blessing, we deprecate thy wrath, we thee return thanks for the past, we ask thy aid for the future; for we are in times of trouble, O Lord, and sore beset by foes, … God prosper the cause. Amen." [412]

The prayer of twenty-five-year-old chaplain, Joab Trout, on September 10, 1777, the eve of the Battle of Brandywine. Trout died the next day in the battle, fighting for liberty.

Endnotes

1 www.merriam-webster.com.

2 Steyn, Mark, "Dependence Day," *The New Criterion*, Jan./11, accessed from www.newcriterion.com/articles.cfm/Dependence-Day

3 Kramnick, Isaac, Moore, Laurence, *The Godless Constitution* (W.W. Norton & Company, Inc., 1997), pp.143,153,179, accessed from books.google.com, 9/25/2011.

4 *The Constitutions of Several Independent States of America* (London: Printed for J. Stockdale, in Piccadilly, 1783), p. 229, Constitution of Delaware, 1776, Article 22, accessed from http://books.google.com, cited 9/26/2011.

5 *The Constitutions of Several Independent States of America* (London: Printed for J. Stockdale, in Piccadilly, 1783), p. 191, Constitution of Pennsylvania, 1776, Chapter II, Section I0, accessed from http://books.google.com, cited 9/26/2011.

6 *A Constitution or Frame of Government Agreed Upon By the Delegates of the People of the State of Massachusetts-Bay* (Boston: Benjamin Edes and Sons, 1780), p. 44, Chapter VI, Article I (June 15, 1780 date ratified) *The Constitutions of Several Independent States of America* (London: Printed for J. Stockdale, in Piccadilly, 1783), p. 90, Constitution of Massachusetts, 1780, Chapter VI, Article I, accessed from http://books.google.com, cited 9/26/2011.

7 Dreisback, Daniel, L., Dr., "A Godless Constitution?: A Response to Kramnick and Moore, Wall Builders," 1997, Wall Builders, www.wallbuilders.com/LIBissuesArticles.asp?id=84

8 Ibid, *The Godless Constitution*, p. 179

9 *The Age of Revelation or The Age of Reason Shewn To Be An Age of Infidelity*, Elias Boudinot (Philadelphia: Published by Asbury Dickins, Opposite Christ Church, Hugh Maxwell, Printer, Columbia House, 1801), Preface, p. XXII, www.books.google.com, cited 10/24/2011.

10 Ellis Sandoz, Political Sermons of the American Founding Era: 1730-1805, 2 vols, Foreword by Ellis Sandoz (2nd ed. Indianapolis: Liberty Fund, 1998). Vol. 1. Chapter: 21: Samuel Cooper, A SERMON ON THE DAY OF THE COMMENCEMENT OF THE CONSTITUTION Accessed from http://oll.libertyfund.org/title/816/69278 on 2012-11-06.

11 Bridenbaugh, Carl, *Mitre and Sceptre: Transatlantic Faiths, Ideas, Personalities, and Politics 1689-1775* (Oxford University Press, 1962) Introduction, chapter XI, p. 290, Internet Archive, www.archive.org/stream/mitreandsceptret000806mbp/mitreandsceptret000806mbp_djvu.txt, Cited 2/13/12.

12 Tocqueville, Alexis de, *Democracy In America* (New York: Edward Walker, 114 Fulton Street: 1847), Vol. II, pp. 152, 327-337, cited from books.google.com, 3/6/12.

13 Ibid, Bridenbaugh, *Mitre and Scepter*, p. 189

14 Columbus, Christopher, *Libro de las profecias* (Book of Prophecies), and *America's God and Country: Encyclopedia of Quotations* edited by William Federer, pp. 113-114

15 *Mayflower Compact*, November 11, 1620, Pilgrim Hall Museum, accessed from www.pilgrimhall.org/compact.htm, cited 9/25/2011.

16 Bradford, William, *History of Plymouth Plantation*, Charles Deane, ed., 1856, p. 24, books.google.com, cited 9/25/2011.

17 Thornton, John Wingate, *The Pulpit of the American Revolution* (Boston: Gould & Lincoln, 1860), Introduction, Preface, pp. XV-XXIV.

18 Allen, William, D.D., *Biographical and Historical Dictionary, Containing An Account of the Lives, Characters, and Writings of the Most Eminent Persons in North America From Its First Settlement, And The Summary Of The History Of The Several Colonies And Of The United States*, president of Bowdin College (Boston: William Hyde & Co., 1832), p. 708, accessed from books.google.com, 3/7/12.

19 *History of the town of Gardner, Worcester County, Mass., from the incorporation, June 27, 1785, to the present time*, p. 474, accessed from www.ebooksread.com/authors-eng/william-dodge-herrick, 3/7/12.

20 Ellis Sandoz, Political Sermons of the American Founding Era: 1730-1805, 2 vols, Foreword by Ellis Sandoz (2nd ed. Indianapolis: Liberty

Fund, 1998). Vol. 1. Chapter: 15: Moses Mather, AMERICA'S APPEAL TO THE IMPARTIAL WORLD Accessed from http://oll.libertyfund.org/title/816/69260 on 2012-11-02

21 Ellis Sandoz, Political Sermons of the American Founding Era: 1730-1805, 2 vols, Foreword by Ellis Sandoz (2nd ed. Indianapolis: Liberty Fund, 1998). Vol. 1. Chapter: 16: Samuel Sherwood, THE CHURCH'S FLIGHT INTO THE WILDERNESS: AN ADDRESS ON THE TIMES Accessed from http://oll.libertyfund.org/title/816/69264 on 2012-11-02

22 Ibid, Thornton, *The Pulpit of the American Revolution,* pp. 207-08.

23 Ellis Sandoz, Political Sermons of the American Founding Era: 1730-1805, 2 vols, Foreword by Ellis Sandoz (2nd ed. Indianapolis: Liberty Fund, 1998). Vol. 2. Chapter: 45: Bishop James Madison, MANIFESTATIONS OF THE BENEFICENCE OF DIVINE PROVIDENCE TOWARDS AMERICA, Accessed from http://oll.libertyfund.org/title/817/69446 on 2012-11-02.

24 Federer, William, *Back Fired, "A Nation Founded For Religious Tolerance No Longer Tolerates The Religion Of It's Founders,"* Amerisearch, Inc., P.O. Box 20163, St. Louis, MO 63123, 2010,2008, p.19

25 Bonomi, Patricia, Professor Emeritus of New York Univ., "*The Middle Colonies as the Birthplace of American Religious Pluralism,*" Kennedy, James, Dr., *Character & Destiny,* Zondervan, 1994.

26 U.S. Religious Landscape Study, The Pew Forum, http://religions.pewforum.org/reports#

27 *The Writings of Washington,* John C. Fitzpatrick, editor (Washington, D.C.: U.S. Government Printing Office, 1932), Vol. XV, p. 55, from his speech to the Delaware Indian Chiefs on May 12, 1779.

28 June 14, 1783 letter from to the States on the Disbanding of the Army, accessed from www.ushistory.org/valleyforge/washington/earnestprayer.html, cited 10/21/2011.

29 George Washington, Farewell Address, September 17, 1796, "The George Washington Papers at the Library of Congress, 1741-1799, memory.loc.gov/cgi-bin/query/d?mgw:0:./temp/~ammem_iU6y:.

30 Benjamin Rush letter to Elias Boudinot on July 9, 1788. Letters of Benjamin Rush, L. H. Butterfield, ed., (Princeton, NJ: American Philosophical; Society, 1951), Vol. I, p. 475.

31 Federer, William, J., *America's God And Country Encyclopedia of Quotations*, William J. Federer (Coppell, Texas: FAME Publishing, Inc., 1994), p. 543.

32 Rush, Benjamin, M.D. (1806). "A plan of a Peace-Office for the United States". *Essays, Literary, Moral and Philosophical.* (2nd ed.). Thomas and William Bradford, Philadelphia. pp. 183–188. Retrieved 9/4/2011.

33 Chase, Samuel, official opinion in Runkel v. Winemiller, 1799

34 Jay, John, *The Correspondence and Public Papers of John Jay (1794-1826)*, ed. Henry P. Johnston, a.m. (New York: G.P. Putnam's Sons, 1890-93). Vol. 4, p. 393, to John Murray, Jr. on October 12, 1816, Online Library of Liberty, Liberty Fund, Inc., oll.libertyfund.org.

35 Jay, William, *The Life of John Jay* (New York: J. & J. Harper, 1833), Vol. II, p. 266, to the Rev. Uzal Ogden on February 14, 1796, cited from "The Founding Fathers On Jesus, Christianity, and the Bible," by David Barton, May 2008, accessed from www.wallbuilders.com, 3/11/12.

36 Ibid, Jay, William *The Life of John Jay*, Vol. I p. 518, Appendix V, from a prayer found among Mr. Jay's papers and in his handwriting, cited from "The Founding Fathers On Jesus, Christianity, and the Bible," by David Barton, May 2008, accessed from www.wallbuilders.com, 3/11/12.

37 Jay, John, *The Correspondence and Public Papers of John Jay, 1794-1826*, Henry P. Johnston, editor (New York: Burt Franklin, 1890), Vol. IV, pp. 494, 498, from his "Address at the Annual Meeting of the American Bible Society," May 13, 1824, cited from "The Founding Fathers On Jesus, Christianity, and the Bible," by David Barton, May 2008, accessed from www.wallbuilders.com, 3/11/12.

38 Jay, John, *The Correspondence and Public Papers of John Jay (1794-1826)*, Henry P. Johnston, editor, (New York: G.P. Putnam's Sons, 1890-93), Vol. IV, Online Library of Liberty, files.libertyfund.org/files/2330/Jay_1530-04_EBk_v5.1.pdf, 9/4/2011.

39 Adams, Samuel, *The Writings of Samuel Adams, 1773-77*, collected and edited by Henry Alonzo Cushing, (New York: G.P. Putnam's Sons, 1907), Vol. 3, p. 286, books.google.com, 9/4/2011.

40 Adams, Samuel, *The Life and Public Services of Samuel Adams*, William V. Wells, editor (Boston: Little, Brown and Company, 1865), Vol. I, p. 504.

41 Adams, Samuel, *Letters of delegates to Congress, 1774-1789*, Vol. XII, February 1 1779-May 31 1779, Samuel Adams to James Warren, February 11, 1779, Electronic Text Center, University of Virginia Library, etext.virginia.edu, 9/6/2011.

42 Adams, Samuel, *Proclamation for a Day of Fasting and Prayer*, March 10, 1793, cited from "The Founding Fathers On Jesus, Christianity, and the Bible," by David Barton, May 2008, accessed from www.wallbuilders.com, 3/11/12.

43 From a Fast Day Proclamation issued by Governor Samuel Adams, Massachusetts, March 20, 1797, in our possession; see also Samuel Adams, *The Writings of Samuel Adams*, Harry Alonzo Cushing, editor (New York: G. P. Putnam's Sons, 1908), Vol. IV, p. 407, from his proclamation of March 20, 1797, cited from "The Founding Fathers On Jesus, Christianity, and the Bible," by David Barton, May 2008, accessed from www.wallbuilders.com, 3/11/12.

44 From the Last Will & Testament of Samuel Adams, attested December 29, 1790; see also Samuel Adams, *Life & Public Services of Samuel Adams*, William V. Wells, editor (Boston: Little, Brown & Co, 1865), Vol. III, p. 379, Last Will and Testament of Samuel Adams, cited from "The Founding Fathers On Jesus, Christianity, and the Bible," by David Barton, May 2008, accessed from www.wallbuilders.com, 3/11/12.

45 Arnold, A. G., *The Life of Patrick Henry of Virginia* (Auburn and Buffalo: Miller, Orton and Mulligan, 1854), p. 250, cited from "The Founding Fathers On Jesus, Christianity, and the Bible," by David Barton, May 2008, accessed from www.wallbuilders.com, 3/11/12.

46 Henry, Patrick, *Patrick Henry, Life, Correspondence and Speeches*, William Wirt Henry, editor (New York: Charles Scribner's Sons, 1891), Vol. II, pp. 591-92, to Archibald Blair on January 8, 1799, Internet Archive, www.archive.org.

47 Will of Patrick Henry, attested November 20, 1798, cited from "The Founding Fathers On Jesus, Christianity, and the Bible," by David Barton, May 2008, accessed from www.wallbuilders.com, 3/11/12, William Joseph

Federer, *America's God and country: encyclopedia of quotations* (Amerisearch, Inc. St. Louis, MO, 2000), p. 290.

48 Ibid, Federer, William, J., *America's God And Country Encyclopedia of Quotations*, p. 290, Ibid, Barton, "The Founding Fathers On Jesus, Christianity, and the Bible."

49 Adams, John, *Works*, Vol. III, p. 421, diary entry for July 26, 1796, cited from "The Founding Fathers On Jesus, Christianity, and the Bible," by David Barton, May 2008, accessed from www.wallbuilders.com, 3/11/12.

50 Adams, John, *The Works of John Adams, Second President of the United* States, Charles Frances Adams, editor (Boston: Little, Brown and Company, 1854), Vol. IX, p. 229, to the Officers of the First Brigade of the Third Division of the Militia of Massachusetts on October 11, 1798, The Online Library of Liberty, Liberty Fund, Inc., oll.libertyfund.org, 9/6/2011.

51 Adams, John, *The Works*, Vol. IX, p. 636, to Benjamin Rush on August 28, 1811, The Online Library of Liberty, Liberty Fund, Inc., oll.libertyfund.org, 9/6/2011.

52 Adams, John, *The Works of John Adams, Second President of the United* States, Charles Frances Adams, editor (Boston: Little, Brown and Company, 1854), Vol. X, pp. 45-46, to Thomas Jefferson on June 28, 1813, The Online Library of Liberty, Liberty Fund, Inc., oll.libertyfund.org, 9/6/2011.

53 Adams, John, *Works*, Vol. X, p. 85, to Thomas Jefferson on December 25, 1813, cited from "The Founding Fathers On Jesus, Christianity, and the Bible," by David Barton, May 2008, accessed from www.wallbuilders.com, 3/11/12.

54 Webster, Noah, *History of the United States* (New Haven: Durrie & Peck, 1832), Vol. II, p. V, books.google.com, 9/7/2011.

55 Webster, Noah, *Defining Noah Webster: Mind and Morals in the Early Republic*, K. Alan Snyder (New York: University Press of America, 1990), p. 253, to James Madison on October 16, 1829.

56 Webster, Noah, *A Collection of Papers on Political, Literary, and Moral Subjects* (New York: Webster and Clark, 1843), p. 291, from his "Reply to a Letter of David McClure on the Subject of the Proper Course of Study in the Girard College, Philadelphia. New Haven, October 25, 1836

57 *Reports of Committees of the House of Representatives Made During the First Session of the Thirty-Third Congress* (Washington: A. O. P. Nicholson, 1854).

58 *Journal of the House of Representatives of the United States: Being the First Session of the Thirty-Fourth Congress* (Washington: Cornelius Wendell, 1855), p. 354, January 23, 1856. See also Lorenzo D. Johnson, *Chaplains of the General Government With Objections to their Employment Considered* (New York: Sheldon, Blakeman & Co., 1856), p. 35, cited from "Is President Obama Correct: Is America No Longer A Christian Nation?," by David Barton, April 2009, accessed from www.wallbuilders.com, 3/11/12.

59 *Holy Trinity vs. The United States*, February 29, 1892

60 Adams, John, *John Adams' Works, Vol. X, pp. 45-46, Letter to Thomas Jefferson on June 28, 1813.*

61 Adams, John Quincy, a speech delivered July 4, 1837 during a celebration at Newburyport, Massachusetts, accessed from http://archive.org/details/orationdelivered00adam, cited 3/13/13.

62 Smith, William, Rev., *The Patriot Preachers of the American Revolution: With Biographical Sketches,* Frank Moore (New York: Charles T. Evans, 1862), Sermon, "The Crisis of American Affairs," June 23, 1775, p. 105.

63 Ibid, Thornton, *The Pulpit of the American Revolution,* Preface, p. III.

64 Morris, B. F., *The Christian Life and Character of the Civil Institutions of the United States* (Philadelphia: George W. Childs, 1864), p. 341, accessed from http://books.google.com, cited 10/5/2011.

65 Barton, David, "A Brief History of the Black Robed Regiment," accessed from brr.wallbuilders.com/the-original-brr/what-is-the-black-robed-regiment.aspx, cited 3/7/12.

66 Baldwin, Alice, *The New England Clergy and the American Revolution* (New York: Frederick Ungar Publishing Co., 1928), p. 134.

67 Ibid, Thornton, *The Pulpit of the American Revolution,* p. 500.

68 *Webster's New World Dictionary, Second College Edition,* The World Publishing Co., 1970,72

69 Irving, Washington, *Life of George Washington,* Vol. I, (London: Harry G. Bohn, York Street, Covent Garden, 1855), p. 145, accessed from books.google.com, cited 9/23/2011.

70 Federer, William, *America's God And Country: Encyclopedia Of Quotations* (Coppell, Texas: FAME Publishing, Inc., 1994), pp. 636-637, *George Washington, the Christian,* William J. Johnson (Nashville, Tenn: Abingdon Press, 1919), pp. 41-42, Marshall, Peter and Manuel, David, *The Light and the Glory* (Old Tappan, NJ: Fleming H. Revell Company, 1977), pp. 285-286, Barton, David, *The Bulletproof George Washington* (Aledo, TX: Wallbuider, Inc., Winter, 1993), pp. 49-51, Williamson, Denise, "Wilderness Fight" (Colorado Springs, CO: Focus on the Family Clubhouse, July 1994), p. 14, referencing the testimony of Billy Brown, who in 1825, at the age of 93 recounted the incident with a historian.

71 The Library of Congress, "The American Revolution 1763-1783" www.loc.gov/teachers/classroommaterials/presentationsandactivities/presentations/timeline/amrev/contarmy/orderone.html

72 Washington, George, *Writings*, Vol. XIII, p. 118-19, General Orders, Head Quarters, Fredericksburg, October 21, 1778

73 Frost, John, *An Illustrated History of Washington and His Times* (Norwich, Connecticut: Published by Henry Bill, 1868), Edited by Rev. William Hutchison, A.M., p. 239, accessed from books.google.com, cited 9/6/12, Ibid, Fitzpatrick, Vol. 5, p. 245, July 9, 1776 Order, Barton.

74 Fitzpatrick, John C., *The Writings of Washington* (Washington, D.C.: U.S. Government Printing Office, 1932), Vol. XI, p. 343, Ibid, Fitzpatrick, Vol. XI, pp. 342-343, General Orders of May 2, 1778, Barton.

75 George Washington, Inaugural Address, April 30, 1789, accessed from www.archives.gov/exhibits/american_originals/inaugtxt.html, cited 5/4/12.

76 Full text of "Carpenter's Hall," by Richard K. Betts (Published by The Company, 1891), Library of Congress, p. 17, accessed from Internet Archive, www.archive.org, cited 3/11/12, *The Southern and Western Literary Messenger and Review* (Richmond, Virginia: Macfarlane & Fergusson, Printers, Law Building, 1847), Volume 13, p. 504, accessed from books.google.com, cited 3/11/12.

77 *The Moral Liberal,* Thursday, March, 29, 2012, www.themoralliberal.com, cited

78 Adams, John, *Letters of John Adams, Addressed to His Wife*, Charles Frances Adams, editor (Boston: Charles C. Little and James Brown, 1841), Vol. I, pp. 23-24, to Abigail Adams on September 16, 1774, cited in *Original Intent*, David Barton, pp. 92-94.

79 Deane, Silas, *The Deane Papers: Collections of the New York Historical Society for the Year 1886* (New York: Printed for the Society, 1887), Vol. I, p. 20, Wednesday, September 7, 1774. See also Barton, David, *Letters of Delegates,* Vol. I, p. 35, as cited in *Original Intent*, p. 93.

80 Ramsay, David, *An Eulogium Upon Benjamin Rush, M.D.* (Philadelphia: Bradford and Inskeep, 1813), p. 103, cited in Barton, David, "Ten Steps To Change America," 4/15/2002, www.wallbuilders.com/LIBissuesArticles.asp?id=117#_ftn19

81 Rush, Benjamin, *The Autobiography of Benjamin Rush*, George W. Corner, editor (Princeton: Princeton University Press, 1948), pp. 165-166, cited from "The Founding Fathers on Jesus, Christianity, and the Bible," by David Barton, May 2008, accessed from www.wallbuilders.com, 3/11/12.

82 Rush, Benjamin, *Letters of Benjamin Rush*, L. H. Butterfield, editor (Princeton, NJ: Princeton University Press, 1951), Vol. I, p. 521, to Jeremy Belknap on July 13, 1789, cited from Barton, David, "The Founding Fathers on Jesus, Christianity, and the Bible," May 2008, accessed from www.wallbuilders.com, 3/11/12.

83 Rush, Benjamin, *Essays, Literary, Moral & Philosophical* (Philadelphia: Thomas & Samuel F. Bradford, 1798), p. 93, "A Defence of the Use of the Bible as a School Book." See also Rush, Letters, Vol. I, p. 578, to Jeremy Belknap on March 2, 1791, cited from Barton, David, "The Founding Fathers on Jesus, Christianity, and the Bible," May 2008, accessed from www.wallbuilders.com, 3/11/12.

84 Rush, Benjamin, *Essays, Literary, Moral & Philosophical* (Philadelphia: Thomas & Samuel F. Bradford, 1798), pp. 94, 100, "A Defence of the Use of the Bible as a School Book," cited from Barton, David, "The Founding Fathers on Jesus, Christianity, and the Bible," May 2008, accessed from www.wallbuilders.com, 3/11/12.

85 Boutell, Lewis Henry, *The Life of Roger Sherman* (Chicago: A. C. McClurg and Co., 1896), pp. 272-273, cited in Barton, David, *Original* Intent, Wall Builder Press, P.O. Box 397, Aledo, TX 76008, p. 138, and in the Winter 1996 newsletter of Wall Builders, www.wallbuilders.com/LIBissuesArticles.asp?id=161.

86 *Correspondence Between Roger Sherman and Samuel Hopkins* (Worcester, MA: Charles Hamilton, 1889), p. 9, from Roger Sherman to Samuel Hopkins, June 28, 1790, cited from Barton, David, "The Founding Fathers on Jesus, Christianity, and the Bible," May 2008, accessed from www.wallbuilders.com, 3/11/12.

87 *The Globe* (Washington DC newspaper), August 15, 1837, p. 1, cited from Barton, David, "The Founding Fathers on Jesus, Christianity, and the Bible," May 2008, accessed from www.wallbuilders.com, 3/11/12.

88 Ibid, Federer, *America's God and Country: Encyclopedia of Quotations*, p. 410.

89 Espinosa, Gastón, "Madison's comments on Proverbs,"

90 Madison, James, *The Letters and Other Writings of James Madison* (New York: R. Worthington, 1884), Vol. I, pp. 5-6, to William Bradford on November 9, 1772, cited in Barton, David, *Original Intent*, p. 208.

91 Madison, James, *The Papers of James Madison*, William T. Hutchinson, editor (Illinois: University of Chicago Press, 1962), Vol. I, p. 66, to William Bradford on September 25, 1773, cited in Barton, David, *Original Intent*, p. 208.

92 Beardsley, Edwards, *Life and Times of William Samuel Johnson* (Boston: Houghton, Mifflin and Company, 1886), p. 184, accessed from books.google.com, cited 1/26/13.

93 Beardsley, Edwards, *Life and Times of William Samuel Johnson, LL.D.* (New York: Hurd and Houghton, The Riverside Press, Cambridge, 1876), pp. 141-143, books.google.com/ebooks, 9/4/11.

94 Jay, John & *John Jay: The Winning of the Peace. Unpublished Papers 1780-1784*, Richard B. Morris, editor (New York: Harper & Row Publishers, 1980), Vol. II, p. 709, to Peter Augustus Jay on April 8, 1784, cited in Barton, David, *Original Intent*, p. 163.

95 Jay, John & Jay, William, *The Life of John Jay* (New York: J. & J. Harper, 1833), Vol. II, p. 266, letter to the Reverend Uzal Ogden on February 14, 1796, accessed from books.google.com, cited 1/26/13.

96 Henry, Patrick, *The Life of Patrick Henry of* Virginia, S. G. Arnold (Auburn and Buffalo: Miller, Orton, & Mulligan, 1854), pp. 249-250, Henry to his daughter Betsy on August 20, 1796, Internet Archive, www.archive.org, 9/6/2011.

97 Wirt, William, *Sketches of the Life and Character of Patrick Henry* (Philadelphia: James Webster, 1818), p. 402, books.google.com/ebooks, 9/6/2011.

98 Franklin, Benjamin, *The Records of the Federal Convention of 1787*, James Madison, Max Farrand, editor (New Haven: Yale University Press, 1911), Vol. I, pp. 450-452, June 28, 1787, books.google.com, 9/7/2011.

99 Webster, Noah, *History of the United States*, (New Haven: Durrie & Peck, 1832), pp. 273-311, books.google.com, 9/8/2011.

100 *Journals of the Continental Congress*, Vol. XXIII, pp. 572-574, by United States. Continental Congress, Library of Congress. Manuscript Division, books.google.com, 9/9/2011.

101 Rules for the Regulation of the Navy of the United Colonies of North America, 28 November 1775, Articles 2-3, Department of the Navy, Naval Historical Center, 805 Kidder Breese SE, Washington Navy Yard, Washington D.C. 20374, www.history.navy.mil/faqs/faq59-5.htm, 9/9/2011.

102 Jefferson's Letter to the Danbury Baptists, Library of Congress, accessed from www.loc.gov/loc/lcib/9806/danpre.html, cited 3/11/12.

103 Adams, James L., *Yankee Doodle Went To Church* (Old Tappan, New Jersey: Fleming H. Revell Company, 1989), p. 12-14.

104 Rehnquist, William, Supreme Court Justice, *Wallace V. Jaffree*, 1985.

105 Allen, Ethan, Rev., (1796-1897), *Historical Sketch of Washington Parish, Washington City, 1794-1857*, www.monticello.org/site/research-and-collections/spurious-quotes, 9/9/2011, Hutson, James H., *Religion and the Founding of the American Republic* (Washington: Library of Congress, 1998), pp. 95-96.

106 Bishop Claggett letter of February 18, 1801, available in the Maryland Diocesan Archives, cited in Barton, David, "Church in the U.S. Capitol," Wallbuilders, 2005.

107 Cutler, William Parker and Cutler, Julia Perkins, *Life, Journal, and Correspondence of Rev. Manasseh Cutler* (Cincinnati: Colin Robert Clarke & Co., 1888), Vol. II, p. 66, letter to Joseph Torrey, January 4, 1802.

108 Smith, Mrs. Samuel Harrison, (Margaret Bayard), *The First Forty Years of Washington Society*, Galliard Hunt, editor (New York: Charles Scribner's Sons, 1906), p. 16, 13.

109 Cutler and Cutler, *Life, Journal, and Correspondence*, Vol. II, p. 119, in a letter to Dr. Joseph Torrey on January 3, 1803; see also his entry of December 12, 1802 (Vol. II, p. 113).

110 Cutler and Cutler, *Life, Journal, and Correspondence*, Vol. II, p. 119, in a letter to Dr. Joseph Torrey on January 3, 1803; see also his entry of December 26, 1802 (Vol. II, p. 114). (cited in Barton, David, "Church in the U.S. Capitol," Wallbuilders, 2005)

111 Smith, Margaret Bayard, "Religion and the Founding of the American Republic," Section IV, Part 2, "Hymns Played at Congressional Church Service," Library of Congress, accessed from www.loc.gov/exhibits/religion/rel06-2.html, cited 9/27/2011.

112 Cutler, Manasseh, Manuscript, *Journal entry, December 23, 1804*, Charles Deering McCormick Library of Special Collections, Northwestern University Library (175), Library of Congress, accessed from www.loc.gov/exhibits/religion/rel06-2.html, cited 9/27/2011. John Quincy Adams. Copyprint, *Diary entry, February 2, 1806*, Adams Family Papers, Massachusetts Historical Society, Boston (177), Library of Congress, accessed from www.loc.gov/exhibits/religion/rel06-2.html, cited 9/27/2011.

113 Franklin and Jefferson notes, Manuscript Division, LOC, (104-105), accessed from http://www.loc.gov/exhibits/religion/rel04.html, cited 9/26/2011.

114 Franklin and Jefferson notes, Manuscript Division, LOC, (104-105), accessed from http://www.loc.gov/exhibits/religion/rel04.html, cited 9/26/2011.

115 Drawing by Benson Lossing, for *Harper's New Monthly Magazine*, July 1856, General Collections, Library of Congress (106), accessed from http://www.loc.gov/exhibits/religion/rel04.html, cited 9/26/2011.

116 Franklin and Jefferson notes, Manuscript Division, LOC, (104-105), accessed from http://www.loc.gov/exhibits/religion/rel04.html, cited 9/26/2011.

117 Bioren, John, Duane, John W., Weightman, R.C., *The Laws of the United States of America, From the 4th of March, 1789, to the 4th of March, 1815, Including the Constitution of the United States, The Old Act of Confederation, Treaties, With Many Other Valuable Ordinances and Documents; With Copious Notes and References,* (1815), Vol. 1, p. 569, accessed from http://books.google.com, cited 9/27/2011. Library of Congress, "Religion and the Founding of the American Republic," Section I, "Religion and the Congress of the Confederation, 1774-89," accessed from www.loc.gov/exhibits/religion/rel04.html, cited 9/6/2011.

118 Treaty With The Kaskaskia Indians, Aug. 13, 1803 (7 Stat., 78.) Proclamation, Dec. 23, 1803, *Indian Affairs: Laws and Treaties*, Vol. II, Treaties, Compiled and edited by Charles J. Kappler (Washington: Government Printing Office, 1904), pp. 67-68, accessed from digital.library.okstate.edu/kappler/vol2/treaties/kas0067.htm#mn6, cited 9/6/2011.

119 Thomas Jefferson, May 15, 1804,Ursuline Academy, Ursuline Convent Archives and Museum, New Orleans, Louisiana, accessed from www.churchstatelaw.com/historicalmaterials/images/thomas_jefferson_letter_1804.pdf, cited 9/6/2011.

120 Ibid, Adams, James, *Yankee Doodle Went To Church*, p. 13.

121 "Jefferson's Gravestone," The Jefferson Monticello, accessed from www.monticello.org, cited 1/26/13.

122 McDowell, Steve, *America's Providential History,* Cofounder and President of Providence Foundation, cited in *Silenced In the Schoolhouse: How Biblical Illiteracy In Our Schools Is Destroying America,* Dr. Michael L. Williams, (Jefferson, Ohio, Wisdom4Today, 2008), p. 98, accessed from books.google.com/books?id=jT8a_BjurkcC&pg=PA97&lpg=PA97&dq, cited 5/28/12.

123 Federer, William, "Harvard Was Founded Upon Christianity," American Minute, *The Moral Liberal,* May 28, 2012, accessed from www.themoral-liberal.com/2010/09/14/harvard-was-founded-upon-christianity-american-minute/, cited 5/28/12.

124 Ibid, Federer, *America's God and Country,* p. 494.

125 Federer, William, "Harvard was Founded Upon Christianity," American Minute, Sept. 14, 2010, www.themoralliberal.com.

126 Ibid, McDowell, Steve, *America's Providential History.*

127 Adams, John, *The Works of John Adams, Second President of the United States*, Charles Frances Adams, editor (Boston: Little, Brown, and Company, 1854), Vol. II, pp. 6-7, diary entry for Sunday, February 22, 1756, accessed from http://books.google.com/ebooks, cited 9/27/2011.

128 Limbaugh, Rush, H., Jr., "Our Lives, Our Fortunes, Our Sacred Honor," accessed from alumnus.caltech.edu/~marcsulf/our_sacred_honor.html, cited 8/8/12.

129 Moore, Frank, *The Patriot Preachers of the American Revolution: With Biographical Sketches* (New York: Charles T. Evans, 1862), pp. 179-80.

130 Ellis Sandoz, Political Sermons of the American Founding Era: 1730-1805, 2 vols, Foreword by Ellis Sandoz (2nd ed. Indianapolis: Liberty Fund, 1998). Vol. 1. Chapter: 31: Elizur Goodrich, THE PRINCIPLES OF CIVIL UNION AND HAPPINESS CONSIDERED AND RECOMMENDED Accessed from http://oll.libertyfund.org/title/816/69311 on 2012-11-04

131 Adams, John, *Novanglus and Massachusettensis* (Boston: Hews & Goss, 1819), p. 45, accessed from books.google.com, cited 3/14/12.

132 Ibid, Thornton, *The Pulpit of the American Revolution,* pp. 143-44.

133 *The Declaration of Independence*, 1776.

134 Hopkinson, Francis, Esq., *The Miscellaneous Essays and Occasional Writings of Francis Hopkinson, Esq.* (Philadelphia: T. Dobson, No. 41 Second Street, 1792), Vol. I, p. 115-16, accessed from www.google.com/search?client=safari&rls=en&q=mdccxcii&ie=UTF-8&oe=UTF-8, cited 11/4/12.

135 Adams, John Quincy, "An Address Delivered at the Request of the Committee of Arrangements for the Celebrating the Anniversary of

Independence at the City of Washington on the Fourth of July 1821 upon the Occasion of Reading The Declaration of Independence," accessed from www17.us.archive.org/stream/addressdelivered00adamiala/address-delivered00adamiala_djvu.txtcited 11/4/12.

136 Ibid, Thornton, *The Pulpit of the American Revolution,* p. 199

137 Ellis Sandoz, Political Sermons of the American Founding Era: 1730-1805, 2 vols, Foreword by Ellis Sandoz (2nd ed. Indianapolis: Liberty Fund, 1998). Vol. 2. Chapter: 54: William Emerson, AN ORATION IN COMMEMORATION OF THE ANNIVERSARY OF AMERICAN INDEPENDENCE, accessed from http://oll.libertyfund.org/title/817/69467 on 2012-11-05.

138 Ibid, Baldwin, Alice, *The New England Clergy and the American Revolution*, chapter 8, pp. 115-16.

139 Ellis Sandoz, Political Sermons of the American Founding Era: 1730-1805, 2 vols, Foreword by Ellis Sandoz (2nd ed. Indianapolis: Liberty Fund, 1998). Vol. 1. Chapter: 12: Samuel Sherwood, SCRIPTURAL INSTRUCTIONS TO CIVIL RULERS, accessed from http://oll.libertyfund.org/title/816/69251 on 2012-11-05.

140 Ibid, Moore, Frank, *The Patriot Preachers of the American Revolution,* pp. 70-71.

141 Ibid, Baldwin, Alice, *The New England Clergy and the American Revolution,* Appendix, pp. 178-79.

142 Ellis Sandoz, Political Sermons of the American Founding Era: 1730-1805, 2 vols, Foreword by Ellis Sandoz (2nd ed. Indianapolis: Liberty Fund, 1998). Vol. 1. Chapter: 15: Moses Mather, AMERICA'S APPEAL TO THE IMPARTIAL WORLD, accessed from http://oll.libertyfund.org/title/816/69260 on 2012-06-01.

143 Ibid, Moore, Frank, *The Patriot Preachers of the American Revolution,* p. 105.

144 Ibid, Thornton, *The Pulpit of the American Revolution,* p. 313.

145 Ibid, Moore, Frank, *The Patriot Preachers of the American Revolution,* pp. 12-14,32,39.

146 Ellis Sandoz, Political Sermons of the American Founding Era: 1730-1805, 2 vols, Foreword by Ellis Sandoz (2nd ed. Indianapolis: Liberty

Fund, 1998). Vol. 1. Chapter: 19: Abraham Keteltas, GOD ARISING AND PLEADING HIS PEOPLE'S CAUSE Accessed from http://oll.libertyfund.org/title/816/69274 on 2012-11-05

147 Ibid, Baldwin, Alice, *The New England Clergy and the American Revolution,* chapter 6, p. 68.

148 Ibid, Baldwin, Alice, *The New England Clergy and the American Revolution,* Chapter 12, pp. 168-69.

149 Ibid, Thornton, *The Pulpit of the American Revolution,* p. 166.

150 Ellis Sandoz, Political Sermons of the American Founding Era: 1730-1805, 2 vols, Foreword by Ellis Sandoz (2nd ed. Indianapolis: Liberty Fund, 1998). Vol. 1. Chapter: 15: Moses Mather, AMERICA'S APPEAL TO THE IMPARTIAL WORLD Accessed from http://oll.libertyfund.org/title/816/69260 on 2012-11-05.

151 Ellis Sandoz, Political Sermons of the American Founding Era: 1730-1805, 2 vols, Foreword by Ellis Sandoz (2nd ed. Indianapolis: Liberty Fund, 1998). Vol. 2. Chapter: 54: William Emerson, AN ORATION IN COMMEMORATION OF THE ANNIVERSARY OF AMERICAN INDEPENDENCE, Accessed from http://oll.libertyfund.org/title/817/69467 on 2012-11-05.

152 Ellis Sandoz, Political Sermons of the American Founding Era: 1730-1805, 2 vols, Foreword by Ellis Sandoz (2nd ed. Indianapolis: Liberty Fund, 1998). Vol. 1. Chapter: 29: Joseph Lathrop, A SERMON ON A DAY APPOINTED FOR PUBLICK THANKSGIVING Accessed from http://oll.libertyfund.org/title/816/69307 on 2012-11-05

153 Mayhew, Jonathan, sermon, "Discourse Concerning Unlimited Submission and Non-Resistance To The Higher Powers," Jan 31, 1749-50, accessed from Internet Archive, www.archive.org, cited 3/14/12.

154 Ibid, Moore, Frank, *The Patriot Preachers of the American Revolution,* p. 68.

155 Ellis Sandoz, Political Sermons of the American Founding Era: 1730-1805, 2 vols, Foreword by Ellis Sandoz (2nd ed. Indianapolis: Liberty Fund, 1998). Vol. 1. Chapter: 10: John Allen, AN ORATION UPON THE BEAUTIES OF LIBERTY Accessed from http://oll.libertyfund.org/title/816/69240 on 2012-11-05.

156 Ibid, Thornton, *The Pulpit of the American Revolution,* pp. 279-283, 313.

157 Mayhew, Jonathan, *Discourse Concerning Unlimited Submission and Non-Resistance To The Higher Powers*, preached in the West Meeting House in Boston 1749-50, accessed from Internet Archive, archive.org, cited 3/27/12.

158 Ibid, Thornton, *The Pulpit of the American Revolution,* pp. 267-322.

159 Ibid, Moore, Frank, *The Patriot Preachers of the American Revolution*, pp. 179-80.

160 Ward, Henry Beecher, Mar 19, 1863, *The Independent* … "*Devoted to the Consideration of Politics, Social, and Ecom Tendencies, History, Literature, and the Arts.*"

161 Ibid, Federer, *America's God and Country: Encyclopedia of Quotations*, p. 235, "Lectures On Revivals of Religion," Rev. Charles G. Finney, Lecture XV, "Hindrances to Revivals," accessed from http://saynsumthn.wordpress.com, cited 10/5/2011.

162 Finney, Charles G., "The Decay of Conscience," *The Independent,* New York, December 4, 1873, accessed from The Gospel Truth, www.gospel-truth.net/1868_75Independent/731204_conscience.htm, cited 1/11/13, "Lectures On Revivals of Religion," Rev. Charles G. Finney, Lecture XV, "Hindrances to Revivals," pp. 274-75, accessed from books.google.com, cited 1/11/13.

163 *The Complete Works Of John M. Mason, D.D.*, edited by Ebenezer Mason (New York: Baker & Scribner, 1849), pp. 560-61, accessed from books.google.com, cited 3/28/12.

164 Ibid, Thornton, *The Pulpit of the American Revolution,* Preface, p. III.

165 Trivers, Howard, "Universalism In the Thought of the Founding Fathers," *The Virginia Quarterly Review*, Summer 1976, pp. 448-62, accessed from www.vqronline.org, cited 3/27/12, *History of Massachusetts From 1764 To July 1775: When General Washington Took Command Of The American Army,* Alden Bradford (Boston: Richardson and Lord, 1822), p. 361, accessed from books.google.com, cited 3/27/12, Baldwin, Alice, chapter 9, p. 123.

166 Ibid, Baldwin, Alice, *The New England Clergy and the American Revolution,* chapter 9, p. 123.

167 Ibid, Adams, James, *Yankee Doodle Went To Church,* p. 64.

168 Ibid, Thornton, *The Pulpit of the American Revolution,* pp. 47-48, 53.

169 Ibid, Thornton, *The Pulpit of the American Revolution,* 53-54.

170 Ibid, Thornton, *The Pulpit of the American Revolution,* p. 197.

171 Ibid, Thornton, *The Pulpit of the American Revolution,* Pp. 320-21.

172 Edwards, Jonathan, Jr. sermon *The Necessity Of The Belief Of Christianity By The Citizens Of The State, In Order To Our Political Prosperity,* to the General Assembly of the state of Connecticut, May 8, 1794 (Hartford: Hudson & Goodwin, 1794), pp. 44-45, accessed from www.unz.org, cited 3/28/12.

173 Smalley, Jonathan, sermon, *On The Evils Of A Weak Government,* to the General Assembly of Connecticut, May 8, 1800, pp. 46-47, 50-51, accessed from www.unz.org, cited 3/28/12.

174 Headley, Joel Tyler, *The Chaplains and Clergy of the Revolution* (New York: Charles Scribner, 1864), p. 27.

175 Ibid, Moore, Frank, *The Patriot Preachers of the American Revolution,* p. 105.

176 Ibid, Bridenbaugh, Carl, *Mitre and Sceptre,* p. 260.

177 Ellis Sandoz, Political Sermons of the American Founding Era: 1730-1805, 2 vols, Foreword by Ellis Sandoz (2nd ed. Indianapolis: Liberty Fund, 1998). Vol. 1. Chapter: 17: John Witherspoon, THE DOMINION OF PROVIDENCE OVER THE PASSIONS OF MEN Accessed from http://oll.libertyfund.org/title/816/69270 on 2012-11-05.

178 Newton, Thomas, *Dissertations on the Prophecies: Which Have Remarkably Been Fulfilled and At This Time Are Fulfilling In The World* (London: Printed for J. and R. Tonson in the Strand, 1766), Vol. I, p. 313.

179 Ibid, Moore, Frank, *The Patriot Preachers of the American Revolution,* pp. 75-76.

180 Ellis Sandoz, Political Sermons of the American Founding Era: 1730-1805, 2 vols, Foreword by Ellis Sandoz (2nd ed. Indianapolis: Liberty Fund, 1998). Vol. 1. Chapter: 22: Henry Cumings, A SERMON PREACE AT LEXINGTON ON THE 19th OF APRIL Accessed from http://oll.libertyfund.org/title/816/69280 on 2012-11-05.

181 Ibid, Moore, Frank, *The Patriot Preachers of the American Revolution* ,pp. 77,79,80,85,87,88-89.

182 Ibid, Sandoz, Introduction, Vol. I, p. XXI.

183 Ibid, Thornton, *The Pulpit of the American Revolution,* Introduction, p. XXIV, Journal of John Winthrop 1630-49, p. 198, accessed from archiver.rootsweb.ancestry.com/th/read/GenMassachusetts/2006-01/1137878434, cited 4/9/12, Sprague, William B., D.D., *Annals of the American Pulpit* (New York: Robert Carter & Brothers, 1857), Vol. I, p. 39, accessed from books.google.com, cited 4/9/12.

184 Ibid, Sandoz, Vol. I, Introduction, p. XX.

185 Ibid, Thornton, *The Pulpit of the American Revolution,* Introduction, p. XXII.

186 Headley, Joel Tyler, *The Chaplains and Clergy of the Revolution* (New York: Charles Scribner, 1864), chapter 2, pp. 21-23.

187 Gordon, William, *The History of the Rise, Progress and Establishment of the United States of America, including An Account of the Late War*, 3 vols (New York: Printed for Samuel Campbell, No. 124 Pearl-Street, by John Woods, 3rd edition 1801), vol. I, pp. 273–74, accessed from books.google.com, cited 8/17/12.

188 Ibid, Moore, Frank, *The Patriot Preachers of the American Revolution,* pp. 280-84.

189 Ellis Sandoz, Political Sermons of the American Founding Era: 1730-1805, 2 vols, Foreword by Ellis Sandoz (2nd ed. Indianapolis: Liberty Fund, 1998). Vol. 2. Chapter: 46: Stephen Peabody, SERMON BEFORE THE GENERAL COURT OF NEW HAMPSHIRE AT THE ANNUAL ELECTION, Accessed from http://oll.libertyfund.org/title/817/69448 on 2012-11-05.

190 Ellis Sandoz, Political Sermons of the American Founding Era: 1730-1805, 2 vols, Foreword by Ellis Sandoz (2nd ed. Indianapolis: Liberty Fund, 1998). Vol. 1. Chapter: 17: John Witherspoon, THE DOMINION OF PROVIDENCE OVER THE PASSIONS OF MEN Accessed from http://oll.libertyfund.org/title/816/69270 on 2012-11-05

191 Ibid, Thornton, *The Pulpit of the American Revolution,* pp. 339-41.

192 Ibid, Thornton, *The Pulpit of the American Revolution,* pp. 373-76,393-95.

193 Ibid, Thornton, *The Pulpit of the American Revolution*, pp. 403,439,489,494-95,499-500.

194 Ibid, Thornton, *The Pulpit of the American Revolution*, p. 298-88.

195 Ibid, Thornton, *The Pulpit of the American Revolution*, pp. 403,503,512-13.

196 Ellis Sandoz, Political Sermons of the American Founding Era: 1730-1805, 2 vols, Foreword by Ellis Sandoz (2nd ed. Indianapolis: Liberty Fund, 1998). Vol. 1. Chapter: 26: Samuel McClintock, A SERMON ON OCCASION OF THE COMMENCEMENT OF THE NEW-HAMPSHIRE CONSTITUTION, Accessed from http://oll.libertyfund.org/title/816/69301 on 2012-11-05.

197 Ellis Sandoz, Political Sermons of the American Founding Era: 1730-1805, 2 vols, Foreword by Ellis Sandoz (2nd ed. Indianapolis: Liberty Fund, 1998). Vol. 1. Chapter: 28: Samuel Wales, THE DANGERS OF OUR NATIONAL PROSPERITY; AND THE WAY TO AVOID THEM Accessed from http://oll.libertyfund.org/title/816/69305 on 2012-11-05.

198 Ellis Sandoz, Political Sermons of the American Founding Era: 1730-1805, 2 vols, Foreword by Ellis Sandoz (2nd ed. Indianapolis: Liberty Fund, 1998). Vol. 1. Chapter: 29: Joseph Lathrop, A SERMON ON A DAY APPOINTED FOR PUBLICK THANKSGIVING Accessed from http://oll.libertyfund.org/title/816/69307 on 2012-11-05.

199 Ellis Sandoz, Political Sermons of the American Founding Era: 1730-1805, 2 vols, Foreword by Ellis Sandoz (2nd ed. Indianapolis: Liberty Fund, 1998). Vol. 1. Chapter: 31: Elizur Goodrich, THE PRINCIPLES OF CIVIL UNION AND HAPPINESS CONSIDERED AND RECOMMENDED Accessed from http://oll.libertyfund.org/title/816/69311 on 2012-11-05.

200 Ellis Sandoz, Political Sermons of the American Founding Era: 1730-1805, 2 vols, Foreword by Ellis Sandoz (2nd ed. Indianapolis: Liberty Fund, 1998). Vol. 1. Chapter: 32: Samuel Langdon, THE REPUBLIC OF THE ISRAELITES AN EXAMPLE TO THE AMERICAN STATES Accessed from http://oll.libertyfund.org/title/816/69313 on 2012-11-05.

201 Ellis Sandoz, Political Sermons of the American Founding Era: 1730-1805, 2 vols, Foreword by Ellis Sandoz (2nd ed. Indianapolis: Liberty Fund, 1998). Vol. 2. Chapter: 40: Samuel Miller, A SERMON ON

THE ANNIVERSARY OF THE INDEPENDENCE OF AMERICA Accessed from http://oll.libertyfund.org/title/817/69407 on 2012-11-05.

202 Ellis Sandoz, Political Sermons of the American Founding Era: 1730-1805, 2 vols, Foreword by Ellis Sandoz (2nd ed. Indianapolis: Liberty Fund, 1998). Vol. 2. Chapter: 42: Jonathan Edwards, Jr., THE NECESSITY OF THE BELIEF OF CHRISTIANITY Accessed from http://oll.libertyfund.org/title/817/69411 on 2012-11-05.

203 Ellis Sandoz, Political Sermons of the American Founding Era: 1730-1805, 2 vols, Foreword by Ellis Sandoz (2nd ed. Indianapolis: Liberty Fund, 1998). Vol. 2. Chapter: 45: Bishop James Madison, MANIFESTATIONS OF THE BENEFICENCE OF DIVINE PROVIDENCE TOWARDS AMERICA, Accessed from http://oll.libertyfund.org/title/817/69446 on 2012-11-05.

204 Logan, Walter Seth, *Thomas Hooker: The First American Democrat* (Kissinger Publishing, 2004), pp. 18-19, accessed from books.google.com, cited 4/10/12, Ibid, Baldwin, Alice, chapter 3, pp. 26-27.

205 Publications of the Colonial Society of Massachusetts (Boston: Published by the Society, 1907), Vol. 10, p. 6, accessed from books.google.com, cited 4/10/12, Ibid, Baldwin, Alice, Chapter 3, p. 26.

206 Ibid, Baldwin, Alice, *The New England Clergy and the American Revolution,* p. 174-75.

207 Ibid, Baldwin, Alice, *The New England Clergy and the American Revolution,* chapter 4, pp. 34, 38-39.

208 Ibid, Baldwin, Alice, *The New England Clergy and the American Revolution,* Ch 3, p. 35.

209 Ibid, Baldwin, Alice, *The New England Clergy and the American Revolution,* chapter 4, p. 40.

210 Ibid, Baldwin, Alice, *The New England Clergy and the American Revolution,* Chapter 3, P. 23.

211 Ellis Sandoz, Political Sermons of the American Founding Era: 1730-1805, 2 vols, Foreword by Ellis Sandoz (2nd ed. Indianapolis: Liberty Fund, 1998). Vol. 1. Chapter: I: Benjamin Colman, GOVERNMENT THE PILLAR OF THE EARTH Accessed from http://oll.libertyfund.org/title/816/69217 on 2012-11-05.

212 Ibid, Baldwin, Alice, *The New England Clergy and the American Revolution,* chapter 3, p. 40, Appendix, p. 175.

213 Ibid, Baldwin, Alice, *The New England Clergy and the American Revolution,* p. 176.

214 Ibid, Baldwin, Alice, *The New England Clergy and the American Revolution,* pp. 29-30.

215 Ibid, Moore, Frank, *The Patriot Preachers of the American Revolution,* p. 269.

216 Chauncy, Charles, sermon, *Civil Magistrates Must Be Just, Ruling in the Fear of God,* May 27, 1747, accessed from The Moral Liberal, centerformoralliberalism.wordpress.com/2009/11/01/, cited 6/7/12.

217 Ibid, Baldwin, Alice, *The New England Clergy and the American Revolution,* chapter 7, p. 87.

218 Ibid, Headley, *The Chaplains and Clergy of the Revolution,* pp. 165, 184-86.

219 Ibid, Headley, *The Chaplains and Clergy of the Revolution,* chapter 2, pp. 25-27.

220 Ibid, Headley, *The Chaplains and Clergy of the Revolution,* p. 30.

221 Ibid, Baldwin, Alice, *The New England Clergy and the American Revolution,* Appendix, p. 181.

222 Ibid, Baldwin, Alice, *The New England Clergy and the American Revolution,* Appendix, pp. 180-81.

223 John Adams to Abigail Adams, (12 May 1780), www.nps.gov, *Familiar Letters Of John Adams And His Wife Abigail Adams, During The Revolution,* p. 381.

224 Ibid, Baldwin, Alice, *The New England Clergy and the American Revolution,* chapter 2, p. 13.

225 Madison, James, *Federalist No. 51, Independent Journal,* Wednesday, February 5, 1788, "Politics From A New Perspective," The George Washington University, Washington D.C., accessed from www.constitution.org/fed/federa51.htm, cited 4/19/12.

226 Rimkunas, Barbara, "The Exeter Combination," July 4, 1639, "What's in a Name," Exeter Historical Society, accessed from exeterhistory.blogspot.com/2011/08/whats-in-name.html, cited 4/20/12.

227 Ellis Sandoz, Political Sermons of the American Founding Era: 1730-1805, 2 vols, Foreword by Ellis Sandoz (2nd ed. Indianapolis: Liberty Fund, 1998), Vol. 1, Accessed from http://oll.libertyfund.org/title/816 on 2012-05-04.

228 Ibid, Baldwin, Alice, *The New England Clergy and the American Revolution*, p. 13.

229 Ibid, Baldwin, Alice, *The New England Clergy and the American Revolution*, p. 12.

230 Ibid, Thornton, *The Pulpit of the American Revolution*, p. XIX.

231 Ibid, Baldwin, Alice, *The New England Clergy and the American Revolution*, Conclusion, pp.134-35, 172.

232 Ibid, Baldwin, Alice, *The New England Clergy and the American Revolution*, p. 138.

233 Ibid, Baldwin, Alice, *The New England Clergy and the American Revolution*, pp. 22-23.

234 Rossiter, Clinton, *Seedtime of the Republic* (New York: Harcourt, Brace and Co., 1953), pp. 328-329, accessed from Barton, David, "What Is The Black Robed Regiment: A Brief History," brr.wallbuilders.com/the-original-brr/what-is-the-black-robed-regiment.aspx#FN10, cited 4/24/12.

235 Ibid, Baldwin, Alice, *The New England Clergy and the American Revolution*, chapter 2, p. 15.

236 Ibid, Baldwin, Alice, *The New England Clergy and the American Revolution*, chapter 3, p. 22.

237 Ibid, Baldwin, Alice, *The New England Clergy and the American Revolution*, chapter 2, p. 15.

238 Ibid, Baldwin, Alice, *The New England Clergy and the American Revolution*, chapter 2, p. 15.

239 Ibid, Baldwin, Alice, *The New England Clergy and the American Revolution*, chapter 6, p. 69.

240 Ibid, Baldwin, Alice, *The New England Clergy and the American Revolution*, chapter 3, 22.

241 Ibid, Moore, Frank, *The Patriot Preachers of the American Revolution*, p. 68.

242 Ellis Sandoz, Political Sermons of the American Founding Era: 1730-1805, 2 vols, Foreword by Ellis Sandoz (2nd ed. Indianapolis: Liberty Fund, 1998). Vol. 1. Chapter: 15: Moses Mather, AMERICA'S APPEAL TO THE IMPARTIAL WORLD Accessed from http://oll.libertyfund.org/title/816/69260 on 2012-11-05.

243 Ellis Sandoz, Political Sermons of the American Founding Era: 1730-1805, 2 vols, Foreword by Ellis Sandoz (2nd ed. Indianapolis: Liberty Fund, 1998). Vol. 1. Chapter: 32: Samuel Langdon, THE REPUBLIC OF THE ISRAELITES AN EXAMPLE TO THE AMERICAN STATES Accessed from http://oll.libertyfund.org/title/816/69313 on 2012-11-05.

244 Ellis Sandoz, Political Sermons of the American Founding Era: 1730-1805, 2 vols, Foreword by Ellis Sandoz (2nd ed. Indianapolis: Liberty Fund, 1998). Vol. 1. Chapter: 12: Samuel Sherwood, SCRIPTURAL INSTRUCTIONS TO CIVIL RULERS Accessed from http://oll.libertyfund.org/title/816/69251 on 2012-11-05.

245 Ibid, Thornton, *The Pulpit of the American Revolution,* Introduction, p. XIX-XX.

246 Ibid, Baldwin, Alice, *The New England Clergy and the American Revolution,* chapter 4, p. 35.

247 Ibid, Baldwin, Alice, *The New England Clergy and the American Revolution,* chapter 3, p. 23.

248 Ibid, Thornton, *The Pulpit of the American Revolution,* pp. 487,495,502-03,506,512-13.

249 Ellis Sandoz, Political Sermons of the American Founding Era: 1730-1805, 2 vols, Foreword by Ellis Sandoz (2nd ed. Indianapolis: Liberty Fund, 1998). Vol. 1. Chapter: 5: Charles Chauncy, CIVIL MAGISTRATES MUST BE JUST, RULING IN THE FEAR OF GOD Accessed from http://oll.libertyfund.org/title/816/69228 on 2012-11-05.

250 Cooke, Samuel, *The True Principles of Civil Government*, May 30, 1770, accessed from www.belcherfoundation.org/civil_government.htm, cited 4/20/12.

251 West, Samuel, sermon, *Natural Law: True Principles of Government, Discourse VI,* May 29, 1776, accessed from www.belcherfoundation.org/natural_law.htm, cited 4/21/12.

252 Sandoz, Ellis, Political Sermons of the American Founding Era: 1730-1805, 2 vols, Foreword by Ellis Sandoz (2nd ed. Indianapolis: Liberty Fund, 1998). Vol. 1. Chapter: 3: Elisha Williams, The Essential Rights And Liberties Of Protestants, Accessed from http://oll.libertyfund.org/title/816/69224 on 2012-04-24

253 Williams, Roger, *The Bloudy Tenent of Persecution,* 1643-44 (Rhode Island: Narragansett Club, Vol. III, 1867), edited by Samuel L. Caldwell, pp. 249-50, accessed from books.google.com, cited 4/23/12

254 Ibid, Baldwin, Alice, *The New England Clergy and the American Revolution,* chapter 3, p. 34.

255 Ibid, Baldwin, Alice, *The New England Clergy and the American Revolution,* p. 34.

256 Ibid, Baldwin, Alice, *The New England Clergy and the American Revolution,* chapter 7, p. 85.

257 Ibid, Baldwin, Alice, *The New England Clergy and the American Revolution,* p. 90.

258 Ibid, Baldwin, Alice, *The New England Clergy and the American Revolution,* p. 97.

259 Ellis Sandoz, Political Sermons of the American Founding Era: 1730-1805, 2 vols, Foreword by Ellis Sandoz (2nd ed. Indianapolis: Liberty Fund, 1998). Vol. 1. Chapter: 3: Elisha Williams, THE ESSENTIAL RIGHTS AND LIBERTIES OF PROTESTANTS Accessed from http://oll.libertyfund.org/title/816/69224 on 2012-11-05.

260 Ellis Sandoz, Political Sermons of the American Founding Era: 1730-1805, 2 vols, Foreword by Ellis Sandoz (2nd ed. Indianapolis: Liberty Fund, 1998). Vol. 1. Chapter: 12: Samuel Sherwood, SCRIPTURAL INSTRUCTIONS TO CIVIL RULERS Accessed from http://oll.libertyfund.org/title/816/69251 on 2012-11-05.

261 Ellis Sandoz, Political Sermons of the American Founding Era: 1730-1805, 2 vols, Foreword by Ellis Sandoz (2nd ed. Indianapolis: Liberty Fund, 1998). Vol. 1. Chapter: 15: Moses Mather, AMERICA'S APPEAL TO THE IMPARTIAL WORLD Accessed from http://oll.libertyfund.org/title/816/69260 on 2012-11-05.

262 Ibid, Thornton, *The Pulpit of the American Revolution,* pp. 305-06.

263 Ibid, Moore, Frank, *The Patriot Preachers of the American Revolution*, pp. 258-288.

264 Ellis Sandoz, Political Sermons of the American Founding Era: 1730-1805, 2 vols, Foreword by Ellis Sandoz (2nd ed. Indianapolis: Liberty Fund, 1998). Vol. 1. Chapter: 32: Samuel Langdon, THE REPUBLIC OF THE ISRAELITES AN EXAMPLE TO THE AMERICAN STATES Accessed from http://oll.libertyfund.org/title/816/69313 on 2012-11-05.

265 Ellis Sandoz, Political Sermons of the American Founding Era: 1730-1805, 2 vols, Foreword by Ellis Sandoz (2nd ed. Indianapolis: Liberty Fund, 1998). Vol. 2. Chapter: 46: Stephen Peabody, SERMON BEFORE THE GENERAL COURT OF NEW HAMPSHIRE AT THE ANNUAL ELECTION, Accessed from http://oll.libertyfund.org/title/817/69448 on 2012-06-12.

266 Ellis Sandoz, Political Sermons of the American Founding Era: 1730-1805, 2 vols, Foreword by Ellis Sandoz (2nd ed. Indianapolis: Liberty Fund, 1998). Vol. 1. Chapter: 21: Samuel Cooper, A SERMON ON THE DAY OF THE COMMENCEMENT OF THE CONSTITUTION Accessed from http://oll.libertyfund.org/title/816/69278 on 2012-11-05.

267 Ibid, Moore, Frank, *The Patriot Preachers of the American Revolution,* pp. 49-73.

268 Ellis Sandoz, Political Sermons of the American Founding Era: 1730-1805, 2 vols, Foreword by Ellis Sandoz (2nd ed. Indianapolis: Liberty Fund, 1998). Vol. 1. Chapter: 15: Moses Mather, AMERICA'S APPEAL TO THE IMPARTIAL WORLD, Accessed from http://oll.libertyfund.org/title/816/69260 on 2012-06-12.

269 Ibid, Thornton, *The Pulpit of the American Revolution,* p. 279.

270 Ellis Sandoz, Political Sermons of the American Founding Era: 1730-1805, 2 vols, Foreword by Ellis Sandoz (2nd ed. Indianapolis: Liberty Fund, 1998). Vol. 1. Chapter: 19: Abraham Keteltas, GOD ARISING AND PLEADING HIS PEOPLE'S CAUSE, Accessed from http://oll.libertyfund.org/title/816/69274 on 2012-06-12.

271 Ibid, Thornton, *The Pulpit of the American Revolution,* pp. 280-81.

272 Ellis Sandoz, Political Sermons of the American Founding Era: 1730-1805, 2 vols, Foreword by Ellis Sandoz (2nd ed. Indianapolis: Liberty

Fund, 1998). Vol. 2. Chapter: 41: Enos Hitchcock, AN ORATION IN COMMEMORATION OF THE INDEPENDENCE OF THE UNITED STATES OF AMERICA, Accessed from http://oll.libertyfund.org/title/817/69409 on 2012-06-12.

273 Ellis Sandoz, Political Sermons of the American Founding Era: 1730-1805, 2 vols, Foreword by Ellis Sandoz (2nd ed. Indianapolis: Liberty Fund, 1998). Vol. 2. Chapter: 45: Bishop James Madison, MANIFESTATIONS OF THE BENEFICENCE OF DIVINE PROVIDENCE TOWARDS AMERICA, Accessed from http://oll.libertyfund.org/title/817/69446 on 2012-06-12.

274 Ellis Sandoz, Political Sermons of the American Founding Era: 1730-1805, 2 vols, Foreword by Ellis Sandoz (2nd ed. Indianapolis: Liberty Fund, 1998). Vol. 1. Chapter: 26: Samuel McClintock, A SERMON ON OCCASION OF THE COMMENCEMENT OF THE NEW-HAMPSHIRE CONSTITUTION, Accessed from http://oll.libertyfund.org/title/816/69301 on 2012-06-12.

275 Ibid, Thornton, *The Pulpit of the American Revolution*, p. 435.

276 Ellis Sandoz, Political Sermons of the American Founding Era: 1730-1805, 2 vols, Foreword by Ellis Sandoz (2nd ed. Indianapolis: Liberty Fund, 1998). Vol. 1. Chapter: 12: Samuel Sherwood, SCRIPTURAL INSTRUCTIONS TO CIVIL RULERS Accessed from http://oll.libertyfund.org/title/816/69251 on 2012-11-05.

277 Ibid, Thornton, *The Pulpit of the American Revolution,* p. 341.

278 Ibid, Thornton, *The Pulpit of the American Revolution,* p. 334.

279 Ibid, Thornton, *The Pulpit of the American Revolution,* p. 392.

280 Ellis Sandoz, Political Sermons of the American Founding Era: 1730-1805, 2 vols, Foreword by Ellis Sandoz (2nd ed. Indianapolis: Liberty Fund, 1998). Vol. 1. Chapter: 21: Samuel Cooper, A SERMON ON THE DAY OF THE COMMENCEMENT OF THE CONSTITUTION Accessed from http://oll.libertyfund.org/title/816/69278 on 2012-11-05.

281 Ellis Sandoz, Political Sermons of the American Founding Era: 1730-1805, 2 vols, Foreword by Ellis Sandoz (2nd ed. Indianapolis: Liberty Fund, 1998). Vol. 1. Chapter: 26: Samuel McClintock, A SERMON ON OCCASION OF THE COMMENCEMENT OF THE NEW-

HAMPSHIRE CONSTITUTION, Accessed from http://oll.libertyfund.org/title/816/69301 on 2012-11-05.

282 Ellis Sandoz, Political Sermons of the American Founding Era: 1730-1805, 2 vols, Foreword by Ellis Sandoz (2nd ed. Indianapolis: Liberty Fund, 1998). Vol. 1. Chapter: 31: Elizur Goodrich, THE PRINCIPLES OF CIVIL UNION AND HAPPINESS CONSIDERED AND RECOMMENDED Accessed from http://oll.libertyfund.org/title/816/69311 on 2012-11-05.

283 Ellis Sandoz, Political Sermons of the American Founding Era: 1730-1805, 2 vols, Foreword by Ellis Sandoz (2nd ed. Indianapolis: Liberty Fund, 1998). Vol. 1. Chapter: 32: Samuel Langdon, THE REPUBLIC OF THE ISRAELITES AN EXAMPLE TO THE AMERICAN STATES Accessed from http://oll.libertyfund.org/title/816/69313 on 2012-11-05.

284 Ellis Sandoz, Political Sermons of the American Founding Era: 1730-1805, 2 vols, Foreword by Ellis Sandoz (2nd ed. Indianapolis: Liberty Fund, 1998). Vol. 2. Chapter: 41: Enos Hitchcock, AN ORATION IN COMMEMORATION OF THE INDEPENDENCE OF THE UNITED STATES OF AMERICA, Accessed from http://oll.libertyfund.org/title/817/69409 on 2012-11-05.

285 Ellis Sandoz, Political Sermons of the American Founding Era: 1730-1805, 2 vols, Foreword by Ellis Sandoz (2nd ed. Indianapolis: Liberty Fund, 1998). Vol. 2. Chapter: 46: Stephen Peabody, SERMON BEFORE THE GENERAL COURT OF NEW HAMPSHIRE AT THE ANNUAL ELECTION Accessed from http://oll.libertyfund.org/title/817/69448 on 2012-11-05.

286 Ellis Sandoz, Political Sermons of the American Founding Era: 1730-1805, 2 vols, Foreword by Ellis Sandoz (2nd ed. Indianapolis: Liberty Fund, 1998). Vol. 2. Chapter: 50: John Smalley, ON THE EVILS OF A WEAK GOVERNMENT Accessed from http://oll.libertyfund.org/title/817/69456 on 2012-11-05.

287 Ellis Sandoz, Political Sermons of the American Founding Era: 1730-1805, 2 vols, Foreword by Ellis Sandoz (2nd ed. Indianapolis: Liberty Fund, 1998). Vol. 1. Chapter: 28: Samuel Wales, THE DANGERS OF OUR NATIONAL PROSPERITY; AND THE WAY TO AVOID THEM Accessed from http://oll.libertyfund.org/title/816/69305 on 2012-11-05.

288 Ellis Sandoz, Political Sermons of the American Founding Era: 1730-1805, 2 vols, Foreword by Ellis Sandoz (2nd ed. Indianapolis: Liberty Fund, 1998). Vol. 2. Chapter: 50: John Smalley, ON THE EVILS OF A WEAK GOVERNMENT Accessed from http://oll.libertyfund.org/title/817/69456 on 2012-11-05.

289 Ellis Sandoz, Political Sermons of the American Founding Era: 1730-1805, 2 vols, Foreword by Ellis Sandoz (2nd ed. Indianapolis: Liberty Fund, 1998). Vol. 1. Chapter: 17: John Witherspoon, THE DOMINION OF PROVIDENCE OVER THE PASSIONS OF MEN Accessed from http://oll.libertyfund.org/title/816/69270 on 2012-11-05.

290 Ellis Sandoz, Political Sermons of the American Founding Era: 1730-1805, 2 vols, Foreword by Ellis Sandoz (2nd ed. Indianapolis: Liberty Fund, 1998). Vol. 1. Chapter: 21: Samuel Cooper, A SERMON ON THE DAY OF THE COMMENCEMENT OF THE CONSTITUTION Accessed from http://oll.libertyfund.org/title/816/69278 on 2012-11-05.

291 Ibid, Baldwin, Alice, *The New England Clergy and the American Revolution,* chapter 3, p. 40.

292 Ibid, Baldwin, Alice, *The New England Clergy and the American Revolution,* p. 40.

293 Ibid, Moore, Frank, *The Patriot Preachers of the American Revolution,* pp. 57-58.

294 Ibid, Thornton, *The Pulpit of the American Revolution,* pp. 275-76.

295 Ellis Sandoz, Political Sermons of the American Founding Era: 1730-1805, 2 vols, Foreword by Ellis Sandoz (2nd ed. Indianapolis: Liberty Fund, 1998). Vol. 1. Chapter: 31: Elizur Goodrich, *The Principles Of Civil Union And Happiness Considered And Recommended,* Accessed from http://oll.libertyfund.org/title/816/69311 on 2012-05-09

296 Jay, John, *The Correspondence and Public Papers of John Jay (1794-1826),* ed. Henry P. Johnston, a.m. (New York: G.P. Putnam's Sons, 1890-93). Vol. 4, p. 393, to John Murray, Jr. on October 12, 1816, Online Library of Liberty, Liberty Fund, Inc., oll.libertyfund.org.

297 Ellis Sandoz, Political Sermons of the American Founding Era: 1730-1805, 2 vols, Foreword by Ellis Sandoz (2nd ed. Indianapolis: Liberty Fund, 1998). Vol. 1. Chapter: 5: Charles Chauncy, *Civil Magistrates Must*

Be Just, Ruling In The Fear Of God, Accessed from http://oll.libertyfund.org/title/816/69228 on 2012-05-08.

298 Accessed from http://www.belcherfoundation.org/civil_government.htm on 5/8/12.

299 Ellis Sandoz, Political Sermons of the American Founding Era: 1730-1805, 2 vols, Foreword by Ellis Sandoz (2nd ed. Indianapolis: Liberty Fund, 1998). Vol. 1. Chapter: 12: Samuel Sherwood, SCRIPTURAL INSTRUCTIONS TO CIVIL RULERS Accessed from http://oll.libertyfund.org/title/816/69251 on 2012-11-05.

300 Hyneman, Charles S., American Political Writing During the Founding Era: 1760-1805, ed. Charles S. Hyneman and Donald Lutz (Indianapolis: Liberty Fund, 1983). 2 vols. Volume 1. Chapter: [33]: Samuel West 1730-1807: On the Right to Rebel Against Governors (Election Day Sermon), Accessed from http://oll.libertyfund.org/title/2066/188670 on 2012-05-08.

301 Ibid, Thornton, *The Pulpit of the American Revolution,* pp. 370-73.

302 Accessed from www.belcherfoundation.org/samuel%20cooper%20sermon%20on%20constitution.pdf, on 5/8/12.

303 Ibid, Thornton, *The Pulpit of the American Revolution,* p. 490.

304 Ellis Sandoz, Political Sermons of the American Founding Era: 1730-1805, 2 vols, Foreword by Ellis Sandoz (2nd ed. Indianapolis: Liberty Fund, 1998). Vol. 1. Chapter: 31: Elizur Goodrich, *The Principles Of Civil Union And Happiness Considered And Recommended,* Accessed from http://oll.libertyfund.org/title/816/69311 on 2012-05-09.

305 Ellis Sandoz, Political Sermons of the American Founding Era: 1730-1805, 2 vols, Foreword by Ellis Sandoz (2nd ed. Indianapolis: Liberty Fund, 1998). Vol. 1. Chapter: 5: Charles Chauncy, *Civil Magistrates Must Be Just, Ruling In The Fear Of God*, Accessed from http://oll.libertyfund.org/title/816/69228 on 2012-05-08.

306 Ellis Sandoz, Political Sermons of the American Founding Era: 1730-1805, 2 vols, Foreword by Ellis Sandoz (2nd ed. Indianapolis: Liberty Fund, 1998). Vol. 1. Chapter: 12: Samuel Sherwood, *Scriptural Instructions To Cicil Rulers,* Accessed from http://oll.libertyfund.org/title/816/69251, on 2012-05-09.

307 Hyneman, Charles S., American Political Writing During the Founding Era: 1760-1805, ed. Charles S. Hyneman and Donald Lutz (Indianapolis: Liberty Fund, 1983). 2 vols. Volume 1. Chapter: [33]: Samuel West 1730-1807: On the Right to Rebel Against Governors (Election Day Sermon), Accessed from http://oll.libertyfund.org/title/2066/188670 on 2012-05-08.

308 Ellis Sandoz, Political Sermons of the American Founding Era: 1730-1805, 2 vols, Foreword by Ellis Sandoz (2nd ed. Indianapolis: Liberty Fund, 1998). Vol. 2. Chapter: 50: John Smalley, *On The Evils Of A Weak Government,* Accessed from http://oll.libertyfund.org/title/817/69456 on 2012-05-09.

309 Ibid, Thornton, *The Pulpit of the American Revolution,* p. 376, 380-81.

310 Ellis Sandoz, Political Sermons of the American Founding Era: 1730-1805, 2 vols, Foreword by Ellis Sandoz (2nd ed. Indianapolis: Liberty Fund, 1998). Vol. 1. Chapter: 12: Samuel Sherwood, *Scriptural Instructions To Cicil Rulers,* Accessed from http://oll.libertyfund.org/title/816/69251, on 2012-05-09.

311 Ibid, Thornton, *The Pulpit of the American Revolution,* p. 373.

312 Ellis Sandoz, Political Sermons of the American Founding Era: 1730-1805, 2 vols, Foreword by Ellis Sandoz (2nd ed. Indianapolis: Liberty Fund, 1998). Vol. 1. Chapter: 31: Elizur Goodrich, *The Principles Of Civil Union And Happiness Considered And Recommended,* Accessed from http://oll.libertyfund.org/title/816/69311 on 2012-05-09.

313 Ellis Sandoz, Political Sermons of the American Founding Era: 1730-1805, 2 vols, Foreword by Ellis Sandoz (2nd ed. Indianapolis: Liberty Fund, 1998). Vol. 2. Chapter: 46: Stephen Peabody, *Sermon Before The General Court Of New Hampshire At The Annual Election*, Accessed from http://oll.libertyfund.org/title/817/69448 on 2012-05-09.

314 Ibid, Thornton, *The Pulpit of the American Revolution,* pp. 165-66.

315 Ellis Sandoz, Political Sermons of the American Founding Era: 1730-1805, 2 vols, Foreword by Ellis Sandoz (2nd ed. Indianapolis: Liberty Fund, 1998). Vol. 1. Chapter: 12: Samuel Sherwood, *Scriptural Instructions To Cicil Rulers,* Accessed from http://oll.libertyfund.org/title/816/69251, on 2012-05-09.

316 Ellis Sandoz, Political Sermons of the American Founding Era: 1730-1805, 2 vols, Foreword by Ellis Sandoz (2nd ed. Indianapolis: Liberty Fund, 1998). Vol. 1. Chapter: 31: Elizur Goodrich, *The Principles Of Civil Union And Happiness Considered And Recommended,* Accessed from http://oll.libertyfund.org/title/816/69311 on 2012-05-09.

317 Ellis Sandoz, Political Sermons of the American Founding Era: 1730-1805, 2 vols, Foreword by Ellis Sandoz (2nd ed. Indianapolis: Liberty Fund, 1998). Vol. 1. Chapter: 32: Samuel Langdon, THE REPUBLIC OF THE ISRAELITES AN EXAMPLE TO THE AMERICAN STATES, Accessed from http://oll.libertyfund.org/title/816/69313 on 2012-11-05.

318 Ellis Sandoz, Political Sermons of the American Founding Era: 1730-1805, 2 vols, Foreword by Ellis Sandoz (2nd ed. Indianapolis: Liberty Fund, 1998). Vol. 1. Chapter: 5: Charles Chauncy, *Civil Magistrates Must Be Just, Ruling In The Fear Of God,* Accessed from http://oll.libertyfund.org/title/816/69228 on 2012-05-08.

319 Ellis Sandoz, Political Sermons of the American Founding Era: 1730-1805, 2 vols, Foreword by Ellis Sandoz (2nd ed. Indianapolis: Liberty Fund, 1998). Vol. 1. Chapter: 12: Samuel Sherwood, *Scriptural Instructions To Cicil Rulers,* Accessed from http://oll.libertyfund.org/title/816/69251, on 2012-05-09.

320 Ellis Sandoz, Political Sermons of the American Founding Era: 1730-1805, 2 vols, Foreword by Ellis Sandoz (2nd ed. Indianapolis: Liberty Fund, 1998). Vol. 1. Chapter: 31: Elizur Goodrich, *The Principles Of Civil Union And Happiness Considered And Recommended,* Accessed from http://oll.libertyfund.org/title/816/69311 on 2012-05-09.

321 Ibid, Headley, *The Chaplains and Clergy of the Revolution,* author's preface, pp. 5-6.

322 Ellis Sandoz, Political Sermons of the American Founding Era: 1730-1805, 2 vols, Foreword by Ellis Sandoz (2nd ed. Indianapolis: Liberty Fund, 1998). Vol. 1. Chapter: 29: Joseph Lathrop, A SERMON ON A DAY APPOINTED FOR PUBLICK THANKSGIVING, Accessed from http://oll.libertyfund.org/title/816/69307 on 2012-05-15.

323 Ibid, Thornton, *The Pulpit of the American Revolution,* pp. 256-57.

324 Ibid, Thornton, *The Pulpit of the American Revolution,* pp. 195-96.

325 Ellis Sandoz, Political Sermons of the American Founding Era: 1730-1805, 2 vols, Foreword by Ellis Sandoz (2nd ed. Indianapolis: Liberty Fund, 1998). Vol. 1. Chapter: 12: Samuel Sherwood, *Scriptural Instructions To Civil Rulers*, Accessed from http://oll.libertyfund.org/title/816/69251 on 2012-05-10.

326 Ibid, Thornton, *The Pulpit of the American Revolution*, p. 225.

327 Ibid, Moore, Frank, *The Patriot Preachers of the American Revolution*, p. 142.

328 Ibid, Moore, Frank, *The Patriot Preachers of the American Revolution*, p. 184.

329 Ibid, Adams, James, *Yankee Doodle Went To Church*, p. 112.

330 Ibid, Adams, James, *Yankee Doodle Went To Church*, pp. 66,112-113.

331 Ibid, Adams, James, *Yankee Doodle Went To Church*, pp. 112,114.

332 Ibid, Thornton, *The Pulpit of the American Revolution*, pp. 242-43,247.

333 Ibid, Thornton, *The Pulpit of the American Revolution*, pp. 311,321-22.

334 Ellis Sandoz, Political Sermons of the American Founding Era: 1730-1805, 2 vols, Foreword by Ellis Sandoz (2nd ed. Indianapolis: Liberty Fund, 1998). Vol. 1. Chapter: 18: John Fletcher, *The Bible And The Sword*, Accessed from http://oll.libertyfund.org/title/816/69272 on 2012-05-11.

335 Ellis Sandoz, Political Sermons of the American Founding Era: 1730-1805, 2 vols, Foreword by Ellis Sandoz (2nd ed. Indianapolis: Liberty Fund, 1998). Vol. 1. Chapter: 22: Henry Cumings, A SERMON PREACHED AT LEXINGTON ON THE 19th OF APRIL, Accessed from http://oll.libertyfund.org/title/816/69280 on 2012-11-05.

336 Ellis Sandoz, Political Sermons of the American Founding Era: 1730-1805, 2 vols, Foreword by Ellis Sandoz (2nd ed. Indianapolis: Liberty Fund, 1998). Vol. 1. Chapter: 26: Samuel McClintock, *A Sermon On Occasion Of The Commencement Of The New Hampshire Constitution* Accessed from http://oll.libertyfund.org/title/816/69301 on 2012-05-14.

337 Adams, John, The Works of John Adams, Second President of the United States: with a Life of the Author, Notes and Illustrations, by his Grandson Charles Francis Adams (Boston: Little, Brown and Co., 1856). 10 volumes. Vol. 3. Chapter: ON SELF-DELUSION. NO. II. Accessed from http://oll.libertyfund.org/title/2101/159682 on 2012-05-14.

338 Adams, Samuel, *The Writings of Samuel Adams*, Harry Alonzo Cushing, editor (New York: G.P. Putnam's Sons, 1908), Vol. IV, p. 253, in the *Boston Gazette* on April 16, 1781, accessed from books.google.com, 5/13/12.

339 Webster, Noah, "The Schoolmaster of the Nation" & the author of *Webster's Dictionary*

Noah Webster, *Letters to a Young Gentleman Commencing His Education to which is subjoined a Brief History of the United States* (New Haven: S. Converse, 1823), pp. 18, 19, accessed from books.google.com on 5/13/12.

340 Webster, Daniel, *The Works of Daniel Webster* (Boston: Little, Brown, and Company, 1853), Vol. II, p. 108, from remarks made at a public reception by the ladies of Richmond, Virginia, on October 5, 1840, accessed from archive.org /stream/worksofdanielweb030653 on 5/13/12.

341 Ellis Sandoz, Political Sermons of the American Founding Era: 1730-1805, 2 vols, Foreword by Ellis Sandoz (2nd ed. Indianapolis: Liberty Fund, 1998). Vol. 1. Chapter: 12: Samuel Sherwood, *Scriptural Instructions To Cicil Rulers,* Accessed from http://oll.libertyfund.org/title/816/69251, on 2012-05-09.

342 Ibid, Moore, Frank, *The Patriot Preachers of the American Revolution,* p. 287.

343 Ibid, Thornton, *The Pulpit of the American Revolution,* p. 386.

344 Ellis Sandoz, Political Sermons of the American Founding Era: 1730-1805, 2 vols, Foreword by Ellis Sandoz (2nd ed. Indianapolis: Liberty Fund, 1998). Vol. 1. Chapter: 31: Elizur Goodrich, *The Principles Of Civil Union And Happiness Considered And Recommended,* Accessed from http://oll.libertyfund.org/title/816/69311 on 2012-05-09.

345 Ellis Sandoz, Political Sermons of the American Founding Era: 1730-1805, 2 vols, Foreword by Ellis Sandoz (2nd ed. Indianapolis: Liberty Fund, 1998). Vol. 1. Chapter: 32: Samuel Langdon, THE REPUBLIC OF THE ISRAELITES AN EXAMPLE TO THE AMERICAN STATES Accessed from http://oll.libertyfund.org/title/816/69313 on 2012-05-15.

346 Ellis Sandoz, Political Sermons of the American Founding Era: 1730-1805, 2 vols, Foreword by Ellis Sandoz (2nd ed. Indianapolis: Liberty Fund, 1998). Vol. 2. Chapter: 42: Jonathan Edwards, Jr., THE NECESSITY OF THE BELIEF OF CHRISTIANITY, Accessed from http://oll.liberty-fund.org/title/817/69411 on 2012-05-15.

347 Ellis Sandoz, Political Sermons of the American Founding Era: 1730-1805, 2 vols, Foreword by Ellis Sandoz (2nd ed. Indianapolis: Liberty Fund, 1998). Vol. 2. Chapter: 46: Stephen Peabody, SERMON BEFORE THE GENERAL COURT OF NEW HAMPSHIRE AT THE ANNUAL ELECTION, Accessed from http://oll.libertyfund.org/title/817/69448 on 2012-05-15.

348 Ellis Sandoz, Political Sermons of the American Founding Era: 1730-1805, 2 vols, Foreword by Ellis Sandoz (2nd ed. Indianapolis: Liberty Fund, 1998). Vol. 2. Chapter: 50: John Smalley, *On The Evils Of A Weak Government,* Accessed from http://oll.libertyfund.org/title/817/69456 on 2012-05-09.

349 Linn, William, 1762-1808. *Serious Considerations on the Election of a President: Addressed to the Citizens of the United States.* New-York: Printed and sold by John Furman, at his blank, stamp, and stationary shop, opposite the City hall, 1800, accessed from http://candst.tripod.com/pol1800.htm, cited 10/6/2011.

350 Ellis Sandoz, Political Sermons of the American Founding Era: 1730-1805, 2 vols, Foreword by Ellis Sandoz (2nd ed. Indianapolis: Liberty Fund, 1998). Vol. 2. Chapter: 51: John Mitchell Mason, THE VOICE OF WARNING TO CHRISTIANS, Accessed from http://oll.libertyfund.org/title/817/69458 on 2012-05-15.

351 *A Secret Life: The Sex, Lies, and Scandal of Grover Cleveland's Presidency*, 2011, Chapter 12, accessed from http://books.google.com, cited 10/6/2011.

352 Ellis Sandoz, Political Sermons of the American Founding Era: 1730-1805, 2 vols, Foreword by Ellis Sandoz (2nd ed. Indianapolis: Liberty Fund, 1998). Vol. 2. Chapter: 43: David Osgood, THE WONDERFUL WORKS OF GOD ARE TO BE REMEMBERED Accessed from http://oll.libertyfund.org/title/817/69413 on 2012-11-05.

353 Ibid, Thornton, *The Pulpit of the American Revolution,* pp. 140-142, 146.

354 Ibid, Thornton, *The Pulpit of the American Revolution,* p. 214, 225-226.

355 Ibid, Thornton, *The Pulpit of the American Revolution,* pp. 255-256.

356 Ellis Sandoz, Political Sermons of the American Founding Era: 1730-1805, 2 vols, Foreword by Ellis Sandoz (2nd ed. Indianapolis: Liberty Fund, 1998). Vol. 1. Chapter: 15: Moses Mather, AMERICA'S APPEAL

TO THE IMPARTIAL WORLD, Accessed from http://oll.libertyfund.org/title/816/69260 on 2012-05-16.

357 Ibid, Thornton, *The Pulpit of the American Revolution,* pp. 256-257.

358 Ellis Sandoz, Political Sermons of the American Founding Era: 1730-1805, 2 vols, Foreword by Ellis Sandoz (2nd ed. Indianapolis: Liberty Fund, 1998). Vol. 1. Chapter: 17: John Witherspoon, THE DOMINION OF PROVIDENCE OVER THE PASSIONS OF MEN, Accessed from http://oll.libertyfund.org/title/816/69270 on 2012-05-16.

359 Ellis Sandoz, Political Sermons of the American Founding Era: 1730-1805, 2 vols, Foreword by Ellis Sandoz (2nd ed. Indianapolis: Liberty Fund, 1998). Vol. 1. Chapter: 20: Jacob Cushing, DIVINE JUDGMENTS UPON TYRANTS Accessed from http://oll.libertyfund.org/title/816/69276 on 2012-11-05.

360 Ellis Sandoz, Political Sermons of the American Founding Era: 1730-1805, 2 vols, Foreword by Ellis Sandoz (2nd ed. Indianapolis: Liberty Fund, 1998). Vol. 1. Chapter: 22: Henry Cumings, A SERMON PREACHED AT LEXINGTON ON THE 19 th OF APRIL, Accessed from http://oll.libertyfund.org/title/816/69280 on 2012-05-16.

361 Ellis Sandoz, Political Sermons of the American Founding Era: 1730-1805, 2 vols, Foreword by Ellis Sandoz (2nd ed. Indianapolis: Liberty Fund, 1998). Vol. 1. Chapter: 21: Samuel Cooper, A SERMON ON THE DAY OF THE COMMENCEMENT OF THE CONSTITUTION, Accessed from http://oll.libertyfund.org/title/816/69278 on 2012-05-31.

362 Ibid, Thornton, *The Pulpit of the American Revolution,* pp. 383-385.

363 *The Writings of George Washington, from the Original Manuscript Sources 1749-1799,* John Clement Fitzpatrick, ed. (Washington, D.C.: United States Government Printing Office, 1931-1944), vol. 26, 2-6-1783 Letter to Maj. Gen. Nathaniel Greene, accessed from *George Washington's Sacred Fire,* Peter A. Lillback (Dickinson Press, 2006), p. 174.

364 Federer, William, *American Minute,* January 16, 2006, accessed from *George Washington's Sacred Fire,* p. 175.

365 Federer, William, *American Minute,* January 16, 2006, accessed from *George Washington's Sacred Fire,* p. 175.

366 Federer, William, *American Minute,* January 16, 2006, accessed from *George Washington's Sacred Fire,* p. 175.

367 Ibid, Lillback, Peter, A., *Sacred Fire,* p. 173.

368 Ibid, Lillback, Peter, A., *Sacred Fire,* p. 173.

369 Ibid, Lillback, Peter, A., *Sacred Fire,* p. 177.

370 Ibid, Lillback, Peter, A., *Sacred Fire,* p. 178.

371 Ellis Sandoz, Political Sermons of the American Founding Era: 1730-1805, 2 vols, Foreword by Ellis Sandoz (2nd ed. Indianapolis: Liberty Fund, 1998). Vol. 1. Chapter: 25: George Duffield, A SERMON PREACE ON A DAY OF THANKSGIVING, Accessed from http://oll.libertyfund.org/title/816/69299 on 2012-05-16.

372 Ellis Sandoz, Political Sermons of the American Founding Era: 1730-1805, 2 vols, Foreword by Ellis Sandoz (2nd ed. Indianapolis: Liberty Fund, 1998). Vol. 1. Chapter: 26, A SERMON ON OCCASION OF THE COMMENCEMENT OF THE NEW-HAMPSHIRE CONSTITUTION Accessed from http://oll.libertyfund.org/title/816/69301 on 2012-11-05.

373 Ellis Sandoz, Political Sermons of the American Founding Era: 1730-1805, 2 vols, Foreword by Ellis Sandoz (2nd ed. Indianapolis: Liberty Fund, 1998). Vol. 2. Chapter: 46: Stephen Peabody, SERMON BEFORE THE GENERAL COURT OF NEW HAMPSHIRE AT THE ANNUAL ELECTION, Accessed from http://oll.libertyfund.org/title/817/69448 on 2012-05-16.

374 *Branch Ministries v. Rossotti,* 211 F.3d 137 (D.C. Cir. 2000), accessed from "Church's Loss Of Tax Exempt Status Letter Turns Out To Be A Victory For Churches," Mathew D. Staver, 2000, www.lc.org, cited 7/3/12.

375 Ibid, *Branch Ministries v. Rossotti.*

376 Staver, Matthew, "Church's Loss Of Tax Exempt Status Letter Turns Out To Be A Victory For Churches," 2000, www.lc.org, cited 7/3/12.

377 *Lemon v. Krutzman*, U.S. Supreme Court, 403 U.S. 602 (1971), Chief Justice Warren Burger, section V.

378 Ibid, Thornton, *The Pulpit of the American Revolution,* Introduction, p. 23.

379 Ibid, Baldwin, Alice, *The New England Clergy and the American Revolution,* p. 134.

380 Coffman, Elesha, "Of Church, State, and Taxes," 2008, Christian History, Christianhistory.net, accessed from www.christianitytoday.com/ch/news/2002/may17.html, cited 6/29/12.

381 H.R. Committee on Ways and Means, *Hearings on Forty Topics Pertaining to the General Revision of the Internal Revenue Code,* 83d Congress 1576 (August 11, 1953).

382 "Churches are Tax Exempt as a Matter of Constitutional Right," accessed from www.opposingviews.com/arguments/churches-are-tax-exempt-as-a-matter-of-constitutional-right.

383 *McCulloch v. Maryland,* 17 U.S. 327 (1819).

384 Ibid, *McCulloch v. Maryland,* p. 427.

385 Stanley, Erik, "ERIK STANLEY: Tax exemption churches' right," September 27, 2008, accessed from oldsite.alliancedefensefund.org/userdocs/2008-09-27MontgomeryAdvertiser.pdf, cited 7/4/12.

386 Internal Revenue Service Tax Code, 1996, Volume I:856.

387 100 Cong. Rec. 9604 (1954).

388 Ibid, Stanley, Erik.

389 Ibid, Thornton, *The Pulpit of the American Revolution,* p. 161.

390 "Old Swamp Church and the first U.S. Speaker of the House," The Bowery Boys, New York City History, January 7, 2011, accessed from theboweryboys.blogspot.com/2011/01/old-swamp-church-and-first-us-speaker.html, cited 12/12/12.

391 *Luther League Review: 1914-1915, Volumes 27-28*, Vol XXVII, Dec. 1914, No. 12, p. 13, accessed from books.google.com, cited 12/11/12, The Lutherans of New York, their story and their problems (New York: The Petersfield Press, 1918), George Unangst Wenner, pp. 12,14, accessed from books.google.com, cited 12/11/12, *The Pennsylvania-German*, Volumes 3-4, Philip Columbus Croll, Henry Addison Schuler, Howard Wiegner Kriebel, Vol. III, April 1902, No. 2, pp. 54-55, accessed from books.google.com, cited 12/11/12, *The Pennsylvania Magazine of History and Biography*

(Philadelphia: The Historical Society of Pennsylvania, 1889), Volume 13, pp. 189-191, accessed from books.google.com, cited 12/11/12.

392 Ibid, "Old Swamp Church and the first U.S. Speaker of the House."

393 Barton, David, April 28, 2010, interview by Glenn Beck, The Glenn Beck program, www.foxnews.com/story/0,2933,591785,00.html.

394 Ibid, Moore, Frank, *The Patriot Preachers of the American Revolution,* pp. 359-61.

395 *The Speeches Of The Right Honourable John Philpot Curran,* (Dublin: Printed by Jay Stockdale And Sons, 1808), "Speech Of John Philpot Curran, Esq.; On The Right Of Election Of Lord Mayor Of The City Of Dublin, Delivered Before The Lord Lieutenant And Privy Council Of Ireland, 1790," p. 5, accessed from books.google.com/books, cited 6/15/12.

396 Whitman, Wilson, *Jefferson's Letters* (Eau Claire, Wisconsin: E.M. Hale and Company, 1948), Thomas Jefferson letter to William S. Smith, November 13, 1787, p. 83

397 Augustine, Confessions I,1,i, *The Journey Toward God In Augustine's Confessions, Books I-VI,* Carl G. Vaught (Albany: State University of New York Press, 2003), p. 23, accessed from books.google.com, cited 6/16/12.

398 *Pensees 10.148,* cited from *Just A Thought ... Manna For The Mind,* Ed Cook (Woodinville, Washington: August Ink Books, 2011) p. 148, accessed from books.google.com, cited 6/16/12.

399 Ellis Sandoz, Political Sermons of the American Founding Era: 1730-1805, 2 vols, Foreword by Ellis Sandoz (2nd ed. Indianapolis: Liberty Fund, 1998). Vol. 1. Chapter: 28: Samuel Wales, THE DANGERS OF OUR NATIONAL PROSPERITY; AND THE WAY TO AVOID THEM, Accessed from http://oll.libertyfund.org/title/816/69305 on 2012-06-17.

400 Ellis Sandoz, Political Sermons of the American Founding Era: 1730-1805, 2 vols, Foreword by Ellis Sandoz (2nd ed. Indianapolis: Liberty Fund, 1998). Vol. 2. Chapter: 54: William Emerson, AN ORATION IN COMMEMORATION OF THE ANNIVERSARY OF AMERICAN INDEPENDENCE, Accessed from http://oll.libertyfund.org/title/817/69467 on 2012-11-05.

401 Obama, Barack, *The Audacity of Hope: Thoughts on Reclaiming the American Dream* (Crown Publishing Group, 2006), p. 90, accessed from books.google.com, cited 6/23/12.

402 Souter, Douglas, Justice, *Lee v. Weisman*, concurring opinion, June 24, 1992, Section II, C, accessed from Cornell University Law School, Legal Information Institute, www.law.cornell.edu/supct/html/historics/USSC_CR_0505_0577_ZC1.html, cited 6/23/12.

403 Ibid, Moore, Frank, *The Patriot Preachers of the American Revolution,* p. 105.

404 Metaxas, Eric, *Bonhoeffer: Pastor, Martyr, Prophet, Spy* (Thomas Nelson, Inc., 2010)

405 Federer, William, *America's God and Country: Encyclopedia of Quotations*, 2000, p. 235, Finney, Charles G., Rev., "Lectures On Revivals of Religion," Lecture XV, "Hindrances to Revivals," accessed from http://saynsumthn.wordpress.com, cited 10/5/2011.

406 Accessed from constitution.org/lincoln/lyceum.htm.

407 Ibid, Moore, Frank, *The Patriot Preachers of the American Revolution,* p. 185.

408 Ellis Sandoz, Political Sermons of the American Founding Era: 1730-1805, 2 vols, Foreword by Ellis Sandoz (2nd ed. Indianapolis: Liberty Fund, 1998). Vol. 1. Chapter: 22: Henry Cumings, A SERMON PREACHED AT LEXINGTON ON THE 19th OF APRIL Accessed from http://oll.libertyfund.org/title/816/69280 on 2012-11-05.

409 "Only One Life," C.T. Studd.

410 Ibid, Thornton, *The Pulpit of the American Revolution,* pp. 395-96.

411 Ibid, Headley, Joel, *The Chaplains and Clergy of the Revolution*, p. 39.

412 *Collections Of The Historical Collections Of The Historical Society Of Pennsylvania,* Vol. I (PHILADELPHIA: John Pennington, No. 10 South Fifth Street, Henry C. Baird, No. 27 South Sixth Street, 1853), p. 70-72, accessed from http://www.archive.org, cited 4/3/13, *Magazine of American History* (30 Lafayette Place, New York City), Martha J. Lamb, editor, Vol. XIII, January-June 1885, March 1885, No. 3, p. 281, accessed from http://books.google.com, cited 4/4/13, Moore, Frank, *The Civil War In Song and Story, 1860-1865* (P.F. Collier, Publisher, 1889), p. 401, accessed from http://books.google.com, cited 4/4/13, McIlhany, Hugh Milton, Jr., M.A.,

Ph.D., *Some Virginia Families* (Staunton, VA: Stoneburner & Prufer, Printers, 1903), pp. 112-113, accessed from http://books.google.com, cited 4/3/13, "Battle of Brandywine," by Allen G. Eastby and originally published in the October 1998 issue of *Military History* magazine, http://www.historynet.com, published Online: June 12, 2006, cited 4/4/13, Library of Congress, http://hdl.loc.gov/loc.rbc/rbpe.14403300, communicated by Mr. John H. Lick of Fredericksburg, Lebanon County.